WELFARE
WARRIORS

WELFARE
WARRIORS

The Welfare Rights Movement
in the United States

PREMILLA NADASEN

Routledge
NEW YORK • LONDON

Published in 2005 by
Routledge
270 Madison Avenue
New York, NY 10016
www.routledge-ny.com

Published in Great Britain by
Routledge
2 Park Square
Milton Park, Abingdon
Oxon OX14 4RN
www.routledge.co.uk

Routledge is an imprint of the Taylor and Francis Group.

Printed in the United Stated of America on acid-free paper.

10 9 8 7 6 5 4 3 2 1

Library of Congress Cataloging-in-Publication Data

Nadasen, Premilla.
  Welfare warriors : the welfare rights movement in the United States / Premilla Nadasen.
    p. cm.
  Includes bibliographical references and index.
  ISBN 0-415-94578-X (hc : alk. paper)—ISBN 0-415-94579-8 (pb : alk. paper) 1. National Welfare Rights Organization (U.S.)—History. 2. Welfare rights movement—United States—History—20th century. 3. African American women political activists—United States—History—20th century. I. Title.
  HV97.N34N33 2004
  362.5'82'06073—dc22

                                                                              2004010468

Table of Contents

Acknowledgments   vii
Abbreviations   xi
Introduction   xiii

1. The Origins of the Welfare Rights Movement   1
2. Dignity and Representation   45
3. More Money Now!   79
4. In the Name of Equality   103
5. Internal Tensions   125
6. The Guaranteed Annual Income and FAP   157
7. Decline of the Movement   193
    Conclusion   231
    Endnotes   243
    Bibliography   273
    Index   287

Acknowledgments

This book was based on archival sources, official published documents, interviews, and the previous research of other scholars. I would first like to thank all those who have provided the groundwork for my research. Many scholars, activists, and participants wrote about the welfare rights movement over the past several decades and produced case studies and analyses upon which I could build. Guida West, who pioneered research on the welfare rights movement, very generously shared her interviews with me early on in this project.

I also conducted a number of interviews for this research. I found the interviews illuminating and was thrilled to have conversations with people who "had been there." At the same time, what people remember about the movement 30 or 40 years later is colored by contemporary welfare politics, their own political development, and pride and/or regret about their own involvement. I would like to extend my gratitude to all those people who took time out of their busy lives to speak with me and reminisce about their participation in the welfare rights movement.

The most valuable information I could gather about the movement was from the archives themselves. Archives are notoriously incomplete, and represent only what people thought worth saving. So much of what transpired in the movement was not captured in print and thus is lost forever to historians. Nevertheless, the written record gives us a limited window into a fascinating historical period. Understanding the words, voices, and aspirations of those involved in the welfare rights movement in the context of the period is part of what makes this such a significant movement. My goal has been to document, in particular, the voices of women welfare recipients and put their vision at the center of my scholarship. In carrying out this project archivists and librarians at the State Historical Society of Wisconsin, the Ohio Historical Society, the Moorland-Spingarn Research

Center, the Lyndon Baines Johnson Library, and the Columbia University Rare Book and Manuscript Library all provided invaluable assistance.

A number of institutions extended financial support enabling me to complete this project. Columbia's Presidential Fellowship saw me through the first several years of the writing of my dissertation. A summer fellowship from the Martin Luther King Paper's Project at Stanford University trained me in analyzing primary sources and fostered a sense of community and collaboration that I hadn't previously experienced in academia. The Lyndon Baines Johnson Foundation gave me a grant to conduct research in the Johnson Presidential Library. The Williams College Bolin Fellowship provided a welcome retreat in a bucolic setting that facilitated writing and also introduced me to some wonderful people. A one-year grant from the Aspen Foundation gave me the time and space to complete the dissertation. Awards from the Research Foundation of the City University of New York as well as the Queens College Presidential Fellowship enabled me to make the revisions that transformed the dissertation into a book.

Queens College has been a wonderful place to work for the past six years. The diversity of the student body, their life experience, and their maturity make it a pleasure to walk in to my classroom. My colleagues and the many people I have befriended at Queens are not only brilliant scholars, but demonstrate an admirable commitment to teaching and public education. It is an academic setting where teaching and scholarship are truly balanced, as it should be. My chair, Frank Warren, is a gem, and has done everything in his power to help me through the difficult processes of manuscript revisions and tenure.

There are many people who have provided support, have generously volunteered (or acquiesced) to read the manuscript, or portions of the manuscript. My dissertation committee members—Eric Foner, Betsy Blackmar, Manning Marable, Phil Thompson—were outstanding for their insightful comments, and the depth and breadth of knowledge they brought to my work. Eric Foner was a responsible and attentive chair, despite his many other commitments. Betsy Blackmar provided much needed encouragement from the very earliest stages of this project. Others who read all or portions of the book include: Eileen Boris, Ula Taylor, Marion Kaplan, Mimi Abramovitz, Daryl Scott, Frank Warren, Nancy Hewitt, Tami Friedman, Nora Eisenberg, the CUNY Faculty Fellowship Publications Program, Charles Dew, and the faculty committee of the Oakley Center for the Humanities at Williams College.

Barbara Ransby has been a political ally and very close friend since my first year of college. Her consistent support, encouragement, and political wisdom has helped me through graduate school and the arduous process of book writing. She read whatever I sent her, pushed me to do my best with her critical eye, and inspired me with her political vision. Barbara, Peter Sporn, Jason, and Asha are very much an extension of my own family. Robyn Spencer is a very dear friend who has been a colleague and companion for many years. Her critical insight, common sense, and communal values are a wonderful combination. Robyn has consistently worked to create communities of support to acknowledge the unacknowledged and to develop an alternative, more egalitarian set of values. She has been a model, both as a scholar and an academic. Many years ago Phyllis Englebert helped me write my first published essay for a progressive weekly paper in Ann Arbor, Michigan. It was fitting that she so generously volunteered to help edit my first published book. Not only a talented writer, Phyllis has also remained committed to an organizing tradition despite the ups and downs of radical politics in the past two decades.

Phyllis was one of a crew of rabble-rousers from my Michigan days. Many of the friends I made during the sit-ins, on the picket lines, and in late-night strategy sessions of the antiapartheid and antiracist groups are still very much a part of my world and impact me in ways they probably don't even realize. They continue to serve as a moral compass in terms of my academic research and life choices. They include David Austin, Nikita Buckhoy, Cathy Cohen, Latrice Dixon, Laura Dresser, Jen Faigel, David Fletcher, Chuck Gattone, Liz Gottlieb, Amy Jordan, Pam Kisch, Thea Lee, Tracye Matthews, David Maurasse, Rajal Patel, Rosalind Reeves, Suzanne Sherde, Kim Smith, Lillian Waller, Brett Stockdill, Gus Teschke, Anthony Vavasis, Mark Weisbrot, and Michael Wilson.

Many nonacademic friends helped me maintain perspective about exactly what I was doing. They include Joanne Bauer, Seth Berry, Karen Ellis, Pablo Foster, Pam Galpern, Adelaida Gaviria, Guadalupe Gonzalez, Reena Karani, David Levine, Kavitha Medirrata, Helen Schaub, Clay Smith, Naomi Smith, and Pam Sporn. Many of them are involved in the kind of organizing and social change I theorize about in this book. Most of them were too busy trying to change the world to take the time to read my book. They serve as a constant reminder that the world is much bigger than the ivory tower; that scholarship is important but must be coupled with a commitment to putting those ideas into practice, or else, what's the point?

I would also like to extend a special thanks to my family. Some of them were intimately involved with this project, charting my progress, and breathing a big sigh of relief at every turning point. Others were only vaguely aware of what I was doing when I spent hours on end in my study or was simply "too busy" to attend family functions. I am very lucky to have such a supportive and loving group of people around me. In no special order, thanks to Jeff and Mary Nadasen and their children, the Calkins clan in Massachusettes, the Hruskas of Masaya, Nicaragua, Kathleen Gladstone, my entire family in South Africa and Michigan, too numerous to mention, but who all provided welcome reprieves from writing and large quantities of good food to eat. My late father-in-law, Richard Gladstone, a man with a big heart and good head on his shoulders, was always interested in what I was doing and would have undoubtedly been happy to see this project finished. Special thanks to my Aunts Saroj and Gonam, who traveled from South Africa to help out with my second child as I was putting the finishing touches on the book. My sister, Denise, also deserves to be singled out. She served as my taskmaster, setting deadlines for me, insisting on the completion of particular chapters, giving advice, and helping proofread the final product. Life would simply not be the same if she, her husband Tom, and children Clay and Jeremy were not a part of my life. My parents, always generous and never critical, made my undergraduate and graduate education possible, helping out whenever necessary and in whatever way possible. My mother, in particular, came at a moment's notice, whenever a child care crisis emerged, staying as long as necessary to help out. She is a model of a self-sacrificing mother. This book would have never been completed without the support of both my parents. That is why I have dedicated it to them.

My son Tyler was born as I completed the dissertation and began my teaching job at Queens College. My daughter, Indira, born as I completed the book, was eleven days old when I received tenure at Queens. They are bookends to an important phase of my life. Their impending births as well as the postpartum period of changing diapers, burping, and sleepless nights all gave me impetus to bring closure to my projects. Their presence was incentive to put my work aside and they brought immense pleasure to my life in the form of pillow fights, tickling sessions, board games, baseball, and an abundance of hugs and kisses. Bill Gladstone, through many years of graduate school and the writing of this book, has been a bedrock of unwavering support. He urges me to stop and notice the fall foliage, keeps me abreast of the latest flicks, and makes me smile every day, as he promised he would many years ago. His love and good humor have been indispensable for both the book and my own sanity. For that, I say thank you.

Abbreviations

ACLU	American Civil Liberties Union
ACORN	Arkansas Community Organizations for Reform Now
ADC	Aid to Dependent Children
AFDC	Aid to Families with Dependent Children
AFDC-UP	Aid to Families with Dependent Children for Unemployed Parents
AFL-CIO	American Federation of Labor-Congress of Industrial Organizations
ANC	Aid to Needy Children
BPP	Black Panther Party
B-WAC	Brooklyn Welfare Action Council
BWRO	Baltimore Welfare Rights Organization
CAA	Community Action Agency
CAP	Community Action Program
CARASA	Committee for Abortion Rights and Against Sterilization Abuse
Citywide	Citywide Coordinating Committee of Welfare Rights Groups
COINTELPRO	Counter-Intelligence Program
COLA	Cost of Living Adjustments
COMBAT	Community Organization Members Build Absolute Teamwork
CORE	Congress of Racial Equality
CUFAW	Citizens United for Adequate Welfare
DWAC	Downtown Welfare Advocate Center
EKWRO	East Kentucky Welfare Rights Organization
EOA	Economic Opportunity Act
ERAP	Economic Research and Action Project
FAP	Family Assistance Plan

FDR	Franklin Delano Roosevelt
GROWL	Grass-Roots Organizing for Welfare Leadership
HEW	Department of Health, Education and Welfare
ICPP	Inner-City Protestant Parish
IFCO	Inter-religious Foundation for Community Organizations
JOIN	Jobs or Income Now
KOCO	Kenwood-Oakland Community Organization
MAW	Mothers for Adequate Welfare
MEJ	Movement for Economic Justice
MFY	Mobilization for Youth
MWRO	Massachusetts Welfare Rights Organization
NAACP	National Association for the Advancement of Colored People
NASW	National Association of Social Workers
NCC	National Coordinating Committee
NCSC	National Council of Senior Citizens
NOW	National Organization for Women
NUL	National Urban League
NWRO	National Welfare Rights Organization
NWRU	National Welfare Rights Union
OAA	Old Age Assistance
OAI	Old Age Insurance
OEO	Office of Economic Opportunity
OSCAW	Ohio Steering Committee for Adequate Welfare
PAPAW	Pittsfield Association of Parents for Adequate Welfare
POWER	People Organized to Win Employment Rights
PPB	People's Poverty Board
P/RAC	Poverty/Rights Action Center
PWRO	Pennsylvania Welfare Rights Organization
SCLC	Southern Christian Leadership Conference
SDS	Students for a Democratic Society
SNCC	Student Nonviolent Coordinating Committee
SRS	Social and Rehabilitative Services
SSI	Supplemental Security Income
VWRO	Virginia Welfare Rights Organization
WIC	Women, Infant, and Children Program
WIN	Work Incentive Program
WRDA	Welfare Recipients Demand Action
WRO	Welfare Rights Organization
WSO	Wage Supplement Organization

Introduction

Welfare is one of the most contentious political issues in the United States today.[1] The debates about welfare are informed by competing views and values on some fundamental issues including: the work ethic, faith in the market economy, compassion for the less fortunate, models of motherhood, mores about sexuality and reproductive rights, and convictions about where our taxes ought to go. These rhetorical welfare wars are steeped in the ongoing politics of race, class, and gender, and give symbolic, as well as social meaning to these categories by casting the typical welfare recipient as a poor black woman. The merits and drawbacks of public assistance are discussed among academics, policy makers, and journalists; in pool halls and coffee shops. People with their own research teams and reams of data about welfare, as well as people who have never met a welfare recipient but suspect that the lady across the street with six kids must be on welfare, all have opinions about public assistance. Conspicuously muted in the public debate are the voices of welfare recipients. Muted is not to say, silent. Since the 1960s, welfare recipients have asserted—in various ways, with varying degrees of success—their right to speak to the issues that impact their lives. The problem that remains is the reluctance of those in power to pay attention.

Welfare came about with the passage of the Social Security Act in 1935. With that act, the federal government initiated what later became Aid to Families with Dependent Children (AFDC) to provide matching funds to states to support poor women with dependent children. Since then, dominant public opinion and policy makers' rhetoric unfolded in such a way as to demonize and silence welfare recipients. In the words of historian Michael Katz, most Americans see welfare recipients as "the undeserving poor."[2] Their needs, desires, concerns, and day-to-day lives are so far removed from the popular debates that when researchers reveal accurate statistics about women on welfare and their employment or fertility rates, many people refuse to believe them. The stereotypes and snap-shot images of the lazy, undisciplined, promiscuous recipient so dominate the discourse about welfare that few people see the reality for what it is. Even fewer consider that welfare recipients might have opinions that matter, or that they ought to have a say in the making of social policy. Simply put, poor people are more palatable to others when they seem to accept their lot without complaint.

There have been periods of successful protest on the part of poor people in this country. The welfare rights movement captured the national spotlight in the mid-1960s as a powerful movement of poor black women on welfare asserting their political and economic rights, shaping welfare policy, and demanding and winning a space at the table, at least temporarily. In the span of a few short years, the movement changed the face of social policy, established legal protections for welfare recipients, and helped shift the political dialogue about government responsibility and economic justice. Although the welfare rights movement did not, in fact, achieve many of its primary goals, its victories are, nevertheless, astonishing given the obstacles it encountered, the resources it lacked, and the internal tensions in the movement that had to be negotiated.

The welfare rights movement at its peak had an estimated following of somewhere between 30,000 and 100,000. These are the same estimates given for followers of Students for a Democratic Society (SDS) at its height, yet SDS has been the subject of countless books, articles, films, and memoirs. In contrast, the welfare rights movement is one of the most understudied sociopolitical movements of the postwar period. With a few exceptions, most notably Guida West's *The National Welfare Rights Movement* and Frances Fox Piven's and Richard Cloward's chapter in *Poor People's Movements,* the struggle for welfare rights in the 1960s has received little attention. In recent years, some historians have begun to write about the movement, paying particular attention to gender and what the activism of this group of poor women can tell us about motherhood, citizenship, and legal reform.[3] Overall, however, compared to other struggles of the 1960s, the welfare rights movement has been essentially glossed over.

Despite this lack of scholarly attention, it is clear that the welfare rights movement was perhaps one of the most important political and social struggles of the 1960s. Its significance goes far beyond the number of members it counted or the following it amassed. The movement emerged in the late 1950s and early 1960s when women on AFDC came together in their local communities to discuss problems with their caseworkers, to try to understand welfare department policy, and to figure out how to make ends meet on a meager monthly budget. They soon formed local groups—sometimes by themselves, sometimes with the help of churches, social services agencies, or civil rights organizations. These local groups initiated the process of reforming the welfare system to meet the needs of its recipients more adequately. In 1967, with the help of middle-class supporters, a number of welfare rights activists from around the country formed a national organization to coordinate the actions of local welfare rights groups. The National Welfare Rights Organization (NWRO) was formally under the control of elected welfare recipient leaders, most of whom were African American women. But in practice, the mostly white, male middle-class staff, through control of finances and the bureaucratic machine of the national office, also strongly influenced the politics and goals of the welfare rights movement during its formative years. The ensuing struggle for power between recipients and staff over organizational control, tactics, and ideology proved important, and contributed to the development of a feminist consciousness among the women recipients. In the end, black female recipients were able to make their voices heard and their power felt, but they struggled on multiple fronts to do so.

The movement carried out several campaigns. It advocated better treatment from caseworkers, sought to reform the administration of welfare, and demanded higher monthly benefits and "special grants" to bring recipients up to what the welfare department considered a decent standard of living. It organized to get credit for welfare recipients from major department stores. The movement created advisory boards, submitted recommendations to welfare officials, and sent representatives to conferences and legislative bodies to involve welfare recipients in policy making. Perhaps the most important struggle was for a guaranteed annual income, a federal income floor that would bring all Americans up to a basic minimum standard of living.

In this book, I have written in part a history of a movement. I chronicle the birth, growth, and decline of the struggle for welfare rights from the early 1960s to the mid-1970s. I examine not just NWRO but those local groups that disaffiliated because of political fallouts and those that chose not to join the national organization for a complex set of reasons. I ferret out how organizers mobilized members and established goals and how those goals evolved over time. I also examine the bitter conflicts that wracked the movement at particular moments—conflicts structured by race, gender, class, and political ideology. As a movement history, this story ends with poor women of color claiming ownership of the politics and agenda of the organization, and putting into practice their newly formulated feminist perspective—reflecting their own gender and class politics.

I tell this story primarily by focusing on the activists, both those in national leadership and those at the grassroots level. I analyze the social and political circumstances under which black feminist politics emerged and examine what feminism, racial liberation, and class politics meant to women on welfare. As such, this is as much an intellectual history as a social and political history. The political consciousness of women in the welfare rights movement was forged not from a theoretical understanding of women's place, but from a world view constructed out of their daily lives. Their reasons for coming together were complicated. Structural changes, such as economic prosperity, urban migration, and a relatively optimistic ideological climate, fed their desire to challenge their economic, political, and social marginalization. The large-scale changes in the political mood of the country and the world—demands by the downtrodden of the globe and the nation—fueled their confidence that their desires could be realized. This, in combination with the women's personal histories of activism and the day-to-day indignities they dealt with as poor black women on welfare influenced their involvement in the welfare rights movement.

During the 1960s, AFDC came to serve African Americans disproportionately. Politicians, the press, and some sectors of the public demanded cutbacks in ADFC, launched investigations of welfare fraud, and described recipients as unworthy and undeserving of assistance. Welfare recipients faced restrictive local and federal legislation, punitive welfare department policies, and overbearing caseworkers, who sought to deny them the option of being full-time mothers. They were routinely cut off welfare because caseworkers, in conjunction with department policy or federal and state directives, characterized them as employable or unfit mothers. Even though African Americans were a minority of welfare recipients, welfare increasingly came to be understood in racial terms and viewed as a program benefiting black women. Race-laden press coverage and public discussions of black migration, "illegitimacy," promiscuity, and laziness transformed the program from one supporting the right of single mothers to stay home to one encouraging work outside the home. There was now a racially defined gender script that said good white mothers should stay at home, and good black mothers must go to work. This became a measure of responsible parenting and a reversal of the standard of motherhood applied to the white predecessors of black welfare recipients.[4] Discourse and ideology became particularly important in the politics of welfare. The language, images, and dialogue about AFDC were part of the reality for welfare recipients and influenced such "material" things as the size of the monthly benefit check. In this way, ideology and materiality were intertwined.

As they began to organize, participants in the movement saw themselves not simply as poor people or welfare recipients, but as women, community members, members of a racial group, mothers, tenants, and consumers. This was reflected in their literature, speeches, and demands. In addition to welfare rights, many of them had dabbled or were immersed in myriad community issues such as housing, education, civil rights, urban renewal, and consumer rights. Clearly, race, class, gender, and sexuality were not separate entities shaping the activism of poor black women. Their activism is truly an example of the "multiple consciousness" that multicultural and black feminist theorists have written about in recent years.[5]

This "multiple consciousness," of course, complicated the notion of political identity for these women. They do not fit easily into one of the standard narratives of race/class/gender of the 1960s, which demarcate struggles of that era into poor people's, black freedom, and women's movements. These women defined themselves in ways that were multilayered and evolving. The self-definitions, then, were not fixed, essential positions, and were elastic enough that despite the internal struggles and transformations that the movement underwent, it remained multiracial and open to both men and women. The question of identity is never only a process of self-definition, however, but always takes places within a larger political context. Individuals are not autonomous subjects and their sense of self, according to Chandra Mohanty, is constituted within multiple social relations.[6] Reform movements—such as the women's and black freedom movements—prompted women welfare rights activists to think of themselves differently and encouraged participants to reconfigure movement strategy to appeal to shifting political discourses. But, in addition, the mainstream American culture and dominant political discourse structured AFDC recipients as racialized and gendered subjects. Welfare rights activists contested the symbolic meaning of public assistance and black womanhood by recasting their subject identities as mothers, consumers, citizens, and feminists.

Women welfare rights activists wove together their multiple identities to create a distinct political ideology and brand of radicalism that differed from what many other people—black and white—articulated. They adopted political positions based on a material understanding of the hierarchies of race, class, gender, and sexuality and the way in which these realities were intertwined and inseparable for all people.[7] Although I call theirs a black feminist perspective, white, Hispanic, and Native American women also subscribed to a form of the same perspective or standpoint. But their material understanding was also a subjective view of how welfare recipients saw themselves in relation to the rest of the world and how the world saw them. The affluence surrounding them, as well as the prevalent rhetoric (of forever eradicating want and need) shaped their notions of poverty. They forged their ideas about class, not on the shop floor but in a variety of places, including government welfare offices, the supermarket, and their homes.

These women's stories show that class formation is, as Paul Gilroy puts it, a contingent process. Class is both socially and culturally constructed.[8] Welfare recipients' experiences with household, family, and reproduction shaped their activism and the terms on which they articulated their liberation. Economic discrimination and racial and gender oppression informed their analysis and critique of the welfare system. They opposed the inadequate welfare budget, as well as close monitoring of their personal lives. They clearly benefited from and identified with the black freedom movement, which was the foundation for much of the political organizing of this era. At the same time, they articulated a version of black empowerment that differed from the widespread patriarchal discourse at the time by rejecting the male-centered solutions to poverty premised on a two-parent, male-headed family model. The welfare rights movement also went beyond the call for civil and political rights and demanded a minimum standard of living, pressuring some civil rights leaders to confront problems of poverty more directly. In this way, welfare rights activists were continually expanding and modifying the notion of "rights," and concepts of freedom and liberation. Their story complicates the trajectory of the black freedom movement of the 1960s.

In addition to its rightful place within the black freedom movement, the welfare rights movement also represented a struggle by women for their autonomy and, therefore, can and should be defined as part of the women's movement of the 1960s. Welfare rights organizers' version of feminism differed from that of many other women of the time.[9] Many liberal and some radical white feminists in the 1960s and 1970s believed that gender was primary and should be distinct from other issues such as poverty and racism.[10] Women on welfare, however, understood gender as mediated by race and class, and their notion of what constituted "women's liberation" was rooted in their experiences of racial and gender discrimination and class exploitation—having to work at low-paying, menial, and, often, dangerous employment outside the home. Thus, their version of women's liberation included the right to stay home and raise their children as well as seek employment outside the home; access to reproductive control over their bodies (not only abortion); and the right to be involved in a relationship with a man if they wanted to and on their own terms. Clearly, then, the welfare rights movement had major importance not just because of what it achieved, but because of how its story can help us to redefine our understanding of the history of reform in the 1960s. The following chapters will show us why.

CHAPTER 1

The Origins of the Welfare Rights Movement

The Beginnings: 1966

On June 30, 1966, 35 people, mostly women and children, arrived in Columbus, Ohio, weary but jubilant, after a 10-day walk from Cleveland. Their 150-mile "Walk for Decent Welfare" drew attention to the inadequacy of welfare benefits in Ohio. When the marchers left Cleveland on June 20 they were 100 strong, and several hundred supporters joined them as they passed through towns and cities along their journey. Indicative of the racial hostility directed at the AFDC program, bystanders heckled and harassed the Ohio marchers, calling them bums and chanting "work, work, work." One night a cross was burned nearby as they slept.[1] Upon their arrival in Columbus a crowd of 2,000 met them at East High School, where they gathered before the last leg of their march to the steps of the state capitol. The Ohio Rally for Decent Welfare sought to ensure that recipients receive 100 percent of the amount of money the state welfare department decided was necessary for a minimum standard of living.[2] At the time, the state paid only 70 percent of the estimated amount. The Ohio Steering Committee for Adequate Welfare (OSCAW), which had planned the demonstration in conjunction with the National Association of Social Workers (NASW), demanded that the governor call a special session of the state legislature to increase welfare grants for the remainder of 1966 and that the budget for the following year meet the full standard of need for all welfare recipients.[3]

Protesters in Ohio were not alone in their efforts to reform the welfare system. On the same day that the Ohio marchers arrived in Columbus, recipients and their supporters around the country gathered at their state capitols, in public squares, and at local welfare departments to stage the first nationwide demonstration of recipients of AFDC, a program for poor single mothers and their children.[4] In Chicago, 200 poor people marched to the city's downtown welfare office. In Newark, 75 welfare recipients went to the state capitol to demand higher welfare benefits.[5] In New York City, 2,000 mostly black women and children demanded an end to "indignities" of the welfare system, as well as an increase in the school clothing allowance for their children.[6] Other protests occurred in Los Angeles, Baltimore, Trenton, Louisville, Boston, Washington, and San Francisco. An estimated 6,000 people demonstrated in 25 cities across the country. Made up overwhelmingly of women receiving AFDC, the movement also included a small number of male and female recipients of Aid to the Blind, Aid to the Disabled, and General Assistance.[7] African Americans constituted the majority of participants with involvement by some whites, Latinos, and Native Americans.

Although the 1966 welfare protests did not receive as much attention as the civil rights marches led by Martin Luther King, Jr., they, nevertheless, managed to grace the front pages of many national newspapers. The protests for economic and social justice signaled a new phase in the struggle for black equality—one addressing more resolutely the problems of poverty. As the Ohio marchers embarked on the first major "walk" for welfare, State Representative Carl Stokes, a recently unsuccessful candidate for mayor of Cleveland, spoke to the participants about the importance of the impending protest. In reference to the concurrent Meredith March in Mississippi, he counseled, "As you go down this road, you must remember that this march is more significant than the Mississippi March, because it's here and it's about our problems."[8] According to organizer George Wiley, the welfare rights movement sought to do "what the civil rights movement did not do."[9] Indeed, for poor people in urban centers untouched by the activities of major civil rights organizations, it seemed their time had come.

June 30, 1966, marked the official start of a nationwide mobilization for welfare rights in the United States. It was a date commemorated annually by welfare rights activists for many years. Comprised of an alliance of grassroots groups, the welfare rights movement gave a political voice to one of the most disenfranchised sectors of U.S. society and worked toward improving the living standards of all poor Americans.[10] Recipients and welfare rights supporters had met a few months earlier at a conference in Chicago and made June 30 a national day of action around welfare, in solidarity with the Ohio Walk for Adequate Welfare, which was already planned. Conference members asked George Wiley, head of the Poverty/Rights Action Center (P/RAC) in Washington, to coordinate and publicize the event. Wiley and his staff at P/RAC traveled around the country informing recipients of the upcoming march and providing technical support to local groups. In addition, Wiley arranged several meetings over the course of 1966 resulting in the founding of the National Welfare Rights Organization (NWRO), which would encompass most, but not all, of the local groups that constituted the welfare rights movement, and would lead the struggle for welfare rights over the next decade. Wiley and many of the recipients participating in the first national demonstration would come to play prominent roles in the national movement.

The welfare rights movement sought to organize poor African American women to reform AFDC and, in the process, make the program more humane. They confronted a welfare system that gave them a meager monthly allowance leaving them unsure day to day whether they could pay rent or feed and clothe their children; that showed them little respect; and that stigmatized them as lazy, licentious, and unfit mothers. Welfare rights protesters rallied and marched, picketed and protested to pressure public officials to address the inadequacies in the welfare system. They demanded that welfare officials enforce regulations guaranteeing them a basic standard of living and eradicate those violating their civil rights. They believed that welfare should be distributed in a nondiscriminatory and dignified manner to everyone who needed it. These demands were the basis of the initial welfare rights protests.

Credit for emergence of the welfare rights movement is often given to the many middle-class organizers and supporters—such as African American civil rights activist George Wiley. Wiley and other civil rights activists began to work with welfare recipients in the mid-1960s.[11] Many welfare recipients, however, initiated groups in the late 1950s and early 1960s in response to their own day-to-day difficulties with the welfare system, which was becoming increasingly harsh, particularly for black women. This, in conjunction with a political climate conducive to social action, encouraged them to organize on their own behalf. But despite the looming presence of welfare in their lives, these women did not understand their situation only as welfare recipients or poor people. Instead, their complicated identities emerged from their experiences with racism in the welfare system, their work as mothers, as well as their involvement in numerous community issues. Their multiple identities informed their participation in the movement and later developed into a clearer ideological position. If we take notice of these early welfare rights groups, we might conclude that even though the national movement made its debut in 1966, the struggle for welfare rights actually began much earlier. The grievances the women harbored and an opportune moment for protest had enabled welfare recipients to come together to question the regulations and administration of welfare.

History of AFDC/ADC

The AFDC program in the mid-1960s was dehumanizing, disempowering, and inefficient. Instituted in 1935 as part of the Social Security Act, Aid to Dependent Children (ADC)—as the program was known prior to 1962—offered a small monthly allowance for children and nothing for the mother. The Social Security Act, a watershed development in public policy, had built into it certain race and gender assumptions that profoundly influenced the political fate of various components of the legislation. Full-time wage earners, most of whom were men, were assured a decent level of economic assistance through unemployment compensation and social security, both of which were social insurance programs and tied to one's past work history. Married women benefited as spouses of wage-earning men. However, part-time and unsteady workers and African Americans benefited the least. Southern and conservative congressmen limited assistance to African Americans by excluding two occupations in which they predominated: domestic and agricultural work.[12]

Part of a gendered and racialized two-track welfare system, ADC provided less generous and more restrictive assistance than social insurance. Along with Old Age Assistance and Aid to the Disabled, ADC was part of the public assistance programs serving the poor and a disproportionately larger number of women and people of color.[13] The federal government provided oversight and matching funds for ADC, but states controlled eligibility criteria, determined budgets, and essentially ran the program. Consequently, local politics, to a large degree, shaped the program.[14] ADC payments varied widely from state to state and were generally far lower than payments in federally run contributory social insurance programs such as social security and unemployment compensation.

Initially a small noncontroversial program, ADC, like its precursor mothers' pensions programs, excluded most, but not all, of the women of color who needed assistance. White women, most of whom were widows or deserted by their husbands, overwhelmingly populated the welfare rolls in the late 1930s.[15] Pitied and considered worthy of support if they met the social and moral standards set by caseworkers, these women were viewed as mothers and caretakers. To deflect potential criticism, caseworkers made assistance available only to recipients they believed were blameless for their current situation, morally pure, and properly disciplining and caring for their children. Consequently, ADC and mothers' pensions contained strict eligibility criteria to force poor single mothers to conform to white middle-class notions of proper motherhood. Mothers' pensions programs, for example, became an avenue for "Americanization" of southern and eastern European immigrant women.[16] Despite these restrictive rules, the idea that single women should be supported in their work as mothers prevailed in the political discourse.[17] In practice, however, most mothers worked or supplemented their monthly allowance, which was simply too little to support their children. Local welfare departments often expected recipients to work even though they saw recipients as primarily mothers.[18]

ADC was, nevertheless, an improvement over the Progressive Era's mothers' pensions and had the potential to be a widespread, nondiscriminatory support system for single mothers. The federal matching system encouraged states lacking mothers' pensions programs to establish ADC programs. And federal oversight and funding gave the federal government some control over how local programs developed. Under ADC the number and proportion of African American families assisted increased. In 1931, of the 93,620 families receiving mothers' aid, an estimated 3 percent were black.[19] In 1940, approximately 17 percent of 372,000 ADC families were black.[20]

Even though more African American women received ADC than had received mothers pensions, patterns of discrimination in the program were widespread. A majority of African American women needing assistance didn't receive it, particularly in the South and other areas where large numbers of African Americans lived.[21] For example, in 1943 the state of Louisiana refused assistance to women during cotton picking season, and Detroit in the 1940s frequently denied assistance to African Americans due to having an "unsuitable home."[22] During the 1940s, the federal Bureau of Public Assistance and advocates in the social welfare community worked to expand benefits and extend eligibility.[23] In 1945 the Social Security Board recommended that states repeal the suitable home law. Fifteen states did so in the 1940s. In 1946 the Board also raised the maximum matching federal payment. The following year it issued guidelines that everyone should have the opportunity to apply for ADC and that the application process must be prompt and efficient. However hesitantly, in the 1940s a network of welfare reform advocates worked to curb the exclusionary policies of states and improve the stature of ADC. Simultaneously, the number of needy women claiming assistance—both African American and white—climbed steadily, and, at times, dramatically.

The Backlash

During the 1950s a welfare backlash by local politicians, the conservative press, and many ordinary white Americans exposed purported welfare fraud and "chiseling." In local areas around the country, including Washington, D.C., Detroit, and New Jersey, special investigative committees documented and ferreted out recipients allegedly unworthy of support. In most cases, hyperbole and inflammatory rhetoric shrouded the dialogue and publicity about welfare. Journalists or investigative committees charged that women recipients had several children out of wedlock, fathers took no responsibility for raising their children, and parents simply did not want to work. In most cases, the stereotypical welfare recipient was an African American woman. Investigations into these claims, however, rarely revealed widespread fraud and found minimal abuse in the system. In Detroit, for example, a 1948 study revealed only two cases of alleged fraud and in neither case was the recipient convicted of criminal wrongdoing.[24] Nevertheless, the investigations aroused public suspicion about welfare and planted in the minds of many Americans an inextricable association among receipt of ADC, African Americans, immorality, and laziness.

The rhetoric and publicity encouraged legislative changes. These changes included a whole new slate of local regulations: "suitable home" laws denying aid to mothers who had children out of wedlock or engaged in other behavior caseworkers considered immoral or inappropriate; "substitute father" or "man-in-the-house" rules denying aid to women if there was evidence of a male present in her home; employable mother laws refusing assistance to women physically able to work; and residence laws denying assistance to migrants from outside the state.[25] During the 1950s, a number of cities and counties, including Washington, D.C., Milwaukee, WI, Los Angeles, CA, Cuyahoga County, OH, Wayne County, MI, and the states of Illinois, Louisiana, and Pennsylvania formed special units within the welfare department to investigate whether a substitute parent resided in the house.[26] Georgia passed an employable mother rule in 1952. Michigan and Florida passed suitable home laws in 1953 and 1959, respectively. In 1962, New York State passed a residence law denying benefits to migrants if it could be proven that they came to the state for the purpose of receiving welfare.[27] By the late 1950s and early 1960s, a number of states implemented punitive welfare laws to reduce the number of people on welfare.[28] These laws were not new, but in the 1950s they were strengthened, formalized, and expanded.

In addition to restricting eligibility, local officials reduced welfare grants. Between December 1961 and December 1962, the average monthly ADC grant per recipient declined in 30 states. Far from being restricted to the South, these cuts also occurred in relatively "liberal" states of the North,

West, and Midwest, including New York, California, Pennsylvania, Illinois, Michigan, and Connecticut. Public assistance budget shortfalls cannot fully explain the decrease. Of the 30 states that cut ADC, only six also cut old-age assistance—a more costly program. On average, people on old-age assistance received two and one-half times the monthly payment received by women on ADC. So cuts in ADC were not only more widespread, but more devastating for those families.

The following year, from December 1962 to December 1963, monthly ADC grants declined again in 26 states.[29] Legislators justified the cuts with charges of cheating, immorality, and laziness by ADC recipients. For example, Cuyahoga County, OH, cut welfare checks in June 1959 by 10 percent and in May 1960 denied assistance to all employable single women and childless couples concurrent with the arrival of large numbers of black southern migrants to the area.[30] An Ohio senator explained the cuts in terms of the public perception of welfare recipients: "Too many people believe that there is too much chiseling among recipients and, while there may be some, I am certain it is a very few and yet many suffer from these people."[31] Thus, welfare policy on the local level shifted away from ensuring that women on ADC maintain proper households toward one of denying or reducing assistance to needy mothers.

Politicians and journalists may have attacked ADC because of increases in the welfare rolls. The number of families on welfare grew from 652,000 in 1950 to 806,000 in 1960, but this hardly warranted the alarmist investigations of this period.[32] Instead, public concern about welfare centered on the particular welfare recipients joining the welfare rolls. The rolls in 1960 looked very different than they did in 1940 in terms of the morality and worthiness—often defined by divorce, a child born out of wedlock, or the racial or cultural background of a recipient. Increasingly, the politics of welfare converged on the stereotypical image of a black unmarried welfare mother with a child born out of wedlock. This image, more than any other, fed the fires of the welfare controversy. So, the public opposed not just more families on welfare, but the greater number of unmarried women receiving assistance. The 1939 Social Security Amendments encouraged this trend by extending old age insurance coverage to widows and their children, in effect, removing "deserving" women and children—whose husbands and fathers had died—from the ADC rolls. In 1961, widows made up only 7.7 percent of the ADC caseload, down from 43 percent in 1937.[33]

Because of poverty, racism, and economic changes the percentage of African Americans on ADC nationally increased from 31 percent in 1950 to 48 percent in 1961.[34] Mechanization and other changes in agricultural production in the postwar South left many African Americans without work, fueling the migration of African Americans to urban areas and the

North. Between 1940 and 1960, more than three million African Americans made their way from the South to northern cities in search of employment. Although many found work, deindustrialization in urban centers in conjunction with widespread race and gender employment discrimination led to a disproportionately large number of unemployed or underemployed African Americans. In 1960, the official unemployment rate was 4.9 percent for whites and 10.2 percent for nonwhites.[35] Those landing in the North may have turned to welfare departments for economic support as a last resort.

In addition, nonwhite and African American women were disproportionately single mothers. In 1960 the official out-of-wedlock birth rate for whites was 23 out of 1,000 births. For nonwhites it was 216.[36] The percentage of single mothers in all racial groups increased after World War II because of social and economic dislocations. Between 1950 and 1960, out-of-marriage births increased by 31 percent for white women and 20 percent for non-whites.[37] White women becoming pregnant, however, were well hidden from the public eye. Many were sent off to birthing homes and their babies quietly put up for adoption. Black women had fewer institutional resources available. The lack of avenues for adoption, in addition to community values discouraging mothers giving up their children, meant that black women kept their children and raised them at a far higher rate than white women.[38] This higher rate of black single motherhood coupled with higher poverty rates translated into a higher ADC rate. Taking into account their poverty and out-of-wedlock birth rates, black women were actually underrepresented on ADC. Even though only a small minority of children born out of wedlock ended up on ADC, the increase in black single mothers on welfare caused public alarm.[39] Politicians and the press hammered away at the apparent overrepresentation of black women on the welfare rolls.

Reflecting hysteria as well as creating it, popular and social welfare magazines in the late 1950s gave undue attention to the rise in out-of-wedlock births among women on ADC and attributed this to black migration.[40] In 1965, *U.S. News and World Report* explained the large percentage of African Americans on ADC by the "mass migration of unskilled Negroes from the South to Northern cities." It reported that black men, unable to get jobs, deserted their families: "Deserted wives, sometimes turning to any man who comes along, add to the high rate of illegitimacy in the self-perpetuating breeding grounds of city slums."[41] Thus, the concern about ADC was shaped and sold to the public in large part by racial ideology. Promiscuity and laziness became synonymous with black women on welfare. No one definitively linked the increase in welfare rolls to the rise in out-of-marriage births, yet "illegitimacy" became a code word for black single mothers on ADC.

Although the language of "illegitimacy" dominated the debate about welfare, the real issues were employment, motherhood, and what was considered the proper social role for black women. Restrictive welfare laws directed primarily at black women, who had a long history of employment outside the household, helped provide an adequate supply of laborers to the workforce. A field supervisor in a southern state reported:

> The number of Negro cases is few due to the unanimous feeling on the part of the staff and board that there are more work opportunities for Negro women and to their intense desire not to interfere with local labor conditions. The attitude that "they have always gotten along," and that "all they'll do is have more children" is definite ... [They see no] reason why the employable Negro mother should not continue her usually sketchy seasonal labor or indefinite domestic service rather than receive a public assistance grant.[42]

Consequently, local officials routinely tightened eligibility restrictions and forced recipients into the labor market, particularly in the South during periods of labor shortage.[43] Thus, black women's status as welfare recipients was bound up with their relationship to the labor market. Black women, more often seen as laborers than as mothers, were considered less deserving of public assistance than other women.[44] In turn, this view of black women shaped the politics of welfare, whether or not black women comprised a majority of recipients. The architects of ADC and mothers' pensions constructed programs to assist women as caretakers, but theirs was a racially specific vision. They had in mind white single mothers. After the establishment of ADC, as black women increasingly applied for this entitlement in local areas around the country, single welfare mothers came to be viewed as wage earners as well as mothers.

Two well-publicized cases, one in Louisiana and the other in Newburgh, NY, reveal the changing nature of ADC. In 1960, Louisiana implemented a "suitable home clause," cutting off public assistance to a family if the mother had a child out of wedlock while on ADC unless she could prove that she "has ceased illicit relationships and is maintaining a suitable home for the child or children."[45] The Louisiana law, applied retroactively, dropped 25 percent of ADC cases from the state rolls. Ninety-five percent of children affected were African American.[46] Of the over 6,000 families cut off assistance, half were later reinstated by a local welfare board, which found their homes "suitable."[47] The state action created enormous hardship for the families, exacerbating their destitution. According to a federal review, a "large group of families were hungry, had 'no place to turn to,' were on the point of eviction from their homes, and would soon have to remove their children from school."[48]

Some local residents were outraged. The editor and publisher of *The Beacon*, a small local paper in Lake Charles, LA, wrote to the American Civil Liberties Union (ACLU) charging that the Louisiana law was unconstitutional.[49] The ACLU agreed that the law violated equal protection laws and the due process clause of the 14th Amendment.[50] Numerous other groups, including the National Social Welfare Assembly, American Public Welfare Association, Child Welfare League of America, and National Urban League, lobbied and pressured the federal government to reverse Louisiana's suitable home clause.

The federal government had rarely challenged a state's right to restrict eligibility. In 1945 the federal government recommended that states repeal the suitable home clause. Merely a request with little power of enforcement, this did nothing to stop the wave of suitable home laws in the 1950s. The federal government had tolerated suitable-home laws since the mothers' pensions programs of the 1920s. A provision in the 1935 Social Security Act allowed states to take into account the "moral character" of the parents. In theory, the suitable home provision encouraged mothers to maintain high moral standards in their homes. In practice, however, the suitable-home requirement was used to exclude families, especially African American.[51] In addition, welfare departments denying assistance did little to protect children from these ostensibly unsuitable circumstances or to improve their living conditions. In 1954 Mississippi passed a suitable home clause and over the next few years removed 8,400 families from ADC, over half because of a child born out of wedlock.[52] By 1961, 23 states, including Louisiana, had suitable-home clauses.

Escalating pressure from activists in the civil rights and social welfare communities impelled the Secretary of the Department of Health Education and Welfare (HEW), Arthur Flemming, to hold hearings to determine whether Louisiana's actions violated federal regulations governing the ADC program. He threatened to cut off federal ADC funds to the state if that were the case. Flemming ruled that the Louisiana law conformed to federal guidelines as they currently stood, but the next day he issued a new federal guideline. The Flemming Ruling, as it came to be known, forbade states from excluding children from ADC because of an "unsuitable home" unless the state made an effort to improve home conditions or put the child in an institution or in foster care. Because of the high cost of the alternatives, Flemming's ruling essentially invalidated the suitable-home clause.[53]

The other case, in Newburgh, NY, received more coverage in the popular press, and in some ways overshadowed the events in Louisiana. In 1961,

Newburgh, a small town 70 miles north of New York City, hired a new city manager, Joseph Mitchell. Mitchell proposed cutting ADC to mothers who bore children out of wedlock, requiring able-bodied men to work full time, requiring recent migrants applying for welfare to prove that they came to the city with offers of employment, and limiting the size of monthly checks. The purported reason for the new rules, according to one reporter, was "that shiftless migrants from the South were flooding the relief rolls and that the city was subsidizing crime, immorality, slums and a general 'pollution' of social standards."[54]

During the 1950s, Newburgh was in economic decline. It was previously a center of textile and carpet manufacturing, but several factories closed down or moved out of town. Between 1958 and 1963, the number of large manufacturers (employing at least twenty people) declined from seventy-one to sixty-two.[55] Since 1957 the region had been classified as one of "substantial unemployment" by the U.S. Department of Labor.[56] Paralleling changes in other urban centers in this period, the economic decline of the central city was linked to the growth of the surrounding area.[57] Federal highway construction, greater reliance on automobiles, and federally guaranteed home mortgage loans fueled the expansion of industry, housing, and retail establishments in suburban areas. Consequently, Newburgh lost much of its industry, downtown businesses, and white population. At the same time, the proportion of African Americans in Newburgh increased from 6 percent to 17 percent during the decade.[58] Indeed many white residents in Newburgh believed that the rise in the black population caused the perceptible economic decline of the city. Rather than examining the changing industrial trends and the impact of federal subsidization of suburbs, they blamed the city's economic woes on black migration, thus providing a base of support for cutbacks by their new city manager.

Liberal policy makers, civil rights activists, and social welfare advocates opposed Mitchell's inflammatory and hostile policies. They issued denunciations, launched legal suits, and lobbied federal and state officials to end what they believed was a discriminatory action. Threatening to end state welfare assistance to the city, the New York State Board of Social Welfare held a hearing to determine if the reforms in Newburgh violated state and federal welfare regulations. The city ultimately lost the battle in the courts and rescinded the regulations, but it won the larger political battle. Mitchell's plan generated widespread support nationally. In an August 1961 Gallup poll 85 percent of Americans favored forcing men who could not find jobs to take any job offered. Seventy-five percent of those polled believed recent migrants wanting assistance should prove that they moved to the area with a job offer. Only about 10 percent advocated continued aid to women with more than one child out of wedlock.[59] Moreover, the Newburgh case focused the country's attention on welfare rolls populated disproportionately by African Americans and unmarried mothers. Regardless of the outcome of Mitchell's reforms, this episode etched into the public mind the image of the unworthy black recipient.[60]

The Newburgh controversy also reveals the parameters of debate about welfare in the early 1960s. Liberals, like conservatives, sought to decrease the number of African Americans on the welfare rolls, to reduce out-of-wedlock births, and to encourage poor mothers to work. Instead of simply eliminating people from welfare, liberal policy makers proposed work incentives, job training, counseling, and other support services to enable families to become independent. Even though their tactics differed, the end result was similar. The Newburgh and Louisiana incidents reinforced the trend toward self-sufficiency and employment.

The 1962 Amendments to the Social Security Act embodied the liberal social welfare philosophy. To help families attain self-sufficiency, the amendments provided more federal money for social services to counsel families. Indicating its new focus, the program was renamed Aid to Families with Dependent Children (AFDC). To stem the rise in single parenthood, it extended the pilot AFDC-UP (Aid to Families with Dependent Children—for Unemployed Parents) program, which provided assistance to two-parent families when both parents were unemployed. The Amendments also contained the first federal work incentive for women on welfare, permitting states to require adult recipients to work in exchange for benefits and to deduct work-related expenses when computing welfare benefits.[61] Thus, even people vociferously protesting the developments in Newburgh and Louisiana sought, through different means, to reduce the welfare rolls and put women and men on welfare to work. The 1962 Social Security Amendments, like the Newburgh debate, signaled the end of the days when welfare encouraged women to stay home and care for their children.

By the 1950s the debate about welfare, particularly among politicians and some sectors of the public, had come to be dominated by discussions of cultural values, "illegitimacy," and immorality, all cast through a racial lens.[62] Many communities attempted to uncover alleged welfare fraud and corruption, limit the size of the welfare rolls, reduce welfare payments, and put welfare recipients to work.[63] Motherhood was no longer the most important factor determining one's status as a recipient. These increasingly restrictive ADC policies made it harder for all women, particularly black women, to receive assistance.[64] Caseworkers routinely checked up on recipients, sometimes conducting "midnight raids" to ensure that a recipient was not involved in a relationship with a man. They applied stringent and humiliating eligibility criteria to prevent women with alternate sources of support from receiving assistance. Under constant scrutiny, recipients had to verify the soundness of their character, their destitution, and, increasingly, their willingness but inability to work. Even when recipients qualified for assistance, their income was not always secure. Caseworkers frequently cut them off assistance without notice or explanation or reduced grants arbitrarily. Those getting a monthly check found the amount hardly enough to provide the basic necessities for their children. Thus, women on welfare in the early 1960s found themselves caught in a harsh and dehumanizing system, which fertilized the soil for a mass-based movement for welfare rights.

Academic Interventions

In contrast to hard-hitting attacks on welfare, in the late 1950s and early 1960s, academics and policy makers discussed, documented, and analyzed poverty and its negative social consequences. The main concern of poverty researchers, however, was not single motherhood or even racial discrimination. Instead, they studied the impact of broad structural changes, especially deindustrialization, on able-bodied but unemployed men. Countless academic reports echoed the concern with male unemployment and its attendant social problems. In 1958 John Kenneth Galbraith wrote in *The Affluent Society* about the persistence of poverty in depressed regions of the country and in families with an unemployed breadwinner. In 1960, Richard Cloward and Lloyd Ohlin analyzed in *Delinquency and Opportunity* the relationship between blocked job and educational opportunities and juvenile delinquency in poor neighborhoods. In 1962, Michael Harrington, in *The Other America,* documented the existence of widespread poverty amid the wealth of the nation. These academics asserted that the tentacles of economic prosperity had not reached every nook and cranny of the nation; that some people had been left behind through no fault of their own. Counseling government intervention through job training and educational programs, these social science experts influenced national government policy, but also laid on the poor the burden to adapt to the new economic circumstances.[65] Addressing the emerging concerns about poverty, President Kennedy in 1961 established the President's Committee on Juvenile Delinquency and Youth Crime. At the same time Congress passed the Area Redevelopment Act providing financial assistance to depressed areas and the next year it enacted the Manpower Development and Training Act, which trained people to develop new skills to become self-supporting.[66]

The antipoverty rhetoric of the early 1960s had a twofold impact on the welfare rights movement. First, it opened up a dialogue about poverty and economic need, suggesting that in the midst of economic abundance no American should be deprived of basic necessities. Many authors argued that the nation could and should do better for its neediest citizens. Although the reports and studies of the early 1960s did not speak to the specific needs of women on welfare or single parents, the antipoverty rhetoric probably heightened recipients' expectations for increases in their own standard of living and gave them hope that a struggle for reform might yield results. Middle-class preoccupations with the social and economic problems of the poor increased the likelihood of recruiting allies and funding for a movement for welfare rights. Second, theorists framed the discussion of poverty within the circumscribed boundaries of male unemployment, and prescribed preparing the unemployed for available jobs, redeveloping deindustrialized areas, and increasing the minimum wage. Lost in the discussion were how single mothers might support themselves, the lack of available day care, and increases in AFDC payments. The emphasis on male unemployment rather than female independence foreshadowed a fierce debate within the welfare rights movement, and in other policy circles, about single motherhood, gender, and poverty.

Another strain of academic research and writing in the postwar period emphasized the deleterious impact of racism and poverty on the black community.[67] This literature, including Abram Kardiner and Lionel Ovesey's *The Mark of Oppression*, outlined the psychological and cultural damage caused by racial discrimination on African Americans. Some of these "damage-oriented" liberal scholars morally critiqued racism, hoping to expand rights and opportunities for African Americans.[68] With surging interest in inner-city black poverty in the early 1960s, scholars such as Kenneth Clark, in *Dark Ghetto*, and Lee Rainwater, in *Behind Ghetto Walls*, examined structural barriers to economic success for urban African Americans and the resulting "pathological" behavior. Whether the point of departure was economic structures, psychological damage, or an inner-city subculture, nearly all of these theorists honed in on the problems of black male unemployment and "female-dominated" families. Like the antipoverty researchers, they resolved to find work for black men and reestablish the two-parent household, an approach at odds with the welfare rights movement's goal of economic support for poor single mothers.

Thus, in the decade preceding the welfare rights movement, activists and policy makers laid the groundwork for the politics of welfare in the 1960s. The optimistic public dialogue about the affluence of the nation and the possibility of eradicating poverty stood in stark contrast to the concerted efforts to cut AFDC budgets, restrict the number of people on the rolls, and attack the character of recipients. Many believed that black women on AFDC were unworthy of support and ended up on welfare because of debauchery and personal failings. On the other hand, unemployed and poor working men, cast as victims of impersonal structural forces, signaled the economic failure of the nation. The parallel trends of AFDC cuts and antipoverty rhetoric produced a formula that encouraged women on welfare to begin to fight back. "Rising expectations" for poor people and trying circumstances for welfare recipients gave welfare activists a reason to organize as well as hope that their organizing might be effective.

Why Women Organized

In this context the first local welfare rights groups formed in the early and mid-1960s, several years before the Ohio march. Welfare recipients in cities, towns, and rural communities began to discuss, and in some cases demonstrate, about their day-to-day experiences with poverty, racism, and the many abuses they endured with the welfare system. Women organizing local groups often met in the cramped kitchens or sparse living rooms of poor single mothers. They initiated neighborhood groups, often informally, to testify about the difficulties of being a welfare recipient. The first welfare rights organizers spearheaded collective efforts that questioned or confronted unfair welfare policies and practices. For example, Ruth Pressley, a recipient in central Harlem, founded Welfare Recipients in Action in 1964, hoping to create an "organized, determined, and united group to fight the power structure" and to train recipients to "handle any welfare problem."[69]

Throughout the 1960s and early 1970s local groups formed and folded as opportunities to organize on the local level arose and diminished. Although middle-class activists and antipoverty workers sometimes helped initiate these groups, recipients' decisions to join the movement for welfare rights was rooted in a multiple consciousness integrating race, class, and gender. Women in the welfare rights movement did not consider themselves only poor people or welfare recipients, but also black, brown, or white, mothers, tenants, community members, and consumers. Some participants were previously involved in other political issues, such as civil rights, housing, and labor organizing. Prior to any major national attempt at organizing a welfare rights movement, women in local settings banded together to resist oppressive welfare policies.

Recipients became involved because of their difficulties with poverty, trying to survive on a meager monthly check, the recurring racism of the welfare system, as well as the reality of their lives as mothers. They dealt with high food prices, exorbitant rent, and dehumanizing treatment by social service caseworkers. The scant monthly allowance and stigma associated with welfare deterred many poor mothers from applying for ADC. Those receiving aid were subjected to constant scrutiny and a bureaucratic maze of rules and regulations, leaving them powerless and at the mercy of caseworkers, who, at some moments, required them to discuss deeply personal matters and, at other times, expected them to be voiceless, passive subjects. One welfare recipient on the Lower East Side of Manhattan said,

> No one cares and you are like a stone on the sidewalk . . . We've got to go on welfare and have the welfare worker come up to see us and tell us how to live, and then she looks in the ice box at what we have. They want to know what kind of clothes you have, and when they see a telephone, they want to know who is paying for it and why that money isn't being used for food.[70]

Some recipients internalized feelings of shame. This may have hindered organizing, but the opportunity to join a welfare rights group often enabled recipients to overcome their hesitation. Mildred Calvert, chairman of Northside WRO in Milwaukee, recounted her initial ambivalence about attending a welfare rights meeting:

> When I first came on welfare, I was ashamed, because society has taught us to be ashamed of something like that . . . We were taught that welfare was begging, charity, and when you have a little pride, you don't want to do that. So, for a while, I hid it. I heard about the Welfare Rights Organization through a cousin of mine. She kept trying to get me to go to these meetings with her and I said, "No, I'd never go to anything like that." But then I had a problem and I went to her with it and she kept telling me that she could take me to people who could help me and I still said "No." So I sat around and sat around and let the problem get out of hand, so finally I did go to the Welfare Rights people.[71]

The indignity of being poor compounded the shame of receiving welfare. In a thriving consumer culture in which acquisition of material goods determined social status, welfare recipients were on the bottom of the social order. The meager monthly allowance relegated many recipients to living in dilapidated housing in dangerous neighborhoods that offered few public services. Many families on welfare lived below the basic subsistence level in the 1960s. In 1967, 24 percent of AFDC families had no running water, 30 percent did not have enough beds, and 46 percent did not have enough money to buy milk at least once in the previous six months.[72] Many recipients did not believe that the degrading and unhealthy conditions were of their own making. The surrounding images of wealth and the public dialogue about eradicating poverty probably led them to consider the injustice of their own poverty. A recipient in New York City explained:

> Every day when I come out of the building through a broken door and the filthy hall and see that abandoned car sitting in the garbage-littered snow, I feel as if I am living in a dump, one for which I am not responsible. I think to myself that the City of New York has abandoned me and my children, and I'm sad and ashamed . . . It doesn't care about its residents or sanitation—not down here at least. But I've heard that it's different on Fifth Avenue. It's clean.[73]

Loretta Johnson, a welfare recipient from Richmond, VA, and later a member of NWRO's National Coordinating Committee, had her own frustrating experiences. Although she struggled with sickness her whole life, she tried hard to be financially independent and care for her two daughters. She held several jobs, but eventually her illness got the better of her. When she applied for welfare, she was turned down. Shortly after that she attended a hunger demonstration planned by the Richmond WRO. Interactions between welfare officials and recipients at the demonstration only fueled her political commitment: "The poor people were talked down to and treated horribly by the Welfare Director and other officials. This action amazed me and I felt only contempt for all who were in the government or some powerful office that they would be so inconsiderate of those less fortunate than themselves."[74]

In countless ways the welfare system made life hard for those depending on it, while also spurring recipients and others to organize. In Cuyahoga County, OH, for example, community members and welfare recipients in the late 1950s responded to cuts in welfare. Welfare in Ohio was administered by the county, but financed by the city. Beginning in 1959, the city of Cleveland found it increasingly difficult to pay its full share of the welfare budget. In May 1959, the county denied assistance to all able-bodied single men. The following year employable single women and childless couples were also denied assistance.[75] When Ohio established a statewide minimum standard for welfare in 1960, the county recalculated ADC budgets to determine the minimum standard, then reduced grants leaving recipients at 80 percent of the established standard of need.

The reasons for the cuts ostensibly revolved around budgetary battles between the county and the city, with city officials claiming a shortage of funds. There may be a measure of truth to this claim, since welfare rolls rose steadily in this period. Yet, ADC payments were well below other public assistance levels in Ohio. Families on ADC received $31 per person. Recipients of old-age assistance, aid to the blind, aid to the disabled, and general assistance received between $75 and $80 per person.[76] Clearly, when budgets tightened officials turned to ADC rather than other programs because of political necessity or expediency. The racial composition of the rolls was a contributing factor in this decision. In Cleveland, 87 percent of the AFDC caseload in 1966 was African American.[77] The Cleveland City Council cut welfare, it stated, because of the rising number of relief cases due to "recent migrants." Indeed Cleveland's nonwhite population had nearly doubled between 1950 and 1960, from 16 percent to 29 percent.[78] As with other urban centers, economic decline had set in. From 1958 to 1963, Cleveland lost forty-two large manufacturers and 12,000 manufacturing jobs.[79] The city council passed a resolution in March 1959 urging the Ohio General Assembly to require three years of residence in the state in order to qualify for welfare. Mayor Anthony J. Celebrezze, noting "the racial overtones in the discussion," vetoed the measure.[80]

In response, a group called Mothers' Campaign for Welfare lobbied state officials in 1957 to increase ADC payments.[81] In 1961, another group, Cleveland Mothers, challenged the impending cuts. These were, for the most part, short-lived efforts. The Inner City Protestant Parish (ICPP), a cooperative interdenominational and interracial church founded in 1954 to assist the poor, initiated more sustained organizing and provided religious leadership for the welfare rights movement in Cleveland. Rev. Paul Younger, who worked with ICPP and the civil rights movement in Cleveland in the early 1960s, helped form in 1962 Citizens United for Adequate Welfare (CUFAW). Cochaired by Erla Jones and Mabel Swanson, the group educated the public about inadequate welfare grants, fair hearings, and the free school lunch program. With the support of churches and other community groups, they organized letter-writing campaigns and public forums and picketed at the State House. In 1962, the South Side Family Council, a group of social service workers and welfare recipients in Columbus, in conjunction with Cleveland Mothers, sent letters to state and federal representatives and welfare department administrators protesting welfare cuts in Ohio.[82] In February it sent a petition with 600 signatures to the Columbus city council demanding emergency funds for families on welfare.[83] Despite their efforts, grants in Ohio were reduced in 1962 to 75 percent of the state standard and to 70 percent in 1963.[84] One lawyer from whom activists sought support revealed the mindset of proponents of reductions when he explained: "I do not think there is an insufficiency of money, but I think that there is a need for improvement in the program so that the truly needy are provided for and the lazy are required to find work."[85]

In other cases a frustrating experience with the welfare department triggered organizing among recipients. An early welfare activist, who became prominent in Mothers for Adequate Welfare (MAW) in Boston, had several run-ins with the welfare department in the 1950s. Two caseworkers, she

explained, "had very peculiar ways of dealing with public assistance families
. . . They visited late at night . . . If . . . you were going to have a male visitor,
you knew that you were subject to visits during any time of the 24 hour period." If the caseworkers suspected something, the client stopped getting a
check.[86] The MAW member explained that prior to the formation of a welfare rights groups, recipients in Boston challenged this kind of treatment:

> Occasionally, [women] who may live in the same building or in the
> same block in the street would go together directly to the local field
> office and quarrel with the welfare office supervisor or they would
> move from the supervisor and go straight to the central office and
> try to get an appointment with the Director . . . This was in the
> early fifties through to about 1957 or '58.[87]

In early 1966 welfare recipients in Detroit organized a group called
Westside Mothers ADC. Their first campaigns were very practical. They
met with postal authorities to get locks on mailboxes in apartment build-
ings to prevent the theft of welfare checks, negotiated with the welfare department to pay for babysitters for mothers in the work experience
program, requested special clothing allowances, and persuaded utility
companies to eliminate deposits for low-income families.[88]

Johnnie Tillmon, chairwoman and later executive director of NWRO,
also attributed her initial welfare rights activity to difficulties with the welfare system. A mother of six children, Tillmon formed the welfare rights
group, Aid to Needy Children Mothers Anonymous in 1963 in a housing
project in Los Angeles. A sharecropper's daughter originally from Scott, AR,
who never finished high school, she washed clothes for a white man for 15
years while working in the cotton fields. Tillmon arrived in California in
late 1959 to join her two brothers because most of her other family members had died. To support herself and her two children she ironed shirts in
a laundry where she organized for better working conditions as a union
shop steward. She also became active in a community association, the
Nickerson Gardens Planning Organization, which planted flowers, arranged
afterschool activities for children, and improved living conditions in the
housing project.

In 1963, Tillmon became sick and was admitted to the hospital. The
president of the neighborhood association suggested she apply for welfare
as a way to take care of herself and her children. Imbued with negative ideas
about welfare, she was reluctant, but eventually applied because she felt her
teenage daughter, who had been skipping school, needed her attention. She
immediately noticed her poor treatment as a recipient. The welfare budget
outlined how to spend her money and caseworkers inventoried Tillmon's

refrigerator and questioned her decision to purchase a television. She later recounted: "When I was working every day, if I wanted to have male company, then I had male company. But when you're on welfare, you can't have too much male company."[89] Welfare recipients like Tillmon were treated alternately like children or criminals. These degrading conditions inspired Tillmon to organize her fellow ADC recipients. She first obtained a list of all ADC recipients in the housing project and visited more than 500 of them. Three hundred people showed up to the first meeting.[90] In August 1963, Aid to Needy Children opened an office staffed by welfare recipients and helped people who had been cut off assistance, who had not gotten a grocery order, or others with similar welfare problems.

In the late 1950s, Dorothy Moore headed another welfare rights group in Los Angeles. The Welfare Action and Community Organization started in 1958 in South Central and East L.A. A group of 10 to 15 people, working out of the home of Catherine Jermany, addressed welfare and voter registration and soon developed a network of neighborhood organizations. Although they came together because of problems with caseworkers, Jermany believed that "you had to change the department and that changing one worker, you could get someone equally as bad. That the whole philosophy of the department had to be changed."[91] As groups emerged in Los Angeles in the late 1950s and early 1960s, local leaders established in 1961 the Los Angeles County Welfare Rights Organization, which acted as a "legislative body to deal with the County Board of Supervisors who administer the welfare program in Los Angeles County for the State of California."[92] Shortly after that, recipients in Northern and Southern California formed a statewide welfare rights organization.

Whatever particular problems recipients encountered with welfare, uniting to address them was tremendously empowering. As a group, welfare recipients could more effectively navigate the welfare bureaucracy, challenge caseworkers, share information, or simply support one another. On the south side of Minneapolis in the fall of 1966, six people with the same caseworker discussed their common complaints. The recipients asked the Minneapolis Community Union Project for assistance in setting up a meeting with welfare officials, and outlined their grievances to the caseworker and her supervisor. They waited two weeks and, after no reply, wrote a letter. In response, the Assistant Director of the Hennepin County Welfare Department met them at the Community Union Project to discuss the matter and within a week rectified most of the complaints. This group founded the welfare committee of the Minneapolis Community Union Project and began to strategize about organizing other welfare recipients.[93] Collective action empowered recipients, most of whom had silently suffered the humiliation of being on welfare. Sharing their experiences taught them that their problems were not exceptional, but that abuse and arbitrary treatment characterized AFDC and was designed to discourage them from applying for assistance or to prevent them from knowing and asserting their rights. In Chicago, for example, according to the West Side Organization, a local antipoverty group, "Stringent and inflexible rules of the system, interpreted and applied by punitive caseworkers, created great frustration among the women recipients."[94] In 1965 the staff of the WSO helped the women to form a union, which provided mutual assistance and enabled them to "take collective action in their own interests."[95] By the summer of 1966, the WSO Welfare Union had attracted over 1,500 welfare recipients.[96] The very act of coming together challenged the stigma long associated with AFDC and embodied the idea that welfare was not charity, but a right. Many women on AFDC, for the first time, publicly identified and spoke about their experiences as welfare recipients.

Yet, the complex rules and regulations, disempowerment of recipients, arbitrary control by caseworkers, and stingy allowances that gave recipients a reason to join or start a welfare rights group also made organizing difficult. Welfare recipients faced constant fear and occasional threats when deciding to form groups or speak out. As welfare organizers in New York City wrote,

> The first step the organizer took was in the direction of instilling confidence in those who attended the mass meetings—confidence that they were capable of standing up for their rights . . . Most of them had never before belonged to an organization and did not believe that they were capable of affecting the Welfare Department; those who did believe it was possible were frightened of the consequences.[97]

Involvement in a welfare rights group was a potentially costly activity for recipients. New York City organizers explained: "When the [welfare rights] group was first formed, some recipients were urged by their Department of Welfare caseworkers not to join the organization, and a few were warned that they would be cut off the rolls if they did."[98] Dorothy Moore in Los Angeles also recognized how fear dissuaded recipients from organizing. She formed a welfare recipients union after the department mistakenly gave her a weekly check for only $1.50 and she had nowhere to turn for help.[99] She described the overwhelming power of caseworkers:

> The worst thing is the way [caseworkers] use fear. People depend on their checks so much that they're afraid to speak up for their rights . . . they are afraid to assert themselves and ask for what's

theirs because if they do the worker may threaten to cut them off entirely.[100]

Leaders of the welfare rights movement worked to overcome this fear of organizing. The Citywide Welfare Alliance in Washington, D.C., distributed a flier encouraging recipients to "Come and learn your rights! Don't be afraid to speak out." Trying to allay the fears of welfare recipients, the organization assured them, "We know we now have power, so don't stand back. Your checks will not be cut off because of your participation in this organization."[101] Despite the innumerable obstacles to organizing, thousands of recipients banded together in the 1960s to reform the welfare system. The seeming omnipotency of caseworkers, recipients' financial insecurity, and shame associated with welfare may have instilled fear, but it did not deter them.

AFDC recipients often coalesced as a result of friendships or connections to a neighborhood association. These kitchen-table discussions enabled recipients to trade stories about the indignities of the welfare system, the first step in the formation of local welfare rights organizations. Through these discussions people came to believe that they should not have to be humiliated in order to receive a welfare check, that the grant should be enough for them to live decently, and that they had rights that ought to be protected. By meeting to talk about their problems, welfare recipients turned social networks into political ones and embarked on a process that ultimately led them to forcefully challenge the rules and regulations governing their lives.

Local organizing was not widespread before the emergence of a national movement in 1966. Nevertheless it illustrates that the impetus for the movement lay not with civil rights and student organizers, but with the daily experiences of welfare recipients and their belief that they could make gains—a belief no doubt influenced by the liberal political climate and the example of other social movements. The heart of the movement was comprised largely of poor, uneducated, single black mothers who were, to use the famous rallying cry of Civil Rights leader Fannie Lou Hamer: "sick and tired of being sick and tired."

Social Movements

The example of other social movements in the postwar period inspired women on welfare to organize in the early 1960s. After World War II, oppressed people throughout the world mobilized for political and economic independence. In India, Gandhi led a struggle for independence. Movements in Southeast Asia and Africa threw off the yoke of colonialism.

In the late 1940s, African Americans in the United States, both North and South, began to challenge segregated public and private facilities and worked to ensure equal access to the ballot and employment opportunities. Through lawsuits, boycotts, pickets, and marches, activists gained a measure of public sympathy in the struggle for racial equality and eventually forced the federal government to protect their basic civil rights. These examples demonstrated that relatively powerless people could successfully reform a social, political, and economic system that excluded and exploited them. The movements served as a model of grassroots organizing, inspiring others to question daily indignities. Although centered in the South, the black freedom movement spanned the nation's borders and in Oakland, Harlem, Chicago, Philadelphia, and countless other non-Southern cities, communities agitated, mobilized, and coalesced for social justice.[102] The movement's counterhegemonic discourse demonstrated that ordinary people could mobilize to transform discriminatory institutions in society, such as government, the legal system, and business.[103] Empowering individuals as agents of social change, the movements gave a voice to the disenfranchised and articulated a moral code of human rights, racial equality, and social justice that superseded the law and custom. Premised on the moral conviction of its participants, they prompted other grassroots groups during this period to organize: labor unions, farm workers, students, women, gays, and lesbians.

Women in the welfare rights movement drew on the example, language, and tactics of other social movements to assess their situation, develop a collective identity, and come together politically. The black freedom movement spoke to the women's concerns about racial equality and social justice and provided a framework for understanding their oppression. For some welfare recipients the connection was more direct because their first political involvement was in the black freedom movement. Whether or not they were active previously, the larger context and political climate of the postwar period gave welfare recipients both the optimism and opportunity to affect change.

Community Organizing, Housing, and Welfare

For most people on AFDC, welfare was part of a web of social problems, which included housing, education, playgrounds for children, urban renewal, police harassment, and high food prices. Recipients in the welfare rights movement had complex identities leading them to address a range of issues. They were not only "poor people" or "welfare recipients," but also mothers, people of color, tenants, consumers, and community members. By voicing their many roles and complicated interests, welfare recipients challenged the stigma associated with AFDC and questioned the belief that people on welfare were "dependents."

Welfare recipients often worked on myriad community issues before joining welfare rights. Many welfare recipients confronted the specific problem of welfare through their involvement in neighborhood and community organizations. In October 1966, welfare clients in Harlem and housewives in Queens boycotted grocery stores to protest an increase in food prices.[104] In the Ocean Hill-Brownsville School strike in New York City in 1968, nearly half of the participants involved in community organizations were members of welfare rights groups.[105] In Boston, the leaders of MAW worked on issues prior to welfare organizing, such as a Congress of Racial Equality (CORE) rent strike in 1962, campaigns with the multi-issue organization the Boston Action Group, an NAACP battle to end de facto school segregation in 1963 and 1964, and the 1964 congressional race of Noel Day.[106]

In the 1960s housing was deeply intertwined with welfare. A Mobilization for Youth (MFY) report stated in 1965: "Poor housing and welfare problems existed side by side and it was artificial to separate the two problem areas . . . Many tenants were found to be welfare recipients and the demand on housing staff to provide constant emergency welfare service threatened to stymie any efforts to deal with housing problems."[107] In Mount Vernon, NY, the Committee of Welfare Families, active around housing issues since at least 1966, had been

> protesting for several weeks against slum housing conditions that welfare recipients are forced to endure. Their action has included a sit-in at City Hall demanding temporary shelter and prompt relocation within Mt. Vernon for those evicted; an end to evictions for filing slum housing complaints. They plan to erect a tent in the center of the city for people already evicted who have no place to live.[108]

At its outset in 1968, a welfare rights group in Waltham, MA, said, "Housing is a main complaint of most of the mothers, since many of them pay more than half their incomes for housing."[109]

Many individuals who later became prominent in the welfare rights movement engaged first with issues other than welfare. Beulah Sanders, chair of the Citywide Coordinating Committee in New York from 1966 until 1971, was born and raised in Durham, NC. Sanders moved to New York City in 1957 in search of work. In 1966, unable to find work, she lived on the Upper West Side of Manhattan on a small welfare check in a neighborhood designated for urban renewal. The urban renewal program, known among some black activists as "Negro removal," sought to eradicate "slum" housing by moving poor people out to make way for better housing and wealthier families. Sanders joined the effort to reform urban renewal policies and end the demolition of homes of the poor. She defended the rights of neighborhood families, many of whom were welfare recipients, to remain in their homes. In the midst of this work she helped organize a city-wide welfare movement in New York.[110]

Another New York City activist, Jennette Washington, moved there from Florida in 1945 at the age of ten to live with her mother who had set out in search of work. Living first in Harlem and then in Washington Heights, she went to school until 10th grade and eventually found a job in a factory, but was laid off during a recession. She turned to welfare to help provide for her three children. Washington was always rebellious, questioning authority and standing up for her beliefs. As a youngster, this landed her in trouble with her mother, school authorities, and a judge, who sent her to a juvenile home for a period of time. As an adult, her indomitable personality was well suited for the political organizing that marked the 1950s and 1960s. Washington organized for many years in urban renewal, housing rights, parent-teacher associations, and a community group called the Stryckers Bay Organization, before getting involved in welfare rights activity. Well before the formation of NWRO she helped form the Westside Welfare Recipients League. Washington was at the founding NWRO convention and served on the executive board of the Citywide Coordinating Committee in New York from about 1968 until 1971.[111]

Both Sanders and Washington were part of a larger network of a Brooklyn-based welfare coalition known as the Welfare Recipients League. The League grew out of a grassroots storefront office, the East New York Action Center, started in the early 1960s by Frank Espada. A Puerto Rican who had served in the U.S. Air Force and worked for an electrical contractor, Espada had a long history of political activism. In 1949 at the age of 19, Espada was arrested and spent a week in jail in Biloxi, MS, for refusing to go to the back of a Trailways bus after his discharge from the Air Force. The handful of people working in the East New York storefront in this predominantly black and Puerto Rican neighborhood organized rent strikes and protested inadequate garbage pickup. They soon identified welfare as a critical community problem. Espada remembered, "We had situations where an investigator would barge in to see if they could find a man in the house without notifying anyone. They would go in and look under the beds for a man's shoes or in the closet." In 1964, they started the Welfare Recipients League and named Espada chair. The League grew quickly, and soon incorporated 24 chapters in Brooklyn, with some meetings drawing hundreds of people. Espada, Washington, Sanders, and other members of the Welfare

Recipients' League drove to the 1966 Chicago meeting where the Ohio march was initially discussed.[112]

In addition to the varied experiences of individual recipients, many welfare rights groups grew out of community organizations. Mobilization for Youth (MFY), funded by the federal government to address juvenile delinquency, turned its energy toward community problems and opened up neighborhood service centers.

> In the fall of 1962, when Mobilization's neighborhood service centers opened their doors offering help to anyone in need, it became very clear that what was needed was very largely help with the Welfare Department. Literally thousands of clients over the years ran into difficulty with Welfare—checks not arriving on time, inadequate allowances, emergencies unmet, personal indignities, and illegal coercion and intimidation.[113]

During the early 1960s MFY's neighborhood service centers aided thousands of individual clients with their problems but this did little to reform the practices and policies of the welfare department. Because of ongoing problems, "several workers suggested the idea of organizing clients to protest the more blatant of these practices."[114] They aided in the formation of the Welfare Recipients' League in 1964. The next year, MFY, and the League, with the assistance of Richard Cloward and Frances Fox Piven, formed a citywide welfare rights organization in New York.[115]

In Chicago welfare emerged out of community activism as well. The Kenwood-Oakland Community Organization (KOCO) had on its agenda, among other issues, education, housing, and urban renewal. In one campaign, for example, it opposed the Board of Education's decision to relocate residents to build a new school. But, again, welfare surfaced as a central problem. KOCO started a welfare union, with recipients designated "union stewards" charged with acting as counselors and advocates to other recipients.[116] In early 1966, KOCO Welfare Commission, as the union was known, published a welfare rights pamphlet and planned sit-ins and pickets to pressure the welfare department.[117] The pattern was repeated in Louisville, KY. The West End Community Council initially addressed problems of housing, education, tenants organizing, and recreational activities. Welfare, however, quickly became the main focus. Members planned "a series of workshops to inform local recipients of their rights; a membership drive; and a presentation of recipients' demands to welfare officials in Louisville and Frankford in conjunction with nationwide welfare demonstrations on June 30."[118] In Steubenville, OH, the Community Organization Members Build Absolute Teamwork (COMBAT) was formed in 1966 because of the failure of urban renewal and the poverty program to empower the poor. Out of this group, a welfare committee formed that joined NWRO.[119] For most AFDC recipients, welfare was not an isolated issue, but part of a broader set of concerns such as education, housing, and public safety.

Although the national demonstration in June 1966 officially launched the welfare rights movement, prior to that recipients organized. Northern urban communities were not apathetic in the middle or early 1960s. Urban political activity in the North was not simply a continuation of the Southern civil rights struggle.[120] Neither heightened expectations as a result of the civil rights movement nor a dawning realization by civil rights leaders that racism also existed in the North fully accounts for the birth of the movement. Before the emergence of a national welfare rights movement, and even simultaneously, welfare recipients addressed issues of poverty, welfare, education, housing, and urban renewal.

Although it is difficult to analyze with precision why recipients chose to get involved in welfare rights activity, certain inferences can be drawn. Personal contact among women on AFDC, such as when friends shared their problems or recipients joined neighborhood or community networks, facilitated the emergence of welfare rights organizations. In Englewood, NJ, "many welfare recipients, through meeting and talking generally with one another, found that they were experiencing some of the [same] difficulties with the Bergen County Welfare Board." When the department denied their requests for better communication between clients and caseworkers and more respect for clients, recipients recruited others to join a welfare rights organization.[121] One study in Hennepin County, MN, confirms the importance of personal networks. It concluded that stable welfare recipients who had moved fewer than four times in the previous ten years were more likely to be involved in welfare rights activity than those moving more frequently. In addition, recipients with a higher level of social participation in clubs, churches, and community organizations were more likely to join a welfare rights organization than recipients with a low level of social participation. In this particular study, factors such as age, education, number of children, and length of time on AFDC did not affect participation rates in welfare rights groups.[122]

By analyzing residential stability and social participation, this research suggests that spatial location and the opportunity for welfare recipients to get to know their neighbors were important in the origins of the welfare rights movement.[123] This explains the movement's strength in urban areas, where black women on AFDC could more easily contact other recipients. During the 1950s the number of black women living in urban areas increased by 2.3 million, the largest documented increase to date.[124] In addition, public housing projects expanded in the 1950s contributing to the ways in which people connected socially and politically.[125] Between 1950 and 1960, the number of low-rent housing units managed by the U.S. Housing Authority increased nearly two and one-half times from 201,736 to 478,153. The increase in low-income public housing in this period was greatest in the northeastern and midwestern states of New York, Massachusetts, Pennsylvania, Illinois, and Michigan, where the welfare rights movement found its strongest base.[126] Even more important, federal regulations, by the end of the 1950s, increased the number of poor black women and recipients of AFDC in public housing.[127] So, women like Johnnie Tillmon, for example, canvassed recipients in her housing project to join a welfare rights organization. Similarly, Ethel Dotson, a member of the Richmond, CA, WRO in 1966, who later joined the NWRO National Coordinating Committee, was introduced to welfare rights through meetings in her housing project community center.[128] Thus, urban migration and expansion of public housing helped bring welfare recipients into more concentrated geographical areas, affording them the opportunity to more easily meet one another and address the difficulties associated with AFDC.

Race, Welfare, and the Black Freedom Movement

Race was an important factor in the formation of the welfare rights movement. The welfare rolls in the mid-1960s were 48 percent African American. The welfare rights movement, however, was overwhelmingly African American, perhaps 85 percent, with some participation by white, Latina, and Native American women.[129] Women in the welfare rights movement believed that racism was the scaffolding for the welfare system, which did not regard all poor people or welfare recipients the same. Black women welfare rights activists articulated their involvement in part because of the racism they experienced as AFDC recipients. MAW in Boston explained the different treatment of black and white recipients:

> White recipients will almost automatically be granted special allowances at some offices, while black recipients in similar circumstances will be met with delaying tactics plus a full quota of red tape, and then will probably be turned down. Likewise, caseworkers are accused of using their power to disapprove moving allowances for the purpose of keeping white recipients out of disreputable neighborhoods while black recipients are kept in.[130]

AFDC had a long history of racial discrimination. The cultural, class, and racial bias of caseworkers, administrators, and local politicians affected the disbursement of welfare funds. After the passage of the Social Security

Act, Southern states routinely excluded African Americans from the welfare rolls, by relying on policies such as the suitable-home clause and man-in-the-house rule.[131] In addition, the political attacks on welfare in the 1950s and early 1960s were framed in racial terms and rooted in stereotypes of black women. The association between race and welfare may have encouraged black recipients to join a welfare rights group.

The numerous ties between the welfare rights and black freedom movements also partly explain the disproportionately large number of black women in the welfare rights movement. Discrimination in welfare policies attracted the attention of many organizations including the NAACP. Both the NAACP and the Nation of Islam, for example, formally protested Joseph Mitchell's plans during the Newburgh drama.[132] In addition, beginning in 1967, the NAACP Legal Defense Fund "launch[ed] a broad attack on what it called the 'widespread abuse of clients' rights in the distribution of public assistance.'"[133] Antiracist groups' challenges to the welfare system highlighted the racially discriminatory nature of the program and may have encouraged black recipients to take similar stands.

The black freedom movement had many strands and in the postwar period could be located in northern cities and southern towns from the late 1940s, pushing in numerous ways for racial justice.[134] It appealed to people of varying political perspectives, not all of whom sympathized with the problems of the black poor. Some civil rights leaders opposed organizing African Americans to claim welfare benefits. When Richard Cloward and Frances Fox Piven sought to convince people that the moment was ripe to encourage African American women to join the welfare rolls, they approached Whitney Young of the National Urban League. Revealing his own class biases, Young responded to Piven and Cloward by saying: "I would rather get one black woman a job as an airline stewardess than I would to get fifty black mothers on welfare."[135]

Nevertheless, many welfare recipients and organizers who first became involved in the black freedom movement later joined the struggle for welfare rights. The black freedom movement raised their consciousness about racism, enabling them to see more clearly the racial nature of the welfare state. A civil rights activist and welfare recipient in Mississippi found that support for civil rights causes, not just the fact that he was African American, led to unjust treatment by a caseworker. He explained: "In April 1964 I was put on welfare . . . In February 1965 Mr. Caldwell called me into his office and asked if I had kept a volunteer for [the civil rights group] the Council of Federated Organization in my house. I said yes . . . I did not get my welfare check in March."[136] George Wiley and his associate at the Poverty/Rights Action Center (P/RAC), Edwin Day, both worked with the Congress of Racial Equality (CORE) before breaking away to launch antipoverty campaigns. Mrs. Mildred Calvert, chairman of the Northside Welfare Rights Organization in Milwaukee, also rooted her welfare rights activity in the civil rights movement. She explained that a local priest, Father James Groppi, led civil rights marches in her city. Although "I was afraid of those kind of things . . . when the kids decided that they were going [on the march] . . . I had to go with them." The newspapers reported that the marchers "were doing all the bad things . . . [but] we were the ones being fired upon with rocks and bricks and sticks." She read the black newspapers and started "seeing things in a different light."[137] This was when she joined the welfare rights movement. The links between the black freedom movement and the welfare rights movement exemplified by Calvert's experience partly explains the overrepresentation of black people in the struggle for welfare rights. White welfare recipients usually did not have the same close ties to the black freedom movement. These black men and women participating in campaigns for black equality slowly linked the concept of racism to the welfare system as well.

Through campaigns for welfare rights, organizers and recipients hoped to alleviate the poverty of African Americans and thus come closer to their ultimate goal of racial equality. More than one local welfare rights group argued that cuts in AFDC disproportionately affecting African Americans were racist and violated the equal protection clause. Welfare rights activists also believed that remedying welfare problems would diminish the poverty of African Americans. Although Wiley, in the earliest years of the movement, underscored the interracial nature of poverty, he believed targeting economic issues through welfare activism addressed many of the hardships African Americans encountered.

For most women on welfare, their race or nationality was inseparable from their day-to-day experiences as welfare recipients. Mrs. Clementina Castro, Vice-Chairman of the Union Benefica Hispana WRO and Sergeant-at-Arms of the Milwaukee County WRO, explained:

> When I first came on welfare, they didn't have any Spanish-speaking caseworkers at all . . . I was so shy because I had never talked to white people, because I had been working in the fields . . . Some whites can speak it, but they just know the language, they don't know the problems. Latins can understand better because they know, they have already passed through the same problems. They know our culture.[138]

Welfare recipients, such as Mrs. Castro, saw race and culture mediating their interactions with caseworkers and their relationship with the welfare department. These welfare recipients articulated their problem with the welfare system as one of racial discrimination as well as poverty. The discretionary acts of racism by caseworkers and the systematic mistreatment of black and Latino recipients fostered among welfare rights activists a consciousness rooted as much in their experiences as black, brown, and white people as their status as poor. As black nationalism gained a firmer foothold in the mid-1960s and racial identity became a salient and more frequent part of political discussion, welfare rights activists employed a language of racial consciousness and voiced their struggle as partly for racial liberation. They combined a racial/gender/class analysis, linking their blackness to their experiences as poor women on welfare.

For welfare activists, however, a racial consciousness did not preclude the possibility of working in an interracial setting; and organizing in a multiracial setting did not mean a movement devoid of an analysis of race. They situated racism as integral to the disbursement of welfare while launching an interracial movement and inviting people of any color to join them. Beverly Edmon, the founder of the Welfare Recipients Union in Los Angeles, said: "There's as many white people, probably a lot more, who have the very same kind of problems we get here from welfare. Poor people have the same problems, black or white. What we have to offer is good for anybody who comes in."[139] Welfare leaders formulated a welfare rights agenda that attempted to toe a line, on the one hand, of addressing the racism of the welfare system and wanting to empower black women and, on the other hand, recognizing the class-based nature of their oppression, welcoming all women on welfare, and suggesting that racist attitudes were not inherent. In the context of the emerging Black Power movement, it was a fine line to walk and one that was not always done successfully or with circumspection on the local or national level.

Mothers on Welfare

Many women in the welfare rights movement identified as mothers and were motivated in large part to provide adequately for their children. They wanted the state to support and recognize their work as mothers. Many local welfare rights organizations portrayed themselves as mothers groups, with the word "mother" in their name. In northern Colorado a group calling itself the AFDC Mothers Club organized to protect their rights.[140] Johnnie Tillmon started ANC Mothers Anonymous in California and, in Minnesota, recipients established AFDC Mothers Leagues beginning in 1964.[141] Many welfare rights groups also framed their campaigns and demands as beneficial for their children. In Pennsylvania in mid-June 1966, 700 mothers on welfare planned a "crusade for children" and asked legislatures for an immediate increase in the basic AFDC grant.[142] The Citywide

Coordinating Committee of Welfare Rights Groups in New York wanted to ensure that "our children . . . have the same advantages, the same education, the same hospital services, the same opportunities as other children."[143] The needs of children were a primary issue for many women joining the welfare rights movement.

Lois Walker, a member of the Rockbridge County WRO in Virginia, understood her welfare rights activity in terms of quality of care for her children. Several of her children had health problems including a son with eczema who needed oil baths twice a day, a nearly blind daughter who needed close supervision, and an epileptic son who required medication daily. She explained,

> I was working at the time I became a member because the Welfare Department had really forced me to leave my five children with just any unreliable babysitter . . . I was told if I didn't work my children would be taken away from me. So by being in the group I learned my rights by being an ADC mother, and I am constantly fighting for the beneficial changes that would improve the living conditions for both me and my children.[144]

Welfare recipients responded, in part, to a shift in national welfare policy in the early 1960s, which sought to encourage women on welfare to enter the labor force rather than to support them in their work as mothers. For many black women in the welfare rights movement, their work as mothers had never been valued as much as their participation in waged labor. At a time when welfare recipients—black recipients in particular—were increasingly attacked as lazy, immoral women not worthy of receiving public assistance, these welfare recipients stood up to declare the importance of their work as mothers and to justify their welfare check as compensation for raising their children. Only much later, in the early 1970s, did they display a more coherent feminist analysis, focusing not just on the rights of children, but on the rights of women. Initially, however, many women participated in the struggle for welfare rights because of concern for their children.[145]

This early agitation and welfare recipients' initiative is an important part of the story of how the welfare rights movement emerged. Later developments within the movement were informed by how women on welfare understood their relationship to the welfare department, what prompted them to organize, and how they conceptualized their political involvement. But their experiences are not the complete story. Women activists received invaluable assistance from middle-class allies, enabling their fledgling neighborhood groups to transform into a national political movement.

The number of welfare rights groups increased dramatically after 1964 because of civil rights, student, and antipoverty activism. After 1964, the welfare rights movement acquired momentum and a measure of visibility. The changing political climate, financial resources, and middle-class assistance proved important in the expansion of this nascent movement.

Middle-Class and Nonprofit Support

Increasing attention to poverty among social movement activists, politicians, and ordinary Americans in the mid-1960s led to an outpouring of resources devoted to eradicating poverty. Middle-class support helped recipients overcome obstacles to organizing, augmenting the welfare rights movement. Local welfare rights groups acquired support in their political work from Students for a Democratic Society (SDS), churches, legal aid societies, civil rights groups, and federal antipoverty agencies. Middle-class allies canvassed neighborhoods to recruit recipients, provided meeting space for recipients, gave legal advice, funded local welfare rights groups, and hired staff to work with welfare rights leaders. Some supporters offered basic necessities like use of a telephone while others helped initiate and maintain welfare rights groups. Whatever the level of support, middle-class organizations and individuals proved indispensable in the creation of a national welfare rights movement.

Transformations within some black freedom movement organizations cultivated the concerns about poverty among the middle class. The black freedom movement was heterogeneous, encompassing people who adopted conflicting tactics and articulated differing analyses. Some Southern black activists framed their struggle in international terms, addressed poverty, or advocated black self-defense in the face of white violence, well before the mid-1960s.[146] This diversity notwithstanding, by the mid-1960s a perceptible shift occurred among many national movement leaders prompting them to see the pitfalls of defining racism solely in terms of southern Jim Crow laws and the fallacy of ending discrimination by simply abolishing those laws. African American political leaders, such as Martin Luther King, Jr., concluded that economic justice was vital for social equality. Although unemployment was at one of its lowest points in the postwar period, millions of Americans lived in dilapidated housing and were malnourished and inadequately clothed. Michael Harrington estimated in 1962 that 40 to 50 million Americans were poor.[147] Although the problem crossed racial and ethnic boundaries, the black community bore the brunt of it. In 1962, for example, 15 percent of white families, but 40 percent of black families, earned less than the poverty line of $3,000.[148] Social movement activists contemplated how to alleviate or, better yet, eradicate poverty. Urban uprisings in the mid-1960s targeted exploitative "ghetto merchants." The Southern Christian Leadership Conference's Fair Housing Campaign in Chicago, the economic project of Students for a Democratic Society, and the Student Non-Violent Coordinating Committee's turn to black power all signaled the change in emphasis from civil rights to economic empowerment within certain sectors of the New Left and liberal reform movements of the mid-1960s.[149]

These developments, buoyed by the academic research of the preceding few years, helped engender a discernible shift in the national mood in the mid-1960s, leading to the passage of the Economic Opportunity Act (EOA) in 1964. Through the EOA, the federal government launched a War on Poverty and organized programs to address the needs of the poor, promising "equality as a fact." Head Start and Job Corps made available education and job training for the poor. But the Office of Economic Opportunity (OEO) also funneled government money into community organizations to aid the poor. Perhaps the most important and certainly the most controversial aspect of the War on Poverty was the Community Action Program (CAP), designed to encourage participation of poor people in neighborhood and community associations. Authors of the CAP wanted representation of poor people in organizations working in their interests and included a clause requiring "maximum feasible participation" of the poor. In practice this meant that CAP funded poor people's and welfare recipients' organizations and inspired middle-class activists working on antipoverty issues to mobilize welfare recipients and other poor people to work with them. Federal grants promoted the activism of poor people and provided the material resources for many welfare rights groups to hire organizers, print leaflets, and operate storefront offices. As Johnnie Tillmon explained, "Community action programs and agencies began to form and we began to participate. I'm sure whoever wrote those words 'maximum feasible participation of the poor,' wished they had not done that!"[150]

OEO employed a group of poverty workers, VISTA, which was a domestic version of the Peace Corps volunteers that helped organize welfare rights groups. In 1969, Hulbert James, the Executive Director of New York's Citywide Coordinating Committee, explained, albeit with some exaggeration, "Welfare rights organizations in this country were developed primarily by VISTA."[151] Because of the important contribution of VISTA, organizers attempted to recruit welfare recipients to work with the VISTA program. A group in Pennsylvania announced in its newsletter: "The Welfare Rights Organization of Allegheny County is still accepting applications from welfare recipients for work as VISTA volunteers for the coming year. These VISTAs will be working to build strong welfare rights and tenants' groups throughout Allegheny County."[152]

On the Lower East Side of Manhattan, Mobilization for Youth (MFY), a Ford Foundation and government-funded antidelinquency agency, started several welfare rights groups through neighborhood service centers.[153] Middle-class organizers for MFY helped form the Committee of Welfare Families in October 1965, the Welfare Action Group Against Poverty (WAGAP), and the Citizen's Welfare Action Group in March 1966. Organizers were instrumental in the development of these groups, especially WAGAP, which they believed needed guidance and participation by MFY staff because members were older, "more shy and less sophisticated . . . [and] a larger percentage were illiterate or semiliterate."[154] In Columbus, OH, the People's Poverty Board (PPB) had a cross-class committee of welfare recipients, caseworkers, and civil rights activists, which became an independent Welfare Rights Organization in August 1966.[155] The PPB, a coalition of inner-city leaders, poor people, and community organizations, formed in opposition to the local CAP agency with the purpose of implementing more fully maximum feasible participation of ordinary people. With their motto "let the people decide," they promised to "take whatever steps necessary to promote and insure the right of the people to effective control over their own destiny."[156]

SDS worked with welfare recipients through their Economic Research and Action Program (ERAP). From 1963 to 1965 students in SDS immersed themselves in community organizing in several cities across the country building "an interracial movement of the poor." Intense discussions within the fledgling organization led many to conclude that students could organize inner-city communities and construct a model of participatory democracy. Intending to organize unemployed men, students were forced to consider the specific problems of welfare recipients by poor women who responded to organizing efforts. Students established community centers to work with the poor and welfare emerged as the central issue.[157] MAW in Boston was one product of ERAP. It originated when several Boston welfare mothers, whose children were in the same after-school program, attended the 1963 March on Washington, where other participants told them about the surplus food program.[158] This group of friends (they did not invite people they did not like) got together when they returned to Boston to discuss problems such as the lack of a surplus food program. In 1965, with the help of SDS organizers, they formed MAW.[159] The recipient convening the first meeting reported that "she had become very scared of what she had started, and had been filled with misgivings and worry that her children might in some way be hurt by the publicity."[160] Despite the early hesitation, the group flourished and recruited many new members. Three years later the organization had six branches in the Boston area with a membership of between fifty and sixty. SDS also made

Cleveland an ERAP site and began to work closely with Citizens United for Adequate Welfare (CUFAW), which had organized around welfare cuts in Ohio in the early 1960s, but lay dormant for a couple of years. Sharon Jeffrey and other SDS organizers moved into Cleveland's Near West Side to recruit recipients into the CUFAW. The infusion of resources and energy revived CUFAW, and it quickly became a functioning organization. Throughout Ohio, recipients, with the help of supporters, organized regional committees for adequate welfare. In the spring of 1966 the local and regional groups in Ohio came together to form the Ohio Steering Committee for Adequate Welfare, which launched the Ohio Walk for Adequate Welfare.[161]

In some cases sympathetic caseworkers encouraged recipient activism. Caseworkers were often a target of recipient discontent, but in the 1960s, many people sensitive to clients' predicaments entered the social work profession. Social work students radicalized on college campuses across the country rejected the traditional casework approach to social welfare as well as the overriding concern for professionalism of many social workers in the early postwar period.[162] This led, according to Richard Cloward, to "an important activist segment that was very supportive" of welfare rights.[163] In the 1960s, for example, public welfare workers unionized in New York, Detroit, and Chicago. In New York 8,000 members of the Social Service Employees Union went on strike in 1965 demanding improvements for themselves and their clients.[164] A significant minority of social workers supported a more generous and liberal welfare system and worked with WROs, becoming advocates for welfare rights. For example, according to one study that surveyed members of the National Association of Social Workers, 45 percent of respondents in 1968 believed that poor people must organize to demand better treatment.[165] These social workers assisted welfare recipients in articulating and pushing for their rights. Betty Niedzwiecki, chairman of a WRO in Milwaukee County, illustrates this point:

> When I went on welfare, they stuck me in an experimental zone. The caseworkers in there were working for the people as much as they possibly could. They even belonged to Milwaukee's Friends of Welfare Rights. They told me about Welfare Rights in the first place. They informed me of a lot of things that go on.[166]

Churches also aided welfare rights organizations. Catholic priests and Protestant ministers worked with a predominantly white MAW chapter in Waltham, MA. In a press release, a leader of the group said, "We are very grateful for the help of the priests and ministers. Having them at the meeting will show the mothers that their churches are behind them and will make them less afraid."[167] In Brooklyn, NY, several Catholic priests set up storefront meeting centers for welfare recipients to inform clients of their legal rights, give them lists of items to which they were entitled, and encourage them to confront the welfare department. On a national level, churches also provided most of the financial support for NWRO. Protestant denominations, including the United Church of Christ, Methodists, Presbyterians, and Episcopalians, funded nearly half of NWRO's budget in 1968. Other support came from Catholic and Jewish groups. The largest single funding source for NWRO was the Interreligious Foundation for Community Organizations (IFCO), an arm of the National Council of Churches. Between 1967 and 1971, IFCO gave $500,000 to NWRO.[168] Formed in early 1967 by the United Presbyterian Church, the United Church of Christ, and the Episcopal Church, IFCO supported community organizing in poor neighborhoods. The formation of IFCO and Protestant and Catholic support for community organizing was part of a religious inclination in the 1960s and 1970s to emphasize social action over service and to advocate liberation and empowerment of the poor and oppressed. In concrete terms, this meant a huge network of financial and political support for the welfare rights movement.

Other institutions with a long history of radical politics, like the Highlander Folk School in Tennessee, also supported welfare rights organizing. In 1932 Myles Horton and Don West founded Highlander as an education and training camp for union activists. But in the 1950s the center branched out to civil rights activity as well. The center's history of support for progressive causes made it a place where recipients could turn for help. A group of welfare recipients from Boone County, a rural coal mining district in southern West Virginia, asked Highlander to assist them in starting a welfare rights organization and hosting a workshop on community organizing. They recruited people, arranged transportation, and drove 350 miles to the Center in Tennessee for a weekend workshop:

> These recipients, most with little or no formal education, in a very short period of time, developed and ran an educational program which dealt with constitutional rights, welfare law, and organizing skills. Out of this small beginning there developed a state-wide group which eventually became a force state legislators grew to fear.[169]

The impetus by recipients in West Virginia came to fruition because of assistance from the Highlander Center as well as lawyers who helped them interpret the laws, students and VISTA with research and technical expertise, and churches that provided funds.

In some cases, middle-class supporters dominated and controlled welfare rights groups, making decisions about campaigns and goals. Although their decisions did not necessarily impact recipients negatively, in these instances, the middle-class organizers, not the recipients, exercised power. Their decisions may have materially benefited women on welfare but did little to challenge their fundamental powerlessness. In some cases, a paternalistic relationship developed between middle-class organizers and AFDC recipients. In New York City, neighborhood service center workers who formed the Committee of Welfare Families first decided to wage a winter clothing drive and then called a meeting of welfare clients.[170] Seventy clients attended the first meeting in October 1965:

> The workers explained their right to winter clothing and that their demands might be more effective if the recipients banded together in a group rather than working as individuals through the neighborhood service centers . . . Thus, the winter-clothing campaign began, and the Committee of Welfare Families was instituted.[171]

Middle-class supporters usually brought with them their own notions about welfare and strategies for change. Some subscribed to the widespread belief that welfare dependency was detrimental and hoped that through participation in a welfare rights organization, recipients would ultimately get off welfare. One organizer stated: "It seems likely that being involved in the fight to better conditions for those on welfare, rather than making people more dependent on welfare, actually has the effect of making it possible for some to leave the welfare rolls."[172] In the movement's earliest years conflicts about decision making and the role of middle-class organizers were not explosive. As other nonrecipient activists became directly involved in helping form a national organization, both the immense benefits and inherent problems with middle-class support became clear.

Civil rights groups, students, churches, and antipoverty agencies provided funding, space, administrative skills, and material resources for welfare recipients to organize. The incipient welfare rights movement swelled in the mid-1960s with increased national attention to poverty and an infusion of resources and support. Middle-class efforts aided recipients in establishing new and sustaining old welfare rights groups. Because of the particular plight of welfare recipients, these alliances proved necessary for the creation of a mass welfare rights movement.

Formation of a National Group

One civil rights activist concerned about the problem of poverty and welfare was George Wiley, a black chemistry professor at Syracuse University who eventually became the first executive director of NWRO. Born in 1931 in New Jersey and raised in Warwick, RI, a semirural, nearly all-white middle-class town near Providence, Wiley attended the University of Rhode Island and earned his Ph.D. in Chemistry at Cornell. After a postdoctoral position at the University of California at Los Angeles, and a teaching stint at the University of California at Berkeley, he took a position at Syracuse University. While at Syracuse, Wiley chaired the local CORE chapter, which initiated a series of protests to integrate the public schools and fight for equal employment and housing opportunity.

In 1964 Wiley left his teaching post at Syracuse to work full time with CORE as associate national director, second in command under James Farmer. When Farmer announced his resignation in late 1965, Floyd McKissick, chairman of CORE's policy-making body, the National Action Council, and Wiley both vied for Farmer's position. Wiley was at a disadvantage, however, partly because of the rising tide of nationalism within CORE. Many believed that Wiley's sophisticated and cultured background would do little to ingratiate him with the young militants. In addition, in his ambitious pursuit for power within the organization, Wiley had curried disfavor with Farmer, who in the end supported McKissick.[173] After the unsuccessful attempt to win Farmer's position, Wiley resigned from CORE. He worked briefly for the Citizen's Crusade Against Poverty, before deciding to branch out and form his own organization.

In April 1966, using money raised from friends and $3,000 of his own savings, Wiley started the Poverty/Rights Action Center (P/RAC) in Washington, D.C. Edwin Day, a graduate student in public affairs at Syracuse who had worked with Wiley in CORE and left the organization with him, helped start P/RAC.[174] Wiley and Day envisioned P/RAC as a communications clearinghouse for poor people's organizations around the country, linking efforts already underway. The increased welfare rights activity around the country and the persistent urging of Frances Fox Piven and Richard Cloward, two Columbia University School of Social Work professors, convinced Wiley to focus on welfare.

Wiley met Cloward and Piven at the "Poor People's War Council on Poverty" in Syracuse in January 1966. That year, the two scholars wrote an article arguing that the current welfare system should be replaced by a guaranteed annual income. After extensive research, they discovered that nearly half the people qualifying for AFDC did not receive it and proposed that organizers recruit these people onto the welfare rolls. This, they predicted, would "precipitate a profound financial and political crisis" in the welfare system. City governments, unable to handle the large influx of new recipients, would pressure the national government to implement a guaranteed annual income.[175] George Wiley, on the other hand, was more interested in building an organization of poor people. He wanted "to unite public assistance recipients around the country into an organized bloc that can push for better welfare legislation and demand with some authority that abuses in the system be corrected."[176] He believed that marches, sit-ins, and threats of disruption would reap electoral leverage and economic power for the poor if they were organized. To this end, Wiley hoped to create a mass-based national organization.[177] Although Piven's and Cloward's strategy was not adopted—NWRO chose to recruit current recipients rather than mobilize potential recipients—the two social scientists, were important in the intellectual development of the movement. Piven and Cloward met periodically with Wiley to discuss the direction of the movement, attended conferences and meetings, and raised money. They differed with Wiley and other organizers about NWRO's strategy, but Cloward's and Piven's idea for a guaranteed annual income would ultimately become a central goal of NWRO.[178]

Wiley recruited Tim Sampson, who managed the welfare rights' headquarters as associate director for three years, to work with him and Day at P/RAC.[179] Sampson, a white organizer and social worker, helped start the Alameda County Welfare Rights Organization in California. The first P/RAC staff members set up shop in an old pink row house in Northwest Washington, D.C., and during the first few months traveled around the country speaking to welfare rights leaders. Day contacted Johnnie Tillmon in Los Angeles. When Tillmon got word that an organizer from Washington was looking for her, she called a friend and asked him to "check out" this guy. When her friend confirmed that Day was "okay," Tillmon met and spoke to him about her work with ANC. Within a year, twenty people worked in the P/RAC office in Washington.[180]

While setting up P/RAC, Wiley attended a conference on Guaranteed Income at the University of Chicago in the spring of 1966.[181] After the conference, recipient and nonrecipient welfare activists from around the country, including a group from Ohio that was planning a Walk for Decent Welfare, met. They came from Chicago, Ann Arbor, Newark, Syracuse, New York City, Detroit, and Cleveland.[182] Johnnie Tillmon, Beulah Sanders, Frank Espada, and many others who would become important national leaders also attended this first meeting.[183] This was, in fact, the first time welfare rights leaders from around the country got together.

This meeting laid the basis for a nationally coordinated campaign. The Ohio group had planned their protest for June 30, and asked other activists from around the country to join them. Since it was impractical for welfare recipients who had little money to travel to Ohio, they decided that groups would hold their own demonstrations to coincide with the Ohio Walk. June 30 would be a national day of action for welfare rights.[184] Frank Espada, of the Brooklyn-based Welfare Recipients League, also proposed that they form a national coordinating committee that would meet again in Chicago in August to discuss plans for a national welfare rights organization.[185] Two days after the Chicago conference Wiley returned to Washington for the official opening of P/RAC. He then turned his energies to making June 30 a success. A shrewd fund-raiser, he got a $5,000 loan from Irving Fain, an industrialist in Providence, RI.[186] He also sought financial assistance from people such as Katherine Graham, publisher of the *Washington Post*, Harold Taylor, former president of Sarah Lawrence College, and Maurice Tempelsman, diamond mine owner in South Africa.[187] He traveled around the country meeting with welfare rights leaders and recruiting help from community and religious leaders and social service workers. He mailed out literature, contacted the press, and helped form local and regional welfare rights committees to coordinate activity.[188]

Although a citywide welfare rights group already existed in New York, Wiley worked with several welfare recipients active there, including Beulah Sanders and Jennette Washington, and spoke to them about coordinating the demonstration. The group decided to hold the June 30 protest at City Hall in Manhattan. By August 1966, New York's Citywide Coordinating Committee included forty-five affiliated groups and claimed to represent 5,000 clients. Wiley asked Hulbert James to serve as executive director of Citywide. Born in the Virgin Islands and raised in Harlem, James was active in the student movement and the NAACP while in college. During the mid-1960s he was working on welfare issues with a Louisville antipoverty agency when he contacted George Wiley during the summer of 1966. James accepted Wiley's offer, and by August 1967, was working full time with the Citywide Coordinating Committee of Welfare Rights Groups.[189]

In addition to working with specific local chapters, Wiley also coordinated welfare rights activity nationally. A savvy political organizer adept at dealing with journalists, politicians, and welfare officials of all colors and stripes, Wiley managed at once to bring both much needed publicity and funding to the efforts of local welfare rights groups. More important, he created a space and an opportunity for welfare recipients from around the country to come together around national campaigns and to lend support to local struggles. He helped transform the local struggles against welfare into a coherent national political movement. An important function of NWRO was, according to Wiley, the "encouragement that the local group gets from knowing that it is part of a movement greater than its own local situation. The national visibility we have given to the welfare problem by linking together what would otherwise appear to be disparate activity pulls together matters of really great importance."[190] Welfare recipients concurred. Beulah Sanders believed that if the "system were to be effectively changed, a strong, cohesive organization would have to be formed to link together the activities and purposes of the many neighborhood welfare rights groups that existed."[191] This networking and organizing for the June 30 demonstration that grew out of the Chicago meeting signaled the emergence of a national welfare rights movement.

Wiley and his allies were important in the development of a national welfare rights movement. They did not, however, start the movement. Welfare recipients around the country were already fighting for their rights on a local level. They discussed problems, provided mutual support, and worked to reform unjust policies. Far from being apathetic, this political constituency tackled, not just issues of welfare, but housing, education, and community service. In fact, Catherine Jermany, participant in the Los Angeles County WRO, explained, "We were not particularly interested in a national organization and being a part of it because we had our own thing going in California."[192] Frances Fox Piven reflected on this period of organizing: "There's a sort of arrogance in the . . . way George and all of the organizers really believed that they were moving people . . . That organizers got people to come to a meeting, or a march, or to get arrested or to scream or erupt . . . Organizers played a role. But people were ready to move. People were ready to join [an] organization."[193] They did not initiate the movement, but Wiley and other middle-class supporters expanded and strengthened organizing on the local level. More important, they created a venue to discuss on a national level the goals of a movement.

In August 1966, 100 representatives from seventy-five welfare rights organizations around the country came to the first NWRO meeting in Chicago to set up a national coordinating committee and to formulate goals and strategies for a nationwide movement. At the next national meeting of welfare recipients, in Washington in the spring of 1967, 375 people attended and laid plans for a formal organization. Because of concerns about domination by middle-class people, NWRO limited membership and voting privileges to the poor.[194] Wealthier supporters were invited to join a Friends of Welfare Rights group, which would provide financial and moral support for the movement. Local welfare rights organizations could affiliate with NWRO when they recruited twenty-five members and sent the national office $1 dues per member per year. This earned them the right to send a delegate to the annual national convention. Most local groups required members to pay yearly dues of $1 to the local welfare organization and another $1 for national membership. In this way, NWRO was more of a federation of local groups than a direct membership organization. The national office encouraged, but did not require, local groups to adopt "WRO" as part of their name to display affiliation with the national association.

The yearly convention of representatives from welfare rights organizations around the country set the general program and goals of NWRO. The

National Coordinating Committee (NCC), made up of elected delegates from each state with affiliated welfare rights organizations, was the policy-making body between national conventions and met four times a year. In addition, an executive committee, composed of nine welfare recipients elected at the national convention, carried out policy decisions made by the membership at the convention or the NCC. The executive committee met eight times a year and decided policy between conventions and NCC meetings.[195] George Wiley, the executive director of the national office in Washington, hired a staff to help him fundraise, distribute information to welfare rights organizations around the country, and coordinate campaigns. The official role of the staff was to implement the decisions of the national convention, the NCC, and the executive committee. At the first convention in August 1967, welfare recipients from around the country elected officers. Johnnie Tillmon, head of ANC Mothers in Los Angeles, was chosen chairman of the new organization.[196] They also decided to wage a several-pronged strategy, outlining four major goals of their organization: adequate income, dignity, justice, and democracy. These goals would be incorporated into specific struggles for dignity and representation, to protect the legal rights of welfare recipients, and launch a campaign to raise recipients' standard of living.

The welfare rights movement began with a sense of optimism about what could be achieved. The example of the civil rights movement, the many efforts already underway to organize the poor, and the success of the June 30 demonstration all strengthened its resolve that the time was ripe for working with the poorest of the poor. In this context, welfare recipients came together to challenge the harsh realities of the welfare system. Through the process of self-empowerment, they exhibited a complex political identity, rooted in the many facets of their lives. This political identity would mature into a firmer ideological position over the course of the next several years. It would be the basis upon which they formulated strategy, developed alliances, and, in their eyes, organized a movement that would become the true test of America's commitment to democracy and social justice.

CHAPTER 2
Dignity and Representation

At the first nationwide welfare rights protest on June 30, 1966, recipients in New York City carried signs that read, "I'm a human being too." One demonstrator reportedly told the press, "The welfare treats you like animals, they want you to be animals and if you let them get away with it, you will be an animal."[1] The sentiment that the welfare system dehumanized recipients and treated them capriciously united participants in the welfare rights movement. Prior to the emergence of the welfare rights movement, many recipients were unaware of their rights; others were too ashamed to make claims for better treatment or had too few avenues to challenge the power of welfare officials. Beginning in the 1960s, welfare recipients organized to change the way welfare was administered, protesting violations of their civil rights, arbitrary rules and regulations, and the lack of dignity. They sought to diminish the power of caseworkers, educate recipients about welfare regulations, ensure fair enforcement of laws, pursue a legal strategy to bring AFDC under constitutional protection, and include welfare recipients in the making of welfare policy. They ultimately wanted to remove the stigma associated with receipt of welfare and empower recipients.

The strategy of reforming laws that governed the welfare system and ensuring their proper enforcement provides an important window into the nature of political action advocated by the welfare rights movement. By demanding that welfare regulations be universally enforced, seeking redress in the legal system, and advocating participation in policy making, welfare rights activists' rhetoric and platform dovetailed with the calls for justice, fair treatment, and participation espoused by many liberal reformers of this period.[2] Their efforts to reform the administration of welfare echoed basic tenets of mainstream liberal political theory in the 1960s: including marginalized groups in the democratic system, protecting civil rights and ensuring equal opportunity. In this sense, the welfare rights movement operated within and accepted much of the mainstream political wisdom.

From the standpoint of welfare recipients, however, these struggles challenged the mistreatment of AFDC recipients. Poor black women on welfare sought accountability from the welfare department. For recipients who had been taught that welfare was shameful, standing up and demanding their rights asserted their dignity and self-worth. For women uninformed about their entitlements, education was empowering. For recipients whose fate was left to the whim of an individual caseworker, subjecting caseworkers to a set of standards that applied equally to everyone was a progressive reform. These struggles empowered recipients, helped them overcome the stigma associated with welfare, and shifted the balance of power between recipients and welfare officials. Their victories gave them leverage to influence the disbursement of AFDC, making life on welfare a little more secure. Some of the political struggles to reform the administration of welfare were carried out by lawyers and located in a courtroom. All of the reforms, however, were part of the larger grassroots movement of welfare recipients. Legal arguments did not win the victories in isolation. The threat of protest and disruption by recipients increased public awareness about the plight of women on welfare and created a propitious political climate for legal reform of the welfare system.

The demands to limit bureaucratic control, end casework investigations, protect the civil rights of welfare recipients, and increase the participation and power of recipients were important components of their assertion that welfare was a right. Welfare rights activists questioned the notion that AFDC was charity for which they should be grateful and demanded that they not be branded second-class citizens by virtue of their status as welfare recipients. In seeking to transform how AFDC was disbursed and, more importantly, demanding participation in the policy-making process, welfare recipients built upon ideas of citizenship and democracy nurtured during the civil rights movement and sought to expand those ideas into the world of social work. They rethought the formulation of social policy. Long a domain of experts and intellectuals, welfare rights activists sought to turn public policy into an arena in which ordinary people, or more accurately poor people, who were the objects of scrutiny, could be active participants. In these ways they began to break down the hierarchy governing AFDC, demystify the power of welfare officials, and loosen the bureaucratic controls that silenced and demeaned them.

The Welfare System and Dignity

The welfare system in the 1960s stigmatized recipients as undeserving and labeled them unworthy. As Jennette Washington, welfare recipient in New York City, explained, "The moment they walk in the door of a Welfare Center to apply for help, people are stigmatized; their dignity is stripped from them. They are lined up like cattle begging for a meal."[3] Caseworkers routinely treated women on welfare like criminals, suspecting immoral behavior, alternate sources of income, and illicit relationships. William Engelhardt, director of the training program in community development at the Penn Center in South Carolina, suggested in 1968, "In the final analysis, being hungry is not as bad as feeling you're not a human being. People cannot go in with their head held high saying, 'I am a human being and I want to talk to you about my rights.'"[4]

In speeches and public pronouncements, women in the welfare rights movement sometimes drew parallels to slavery, illustrating their powerlessness and dehumanization, as well as the racism characteristic of AFDC. Etta Horn of the Washington, D.C. Citywide Welfare Alliance said before a session of Congress in 1969,

> You control our lives and so far you've treated us like slaves. You're responsible for the health and welfare of our children but you're not interested in how we live . . . You sit up here on the Hill and talk about building subways and bridges and parking lots for the tourists and people from suburbia . . . It's time to talk about the people who live here. It's time to treat us like human beings.[5]

Recipients, in some cases, made better treatment from caseworkers their first priority. An organizer in New York City reported in 1965:

> The demand for respect is foremost on the list of every welfare-client organization in the country, and the New York groups are no exception. During the mass meetings held on the Lower East Side it was noticeable that more applause was given to the suggestion that clients be treated with dignity than for the suggestion that there be a 25 percent increase in the welfare budget.[6]

The stigma attached to public assistance dates back to the poor relief programs of the colonial era. Local officials, fearing people would needlessly take advantage of public assistance or that overly generous benefits might discourage the able-bodied from working, gave very small allowances, attached work requirements to receipt of aid, and instilled shame in recipients. The obsession to aid only the deserving and scrutinize recipients closely carried over into the state-run mothers' pensions programs of the Progressive Era.[7] Mothers' pensions, the precursor of ADC, were available to only a small proportion of needy mothers. To guard against potential public criticism of the programs, social workers established high qualification standards. They evaluated the quality of recipients' mothering and their personal behavior, and took stock of their assets, frequently denying support to women considered unworthy. However, even women receiving assistance resented the meager monthly allowance and the continual monitoring by caseworkers to ensure continued eligibility.

The federal ADC program established in 1935 incorporated many of the components that shaped mothers' pensions programs. Casework investigation of each applicant determined recipients' eligibility for assistance. Both the moral fitness and financial status of recipients came under scrutiny. States implemented a variety of rules, including the suitable home and no-man-in-the-house laws, which inspected a mother's parenting skills and sexual behavior, and employable mother laws, which denied aid if caseworkers decided the mother was physically able to work, to determine who qualified for assistance. For example, some caseworkers relied on the notorious "midnight raids" to determine whether women on AFDC were involved in a relationship with a man. They appeared at recipients' homes at odd hours—often in the middle of the night—searching for evidence of male presence. If they found anything, the woman was cut off welfare because, presumably, her male partner could support her and her children. Majorie Caesar, a mother of three who joined the Pittsfield Association of Parents for Adequate Welfare (PAPAW) in Pittsfield, MA, went on welfare after leaving her abusive and alcoholic husband. The welfare department supervisor, she said, "threatened to take my children away when he thought I was going out on dates with men."[8] Under pressure to limit the rolls, ensure an adequate supply of labor, and/or reserve assistance for those perceived as most worthy, caseworkers applied these criteria more stringently to women of color. As written or interpreted, the rules were laden with cultural and class biases about what constituted proper motherhood and acceptable personal behavior. Caseworkers searched for clues of neglect or poor housekeeping or perhaps simply sought to harass and humiliate clients. The Cuyahoga County, OH, Welfare Department sent out "housing inspectors" to examine the homes of welfare recipients. "Unfit" recipients were evicted from public housing and removed from the rolls. The local WRO warned its members that "breakfast dishes and unmade beds brand you a filthy homemaker. Beware!"[9] Caseworkers often assumed recipients were unworthy until they proved otherwise. The elaborate bureaucracy governing the disbursement of ADC discouraged recipients from applying for welfare. The application process, consisting of extensive documentation, probing questions, and a long waiting period, was an exasperating experience. Caseworkers gave recipients little information about their rights or welfare regulations, while demanding that recipients disclose finances, divulge information about their personal lives, and open their homes to caseworkers for searches on demand. The bureaucracy created structures of hierarchy between caseworker and client, giving caseworkers an enormous amount of power over recipients and making recipients dependent on them.[10]

The 1967 Social Security Amendments, which froze federal AFDC payments to states for increases in rolls due to out-of-wedlock births, divorce, or desertion, tied morality to receipt of welfare much more explicitly on a federal level.[11] Some states had for many years considered the sexual practices and moral behavior of women when determining welfare eligibility. The 1967 amendments, however, sanctioned and institutionalized on a national scale a policy uneven on the local level. Although the freeze was repealed in 1969, before it took effect, its passage nevertheless reflected the preoccupations with the personal lives of AFDC recipients. The amendments also gave states greater authority to remove children from "unsuitable" homes and provided more money for foster and institutional care for children. Thus, welfare in the 1960s not only financially supported AFDC recipients, but monitored and controlled their behavior.

The Struggle for Dignity

When welfare recipients began to organize in the early and mid-1960s they addressed the bureaucratic and dehumanizing procedures that characterized the disbursement of welfare. They sought to diminish the power of caseworkers, provide information to recipients about the operation of the welfare system, and overcome negative public perceptions. Estell Davis, with the Citywide Welfare Alliance in Washington, D.C., was baffled about why her status as a welfare recipient reflected her character. She wrote,

> I am not ashame [sic] of being on Public Assistance. For a number of years I served my gouverment [sic] as a secretary. Why should my government frown upon me because of my temporary position. I am the same individual who worked, so why aren't I still treated with dignity as I would have if I were still holding my position in the government.[12]

Joy Stanley, of the Los Angeles County WRO, said quite succinctly, "We resent the 'image' of recipients as chiselers or immoral persons."[13] Recipients like Davis and Stanley worked to overcome the stigma associated with welfare by educating and empowering themselves and demanding better treatment and less arbitrary welfare procedures.

For most welfare recipients, the lack of dignity was most frequently played out in the way social workers interacted with recipients. The dominant approach to social work in this period was casework, which emphasized the personal characteristics or moral deficiencies of the recipient, rather than social reform. In some cases the perceived dysfunction was grounds for denying assistance. In other periods, social workers offered more services, such as counseling, education, job training, and moral guidance, to aid families. For example, the 1962 welfare amendments, in response to postwar antipoverty rhetoric, sought to reduce poverty among welfare recipients by allocating more money for services. Rather than explore the larger structural issues contributing to poverty, caseworkers sought to counsel recipients about their psychological problems and teach them the value of hard work, employment, family stability, and self-sufficiency.[14] Casework fostered a paternalistic and demeaning relationship between social workers and clients.

Caseworkers wielding power over welfare recipients could make being on welfare either tolerable or very difficult. An organizer in New York City explained:

> A caseworker is the person who has the most opportunity for showing respect or disrespect to the welfare client. Attitudes of welfare clients toward their caseworkers are described not so much in terms of what they receive in their checks but rather in terms of the relationship that they have with the caseworker—the importance of the caseworker's confidence that clients are telling the truth; respect for their personal lives, which can be shown by keeping appointments; not demanding to know everything; being polite and generally treating their clients as if they were decent human beings.[15]

Many caseworkers did not use their power in the positive ways this organizer described. Women on welfare commonly encountered the attitude that caseworkers' decisions should not be questioned, but rather accepted at face value. In one instance in New York City, a client refused to allow a caseworker to examine her wardrobe after requesting additional money for winter clothing. Subsequently, seven police officers took her to Bellevue Hospital where she was kept for ten days for psychiatric evaluation because she "threatened trouble for city Department of Welfare caseworkers."[16] This kind of overreaction drew a clear line of power between those receiving and disbursing welfare. Mrs. Cassie B. Downer, chairman of the Milwaukee County WRO, explained how the welfare system disempowered her and elevated the status of her caseworker. "When I first came on welfare . . . I had no idea about what was going on. I was like a child looking to my caseworker as a god. Whatever she said was law. It just never entered my mind to question anything the worker said."[17] Many welfare recipients in the 1960s, like Downer, were apprehensive about questioning their caseworkers.

Consequently, caseworkers became a focus of welfare rights activity. Joy Stanley, of the Los Angeles County WRO, explained one of the four basic aims of her group: "To see that welfare recipients are treated with dignity and understanding by any and all administrators and social workers."[18] In western Massachusetts, the PAPAW, a predominantly black but interracial group, devised a plan to resist the welfare department policy of visiting without advance notice. To discourage caseworkers from showing up unexpectedly, it suggested recipients tell social workers "We are leaving" or "We have company, please come back later."[19] In June 1968, members of the Englewood WRO in New Jersey, met with the Bergen County director of welfare and charged the welfare department supervisor with "five specific cases of discrimination and intimidation, of unnecessary delays and unclear statements."[20] Their complaints led to the supervisor's dismissal. Thus, in their campaigns, welfare rights organizers targeted specific caseworkers or patterns of behavior to improve the client-caseworker relationship.

In a three-page, single-spaced "Petition for Rights and Respect" presented to the County Board of Assistance, the Philadelphia WRO outlined their ongoing problems with caseworkers:

> Caseworkers and other public officials are not the judges, but rather the servants of those people entitled to public welfare benefits. Too often, however, we have found the attitudes and practices of many employees in the Department of Public Assistance to be grudging, distrustful, judgmental and even abusive.[21]

The Philadelphia WRO demanded that caseworkers stop delaying aid to needy families, ensure privacy, inform recipients of their rights, avoid extensive documentation, and maintain open lines of communication.[22]

Lack of dignity and abusive treatment by caseworkers was compounded by racism. Jennette Washington, a recipient in New York City, recounted her experiences with the stigma of poverty, welfare, and racism:

> When you went to school, you were labeled. "Their family is on Welfare." People looked at you as if you were a different kind of

person than the other children because their mothers and fathers had jobs . . . As it gradually got worse, it turned into a racial situation, with certain races getting into the unions and getting jobs while others were excluded.[23]

An organizer in South Carolina explained, "The thing probably most devastating of all is that the people serving us in the welfare department just don't understand black people."[24] In addition to a lack of understanding, many caseworkers were imbued with dominant beliefs that black women did not deserve welfare and should be employed rather than receive AFDC. Black welfare recipients increasingly faced discrimination in the welfare system and were often portrayed as licentious and disreputable. Caseworkers' biases about who was deserving of welfare became evident in the decisions they made. Thus, the informal procedures of the welfare system boosted the power of individual caseworkers and often worked against African American and Latina recipients.

To address more permanently recipients' problems with caseworkers, NWRO and local WROs advocated ending casework welfare and separating eligibility, whether one was financially qualified for welfare, from the moral and social issues that had historically defined casework. A recipient with the Massachusetts WRO in Boston suggested that people on AFDC needed economic assistance, not social work: "Simply because we are poor, we do not need any social workers, because we don't have any social problems . . . I need money and I need it now."[25] Instead of casework, NWRO supported a declaration system to determine welfare eligibility.[26] Under this plan, recipients simply signed an affidavit declaring their financial need in order to obtain benefits. The affidavit would reduce the workload for caseworkers and protect recipients' privacy and dignity. The national office planned a letter-writing campaign to support the affidavit system.[27] In New York City, as a result of demonstrations in 1966 by the Citywide Coordinating Committee of Welfare Groups, the Welfare Commissioner agreed to adopt an affidavit system eliminating some of the bureaucratic and humiliating application procedures.

Knowledge and Power

Recipients were also at the mercy of welfare officials because they knew little about welfare regulations or about their basic rights. Caseworkers could exert control and arbitrarily enforce rules, in part, because recipients were uninformed and disempowered. A recipient could not predict whether a request would be granted or denied. A leader of MAW in Boston explained:

It is the way in which many social workers do their job that arouses great bitterness and anger in the MAWs. To begin, the workers are accused of being arbitrary and unfair: One worker may allow such things as a new living room set or fluoride treatments, while another does not, and workers often refuse to grant allowances which are clearly deserved. Even worse, from the MAW's viewpoint, are the worker's attitudes. These are characterized as "sick," "condescending," "insufficiently interested in humanity," "manipulative" and "punitive." "Everything the social workers do screams out that they still love the fact that they have people under their control."[28]

Caseworkers, at a whim, reduced monthly benefits, refused requests for emergency grants, and cut recipients off without giving them official notification or the opportunity to appeal. They could force women into the labor market at their own discretion, selectively enforcing laws that encouraged women on welfare to take paid employment outside the home. These practices discouraged people from applying for welfare and ensured that those on welfare would not remain there for very long. The manner of distributing welfare sent a message not only to those people on welfare, but to those not receiving assistance that welfare was an unpleasant alternative to wage work.

Welfare rights activists around the country educated themselves and their fellow recipients about the rules and regulations of welfare. They obtained welfare manuals to learn their rights and wrote easy-to-use handbooks for other recipients. In many cases, however, local welfare departments refused to hand over copies of the AFDC manual to recipients. In the spring of 1967, members of the Minneapolis Community Union Project Welfare Committee wrote letters to the assistant welfare director requesting copies of the county welfare manual so they could draft a welfare rights handbook. After a series of protests, the county welfare board insisted the manual was not for public use and offered to write its own welfare rights handbook. As a last resort, the organization tried unsuccessfully to take the welfare department to court.[29] In another case, in May 1968, thirty-five members of the Englewood Welfare Rights Organization in New Jersey met with the director of the Bergen County Welfare Board and department caseworkers and presented a list of demands, one of which was for a copy of the New Jersey Bureau of Assistance Manual. The welfare department refused, citing Department of Health, Education, and Welfare (HEW) regulations that "if recipients visiting the county welfare office ask to see any of the welfare regulations, they could be shown only those regulations pertaining to the immediate problem they were concerned with."[31]

The refusal to share manuals indicated that welfare officials had an interest in keeping recipients uninformed and powerless.

Because of the difficulty of obtaining welfare manuals, local groups often relied on other sources. NWRO informed local welfare groups about national welfare policy and issued guidelines for writing handbooks. In addition, sympathetic social workers, nonprofit organizations, and legal aid societies helped recipients pull together information about their rights, assisted them in obtaining welfare manuals, and developed handbooks with them. As important allies of welfare rights activists, lawyers advised recipients and represented them in their dealings with social workers and in court cases. Legal aid societies, a product of the War on Poverty, defended clients at fair hearing procedures and trained them to defend themselves. The Center on Social Welfare Policy and Law, a project at Columbia University's School of Social Work formed in 1966 and funded by the Office of Economic Opportunity, provided recipients with information on how to prepare their own welfare rights handbooks, educated them about laws and defense procedures, and represented them in court.[31] The ACLU's Welfare Civil Liberties Project informed welfare recipients about their right to privacy, right to protest, rights when arrested, and right to obtain a hearing to challenge a caseworker's decision.[32] This legal assistance was in part responsible for many of the movement's successes.[33] In the words of another historian, lawyers gave welfare rights activists "considerable status" and caseworkers were often aware when dealing with welfare rights activists that the legal buttressing for their claims was "only a phone call away."[34] This legal backing helped shift the balance of power between caseworker and client.

With the help of the ACLU, the Center on Social Welfare Policy and Law, and other middle-class allies, many local welfare rights organizations around the country developed and distributed handbooks to recipients informing them of their rights.[35] In Long Beach, CA, Citizens for Creative Welfare circulated a ten-page booklet called "Poor Man's Bible: A Welfare Rights Handbook."[36] MAW in Boston wrote "Your Welfare Rights Manual," which addressed topics such as "What Do I Get on AFDC?" "What About Sheets and Furniture?" "Can My Children go to College?" and "How to Appeal a Decision by Your Caseworker."[37] The Hinds County Welfare Rights Movement in Mississippi developed a handbook called "Your Welfare Rights," counseling recipients: "Welfare is not charity. If you are in need and meet the other standards, you have a *right* to welfare help."[38] The handbook also described common predicaments with caseworkers, informing recipients what they could do:

YOU: My children need help
WELFARE WORKER: Where is the father?

YOU: I don't know. Last I heard he was in Chicago.
WORKER: You won't get any help until you find him and bring
him to court. He's got to support your children.
DISCUSSION: The worker is wrong. You do not have to find him
and take him to court. To get help from the Welfare, you must sign
a form against the deserting father. This tells where he is now, or
where he was the last you knew. Then they may try to find him and
get him to give some support to his children, if he can. They may
take him to court for the support, and ask you to testify.[39]

Activists also educated recipients in other ways about their rights. In
Virginia, the Fayette County WRO and the Raleigh County WRO, with the
help of Mount Hope Baptist Church, held a training session for low-
income people and welfare recipients "to instruct people how to read and
interpret the Department of Welfare manual and how to make and conduct
appeals."[40] Other groups started newsletters, handed out fliers, set up information tables in welfare waiting rooms, or wrote pamphlets and brochures
to keep recipients informed of their rights. The Los Angeles County WRO,
for example, published a regular newsletter updating recipients on new
laws, informing them of current legislation, and advising them how to seek
help when they had a problem.[41]

Legal education turned out to be one of the most important strategies
pursued by welfare rights organizers. A report by the Virginia WRO
summed up:

> The legal counselling [sic] of VWRO has probably been the most
> far reaching of its legal programs . . . This approach has had quite
> a dramatic effect in the areas of Virginia where the welfare pro-
> grams are run as political fiefdoms and your "worthiness," race, or
> some other irrelevant factor determined whether or how much as-
> sistance you got.[42]

Legal education also encompassed training recipients to act as "lay advocates." In July 1967, the Center on Social Welfare Policy and Law began a
project in New York City with the West Side Welfare League, the United
Welfare League, and the Stryckers Bay Community Action Project to train
ten recipients in welfare law. They wanted to expand the number of trained
welfare advocates and "to give [them] the confidence and skills needed for
effective exercise of their rights."[43] In another case, Nashco, a nonprofit arm
of NWRO, requested from OEO a one-year demonstration grant in 1968 to
train welfare recipients as legal representatives in "judicial and quasi-judicial
settings."[44] When welfare recipients in Boone County, WV, organized an

educational program to inform recipients of their legal rights, they asked the question: "Who would be the teachers?" Their answer: "Welfare recipients themselves. They reasoned that they knew the problems best and that they could be the best teachers of their own people."[45]

The welfare rights movement was not alone in its use of lay advocates or paraprofessionals. Architects of the federal government's War on Poverty also sought to promote the use of paraprofessionals. In a wide variety of fields, including law, medicine, education, and social welfare, paraprofessionals, according to historian John Ehrenreich, "turned the professional model on its head" and became an important component of service delivery.[46] Empowering recipients and opposing professionalism was at the crux of the welfare rights movement's strategy to train recipients in the workings of welfare law. It narrowed the divide between caseworker and client, enabling recipients to advocate for their rights and challenge the power of caseworkers.

Fair Hearings

Welfare recipients' newfound knowledge put them in a position to question caseworkers and thus transform the patron-client relationship so characteristic of AFDC. This was most evident in the campaign for fair hearings, a formal nonjudicial hearing before a state board of welfare to review a caseworker's decision. In 1950 federal legislation guaranteed AFDC recipients the right to a hearing to contest decisions about their case. Clients could appeal decisions by the local welfare center to the state welfare department, which would review the case. Intending to protect clients from unfair decisions by caseworkers or their supervisors, the law gave recipients a venue outside the local welfare department to dispute decisions. Few welfare recipients, however, knew about this right or took advantage of it. Even when they did know of their right to appeal a decision, they often did not have access to legal counsel to present a compelling case. In other instances, local officials illegally denied recipients the right to a fair hearing, or conducted the process unfairly.

Welfare rights activists in New York City organized recipients to take advantage of fair hearings. Thirty-four welfare recipients on the Lower East Side, represented by attorneys at Legal Aid Society and Mobilization for Youth, testified before the State Board of Social Welfare in 1967 about repeated violations in fair hearing procedures, including an extensive waiting period once a complaint was filed.[47] Because of recurring problems in the appeal system, the Citywide Coordinating Committee for Welfare Rights Groups launched a campaign to guarantee recipients' right to fair hearings.

Citywide used fair hearings in conjunction with other campaigns, such as the demand for special grants for items they did not have, as a way to overload the welfare system. If caseworkers denied special grants, recipients immediately appealed the decision and requested a fair hearing. By inundating welfare officials, Citywide members hoped to pressure the welfare department to grant concessions to welfare rights activists. According to executive director Hulbert James, Citywide sponsored 3,000 fair hearing cases from August through October of 1967, a huge increase over the usual fifty cases a year. James estimated that each fair hearing case cost the state $300 a day.[48]

Welfare rights activists in other states conducted similar fair hearing struggles, encouraging recipients to challenge unfair or arbitrary decisions through the fair hearing process. In Ohio, OSCAW asked HEW to investigate the Ohio Department of Welfare because it failed to hold fair hearings after recipients were denied special grants.[49] In Massachusetts, MAW worked to ensure recipients' right to a fair hearing. Previously, "a hearing of any sort, before the welfare department . . . was almost unheard of."[50] The organization "successfully fought to bring about a citywide policy to the effect that no recipient's aid will be cut off without an investigation in which she will be able to see the evidence brought against her."[51] The Englewood WRO demanded that the Director of the Bergen County Welfare Board in May 1968 ensure "that clients be made aware of their right to question all decisions of the department and to be advised of the right to a fair hearing if they are not satisfied."[52]

Despite the potential benefits of fair hearing trials, many local groups encountered problems. Some organizations simply did not have the time or resources to accompany clients to fair hearings. In Ohio, the legal services program would not assist the local WRO with fair hearings or welfare cases. In Mississippi, welfare departments scheduled hearings in many different locations, making it hard for recipients and their counsel to attend. In Chicago, recipients found the fair hearing process "too complex" and preferred collective bargaining. Recipients complained most commonly, however, that attorneys dominated fair hearings, inhibiting recipients from speaking for themselves. In these cases, recipients believed that the scrutiny and disempowerment they experienced with caseworkers only repeated itself in the hearings.[53] This discontent points to patterns of domination between the educated middle class, and the poor—a problem that would resurface in the welfare rights movement.

The welfare rights movement relied on the fair-hearing strategy because it challenged the power of caseworkers. Fair hearings threatened caseworkers by flatly questioning their decision and forcing them into a formal setting to explain and defend their actions. Even if the state did not over-turn most caseworker decisions, the appeals process nevertheless put case-workers—both those brought before state welfare boards, and those who only feared the possibility—on notice that they were being monitored.[54]

Power in Numbers

Recipients also used group power as leverage in their battles with the wel-fare department. In many cases, welfare officials treated recipients better or resolved grievances more quickly because of recipients' association with a welfare rights organization. In Washington, D.C., the United Welfare Rights Organization explained: "NWRO buttons are well known at the welfare de-partment. Our members find that when they go down to the department with buttons on, they receive prompter and better service. Everyone there seemed a little scared of NWRO."[55] In Boston a mother of ten called a mem-ber of MAW about getting Easter clothing for her children. The MAW member, aware of the rules and regulations, persuaded the caseworker to give the mother money for Easter clothing.[56] This kind of mutual support when dealing with the welfare department was an important component of welfare rights work. Even when the Minneapolis Community Union Project Welfare Committee had few direct actions, its members "back[ed] each other up on individual complaints." They went "in groups of 4 or 5" to show one another support and resolve grievances.[57]

In this way knowledge and group association empowered recipients. They checked the power of caseworkers, questioned decisions, and pre-vented subjective and unfair treatment of recipients. In some instances, welfare activists were better apprised of complex, ill-defined, and ever-changing rules than caseworkers.[58] Activists sometimes corrected case-workers because they had access to new information, high-ranking welfare officials, and poverty lawyers. This potentially reversed or altered the power dynamic between recipient and caseworker. In addition, the visibility of welfare rights demonstrations instilled confidence in other recipients, prompting them to organize as well. The WRO in Erie Pennsylvania formed in the spring of 1968 after they "read and heard about groups in other cities. We got together in a home one evening and decided to *do* something instead of talking."[59]

For many welfare recipients, education and activism were personally empowering, helping them overcome the public stigma or personal shame associated with welfare. According to an organizer in New York, participa-tion in the welfare rights movement, gave people a "feeling of self-worth, a sense of mastery."[60] A welfare recipient in Virginia explained how the wel-fare rights movement transformed her life:

> WRO has been the backbone and power I've needed to make my
> voice heard, to get action and bring to light the ill-treatment and
> lies the people in power have given the poor, voiceless, helpless,
> elderly, the blacks, and the oppressed people in this country, which
> really shouldn't have any poverty . . . I will never, can never, shall
> never give up this fight for human dignity.[61]

Recipients also began to think differently about the welfare system. Many
welfare recipients overcame their own ambivalence about being on welfare
by learning that they had a right to welfare; that disbursement of AFDC was
not simply an act of charity by caseworkers. Lois Walker, a recipient who
worked with the Virginia WRO, said, "The organization has meant a great
change in the feelings I used to have about poor blacks and whites. I used
to be ashamed to even mention or tell anybody that I'm on welfare. But
now, by knowing my rights, me and other people feel that its really a right
instead of a special privilige [sic]."[62] Reclaiming their dignity proved as important as other reforms advocated by welfare rights activists. It challenged
their silence and shame, enabling recipients to join a welfare rights organization and stand up to mistreatment by caseworkers.

Because welfare recipients' disempowerment was predicated on their lack
of knowledge, clearly defined and publicly accessible rules and regulations
improved a system that had concentrated power in the hands of caseworkers. By getting access to information and marshaling the strength to stand
up for themselves, either individually or collectively, they challenged arbitrary rules and shifted the balance of power. Knowledge gave women on welfare the ammunition and assurance to fight for reforms within the system.

The Legal Strategy

The welfare rights movement also pursued a legal strategy, using test cases
to expand and more clearly define the rights of welfare recipients.
Paralleling some of the strategies of the civil rights movement, it relied on
courts to protect recipients' rights. A lawyer with the ACLU noted, "Just as
black people sought to establish their legal rights through litigation as well
as lay organization, poor people today are working on the very same problems."[63] In contrast to the strategy of representing individual recipients in
their battles with caseworkers or the welfare department, test cases sought
to reform welfare law. Rather than just giving poor people legal advice,
these new "poverty lawyers" used the law as an instrument of policy change
to benefit the poor.[64] They challenged the capricious and racially discriminatory application of welfare rules, and worked to ensure that receipt of
welfare was protected under the due process clause of the Constitution.

The test cases addressed the most egregious violations of recipients' rights. The Roger Baldwin Foundation, an ACLU affiliate, and the Center on Social Welfare Policy and Law, for example, joined together to overturn a substitute-father law in Alabama. Mrs. Sylvester Smith, a recipient in Alabama, was denied her welfare check for refusing to prove that she did not have sex with a man. The Foundation and the Center argued that the substitute-father law in Alabama violated due process, the right to privacy, and equal protection because 95 percent of affected recipients were black. The real motive, they argued, was to keep African Americans off the welfare rolls.[65] This case worked its way up to the U.S. Supreme Court. The Court decided in *King v. Smith* (1968) that substitute-father laws did not conform to the Social Security Act. In another important welfare rights case, lawyers challenged the constitutionality of residency laws. Many states employed residency laws in the 1950s to prevent poor people from moving into their state for the purpose of collecting welfare. The Supreme Court declared residency laws unconstitutional in a landmark 1969 decision, *Shapiro v. Thompson*. This decision invalidated laws restricting the mobility of welfare recipients, striking a blow to the notion that public assistance was a "local concern."

One of the most important legal victories for welfare recipients was the 1970 *Goldberg v. Kelley* Supreme Court decision. In that case, the Court ruled that welfare benefits were protected by due process and could not be terminated without a hearing. Waged in conjunction with a mass campaign by the welfare rights movement around the right to a fair hearing, the case demonstrated how legal aid associations and welfare rights organizations could work together. The fair hearings were a useful political tactic, but they did not prevent unfair or arbitrary decisions. Rather, they gave recipients the power, after considerable time, energy, and argument, to reverse such decisions. In other words, recipients could challenge a caseworker's decision to cut them off assistance, but only after the fact. The caseworker's decision would stand until it could be overturned. The *Goldberg* case sought to rectify this and guarantee recipients a fair hearing before caseworkers cut off benefits.

The first plaintiff in the case was New York City resident John Kelley, a twenty-nine-year-old homeless black man. Disabled by a hit-and-run driver in 1966, Kelley went on home relief. In December 1967, his caseworker told him to move from the Broadway Central Hotel, where he resided, to the dangerous and drug-infested Barbara Hotel. Kelley instead stayed with a friend but used the Barbara Hotel's address to receive his welfare check. When his caseworker learned he was not living at the Hotel, she cut off his assistance and refused to see him. Kelley contacted a neighborhood service center, which put him in touch with a lawyer. In late January 1968, Kelley and five other welfare clients, represented by lawyers from Mobilization for Youth, the Legal Aid Society, the Roger Baldwin Foundation, and the Columbia University Center on Social Welfare Policy and Law, filed a suit in federal district court against the New York State and City Commissioners of Social Service and the State Board of Social Welfare to establish the right to a hearing before relief payments were cut off. Lawyers argued that a recipient's right to a hearing before termination of benefits was guaranteed under the due process clause of the fourteenth amendment of the Constitution. Recipients won the case in November, when a three-judge U.S. district court ruled that "under all circumstances" welfare recipients have a right to "an adequate hearing" before termination of benefits. The court reasoned that, if on AFDC, welfare recipients should expect to receive benefits and plan their life accordingly without arbitrary changes. Although the city appealed, the Supreme Court in 1970 affirmed the ruling of the lower court.[66]

Thus, the *Goldberg* decision set an important legal precedent by successfully establishing the right to due process for welfare recipients. Arguing that AFDC benefits should be treated and protected as any other form of property, the Court affirmed that welfare would not be regarded as charity, but a right.[67] This was important because welfare had historically been considered charity and thus the property of the state—to be disbursed and taken away whenever the state decided. The *Goldberg* decision made welfare an entitlement, not just in theory, but in practice, and gave recipients a measure of protection from having benefits cut unexpectedly. The various legal cases, including those striking down residency and substitute-father laws, began to transform the welfare bureaucracy and empower recipients. These cases won procedural rights for welfare recipients. That is, a right to welfare was not guaranteed, but everyone was ensured equal access and fair treatment once on welfare.

While the *Goldberg* decision was consequential, it also revealed the limitations of the court. By guaranteeing procedural rather than substantive rights, the court decisions did not address other questions of whether the grant was large enough to actually support a family, whether AFDC's lower benefit levels compared to other programs constituted discrimination, or whether a state could implement stringent eligibility criteria. In many of the preceding cases, as well as others, lawyers and recipients argued for a substantive right to welfare. In 1968, for example, two Columbus WRO members took the Ohio Department of Welfare to court for discrimination. They argued that because AFDC, which in Ohio was 55 percent black, paid less than disability, blind, or old-age support, which was 82 percent white, the department denied equal protection to black welfare recipients.[68] Cases dealing with whether the state could reduce the grant or set a maximum grant limit, found little sympathy among the justices. As will be discussed in a later chapter, the justices were unwilling to move from a discussion of equality in procedure and process to one of endorsing the idea that poor people had a right to a basic minimum standard of living. As long as states treated everyone the same, they could reduce grants and reject as many applicants as they saw fit.

Despite the limitations, the legal victories had a tangible impact on welfare policy. Although the *Goldberg* decision did not guarantee receipt of welfare—recipients could still be cut off welfare after a hearing or their application for assistance might be denied altogether—it, nevertheless, protected the civil rights of welfare recipients. Moreover, the welfare rights movement could, and later did, use these legal decisions as ammunition to oppose state policies designed to reduce the welfare rolls. By demanding protection of their due process rights, questioning the discretionary powers of the welfare department, and advocating public and formal procedures in the welfare system, recipients addressed a key source of their oppression and gained a measure of dignity and respect.

Nonprofit organizations and legal aid societies worked hand in hand with the NWRO national office to win the legal decisions. Initially, the relationship was congenial. But over time tensions increased between NWRO and its primary ally, the Center on Social Welfare Policy and Law.[69] Some of these tensions percolated over differences about the relative weight of grassroots mobilization versus litigation. Catherine Jermany, a welfare recipient with the Los Angeles County WRO who also served on the board of the Center on Social Welfare Policy and Law, explained that "sometimes the zealousness of the lawyers interfered with the programs that we had going on at the grass roots."[70] Thus, welfare recipients and the NWRO leadership had relatively little input in the test case strategy, which was mapped out and waged by sympathetic lawyers.

Lawyers argued and won the court cases. In the long run, however, the legal victories were only sustained with a social movement. Legal victories had to be enforced. Even if clients had legal protections, their rights were not always secured inviolably. Laws might be changed, disregarded, or circumvented in technical ways. This became evident to members of the welfare rights movement one year after the *Goldberg* decision, when the state of Nevada removed a number of recipients from the welfare rolls as a cost-cutting measure. NWRO and the local WRO joined forces to reverse the state decision. Welfare recipients in Nevada battled to enforce the *Goldberg* decision and ensure that recipients would not be cut off without a hearing. After massive street demonstrations, wide ranging publicity, and numerous legal challenges to the state's actions, the movement successfully restored recipients' benefits. The actions of Nevada (and subsequently other states) revealed that legal protections required political pressure. Thus, the social struggle and the legal struggle were intertwined. The court victories, the leverage recipients wielded with legal backing, and the legitimacy that sprouted from the legal alliance fueled the grassroots movement. At the same time, the legal victories could best be secured by the political pressure emanating from social activism.[71]

The 1960s and Ideals of Participation

Recipients also attempted to reclaim their dignity by seeking greater participation in the decisions affecting their lives. They demanded that their representatives sit on welfare governing boards and local welfare advisory committees, and that they contribute to any debate or discussion about welfare. The poor, they believed, must not just have good decisions made for them, but must be allowed to make good decisions for themselves. At a statewide New York conference on "The Dilemmas of Municipal Welfare Policy," Beulah Sanders, NWRO executive committee member, explained. "You can't come up with an answer unless you talk to the people. This country has been run too long with the experts making the decisions."[72] George Wiley summed up this goal of the welfare rights movement:

> It is the basic premise of the organization that democracy means having an effective voice and participation of poor people in all levels of decision making in this country. Recipients are very concerned about the degree to which other people have formulated policies and programs allegedly in their interests but which ultimately do not effectively serve them.[73]

By the mid-1960s participation of the poor had become a guiding principle for antipoverty reformers. Policy makers in this era latched onto the idea of participation of the poor because they valued the principle of inclusion, but also as part of a larger strategy to fight poverty. Advocates for the War on Poverty believed that economic resources were vital, but that poverty also fostered a distinctive culture, making it difficult to emerge from its depths. Poverty might lead to depression, marital breakup, drug and alcohol abuse, and a whole host of other psychological traumas and self-destructive behavior. To counteract this lack of power and emotional instability, they believed poor people should engage in the process of social change. That is, participation will enable them to regain their self-confidence and facilitate the process of getting out of poverty.[74] In 1963, the Chairman of the Council of Economic Advisors, Walter Heller, outlined the Johnson administration's approach for fighting poverty which included the tax bill, the Civil Rights bill, job training, and amendments to the Social Security Act. But, he explained, some poor people would be un-affected by this legislation. "For these Americans, we seek ways and means to promote their dignity as human beings by providing access to opportu-nity and encouraging their participation in a democratic society."[75] In his eyes, democratic participation became a means to remedy the social effects of poverty.

A similar philosophy guided the federal government's Community Action Programs (CAP). "Maximum feasible participation," the theory be-hind the CAPs, mandated participation of the poor in federally funded community agencies and projects and rested on the assumption that effec-tive social policy must include those who were directly impacted. The offi-cial history of the OEO made this point:

> For the first time in the experience of many of the agencies dealing with the poor, their clients had a mechanism for evlauating [sic] their services in a way which demanded attention and could, in a manner which could not easily be ignored, demand improvement . . . CAP gave a vocabulary, and then a language, and then a voice, to the poor. They did not, any longer, have to be silent.[76]

By encouraging participation of the poor, federal CAP programs dimin-ished the power of bureaucrats and administrators. Most activists and pol-icy makers believed participation of the poor in community programs would make those programs more responsive to the needs of its con-stituents and improve the delivery of services. In sum, both the quality and effectiveness of social programs rested on the input and participation of the people served.

Although OEO professed support for participation of the poor, when poor people demanded a greater role in decision making, OEO officials often wavered. Throughout the country, community groups, poor people, parents, welfare recipients, African Americans, tenants, and other groups grabbed hold of the notion of participation and ran with it, sometimes de-manding control over OEO projects. The criteria of "maximum feasible participation" according to an OEO official fostered a "violent reaction of poor people and poor neighborhoods to the opportunity to affect their own lives through CAPs."[77] Community activists challenging the power of local bureaucracies and governing coalitions encountered stiff resistance. The federal government, under pressure from local politicians, usually equivocated about backing claims of community groups, which found themselves with little recourse. As a result, CAPs never lived up to their promise of giving voice to the poor and this created bitter resentment among the very "community" people they were supposed to serve.

Demands for Representation

NWRO, and other grassroots groups, criticized the War on Poverty and its half-hearted attempt to involve the poor in policy. In 1967, the NWRO national conference passed a resolution attacking OEO:

> Instead of making it easier for the poor to organize and stand up for their rights many OEO-financed agencies are interfering with or attempting to suppress spontaneous organization of poor people including the WRO.[78]

Local welfare rights groups found the War on Poverty either unhelpful or a hindrance to their political work. In 1965, in Chicago, where OEO funneled money through the mayor's office, the grassroots Woodlawn Organization issued an eleven-page "black paper" labeling the antipoverty program a "war against the poor." The organization explained, mincing no words: "We are sick unto despair of having rich whites and their carefully chosen black flunkies tell us what our problems are, make decisions for us and set our children's future."[79] Other welfare rights organizations bowed out of a process in which they believed they had no power. Beverly Edmon, founder of the Welfare Recipients Union in Los Angeles, said,

> The money is a terrible problem, but when you get into the Poverty Program business—you know, it's their money and they start making deals and making some people into VIP's and after a while the whole thing's up in the clouds and the people down here who know what's happening can't participate except according to how the man says. It's not for us.[80]

Many in the welfare rights movement rejected the tokenism of the community action programs—the claims for participation without the substance. They wanted to participate as citizens: for poor people to have a presence in policy making and for their ideas to be taken seriously. Welfare recipients' political actions—whether it took the form of sitting on an advisory board or sitting-in at the welfare department—constituted a form of citizenship participation.[81] In the 1960s, the welfare rights movement reconceptualized the meaning of democracy and citizenship. Like other social movements in the 1960s, it sought to incorporate disenfranchised sectors of the American population in the nation's governing institutions and democratize the political process. The black freedom movement, by the late 1960s, had developed platforms to include African American representatives in policy-making bodies and the electoral arena. A founding principle of the Student Non-Violent Coordinating Committee (SNCC) and

Students for a Democratic Society (SDS) was participatory democracy to ensure that all members have input in making decisions.[82] These New Left organizations rethought socialism in democratic (rather than economic) terms. They analyzed the multifaceted ways power was manifested—whether it was the power of whites over blacks, men over women or large-scale organizations or bureaucracies (such as universities) over individuals. To address this power imbalance, student groups, civil rights organizations, feminists, and other New Left groups called for decentralization and participatory democracy. New governing structures, they argued, might achieve the ideal of "radical citizenship."[83] Welfare recipients similarly advocated a kind of radical citizenship. Defining their problems more broadly than economic, they attempted to whittle away at the power caseworkers wielded over AFDC recipients and sought to participate in and influence the making of welfare policy. Bureaucratic structure and political process was as important to them as economic inequality.

With these goals in mind, members of the welfare rights movement demanded participation of the poor and welfare recipients in both electoral politics and welfare policy. They hoped to be included in the policy-making process as a group with special concerns; to be recognized as a community with a collective voice and shared interests. In a letter to a Democratic Party official, George Wiley and Beulah Sanders expressed "disappointment and dismay" that politicians mentioned the input of other special interest groups, but not "the vast number of people in this country who are forced to subsist in poverty."[84] Johnnie Tillmon echoed the need to acknowledge the existence of the poor:

> A major problem we had to face was to get recognition. That was a hard thing to do. The fact is that we do have recognition now—whether it is on the subversive lists or whatever. We are still recognized. Maybe people aren't saying the kind of things that we want them to say about us, but the point is that they at least recognize that we are here.[85]

Leaders of the welfare rights movement demanded representation on the local and national levels. Both OSCAW and NWRO wanted representatives on the President's Income Maintenance Commission.[86] When Beulah Sanders spoke before the Commission she reiterated the importance of recipient participation. "We have our own ideas on what kind of system we should have. It seems to us as organized welfare recipients . . . that the recipients of the program should have the largest say as to what goes into it."[87] On the local level, MAW in Boston worked to get recipient representation on welfare committees and advisory boards. After a massive sit-in for uniform price guidelines for furniture, the welfare commissioner in Boston set up an advisory committee, half of which was comprised of welfare recipients.[88] A MAW leader appointed to the State Advisory Welfare Board felt that participating in welfare committees was more effective than demonstrating. An interviewer wrote, "She feels that through her role [on the State Welfare Advisory Board] she can better represent the needs of welfare mothers and other poor people."[89] Other WROs pursued similar strategies. In 1969, the Philadelphia WRO, led by Roxanne Jones, successfully fought to place a welfare rights representative in each local office of the Welfare Department "to assure that welfare clients were not denied their rights to assistance."[90] A welfare rights activist from Beaufort County, SC, testifying before Congress about the food stamp program argued,

> We came to participate in the formulation of plans that would get at the needs of hunger and malnutrition in Beaufort County. For too long, people have been making decisions about what will affect other peoples' lives. The people that these programs will affect directly have nothing at all to say about them. We want to participate in some of those decisions about how the new program can best meet the needs of the poor people.[91]

Many welfare rights organizations broadened their demands to advocate community control rather than just participation. They didn't want to be one lone voice among many setting the agenda for poor people; they wanted to determine that agenda themselves. Local, national, and international movements of poor and oppressed people during this time defined liberation in similar terms of community empowerment. In the United States, the black power movement demanded control of schools, housing and development projects in black communities.[92] Some welfare rights activists made similar demands. In Kansas City, a Native American welfare rights group attending a conference advocated local reservation control of welfare assistance as part of a general call for self-determination.[93] The Brooklyn Welfare Action Council in 1969 called for community control of welfare. They wrote in the newsletter:

> We want to have a say in what is going on in our community, including in our welfare centers. Whatever the problem is in the welfare center where our clients go, we must solve it. Are there certain caseworkers that should be fired? Are clients given prompt servicing? Are emergency grants handled the way we would like? Are the bathrooms, water fountains, and telephones working properly. These are some suggestions for the kinds of issues we can work on

in the centers. But the important thing is that the centers are our centers and we control what goes on inside them.[94]

Thus, NWRO and local WROs pushed to have their voices heard and craft policies affecting their lives. Organizing around group interest, collective action, and representation in the policy making was a product of 1960s liberalism.[95] On the surface the demands of the welfare rights movement didn't sound that different from the liberal agenda of the 1960s—democratizing politics and including disenfranchised groups in policy making. In a sense the welfare rights movement demanded that liberals favoring an inclusive democratic society live up to their professed ideals. The two groups diverged, however, on the meaning of participation and how to implement it. Liberal calls for input from the poor were often perfunctory. Members of the welfare rights movement, on the other hand, craved real power and control over policy making.

The Poor and Policy Making

In the 1960s, democratic participation was a broader concept than simply voting, placing a representative on a board, or submitting a proposal for reform. Many grassroots groups organized people to participate in political institutions, community boards, and policy-making bodies. They did not believe that participation was a means of social uplift. For them, participation might transform individuals, but, more importantly, it would transform institutions.[96] Jon Van Til, a sociologist and participant-observer of three welfare rights organizations in Delaware County, PA, explained:

> [Welfare recipients] participated intelligently. They participated in a civil fashion. And they participated in a productive fashion. It's a real testimony to the ability of individual citizens who are [recipients] . . . These folks know the system. They know how it works. And actively having them participate in shaping it, and critiquing it, and tweaking it, and fine tuning it, and improving it . . . makes for better policy.[97]

Recipients' expectations to transform the system through democratic participation paralleled the idea of some union organizers that if workers participated in running factories, the factories might look quite different. Similarly, for welfare rights activists, democracy was a model of social change rather than an end in itself.[98] By speaking out, demanding representation, and insisting that their voices were heard, welfare recipients challenged their social/political/economic marginalization. As bell hooks suggests, the very act of speaking out begins a process of political empowerment.[99] Through participation recipients transformed a political landscape that silenced and rendered them powerless.[100] Thus, the welfare rights movement did not just reinforce the traditional liberal notion of democratic participation, but used it as a method of social reform.

Including the poor in policy making was not always successful and even when it was, the question loomed of exactly how much power and influence a few welfare recipients had. In Columbus, OH, welfare recipients demanded to sit on welfare department committees, assist with the orientation of new caseworkers, meet regularly with welfare officials, and be allotted a page in the welfare department newsletter.[101] The Director of the Franklin County welfare department recognized the WRO as a representative of welfare recipients and conceded to their demands. But shortly after reaching an agreement, the Franklin County Welfare Commissioners fired him.[102] In this instance, more powerful welfare officials cut short the WRO's progress on implementing policy changes. Welfare administrators sometimes placated protesters by giving them nominal positions without real power or influence. Or, they encouraged recipient participation as a way to defuse political mobilization. A Massachusetts state official suggested that members of MAW "have been brought into the system via the appointment of [a welfare recipient] to the State Advisory Board" and consequently, they no longer have a power base.[103] In this case, the real power to make decisions lay with the welfare department and not the clients. Although community control may have circumvented this problem, it was never realized.

Nevertheless, including the poor in decision making was a watershed development in the history of social welfare. Prior to the 1960s there was no precedent of recipient participation. Caseworkers and administrators rarely recognized recipients as active agents. The 1962 Amendments to the Social Security Act, however, included a provision for local welfare centers to create advisory committees to improve communication between welfare centers and clients. In most cases, administrators only formed advisory committees after clients began to organize as a way to either preempt or undermine their political organizing. In New York City, for example, advisory committees were set up only after recipients formed a citywide WRO.[104] So, the impetus for recipient participation in policymaking came from the welfare rights movement, and this dramatically impacted policy making. As scholar Neil Gilbert summed up,

> Over the past fifteen years a significant increase in client-group-member participation on governing boards of public and private nonprofit social welfare agencies has reinforced the mission and

capacity of these bodies to represent the varied interests of the community. This marked change in board composition was perhaps the most important legacy of the citizen participation movements of the 1960s. One might almost say that those movements fashioned a new norm which mandates client-group representation on social welfare agency boards.[105]

An OEO official similarly pointed out how participation of the poor transformed welfare policy:

> The concept of participation in program operation and decision making by the resident of the target areas, thought to be completely unworkable, has become an accomplished fact . . . Prior to this development, social welfare could be adequately characterized as a noblesse oblige responsibility of one group for the less fortunate.[106]

Thus, the demands for participation altered recipients' relationship to the welfare department as well as its governing processes. Previously shut out of decision making, recipients began to have a voice in and shape the welfare system. Historian Nancy Fraser has argued that even though state processes operate in such a way as to make the interpretation of welfare recipients' needs a foregone conclusion, how we define need is very much a site of contestation. This is precisely where the welfare rights movement had an impact. Their articulation of their needs and how welfare ought to be disbursed became a part of the dialogue and discussion about what our welfare system should look like. The discourse about needs is important, according to Fraser, because it "functions as a medium for the making and contesting of political claims."[107] The welfare rights movement's participation in this discourse reframed the welfare debate and made consulting poor people a necessary feature of implementing welfare policy.

Lobbying and Electoral Politics

Welfare organizers also lobbied legislators, believing they could affect welfare legislation and electoral politics. There are countless examples of local WROs holding meetings and forums, writing letters, and making proposals to influence legislation. In 1967, the Ohio Steering Committee for Adequate Welfare invited their state representatives to lunch and planned a legislative assembly.[108] In Massachusetts, facing cuts in welfare and Medicaid, the MWRO issued a "legislative alert" to its members urging them to write, telegram, and visit their elected representatives.[109] In Des

Moines, IA, the WRO attended the 1968 Democratic Platform Committee hearings and submitted welfare resolutions, which the committee wrote into the state party platform.[110] The Brooklyn Welfare Action Council planned a voter registration contest for its local chapters, giving a cash prize to the group registering the most people.[111] As these examples illustrate, welfare recipients believed that poor people could collectively convey their interests in the electoral arena and influence welfare legislation. Etta Horn, of Washington, D.C., and Catherine Jermany, of California, wanted recipients and potential recipients to form a unified political bloc: "There are more poor than rich people in this country, but Congress doesn't seem to know it. If we organize, they'll have to listen."[112]

More often, welfare rights organizations disrupted meetings, sat in, and took over offices to pressure legislators. But they usually turned to a militant approach only after less confrontational tactics proved ineffectual. In Minneapolis, welfare rights activists reported that after pursuing legal strategies some people in the AFDC Leagues, in particular a group of Native American women, "are talking about direct action" to influence the legislature.[113] At a meeting of the West Center City Welfare Rights Committee in Wilmington, DE, in September 1967, welfare recipients drew up a list of grievances, including increasing the monthly AFDC allowance and appointing recipients to the state welfare board. After attending several legislative sessions and scheduling meetings with the governor, they became frustrated. Three months later, fifty members of the WRO sat in at the governor's office until he agreed to meet with them.[114] In another case, MAW in Boston brought welfare recipients to the capitol from around the state to lobby for a pending legislative bill. The President of the Senate only spoke with them when twelve angry black welfare mothers from Springfield spontaneously sat in and demanded a meeting. Shortly after that, the bill passed.[115] These local welfare organizations used traditional lobbying tactics and when those failed, they turned to direct action strategies.

The Poor People's Campaign

In 1968, NWRO participated with other anti-poverty and black freedom groups in the Poor People's Campaign. The Southern Christian Leadership Conference (SCLC) planned the Campaign to raise public awareness about poverty, inadequate housing, urban blight, welfare abuses, and unemployment. Hoping to bring thousands of poor people to Washington to camp out for an extended period in a campaign of mass civil disobedience, Martin Luther King, Jr., head of SCLC, sought NWRO's endorsement for the Campaign. But the women leaders of NWRO, having been previously rebuffed by requests to meet with King, insisted that if he wanted an endorsement, he should come to their meeting in Chicago to request it personally.[116] At the meeting, King, who was on a panel with Johnnie Tillmon and George Wiley, seemed unprepared for a barrage of questions regarding the pending welfare legislation about which he clearly knew very little. Finally, Tillmon leaned over to King and said, "You know, Dr. King, if you don't know, you should say you don't know." King immediately sat up straight, looked at Tillmon, and said, "Mrs. Tillmon, we don't know about welfare and we have come to learn."[117] In this telling example, one of the most powerful black political leaders publicly deferred to poor welfare mothers on the issue of welfare policy. Thus, members of the welfare rights movement affirmed that welfare recipients most directly affected by welfare legislation were in the best position to make proposals and recommendations. As they persuaded King to look to them for guidance regarding welfare legislation, they hoped to convince their congressional representatives of the same thing.

The welfare rights movement did eventually endorse and participate in the Poor People's Campaign, using it to influence welfare legislation, much as the 1963 March on Washington assisted in the passage of the 1964 Civil Rights Act. Recipients planned a mass presence in Washington and intended to contact politicians and welfare officials. Welfare rights groups came from around the country. The Campaign as a whole had a list of demands, but local groups came with individual grievances as well. A welfare rights organization from Arizona sent a caravan of mostly young people who spent six days on the road in makeshift accommodations. They "visited [their] Arizona congressmen; called on representatives of Departments such as Health, Education and Welfare, Agriculture, and Justice; they appeared at the Supreme Court to peacefully protest the issue of the continually broken Indian treaties."[118] In another case, a delegation of Mexican American welfare recipients met with Ralph Huitt, assistant secretary for legislation at HEW. Among their many concerns was that local welfare officials threatened to take away one member's children unless she returned from the Poor People's Campaign in the next three days. After the meeting, Huitt wrote in a letter to his supervisor, Mary Switzer: "The leaders of the groups pressed this letter to me and urged that we take care of it. I think it is important that we produce results if we can."[119]

Huitt, as well as other HEW officials, seemed sympathetic and responsive to the demands of the Poor People's Campaign. Immediately after the Campaign, the federal agency sent a memo to all state welfare agencies urging compliance with the demands of welfare rights activists. Stating in part:

> In the days and weeks ahead, we will be issuing directives to fulfill
> the commitments in this response. Meanwhile, I call on all agen-

cies to review their policies, procedures, and practices in the administration of the public assistance program, and to eliminate anything which suggests distrust, lack of respect, or lack of concern for human rights. Our goal is to meet need while supporting recipients in maintaining their dignity and sense of worth.[120]

HEW expressed agreement with activists' demands and was ostensibly committed to making reforms. Mary Switzer, administrator of Social and Rehabilitative Services (SRS), which in 1967 replaced the welfare division within HEW, wrote to all SRS employees about the demands of the Poor People's Campaign: "I think we would all agree that the changes they seek in some of our programs are morally just, and in consonance with the mission of SRS."[121] HEW sketched a six-page chart of the demands presented by Ralph Abernathy, who led the Poor People's Campaign after King's assassination. The chart included a target date for completion and the person responsible for follow-through.[122] Responding to the demand for participation, one administrator explained the benefits of having representatives of the poor in SRS, "The contribution of the 'poor' on such committees would be the focusing of policy, program and grant considerations more sharply in terms of the delivery of needed social, health and rehabilitation services."[123]

Four months later, long after the exhausted and rain-soaked residents of the Poor People's encampment in Washington went home, HEW, still intent on implementing the welfare-related demands, strategized about how to force states to adhere to the federal commitment to meet the demands of the protestors. An SRS administrator wrote,

> We believe that it is urgent that States receive official notification of our intentions as quickly as possible. We know of several instances in which States have taken the position that the commitment in the Abernathy letters are not binding on them. A State letter offers the most rapid way of putting States on notice.[124]

As a follow-up the Secretary of HEW regularly asked the regional directors to fill out a chart documenting their progress on the Poor People's Campaign demands.[125]

NWRO joined the Poor People's Campaign hoping to reform the administration of welfare. Although the Campaign is often considered a failure, HEW took its demands seriously and attempted to implement them. Several months after the Poor People's Campaign, the New England regional commissioner of HEW wrote to Wiley asking to meet with NWRO representatives, assuring him "I subscribe wholeheartedly to the philosophy that a continuing dialogue and a sharing of experiences and viewpoints is one of the major methods that can be used to improve public assistance programs and their administration."[126] The Poor People's Campaign exemplifies a level of consensus between protest movements, such as the welfare rights movement, and government officials. Both acknowledged the importance of input of poor people in policy making and sought open lines of communication. NWRO and the HEW undoubtedly had very different notions of welfare administration, how much money poor people needed for subsistence, and other critical issues. Nevertheless, they agreed that bureaucracies must respond in some way to the demands of the poor, that a dialogue ought to be opened up, and that social reform should involve poor people. Even though welfare recipients and their allies did not dictate welfare policy, they contested the terrain of welfare, expanding their right to assistance, addressing inadequacies in the system, and pushing for a role in policy making. Their success was limited, but discernible. After the 1960s, social workers and administrators routinely included recipients on advisory councils and social welfare boards and invited them to meetings and conferences. While recipients did not determine policy, they influenced the content and direction of change. In this way, they contributed to the ongoing discussions about welfare policy, making suggestions, voicing their opinions, and presenting an alternative point of view.

Many welfare recipients believed the political system was potentially democratic and that they could influence it through lobbying or voting. In the 1960s, other activists, both black and white, combined mass protest, international pressure, and legislative change to win some limited victories. The most noteworthy example was the black freedom movement.[127] Disenfranchised African Americans had amassed enough power to compel the federal government to grant and protect its formal civil rights. In the late 1960s, as the black freedom movement fractured, many black power activists, including the Black Panther Party, ran third-party electoral candidates. Stokely Carmichael and Charles Hamilton, in their seminal book, *Black Power*, counseled black communities in the North to form "independent party groups to elect their own choices to office."[128] Campaigns for black electoral power culminated in the 1972 Convention in Gary, Indiana, the largest black political convention in U.S. history, representing African Americans from across the political spectrum. These activists, however, connected their electoral strategy to a mass-based political movement.

Likewise, the welfare rights movement's impact on legislation and social policy cannot be separated from the political pressure generated by protests and demonstrations. The legal reforms advocated by welfare recipients and their representatives were part of a larger grassroots political movement. Lucie White argues that the legal decisions "placed a versatile tactical weapon in the hands of the poor."[129] The victories achieved in the court-room and the legislative halls legitimated the struggle of welfare recipients and emboldened many to become involved. In addition, the momentum for change among politicians and public officials was a response to mass protest. When viewed in light of the grassroots movement, the successes cannot be attributed solely to the persuasiveness of legal arguments. Writing about the *Goldberg* decision, White suggests that it was only "in response to [the welfare rights] movement that dominant groups momentarily acknowledged the gravity, indeed the justice, of the plaintiff's claims."[130] The legal arguments and the political movement worked together to empower recipients, expand their legal rights, and give them a greater measure of control over their lives.

The strategies of advocating more formalized welfare procedures, seeking redress through the legal system, and demanding participation in welfare policy making legitimated important elements of the liberal democratic political system. Women in the welfare rights movement did not intend to transform the political system. Instead they sought to reform it to more effectively meet their needs. An organizer from Massachusetts said, "We do not ever say to the ladies that we are out to tear down the system, because that is their bread and butter. They do not want that system torn down. I will admit that the system is crumbling under the stuff, but that isn't my idea."[131] Rather than destroy it, many welfare recipients sought to share in what the welfare system and the electoral system had to offer. A supporter of the movement observed: "There are no revolutionaries among the welfare mothers I know. Their values are solidly middle-class American values. They want what you and I want: food and shelter and a good education for their kids and a chance to learn or use a skill themselves in useful work outside their home."[132] Indeed many of the strategies pursued by welfare rights activists worked to include them in the political processes and formal welfare procedures.

Welfare recipients' struggle for dignity, participation, and protection of civil rights was a product of their experiences as poor black women on welfare.[133] The welfare system silenced, marginalized, and disempowered women on AFDC, and denied their basic civil rights. In this context, participating in the political and policy-making processes and seeking formal rights helped them overcome their oppression. Patricia Williams argues that "for the historically disempowered, the conferring of rights is symbolic of all the denied aspects of their humanity."[134] For poor black women on welfare with relatively few rights, the struggle for their rights became an important site of battle. Arguing that AFDC was a right chipped away at the building blocks that made the welfare system punitive and repressive. It transformed the very meaning of AFDC assistance: rather than a form of public charity, it would be an entitlement with little cause for stigma or shame. Scholar Hilary Lim argues, "For those whose experience is such that to speak of themselves as having rights is comparatively new, to have in their hands the magic quality of legal concepts is a positive and transforming sensation."[135]

Welfare recipients found most unbearable the arbitrary nature of AFDC and worked to formalize and define the procedures of welfare.[136] The concentration of power in the hands of caseworkers left recipients with few avenues to contest decisions. Although caseworkers could be sympathetic and supportive, many welfare recipients did not experience this. Caseworkers frequently exhibited the same stereotypes and biases about black welfare recipients that dominated the public discussions about welfare in the 1960s. They were not sheltered from the larger society that assumed that black women were undeserving of assistance, promiscuous, or unfit mothers. Patricia Williams comments on how race and racial stereotypes impact the distinction between formal and informal decision making systems:

> If one assumes, as blacks must, not that the larger world wants to overcome alienation but that many heartily embrace it, driven not just by fear but by hatred and taboo, then informal systems as well as formal systems will be run principally by unconscious or irrational forces.[137]

Thus, welfare rights activists did not advocate formal procedures out of ignorance about the limits of liberal political processes, but out of knowledge about how the welfare system operated.

Influencing legislation and policy empowered recipients, helping them overcome the dehumanization and stigma associated with AFDC. By publicly identifying as welfare recipients, demanding participation in the making of welfare policy, and claiming their rights, they challenged the welfare status quo and helped recharacterize the public perception of welfare. Intelligent recipients articulating why they deserved assistance contrasted sharply with the image of the lazy, promiscuous, and ignorant single mother on assistance. By participating in the policy-making process, welfare rights activists helped break down the stereotypes of welfare recipients and challenged a hierarchical, bureaucratic system that functioned to keep them passive and silent. Through their association with welfare rights organizations they brought dignity to their lives and asserted their right to assistance. They diminished the power of caseworkers, modified rules and regulations, and ended the most flagrantly abusive welfare practices. Women in the welfare rights movement struggled for basic rights and privileges ostensibly available to everyone in a liberal democratic political system. But because they were black women on welfare, whose race, sex, and status as welfare recipients disempowered them, their demands for dignity, due process, and representation did not legitimate, but challenged the status quo. Although welfare activists in many ways worked within a liberal framework, the demands and goals of the women in the welfare rights movement were nevertheless an important departure from the way AFDC was perceived and disbursed.

CHAPTER 3
More Money Now!

In addition to reforming the administration of AFDC, the welfare rights movement also worked to improve the living standards of recipients. This was the crux of the movement's campaign for "more money now."[1] The struggles for economic and administrative reform occurred simultaneously, fueling one another and together addressing the myriad problems of recipients. The campaign for dignity ensured the right to due process, while the demands for material benefits addressed the substantive issue of the standard of living. The dual problems of lack of dignity and low benefits were linked. The meager monthly sum indicated the lack of respect afforded to both the AFDC program and its recipients and sent a message that recipients' work as mothers was not valued. Consequently, welfare rights activists sought to remedy the problem of inadequate monthly budgets. This first took the form of a campaign for special grants. They demanded grants from welfare officials for household items that welfare departments had defined as necessary. They took advantage of existing regulations to request clothes, household furnishings, and money to enjoy holidays and other special occasions, arguing that these were basic rights.

Welfare recipients redefined the terms of welfare through the campaign for more money, challenging the core features of a program that sentenced them to poverty and locked them into a system as dependent individuals. Unlike the struggles for dignity and representation, which involved applying for fair hearings, bringing lawsuits, lobbying, and seeking participation by welfare recipients and found its strength in lawyers and knowledge of welfare regulations, the demands for more money centered on a militant strategy of protest and disruption by massive numbers of poor people.

Armed with a sense of entitlement and emboldened by the power of numbers, welfare rights activists marched into welfare offices demanding the items to which they were entitled. They negotiated with caseworkers, lobbied welfare officials, held mass rallies, and took over welfare and state offices. Rather than submitting to a system designed to control and regulate their behavior, welfare recipients sought to make the AFDC program work for them and improve their children's lives. And, in the process, they transformed the meaning of welfare.

The special grant campaign was one of the welfare rights movement's most visible and successful strategies. Initiated on a local level, it turned into NWRO's national campaign for "More Money Now!" bringing in thousands of new members and palpably affecting welfare policy on the local level. Many welfare recipients were drawn into the welfare rights movement through the special grant campaign, which instilled in them a sense of empowerment and convinced them of the benefits of organizing. The male staff of NWRO hoped the campaign would build a mass-based organization with national influence. Women recipients organizing special grant campaigns made their claims as mothers who were victims of structural forces that left them in circumstances of poverty. Despite these differences between staff and recipients, the movement achieved impressive victories that demonstrated the power of mass mobilization and coordinated strategy.

Emergence of Special Grants

Welfare recipients on the local level supplemented the inadequate monthly benefit by requesting special grants from the welfare department. Welfare departments provided special one-time grants for things such as furniture, school clothing, and household items that were not included in the regular monthly allowance and that recipients could apply for as necessary. In assessing what items warranted special grants, local welfare departments developed formulas for determining the minimum living standards for recipients. It might have included, for example, one bed per person, a new winter coat every three years, or costs associated with high-school graduation. Prior to joining a welfare rights groups, many recipients did not know about special grants. And when they did, welfare departments often refused to award them.

Lawyers, caseworkers, and other activists with access to welfare department policy manuals informed welfare recipients of their right to special grants. Across the country, welfare rights organizations mobilized women on welfare to apply for special grants, notifying recipients of their right to certain items, assisting them in filing applications for the grants, and encouraging them to demand a prompt response from the welfare department. Some groups mimeographed checklists of "minimum standards," and distributed the lists to friends and neighbors. They organized groups of recipients—anywhere from ten to several hundred—to collectively request special grants and sat in or disrupted welfare offices until caseworkers granted all of the requests. They also insisted that welfare departments process forms quickly and without question.

The special grant campaign sought to remedy the poverty of welfare recipients by acquiring for them basic necessities, such as clothes, furniture, and working appliances. But more significantly, welfare rights activists turned to the state for an assurance of a minimum standard of living. They did not believe that individuals, charitable organizations, or the business sector was responsible for ensuring that everyone lived decently and comfortably. It was the duty of the government. In the 1960s the state's responsibility to its citizens expanded. The state became regulator and enforcer, shaping business conduct and the everyday lives of Americans.[2] The civil rights movement, for example, pushed the federal government to end institutional patterns of racism and discrimination. Environmental groups demanded state regulation of air and water quality. Women's groups advocated governmental assurances of an end to job discrimination. The welfare rights movement similarly sought to broaden the government's role in alleviating poverty.

In making demands upon the state, welfare rights activists confronted a bureaucratic system theoretically unaccountable to them. They were not workers whose labor was essential to the functioning of the system. They were not consumers who could withhold the purchase of services until the program improved. They were unable to initiate an economic boycott to demonstrate their dissatisfaction with AFDC. Welfare recipients desperately needed welfare services, but, as individuals, they wielded little leverage over the program. Protests against the state were hardly new, but welfare rights activists in the 1960s forged a new road. They consciously tried to make the AFDC program more accountable to its clients and consequently fashioned a new relationship between the state bureaucracy and the people it served.

In New York City the Committee of Welfare Families and the Welfare Recipients League demanded special allowances for winter clothing for their children as early as 1964. Learning of special grants from Richard Cloward, the League found some welfare directors sympathetic, but filed fair hearings when their requests were denied.[3] The Committee of Welfare Families sent individual letters to the welfare department asking for money for winter clothes. The department granted eighty of the 100 requests for additional money for winter clothing.[4] Over the next couple of years, the special grant campaign spread rapidly throughout the country.[5] The Welfare Grievance Committee in Cleveland, OH campaigned in June 1966 for telephones for clients.[6] The Ohio Steering Committee for Adequate Welfare (OSCAW) staged a two-and-a-half-week vigil at the governor's office in October 1966 to pressure him to grant a $100-a-year clothing allowance for school children.[7] And in Detroit in late 1967 the Westside ADC Mothers refused to send their children to school until the department increased the $5-per-month clothing allowance for their children.[8]

In New York City, the special-grant drive peaked in the spring of 1968. The Citywide Coordinating Committee of Welfare Rights Groups (Citywide) coordinated activity and provided support for local groups demanding money for spring and Easter clothing, Mother's Day clothing, graduation clothing, camp supplies, and telephones. The sheer magnitude of the protests, the persistence of welfare recipients, as well as their knowledge of department regulations coerced many welfare officials to accede to the demands of welfare rights activists. In 1968, over 100 people sat in at the Melrose welfare office in the Bronx for three days and two nights. After almost continuous protests for a month, the department granted recipients $35,000 for Easter clothing. In upper Manhattan a small group of nine mothers, members of Langston Hughes Welfare Rights, met with the administrator of the Dyckman Welfare Center and walked out with over $4,500. At the same time, 200 mothers and their children spent four nights at the Tremont Welfare Center in the Bronx requesting money for "beds, lampshades, dust mops and clothes pins." The staff worked into the evening for two days screening applications and issuing checks.[9] Sit-ins, demands for fair hearings, and blockades of welfare center entrances sometimes prompted caseworkers to walk off the job and welfare directors to shut down the centers.[10] When welfare officials could not award money for special grant items immediately, activists demanded emergency checks.[11] Regulations required caseworkers to visit a client's home before issuing a check, but protesters insisted that caseworkers bypass the regulations and grant money on the spot. On the Lower East Side groups were given checks for graduation clothing without the usual mandatory verification from the school.[12] At the Jamaica Welfare Center in Queens, the director appointed a task force to process application forms for new cases and provide emergency cash grants the same day.[13] The threat of protest and disruption convinced many welfare officials to circumvent bureaucratic regulations and meet the demands of irate welfare recipients.

At NWRO's August 1968 annual convention in Chicago, dubbed an "Action Conference," participants decided to wage a national campaign for school and winter clothing and Christmas grants. The campaign for More Money Now! coordinated special-grant protests already in progress. Staff members in Washington sent out packets of literature to affiliated local groups, instructing organizers to develop minimum-standards checklists.[14] Over the next year welfare rights activists employed direct-action tactics, including rallies, pickets, and sit-ins, to force concessions from local welfare centers. Angry clients demanded money for clothing, furniture, and household supplies, and more prompt and efficient service from caseworkers.[15] The national office gave direction to local struggles, reinvigorating the local movements. In early 1969, Ohio welfare recipients demanded a Thanksgiving and Christmas bonus so "welfare children may attach the same significance to traditional American holidays as other children."[16] In Detroit, Westside Mothers ADC Group requested $25 per person for the Christmas holidays in 1968. When their request was not granted they sat in for two weeks at the Department of Social Service.[17] Similar campaigns occurred in Toledo, Boston, Philadelphia, Providence, Washington, D.C., Newark, and Youngstown, OH.[18]

Special Grants and Building a Movement

Most staff members valued the special grant campaign because it materially improved recipients' lives and enabled recipients to confront the welfare bureaucracy. But some staff members also used the campaign as a way to boost the power of the national organization and build the membership of welfare rights groups. Tim Sampson, the point person for the campaign in the national office, said, "I was very interested in . . . creating a membership organization . . . So, we set up a membership system."[19] They required recipients to join the organization and pay the yearly dues of $1 in order to participate in the special grant campaign. This brought into welfare rights organizations thousands of recipients who wanted additional money from the welfare department. The Wyandotte County WRO in Kansas City, KS waged a campaign at the start of the 1968 school year to increase the $9-a-month clothing grant. Members of the WRO met with the County welfare director and the County Commissioners, who told them that state regulations prohibited increases in the clothing allowance. Welfare mothers persisted, referring to the welfare manual that allowed for an increase in the clothing grant when necessary. In mid-September Commissioners granted members of the WRO $15 per child for clothing. Within a week the local group's membership doubled.[20] The Brooklyn Welfare Action Council (B-WAC) brought local WROs participating in the special-needs campaign into a borough-wide structure, which had 3,000 dues-paying members shortly after it formed in the fall of 1967. Organizer Rhoda Linton set up tables outside the welfare offices, where they "recruited a lot of new members" into NWRO.[21] Nationally, as well, participation ballooned during the special grant campaign. Between 1968 and 1969, at the peak of the special-grant tactic, NWRO membership more than doubled from 10,000 to 22,500.[22]

Relying on special grants, NWRO organizer Bill Pastreich had substantially increased membership in Massachusetts. In 1963, recipients in Massachusetts, with the help of SDS, formed local groups called Mothers for Adequate Welfare (MAW). In 1966 and 1967, MAW conducted special grant campaigns for Thanksgiving dinners and for school clothing for their children.[23] Under the direction of Pastreich, hired by George Wiley, welfare recipients in the Boston area began a mass campaigns in 1968 to demand grants for furniture. If departments refused to award money, recipients sat in, marched, and picketed.[24] Pastreich, twenty-eight years old, married with an infant son, was from Manhattan Beach, a prosperous neighborhood in Brooklyn. He had a master's degree in social work and spent two years in the Peace Corps in Peru.[25] Pastreich's organizing style was aggressive and goal-oriented. He collected the names of welfare recipients from caseworkers or went to the supermarket on the day welfare checks were distributed. Then he door-knocked, often taking a welfare recipient along with him. Once in the home of the recipient, Pastreich assessed whether they qualified for welfare or, if they were already on welfare, special grants. If, in his judgment, they had too much money, he moved on to the next family. If not, he looked over their furniture and household items. As one reporter described it: "His hand feeling couches to determine worn-out springs, his eyes sweeping the kitchen to note missing appliances—he starts telling tales of all those stoves, pots, endtables, hampers, cribs he can get you from 'the welfare.'"[26] If the recipient expressed interest he informed them of the next welfare rights meeting, promising them money for the items they needed.[27] Using this method, Pastreich could organize a new welfare rights group in as little as three weeks. As he exhausted special grants in one geographical area, Pastreich moved on to organize another. He started groups in Cape Cod, Adams, North Adams, and other cities and towns across Massachusetts.

Interested primarily in the issue of power, Pastreich and other Massachusetts Welfare Rights Organization (MWRO) staff followed political theorist Saul Alinksy. While a student at Syracuse University, Pastreich worked at the Community Action Training Center, run by Fred Ross and Warren Hagstrom. Alinksy flew to Syracuse four times a month in the mid-1960s to work with graduate students and staff associated with the Center.[28] He had organized the Back of the Yards neighborhood in Chicago in the 1930s and, more recently, the Woodlawn Organization, a predominantly black community group in Chicago. Alinksy believed that if poor communities organized, they could effect political, economic, or social change or negotiate to improve their living conditions. According to Alinksy, the poor only had the power of numbers:

You can get jobs, you can break segregated housing patterns. But you have to have power to do it, and you'll get it only through organization. Because power just goes to two poles—those who have money and those who've got people. You [poor people] haven't got money so your own fellow men are your only source of strength.[29]

Alinsky saw poor people as one of many contending interest groups. Welfare recipients and other poor people with minimal political influence or financial resources needed to mobilize in order to exert power. Pastreich similarly hoped to develop an interest group for the poor:

Democracy in the United States works on a pressure basis and . . . everybody has their pressure group. The doctors have the A.M.A. The lawyers have the American Bar Association. Social workers have the National Association of Social Workers. The poor don't have anything. What we're doing now is working the way the system works. We're building a pressure group for poor people.[30]

Adopting a pluralistic view of American society, these NWRO organizers sought to form associations in communities lacking political influence so they could compete in the political arena and marketplace.[31]

Many other NWRO staff members and organizers had worked with Alinsky or were his disciples. Wiley, for example, taught at Syracuse at the same time that Alinsky supervised the Community Action Training Center. And MWRO invited Alinsky to lead training sessions for its organizers.[32] Despite the overlapping ties, some NWRO organizers defined themselves differently from Alinsky by highlighting the power of individual participation rather than collective influence. For example, Tim Sampson, who was trained by Alinksy and worked closely with Wiley at NWRO headquarters, believed:

A central problem in the United States for everybody is that we don't participate in our government . . . If people who are economically dependent on the government, namely welfare recipients . . . could find a method to organize and participate in relationship to the programs that were their lifeline to economic subsistence, what we could learn about organizing and participating in our government would benefit the rest of us.[33]

Sampson advocated a form of democratic participation for all people as a way to overcome alienation, disempowerment, and injustice. Similarly,

Rhoda Linton emphasized individual consciousness. From upstate New York, Linton completed her masters in social work at Syracuse University, where she met Wiley and worked at the Community Action Training Center. Influenced more by Hagstrom than Alinsky, Linton believed in changing individuals by involving them in social action in order to effect bigger transformations. After forming B-WAC Linton started the Brooklyn Leadership Development Project in 1968 to educate and train recipients in welfare law.[34] Linton's position on individual participation in social action diverged from that of hard-core Alinsky-style NWRO organizers like Pastreich.

Pastreich lured in recipients with the promise of material goods in order to build a powerful organization of poor people. More important than the reasons people joined was the number of people mobilized to advocate reform of the system.[35] Pastreich tied receipt of special-grant items to membership in the welfare rights group, and believed that organizational goals outweighed material benefits to recipients. In one case, he discouraged a caseworker from helping clients get new furniture, so he could use it as an enticement. He told the caseworker, "I need the furniture as a benefit to offer guys who may have supplementation already but need a new kitchen range, sofa, bunks for the kids. So go easy on the furniture for now." The caseworker agreed.[36] In the short run, Pastreich's strategy proved successful. During the special-grant campaigns, MWRO membership increased dramatically: more than 4,000 recipients joined MWRO between the summers of 1968 and 1970.[37] By the time of the NWRO conference in Detroit in August 1969, it had the second largest delegation in the country.[38] The "Boston model," as Pastreich's organizing style came to be known, successfully established a mass base.

Activists such as Pastreich and Alinsky assumed that people, especially poor people, would organize only around their immediate self-interest. Consequently, they downplayed ideology and peddled their strategies as financially beneficial for recipients. The analysis was flawed in two ways, however. First, organizers committed to mobilizing welfare recipients around a narrow definition of self-interest, centering on "getting what I can for myself," found it more difficult to build a radical, sustained political movement. The groups started by Pastreich and MWRO dissipated as quickly as they grew. Once recipients got their furniture or clothing—the reason they joined—they left the organization. These groups could not carry on unless they routinely brought in new members. Participants who joined solely for a special grant lacked a deeper commitment to the vision of more seasoned organizers. MWRO staff excluded most recipients from decision making, discussions about political strategy, and planning for political protests. Staff members viewed them as bodies to carry out the plans outlined by middle-class organizers. In fact, MWRO and MAW split in October 1968 because of MAW members' discontent with staff domination and Pastreich's control.[39] The pattern of recipient exclusion and goal of building membership was also evident on the national level. At a national conference on the minimum standards campaign in January 1968, recipients complained of "lack of participation" and "lack of . . . involvement in decision-making regarding national organizational strategy and tactics."[40] The NWRO information packet on the winter action campaign in 1968 also reflected the aim of bringing in recipients: "The main idea of action is to win benefits—*MONEY and BUILD MEMBERSHIP*."[41] So, organizers achieved short-term goals, such as winning special grants for furniture, but were less successful at developing among recipients a long-term commitment to social change. Recipients, like middle-class activists, were capable of working toward ideological goals such as social equality and economic justice. Recipients in the movement for the long haul remained active, not for personal benefit, but because they believed deeply in a more egalitarian and just society. These recipients may have joined the movement because of immediate self-interest, but through the process of political organizing, they came to advocate long-term social change.

Second, organizers' strict cost-benefit analysis was not a clear-cut issue for women on welfare, making organizing around self-interest tricky. Progressive political and economic reforms would likely improve living standards for most poor people. Indeed, thousands of welfare recipients benefited from the special-grant campaign by acquiring new household items. But many recipients also paid a price for participation in the welfare rights movement, giving up time spent with their children, their limited financial security, their sense of safety in the face of police or welfare department harassment, and their anonymity, which was important because of the shame and guilt tied to receipt of AFDC. If recipients were drawn into welfare rights organizing solely on promises of immediate benefits and never developed a devotion to the long-term goals of the movement, once the practical costs of organizing became clear, they would likely cease participating. The costs of organizing might outweigh the benefit of a new TV set or a new pair of shoes. The balance was tipped especially during periods of limited activity or when recipients encountered resistance to their demands by welfare officials. Prolonged involvement required participants to connect short-term goals to long-term change. Thus, it seems that some organizers' exclusive focus on amassing membership lists did little to contribute to the goals of building a sustained movement.

Recipients and Special Grants

Recipients, like staff members, appreciated the material benefits of the special-grant campaign. In fact, many recipients participated in welfare rights activities hoping to raise their standard of living. Two Mobilization for Youth organizers, Birnbaum and Rabagliati, summed up the importance of material benefits in their report on welfare organizing in New York City:

> The right to have telephones has been won for certain categories of clients. Automated school-clothing allowances have been obtained, and clients now have a right to burial money . . . The benefits of the organizations can be described in terms of better living conditions, more respect from the caseworker, more hope for the future, more understanding of the system, and more knowledge about how to master the situation in terms of material benefits and human dignity.[42]

Local welfare rights leaders participated in special-grant campaigns, but differed with middle-class organizers about the significance of special grants. Many recipients agreed with the staff that special grants might persuade people on welfare to formally join local and national organizations, but some believed the movement needed to be more concerned with the overall plight of recipients than shoring up membership. The Virginia WRO saw its goal as more expansive.

> Though VWRO is a membership organization, our primary goal is not membership. We are an organization of poor people *for* poor people and our primary function is service to impoverished communities and individuals . . . [During our campaigns] it was the decision of the VWRO leadership not to solicit members. Neither of the VWRO groups wanted dues or ideologies to get in the way of getting healthier living conditions or warm clothing for all of the poor children possible.[43]

In the school clothing campaign, VWRO submitted 300 applications to the welfare department: only forty were from its members. In another case, a woman unexpectedly hospitalized had left four children at home when her landlord tacked an eviction notice onto her door. "Somebody telephoned the city-wide VWRO chairwoman. Three hours later the woman's rent was paid and her children fed. The woman was never asked to join VWRO. If she joins it will be because she too wants to help her fellow poor."[44] The VWRO, like many other local welfare groups, was less concerned about the organization's fate than the conditions under which poor people lived.

Recipients also attached different meanings to special grant items. They considered the social significance of material goods, the circumstances under which items were given, and the reason for assistance. Claiming special grants as a right, recipients refused, for example, to accept anything at the expense of their "dignity." Maintaining dignity meant being treated with respect, not being stigmatized, protecting their individual civil rights, and, ultimately, deciding for themselves what was in their best interest. They rejected anything that smacked of charity:

> In Washington, The District government has responded to the drive for winter clothing grants with appeals for private donations . . . The mothers do not want private charity . . . Mrs. Etta Horn, the President of the Citywide Welfare Alliance, put private donations in the right perspective when she returned a $500 donation and said, "From slavery on, it's been tokenism. The day of tokenism is over. The $500 is nothing but hush money."[45]

In Columbus, OH, recipients refused second-hand clothing because it was out of style and did not include items they needed.[46] In Worcester, MA, MAW refused vouchers for new furniture and insisted on cash so they could shop anywhere they wanted.[47] Similarly, just before Christmas, recipients in Columbus picketed the local "Toys for Tots" program. Their leaflets read, in part,

> Christmas is perhaps the only time every year when almost everybody wants to help someone else. And so we are given Christmas baskets, Christmas clothing and Christmas toys. This is maybe nice but people need food, clothing and a place to live the whole year round—not just at Christmas time.[48]

Thus, recipients believed they were entitled, not just to hand-me-downs, but to fashionable clothing; not just to what others did not want, but to items of their own choice. They wanted assistance not only when donors were in the spirit of giving, but when they needed particular items. So, the needs and desires of the recipient, not the generosity and excesses of the giver, should determine the terms of the transfer. This would diminish the stigma historically tied to receipt of welfare. Welfare recipients wanted to live their lives no differently from the nonpoor around them. In this way, they subscribed to the politics of respectability that had historically informed so many poor people's struggles.[49]

Many welfare recipients justified assistance by their poverty and their status as mothers, believing that material benefits would improve their living standards and enable them to raise and properly care for their children. Most special grant campaigns were for school clothing, winter clothing, summer camp items, or other things for recipients' children. The Pittsfield Association of Parents for Adequate Welfare (PAPAW) in western Massachusetts conducted surveys to determine the main complaints of welfare recipients. Children's needs topped the list of concerns.[50] The Philadelphia WRO, as well, believed special grants could vastly improve the quality of life for children. In an internal document the organization argued:

> The frequent inability of children on assistance to participate in the more formal events of community life (such as graduation ceremonies) because of lack of appropriate clothing sets these youngsters apart from their friends . . . The careful use of special grants would go far toward helping such deprived children take part in the more constructive experiences society offers.[51]

The Philadelphia WRO worked to better the lives of children of welfare recipients.

In Ann Arbor, MI, welfare recipients campaigned for school clothing for their children. Throughout the summer of 1968, women on welfare in Ann Arbor requested money for school clothing from their caseworkers. They argued that the $9-a-month allotment, based on 1960 cost-of-living estimates, was not enough and their children had only shorts and sandals to wear to school. In September, they took over a meeting of the County Social Services Board for nine hours to get $100 a month for school clothing. With school beginning the next day, the mothers, threatening an all-night sit-in at the welfare office, demanded the grant be issued immediately.[52] The following day, after a late-night meeting of the Board of Supervisors, the county agreed to give $40 to all mothers for school clothing. When protesters rejected this offer, the county promised to assess needs individually and award up to $60 for each recipient. Sticking to their original demand of $100, the welfare rights organization sat in at the County Building.[53] Garnering support from University of Michigan students, the sit-in grew to 800 after the county began to process the $60 grant requests. On the third day of the sit-in, frustrated by the impasse, the Director of the Social Service Department ordered the arrest of 200 people and declared, "We aren't going to put up with this anymore."[54]

The protest in Ann Arbor is one example of how welfare mothers organized on behalf of their children's needs. The special-grant protest empowered them as mothers, giving them a platform to publicly and vocally place value on motherhood. Welfare recipients tied the raising of their children in an appropriate manner to the availability of special grants. The grants provided items or opportunities that would foster in their children the self-esteem and self-confidence necessary for success. For example, at a meeting in 1966 in New York City, welfare mothers emphasized the psychological impact of the lack of adequate clothing on the well-being of their children. Appropriate clothes and their children's participation in social activities, they believed, were indispensable for healthy development. "Our children always have to feel an inferiority complex because they can't participate in some social programs, because they can't dress properly and we can't afford to buy their outfits."[55] A group in Rhode Island argued that more money for school clothing "will improve children's attendance, attitudes, and performance at school . . . Authoritative studies show that children do poorly in school if they don't have proper clothing. Clothing is an essential ingredient in a child's self-image."[56] Some recipients claimed that poverty was not just an obstacle to success, but the source of damaging and dangerous behavior. Stark poverty may alienate children, profoundly impacting their psyche. A Philadelphia welfare rights organizer quoted one mother:

> "Children who feel different, act different." Habitual "different-ness" of this kind tends to lessen a child's respect for his parents and for the society from which he feels estranged. It may lead to destructive behavior or to illegal acts that will finance special items or activities enabling such a child "to be like his friends for once."[57]

Thus, these mothers believed their children should be treated the same and experience the same things as other children. They justified special grants for school clothes, graduation clothes, and summer camp as mothers concerned about their children, rather than just as welfare recipients.

By framing special grants as necessary to enable them to raise emotionally stable and successful children, welfare rights activists did several things at once. First, they tapped into popular discussions about psychological health and emotional well-being. Since World War II, psychologists, sociologists, social workers, educators, and even economists had stressed the importance of emotional health. Countless intellectuals and authors in the 1950s and 1960s, including David Reisman, Daniel Bell, and Betty Friedan, analyzed the psychological state of sectors of the American population.[58] The heightened concern about mental health convinced President Kennedy in 1963 to urge Congress to allocate money for community mental health centers, which it did. The number of mental health clinics in this period increased dramatically. Thus, psychological health became a topic of public concern, woven into discussions of medical care, workplace issues, family status, public policy, and civil rights.

The connection between mental health and civil rights was most obvious in the *Brown v. Board of Education* Supreme Court decision, which argued that segregation psychologically damaged black children and stigmatized them as inferior. The Supreme Court based its decision in part on research by psychologists Kenneth Clark and Mamie Clark. The Clarks tested children in segregated settings to determine whether they would identify with black or white dolls and which ones they would describe as good, beautiful, and nice. The Clarks found that most black children living in the segregated South associated negative traits with the black doll and positive traits with the white doll. Moreover, many of these black children represented themselves as white or identified with the white doll.[59] This, the Clarks concluded, indicated self-hate and was evidence that segregation destroyed the emotional health and self-esteem of black children. This argument helped convince the justices of the Supreme Court to declare school segregation unconstitutional in the landmark 1954 *Brown* decision.[60]

Along the lines of *Brown*, welfare recipients analyzed the way society categorized people as different and inferior based on economic status and how this negatively impacted their mental state and translated into a form of discrimination. They crafted arguments—about the psychological well-being of their children and how the stigma of poverty created in them an inferiority complex—to demand greater allowances for clothing and other necessities. For them, equal opportunity meant not only access to school, but an emotional and psychological state that allowed them to take full advantage of educational opportunities.

In making claims as mothers, welfare rights activists also wanted to recast the dominant image of the lazy welfare recipient who did nothing of value and ought to be working outside the home. Highlighting their children's needs drew attention to their work as mothers and helped reconstruct the popular view that welfare recipients were undeserving of assistance. At a time when motherhood was highly touted as a foundation of civil society, a bulwark against Communism, and a source of economic prosperity, welfare mothers sought to integrate their own work as mothers into the larger discussion of the importance of motherhood.[61]

Recipients' attention to children looking and dressing properly also points to the social significance of clothes. Clothing reflected identity and status. Members of the countercultural movement in the 1960s often rejected their own middle-class or privileged background by shedding outward appearances. They grew their hair and wore tattered t-shirts and ripped jeans. These cultural rebels challenged social norms by dispensing with the accouterments that others expected of them. Welfare recipients and other poor people who sought to dress their children in new clothing also defied the social norms of someone of their class background and, especially, welfare status. They believed that the way an individual dressed shaped self-respect, affected personal behavior, and influenced success. By dressing fashionably and neatly welfare recipients could begin to break down the class and cultural barriers distinguishing them as different and inferior.

The special-grant campaign brought thousands of recipients into the welfare rights movement, collectively won millions of dollars for women on welfare, and legitimated the welfare rights movement as a force to be reckoned with. It soldered bonds among local groups more concretely than could national meetings or membership buttons. Moiece Palladino, who worked with the San Francisco WRO, explained the importance of this connection: "A lot of our campaign activity was focused as a result of . . . national campaigns. And that's what we pushed. We pushed the national campaigns . . . I think [our local work] would have been very difficult if we hadn't . . . felt that we were part of a larger scheme."[62] Through the campaign staff members worked to improve the lives of the poor and build a mass organization of poor people, which they hoped would reform the welfare system. Recipients hoped to improve the lives of poor people, to remove the stigma of charity, and to enable mothers to raise their children. These differences did not become an obstacle in the special grant campaign. Staff members and recipients cooperated, even after local officials abolished the special-grant system.

Limits of the State: Flat Grants and Repression

The special-grant campaign's success at winning concessions from the welfare department created a sense of crisis for welfare officials. During the spring and summer of 1968, for example, welfare rights activists inundated New York City welfare departments with demands for special grants, threatening sit-ins or disruption. Demonstrations in the city became so frequent and troublesome that it established an emergency communications room to monitor protests.[63] Local welfare officials, unable to cope with the massive protests, often processed forms quickly, overlooking department regulations. They granted $12 to $13 million a month at the height of the campaign, five times more than the previous year. The earliest demonstrations succeeded because of the tactics of mass protest and because clients requested items according to welfare department guidelines. This demand to enforce existing regulations initially made it difficult for welfare administrators to turn down recipients. But that soon changed.

As the demonstrations gained momentum, welfare officials around the country became less sympathetic to recipients' demands, had demonstrators arrested with more frequency, and modified regulations to eliminate special grants. A Massachusetts Department of Public Welfare memo to regional administrators instructed that if recipients disrupt offices, enter staff areas, arrive in a group, or refuse to leave the building, special grants should not be authorized and "a police detail" should remove recipients.[64] In the spring of 1969 members of MWRO went into welfare offices in Boston demanding Easter and spring clothing. Welfare officials refused to issue special grants, insisting that each recipient meet individually with her caseworker. MWRO tried this, but few were given grants. They went back in mass, but were still unsuccessful.[65] Despite several months of continuous protests, officials in Boston refused to meet the requests of welfare rights protesters.

In other instances, law enforcement and welfare officials treated welfare mothers and organizers with outright hostility. As the welfare rights movement mushroomed, officials routinely harassed recipients. In Somerville, MA, after the formation of a local welfare rights organization in November 1968, the mayor asked the attorney general to take "aggressive action" and arrest "professional agitators who cross state lines to organize disturbances," claiming these NWRO employees obstructed work at government offices and incited riots.[66] In another case, Mrs. Nick, a welfare mother in Goldsboro, NC, organized an NWRO chapter in August 1968. The department subsequently suspended her public assistance payments, presumably because of an intimate relationship with a man. In a letter to NWRO staff person Tim Sampson, a member of the NAACP wrote, "It is fairly clear that Mrs. Nick was suspended in retaliation for her organizing work and for her statements concerning the welfare department."[67] In another case, after a sit-in for school clothing by the Cleveland Welfare Rights Organization, police picked up a leader of the demonstration when she was on her way home with her four small children. Held on charges of welfare fraud, the woman was questioned by police about a number of things, including her political choice for mayor. After 72 hours, police dropped the charges and released the family.[68]

This kind of harassment had been present since the welfare rights movement's inception. Sometimes the attempts to snuff out activism originated with the welfare office, sometimes law enforcement officials acted on their own or on behalf of political leaders. Another source may have been the uneasy relationship between cops and the black community, a relationship permeated with distrust since many white police officers had little connection to or regard for residents of poor black communities. The National Advisory Commission on Civil Disorders, which analyzed the causes of urban uprisings in the late 1960s, concluded that "abrasive" police-community relations caused much of the unrest in the inner city. White officers, the report claimed, often exhibited racist attitudes and people in the inner city frequently perceived police officers as symbolic of white racism and repression.[69] As the welfare rights movement expanded and became more militant, harassment increased, reflecting broader patterns of police repression in the 1960s. Cops in the 1960s were charged with preventing disruption, containing political protest, and maintaining the status quo. The FBI instituted the Counterintelligence Program (COINTELPRO) to gather information about protesters and ultimately to quell and discredit these movements. Welfare rights activists were not direct targets of COINTELPRO, but they, nevertheless, experienced a considerable share of political and economic harassment.

City officials also stymied demonstrations by replacing special grants with a flat grant, which gave recipients a set amount of money each year for additional needs, rather than permitting them to request money for specific items. For welfare officials the flat grant was a lifeline out of the political quagmire of having to concede to the demands of militant welfare mothers. Hugh Jones, Chairman of the Board of Social Welfare in New York, indicated in the summer of 1968 that the "volume of [special grant] applications has come close to breaking down the system." Special grants inflated the budgets of local welfare departments, engendering an image that municipal politics were out of control and too much money was spent on welfare. The special-grant protests, in effect, created a political crisis for officials. Mitchell Ginsberg, Director of the New York Human Resources Administration, warned that special grants cost the city an enormous amount and that it "desperately needed" a flat-grant system. The *New York Times* editorialized: "'Flat grants, used virtually everywhere else in this country, will not cure this situation, but they are an immediate necessity to help meet the city's current welfare crisis."[70]

New York City adopted the flat grant in August 1968. Under the new system, AFDC recipients received $100 a year per person to buy household items, furniture, and clothing not covered in the monthly grant. The city rationalized that all recipients, not only those requesting special grants, benefited from flat grants. In addition, clients could plan for their own needs, without the indignity of investigations, which were routine for special grants.[71] The city expected to save close to $40 million a year. Other states adopted flat grants as well. The Massachusetts State Welfare Department in April 1969 froze special grants for furniture and household items in order "to meet the basic budgetary needs of recipients in the period ahead."[72] A few months later, in December 1969, the Massachusetts governor announced he would implement a flat grant.[73] A flat grant was also proposed in Washington, D.C., in 1972.

Members of the welfare rights movement vehemently opposed flat grants. In New York City, they argued that $100 a year per person for all items not included in the monthly grant was too little. Sarah Martinez, member of the United Welfare League, said, "I was on welfare myself, so I know $25 every three months for each child just isn't enough for clothing and all household replacements."[74] Citywide calculated that a family of four would be given $4,119 a year with their monthly benefit and the flat grant. But with special grants, a family potentially obtained up to $4,591 a year.[75] So, although the flat grant increased the yearly allowance for the majority of welfare recipients in the city, those most active and knowledgeable would get less. According to Beulah Sanders, the flat grant would be "a raise for people who are not organized, but could be a cutback for those who had been able to win special grants."[76]

The flat grant generated tension about whether the political future of the movement or the needs of welfare recipients not in the movement ought to take priority. The flat grant's simplified procedures of automatic payment without an application for each item were appealing. It divested caseworkers of power, giving recipients greater freedom to decide how to spend their money. However, welfare officials, intent on quelling political protest and saving money, implemented the flat grant with little regard for bettering the lives of welfare families. Couching their reforms in a language of "unfairness" of a system that only benefited the organized was merely a political ploy to make the flat grant more palatable to welfare recipients and their liberal constituency and to put the welfare rights movement on the defensive. Politicians cared little about the fairness of the system when only a handful of recipients knew about or applied for special grants. The struggle over special grants and flat grants was fundamentally about the power of welfare rights groups versus the power of city officials.

As welfare officials had hoped, the abolition of special grants meant the loss of a crucial organizing tool for the welfare rights movement. The special grant campaign pressured local welfare departments, brought visibility to the movement, recruited new members, and demonstrated the power of welfare rights organizations. Implementation of the flat grant undermined a tactic that had won millions of dollars worth of items in the previous months and helped activists build membership. Welfare rights activists vigorously organized against the flat grant reforms to sustain the political life of the movement.

New Strategies

The flat grant became a flashpoint of political protest. At the Kingsbridge Center in New York City recipients ripped phones off the walls and overturned furniture. Hulbert James, executive director of Citywide, threatened to call on members of the Black Panther Party, the Student Non-Violent

Coordinating Committee, and the Columbia University chapter of Students for a Democratic Society to "send men to protect our women," if the arrests and harassment of welfare recipients continued.[77] This threat reflected a position taken by many men in the welfare rights movement that women recipients needed male protection. George Wiley, for example, told a mayor's commission in 1969 on "The Crisis in Welfare in Cleveland" that "the man related to the welfare mother is not going to sit idly by and see black women brutalized."[78] In Massachusetts, organizer Bill Pastreich speculated that if men from black power organizations participated in a planned sit-in, the welfare department would yield to the demands of the welfare rights organization and change its policy under the threat of a riot.[79]

The Black Panther Party and the welfare rights movement shared a political outlook and the concomitant goal of addressing black inner-city poverty. But male staff members of the welfare rights movement exploited this relationship to intimidate welfare officials. They painted a picture of passive and defenseless black women needing the protection and support of militant black men in order to wage a successful struggle. This strategy promoted an image of groups like the Black Panther Party as predominantly male, even though black women were active, visible members.[80] It also reinforced gendered racial stereotypes of the militant, "bad" black man —a perception permeating both activist and nonactivist circles in the 1960s. Organizers used the stereotypes to frighten public officials and capitalize on widespread trepidation about urban riots. The fear of disruption and political disorder were really the only power recipients had, and organizers relied on this to reform the welfare system.

Welfare rights organizers threatened unrest in part because this spoke to the moment of the late 1960s. Black northern urban communities, such as Newark, Harlem, Detroit, Cleveland, Tampa, Chicago, and Watts, experienced civil disturbances in the middle and late 1960s. Participants rioted, looted, and destroyed property, causing millions of dollars worth of damage. In some cases, as in Detroit and Newark in 1967, local law enforcement officials had simply lost control and were forced to call in the National Guard. Even without resorting to this drastic measure, local officials had difficulty containing the turmoil or alleviating the discontent of inner-city residents who were lashing out at a broad spectrum of issues, including housing, welfare, poverty, unemployment, and police conduct. These ostensibly spontaneous protests in combination with the visibility of black power groups, such as the Black Panthers, the Revolutionary Action Movement, and the Republic of New Afrika, which threatened more calculated and politically directed disruption, instilled apprehension in politicians and the mainstream public. Political leaders found themselves treading lightly and carefully in black urban centers for fear of igniting a political wildfire. Welfare rights organizers hoped to tap into these fears to bend the hand of local politicians, but they did not always do so with success.[81]

In New York, Citywide's massive protests in response to the flat grant system achieved few tangible gains.[82] The city's response was intransigence and, usually, arrest. Cops and welfare recipients often clashed violently. During a two-week period of nearly continuous demonstrations in 1968 after the adoption of the flat grant, police arrested hundreds of people and dozens of injured were taken to the hospital. At one of several demonstrations of 600 to 700 people at City Hall, 200 foot patrolmen and nine mounted police, in the words of one journalist, "herded" the group of mostly black women away as they attempted to enter the building. One recipient caught up in the melee screamed as she ran from mounted officers that the police "wouldn't do this to white people!" Other participants were arrested for blocking traffic and crossing police barricades.[83] Welfare rights activists also demonstrated at local welfare centers in Brooklyn, Queens, Manhattan, and the Bronx, tying up nearly two-thirds of the city's thirty-eight welfare centers during the two weeks of protest. Anywhere from 50 to 500 demonstrators usually took over a building and sat in until arrested or threatened with arrest.[84] Although a number of welfare centers were effectively shut down, the protests yielded little. The city refused to budge. The flat grant system remained in effect.

Recipients in New York decided that if the city would not give them special grants, they would simply take money from another source—their rent. The "rent revolt" was outlined a few months earlier by Francis Fox Piven and Richard Cloward, who argued that, to improve housing conditions, activists should manufacture a crisis to pressure politicians to make changes. The best way to do that was to withhold rent:

> Widespread action of this kind would throw the slum housing economy into chaos, for many landlords would have to abandon their property, leaving thousands of tenants in buildings without services or even minimal maintenance. As health hazards multiplied and the breakdown of landlord-tenant relations threatened to spread, the clamor would mount for governmental action to solve the crisis.[85]

Welfare clients participating in the rent revolt in New York used their rent money for clothing, food, and household furnishings to protest the flat-grant system and dilapidated housing conditions. Recipients pledged to withhold rent until the mayor and welfare commissioner agreed to "stop paying rent for illegal rattraps and begin to prosecute landlords and rebuild the slums." In a working paper, Citywide projected that recipients would gain between $60 and $100 a month through the rent revolt. Invoking the urban unrest in Detroit, Newark, Washington, D.C., and numerous other cities, the organization wrote, "The present black militancy in the ghettos" made the time right for a rent revolt. Citywide enlisted lawyers to deal with possible evictions but also proposed to resist evictions by "sitting on furniture [and] blockading apartments." In addition, they planned to move families downtown to "Resurrection Cities," occupy luxury hotels, and take over the office of the welfare commissioner.[86]

Responding instantly and unequivocally to the possibility of a rent revolt, the welfare commissioner stated: "We're not going to stand for people not paying their rent." The Department decided to issue rent vouchers or deduct money from the basic monthly allowances, demonstrating once again the weakness of a constituency with little economic clout. By the beginning of the rent revolt, only 600 people had signed up, far fewer than anticipated. Citywide called off the plan, explaining that recipients feared arrest and eviction.[87]

The rent revolt and the special-grant campaign drew on the mass power of recipients to address the poverty of women on welfare. As clients of a government program, welfare recipients' range of protest possibilities was limited. Economic boycotts, a primary political tactic in the 1960s, were not a viable strategy for women on welfare, since refusing the services of the welfare department might jeopardize their survival. Instead, they inundated the department with requests, took over offices, threatened disruption, and proclaimed their basic needs to the public. Using collective power and framing their goals in moral terms, they expanded the welfare rights movement and won concessions for members. By engaging in militant protest to wield leverage over a program that demonstrated little accountability to its recipients, the movement sought to expand the role of the state in providing for its citizens. This created a crisis for many municipalities. The inability of local governments to cope with the incessant protests also built pressure for greater federal control of the system. For some sectors of the public, however, the images of welfare protesters reinforced beliefs that women on welfare were undeserving and ungrateful for assistance. Citywide, and other welfare rights organizations around the country, did not stop the trend toward flat grants, which was a direct response to the political crisis caused by the special grant campaign. But the campaign demonstrated the power of welfare recipients to initiate reform as well as the ultimate power of local welfare officials to stifle those changes.

One of the more successful tactics used by organizers, the special-grant campaign brought thousands of new members into the welfare rights movement. Recipients gathered information about welfare department rules, and requested those items to which they were entitled. Many people who previously had little contact with welfare rights, upon the promise of a new couch or clothes for their children, paid their dues. And organizers tapped into this desire for an improved standard of living to build the national and local groups. This approach to membership building also revealed fissures within the movement. Some welfare recipients questioned a tactic designed to increase the membership of the organization while refusing to help needy people who were not members. Many grassroots participants valued the campaign because it met some basic needs of mothers on welfare seeking to make a better life for their children. They wanted to raise emotionally and psychologically healthy children, who were not tainted with the stigma of poverty or charity, who dressed and lived in dignity, and who could participate fully in social activities.

Welfare recipients asserted that a basic standard of living was a right. They insisted that AFDC provide an adequate standard of living that included household items, clothing, and participation in social and cultural activities. In this way, they chipped away at a cornerstone of the welfare state: the idea that relief should be discouraged and welfare should not be an attractive alternative to work. They questioned the long-standing assumption that the poor caused their own poverty, which informed the War on Poverty and the social work profession in the postwar period. Many social workers, believing that the structure of society was infallible, counseled, advised, trained, and aided the poor to take better advantage of opportunities. Permanent income support was not a central premise of the welfare system, which wanted to help people attain independence. The economic prosperity of the time bolstered the notion that ample opportunity was available for all. The welfare rights movement—both staff and recipients—had a different view. They believed that welfare recipients were not culpable for their economic circumstances. In claiming more public assistance, recipients in Washington, D.C., explained their poverty as a result of larger structural forces: "We are forced into poverty because of circumstances beyond our immediate control. We are kept in poverty because of a pitiful inadequate allowance . . . We are living like dogs because you all will not give us enough to live decent lives."[88]

Recipients used the special-grant campaign to transform the meaning of welfare on their own terms. The welfare system did not function only in the interests of the powerful to control and regulate the less powerful. Nor did the poor have complete freedom to shape it. The struggles of the welfare rights movement demonstrate that the meaning of welfare was contested terrain. Sometimes welfare rights activists organized on terms set by welfare departments, but they sought to fashion these in their own interests. In other ways, the women on welfare defined their needs and the nature of their claims. In sum, welfare policy was an evolving process. As welfare activists organized and found strength in numbers, they questioned decisions by caseworkers about their monthly budget and standard of living. They rejected anything tainted of charity, made claims as mothers, and sought to make theirs and their children's lives more comfortable. While the campaign was initially successful, once departments eliminated special grants or refused to concede to recipients' demands, welfare rights organizations again faced the conundrum of how to address the problem of inadequate grants.

CHAPTER 4
In the Name of Equality

Once the avenues for protest in local welfare departments narrowed, organizers searched the political landscape for alternate routes to address welfare recipients' inadequate standard of living and political disempowerment. Between 1967 and 1969 various local welfare rights groups campaigned to boost recipients' purchasing power by forming buying cooperatives and credit unions, protesting high credit charges, or seeking credit at local stores. In 1969 the national office advocated two tactics that grew out of these local efforts: one attempted to obtain credit cards for welfare recipients from major department stores and the other was a live-on-a-welfare-budget campaign, which organized middle-class people to feed their families on the amount of money allotted in the average welfare budget. Both strategies sought to rectify the consumer problems of welfare recipients. In addition, the credit campaign redirected the locus of political activity from welfare departments to private institutions. Recipients protested the practices of corporations, which, they contended, contributed to their poverty—or at the very least did little to alleviate their hardship. Families on AFDC routinely faced unfair consumer practices such as inflated prices, high interest charges, and an inability to obtain credit. By addressing these problems, welfare rights activists attempted to gain some economic control over their lives and find ways to better provide for their children. They wanted their welfare benefits to be recognized as income and fought for the same credit and purchasing opportunities as other Americans. In these campaigns, welfare recipients spoke of their rights as consumers, mothers, and citizens.

The credit strategy and the live-on-a-welfare-budget campaign addressed the relative poverty of welfare recipients. Their meager food budget, lack of access to credit, and paucity of material goods contrasted with the wealth and affluence surrounding them. Welfare rights activists raised the issue of what was an adequate standard of living, suggesting that poor families could and should live more comfortably. They demanded a share in the economic abundance that had come to define American society. By doing so, they critiqued not just poverty, but inequality in the United States. Partly a battle for the public mind, these campaigns shifted the political debate about welfare in a direction that recognized the relative deprivation of women on welfare. Moreover, the campaigns attempted to refashion the public image of welfare recipients as one of consumers in the marketplace rather than dependents on the welfare state.

Consumerism in the 1960s

In the postwar years economic theories rooted in the belief of the strength and resilience of the American economy gained currency. Keynesian economists, whose ideas dominated the period, argued that the government could regulate the economy to control inflation or forestall a recession by expanding or contracting government spending and the supply of currency. Central to this economic model was the notion that private demand and consumption stimulated growth. Many liberal economists believed that government spending and consumer purchasing power improved the overall health of the economy. President Kennedy's 1963 income tax cut, designed to increase consumer spending and stimulate growth, demonstrates the reliance on Keynesian economics in this period. Thus, for many economists and politicians in the 1960s, consumption was the engine driving the economy.[1]

Moreover, some Keynesian economists suggested that by generating sustained economic growth, spending and consumption reduced unemployment and poverty. For them, the long-term answer to economic problems lay not in redistribution of wealth, but in government and consumer spending, which led to increased production. Increased production created more jobs. More jobs resulted in more disposable income for working Americans. And more disposable income meant greater consumption, which in turn led to more production. A robust and expanding economy, they argued, raised the standard of living for all classes of Americans. Although modified in the 1980s into a new version of "trickle-down" economics and advocated primarily by conservative economists and politicians who favored consumer spending but opposed government spending, in the 1960s this economic theory was a cornerstone of the liberal agenda.[2]

As one participant in the White House Conference on Civil Rights in 1965 explained,

> Current policy has approached the problem of unemployment in this country primarily through the route of stimulating aggregate demand. The attempt was made to create jobs by increasing purchasing power and investment incentives through fiscal and monetary policies while implementing manpower development programs to get at the structural problems of the labor force.[3]

Some Keynesian economists also supported expanding the welfare state. Cash assistance to the poor, they argued, put more income into the hands of American consumers. As historian Alan Brinkley summed up, "The renewed wartime faith in economic growth fused the idea of the welfare state to the larger vision of sustained economic growth by defining social security mechanisms as ways to distribute income and enhance purchasing power."[4] Advocates of this view saw no inherent tension between capitalism and the welfare state. Rather than draining the public treasury and inhibiting economic growth, welfare, they argued, benefited capitalism by increasing the purchasing power of the poor. These economists rationalized increased government spending and expansion of the welfare state by linking welfare grants directly to consumer spending.

As a result, more people in the 1960s connected poverty and consumption. Some policy makers took the analysis further, suggesting that the urban upheavals, such as in Watts, Newark, and Detroit, were rooted in consumer dissatisfaction. The Office of Economic Opportunity (OEO), created in 1964 to address poverty across the nation, saw its mission closely tied to securing the interests of poor consumers. An OEO official explained:

> There is increasing evidence to suggest that discontent and disorder in cities across the country are in no small part consumer revolts against a system that has for years permitted the unscrupulous to take advantage of those least able to pay—a system that has at the same time deprived the poor of any real choice in the quality of goods they can buy, the prices they pay or the method of financing or source of credit available to them. OEO is convinced that the consumer problems of the poor must be solved if they are ever to be victors in the war against poverty.[5]

In the postwar period, policy makers, politicians, economists, and the business sector recognized poor people as a class of consumers and identified their distinct problems. Prior to World War II, most poor and working-class families had, in the words of historian Susan Porter Benson, "modest and prudent" consumption goals.[6] Since the advent of mass production at the turn of the century, advertisers targeted middle-class families as potential consumers, while poor families were more often gripped with the struggle for basic survival by simply trying to make ends meet. After the war, however, rising working-class wages and greater availability of consumer goods put the therapeutic ethos of consumption—or at least that ideal—within reach of working-class families. Many people viewed this new form of working-class consumption as vital for the well-being of poor families and an asset to the American economy.

Consumption in the postwar period to a large degree, was dependent upon the availability of credit. Consumer debt increased sixfold from 1950 to 1970.[7] Both middle- and working-class people borrowed money to purchase big-ticket items, enabling them to live at a higher standard of living than their yearly income may have otherwise allowed. Welfare recipients and other poor people wanting to participate in the postwar consumer society needed access to credit. However, African Americans and the poor were subject to high prices and high-interest loans.[8] David Caplovitz in a pioneering study in 1963 documented the problems of poor consumers and found that poor people could often only get credit from small neighborhood merchants, who charged higher interest rates than large department stores, sold low-quality merchandise, and marked up the price of goods 100 to 300 percent.[9] In 1968 the Federal Trade Commission studied low-income merchants in Washington, D.C. and revealed that 93 percent of durable goods were purchased on installment with an average interest rate of 23 percent a year.[10] Poor consumers also turned to door-to-door credit salespeople, who sold items at greatly inflated prices. Caplovitz discovered that, despite the high interest rates and poor-quality merchandise, 75 percent of poor people, and a disproportionately higher number of black and Puerto Rican families, relied on credit as a means to purchase costly items or survive the month on a meager salary.[11] Thus, despite the increasing importance of consumption, poor people were disadvantaged in the marketplace and had inadequate access to information and fewer choices than other consumers.

To address these problems, in 1964, Congress created the Committee on Consumer Interest, which President Johnson instructed to promptly develop ways to inform poor families about getting the most for their money.[12] OEO suggested that resolving the problems of low-income consumers would bridge the gulf that left the poor "outside the mainstream of American Life."[13] Thus, addressing poor people's lack of disposable cash— and related problems of high prices and lack of access to credit—would narrow the gap between the rich and the poor, promote social stability, and, ultimately, strengthen capitalism.

Grassroots activists also saw consumption as a cure for social ills. From the slave South to the urban North, African American activists had historically channeled consumer clout to challenge their subordinate position and assert independence.[14] The "Buy Black" campaigns of the 1940s and the Detroit Housewives Leagues in the 1930s harnessed consumer power to foster community development and initiate political reform.[15] In the 1960s, civil rights activists boycotted buses to demand courteous treatment, the hiring of more African Americans, and an end to Jim Crow. A viable tactic because of the political unity among African Americans, consumer boycotts also indicated the growing economic clout of the African American community. During civil rights protests, for example, white southern businessmen fearful of losing black patronage and their profit margin pressured white politicians to moderate or eliminate Jim Crow legislation.

In addition, other political activists—including Latinos, women, and trade unionists—relied on consumer strategies. Since the emergence of consumer capitalism, women, as primary purchasing agents in the household, were considered a key consumer group.[16] In many cases, women's participation was the linchpin to the success of consumer tactics such as boycotts, cooperatives, and union label purchasing.[17] Women also organized against inflation and the high cost of living. For example, in the mid-1960s tens of thousands of housewives nationwide demonstrated and protested at supermarkets against false advertising, promotional gimmicks, and high food prices. They were part of a broader consumer movement through the 1960s and 1970s that included the elderly, students, unionists, poor people, policy makers, and government officials. The consumer movement gained a foothold in this period in part because of economic prosperity, new advertising techniques, and changing personal expectations and values.[18] Welfare rights activists drew on these examples and traditions, as mothers, African Americans, and poor people, to assert their rights as consumers. In doing so, they hoped to direct company executives to their bottom-line interest of money making. With little power to halt the wheels of production, women on welfare hoped to have more influence in the arena of consumption.

The Consumer Campaigns

By the late 1960s, recipients in the welfare rights movement began to make claims as consumers and assert that their spending promoted economic expansion. Paralleling discussions in other political and economic circles, they suggested that welfare aided economic growth and argued that everyone had a stake in providing assistance to the poor. In Franklin County, OH, in 1969 welfare recipients compared sales generated by the purchasing power of welfare recipients to the taxes local residents paid toward the welfare budget. They concluded that county residents paid only 9.5 percent of the welfare budget, yet local businesses reaped enormous financial benefits from the money welfare recipients spent.[19] In another case, George Wiley asked the Coca-Cola Company to provide complimentary beverages for the 1969 NWRO National Conference, explaining that this would serve as a form of advertising: "I know this will give an important visibility for your products to your constituency."[20]

Simultaneously, welfare rights activists worked to protect their rights as consumers and oppose unfair credit and pricing practices. Mobilization for Youth (MFY), a community action program in New York City, submitted a proposal to OEO in 1966 for a Community Program in Consumer Affairs to address the problems of low-income consumers.[21] In another case, in 1969 in Washington, D.C., the Citywide Welfare Rights Organization picketed the Walker Thomas Furniture Store, accusing it of "unjust credit methods, over pricing merchandise, high interest rates and re-possing [sic] furniture unfairly."[22]

A number of welfare rights groups around the country formed consumer cooperatives and credit unions to pool their limited resources and increase their buying power. In Cleveland, members of the welfare rights organization rented church space and set up a Buyer's Cooperative for welfare recipients, selling soap at cost and eventually expanding to other household items.[23] Similarly, the welfare committee of the Jobs or Income Now (JOIN) organization in Chicago started a food co-op to stretch the dollars of welfare recipients and the poor.[24] In New Haven, CT, the Hill Resident Welfare Moms organized a nonprofit food co-op as "an alternative to sky-high supermarket prices."[25] In 1968, the WRO in Des Moines, IA, and the local Unitarian Church, formed a credit union, a food bank, and two preschools, which were run by and served WRO members.[26]

Most of the cooperatives and credit unions begun by welfare recipients in the late 1960s could not sustain themselves in the long run. Often, recipients did not have the skills or time necessary to carry out such projects. In addition, financial losses—likely at some point—were devastating for a group of people already living on the margins of destitution. Hulbert James, an organizer in New York, summed up in a training session for VISTA volunteers:

> I do not know of a successful poor people's cooperative in this country. The only ground on which I might permit you to form a cooperative is if you are using it as a step for organizing welfare recipients . . . The same thing holds for credit unions. They don't

work for poor people. You are talking about people going to pool their money when all they have is a nickel.[27]

The condescending tone of James' remark aside, he correctly identified some of the difficulties poor people encountered in their economic ventures. But the potential success or failure of the cooperatives and credit unions is less important than the fact that so many welfare recipients turned to such efforts to alleviate their poverty and enhance their power.

Department Store Credit

To advance its members' interest as consumers, NWRO coordinated a national campaign to force major department stores to extend credit to welfare recipients. Dubbing it the credit campaign, welfare rights activists targeted several department store chains including Sears, Montgomery Ward, and Abraham and Straus. The campaign was initiated on the local level when the Philadelphia WRO, led by Roxanne Jones, picketed and demonstrated until they got $50 worth of credit for each recipient at several department stores in the summer of 1968.[28] NWRO officially adopted the credit campaign at the August 1968 conference in Chicago, but made little headway until 1969. The decline of special grants during this period made the credit campaign more appealing to activists as they sought alternative mobilization strategies.

Beginning in late 1968, local welfare rights groups around the country campaigned for credit from department stores. In New York City, 150 members of the Brooklyn Welfare Action Council and Citywide went to the E.J. Korvette's store in downtown Brooklyn at ten-thirty in the morning, picked out several garments, and, instead of paying for them, demanded charge accounts at the checkout counters. They did nothing illegal, but the clerks had to take the time to return the clothing to the racks and, consequently, long lines formed at the checkouts. Demonstrators then went to the shoe department to occupy all the seating space. Later in the afternoon, the unruly crowd picketed on the sidewalk for credit and winter clothing and "to force the downtown Brooklyn stores to join our fight against the city for an increase in our quarterly [flat] grants." In response, the general manager of Korvette's promised to expedite the processing of credit applications. The store eventually offered recipients $25 in credit, which they refused because the amount was too little. Similar credit protests continued at New York City department stores throughout the winter.[29] In Kansas City, KS, welfare recipients in the Wyandotte County WRO sent letters to J.C. Penney, Montgomery Ward, W.T. Grant, and Sears, asking them to consider welfare recipients for credit. Eighty people went to Montgomery Ward to apply for cards. Of the fifty applications processed, forty were approved for credit.[30] At Sears, only four out of thirty-three recipients applying received credit. The WRO picketed Sears for two days while leaders of the protest negotiated with the regional credit manager for the remaining recipients. A Friends of Welfare Rights chapter joined the pickets and some turned in their own Sears credit cards. In the end, Sears granted credit to one-third of the recipients.[31]

In March 1969, NWRO met with the national Sears management to discuss extending credit to welfare recipients on a group basis upon recommendation from a WRO. NWRO hoped to pressure Sears to give $150 of credit to recipients with a letter of reference from the local welfare rights organization and "NO OTHER QUESTIONS ASKED."[32] Sears refused to grant group credit to recipients, insisting that it would give credit only to qualified recipients. Sears quickly became a focus of NWRO activity. In a national campaign they called "Sock it to Sears," NWRO planned pickets, leafleting, and shop-ins at Sears stores around the country.[33] It called on welfare rights supporters to boycott Sears "until a satisfactory credit agreement is reached."[34] The national office prepared "how to" packets, sent them out to local chapters, and followed up with telephone calls urging local participation in the campaign.

Local groups protested and picketed at their neighborhood Sears stores with limited success. In Pennsylvania, a number of stores gave recipients $50 worth of credit.[35] In Michigan, Sears nominally agreed to NWRO terms, but retained the right to conduct individual investigations of families. Arguing that this was unacceptable, the WRO wrote, "If they investigate each family, what good is the letter of reference? What that means is that the WRO organization REALLY doesn't have the power—Sears could investigate each person and then turn them all down. And where would we be then?"[36] In Cambridge, 250 members of the Massachusetts WRO "shopped in" at Sears during the busy Easter sale, but did not reach a group agreement.[37]

In May 1969, 300 people, attendees of the National Conference on Social Welfare and members of NWRO, marched to a Sears store in New York City. People with Sears' credit cards ceremonially burned them in front of the store. The group then marched inside, some ordering televisions, radios, sewing machines, and washing machines, while others applied for credit. They accused Sears' executives of discriminating against welfare recipients and demanded the store grant $150 of credit to recipients with a letter of recommendation from a welfare rights organization. They threatened a boycott if recipients were not given credit. Despite several months of protests and four months of negotiations between Sears and NWRO, Sears' officials remained intransigent. Credit, they steadfastly maintained, was decided individually and "terms must apply equally to all customers."[38]

Although NWRO made little headway with Sears, other department stores, feeling the heat generated by the Sears campaign, extended group credit to welfare recipients. Hoping to avert protests, the Klein Company agreed to meet with NWRO and discuss credit for WRO members.[39] In mid-July, after a massive Sears protest by Citywide, Gimbel's, Abraham and Straus, and E.J. Korvette in New York, announced they would extend credit to welfare recipients and expressed agreement that excluding recipients was "discriminatory" because recipients' welfare benefits qualified as income.[40] In Massachusetts, after a series of protests at Sears, MWRO "establish[ed] $50 worth of credit for welfare recipients at Jordan Marsh, Filene's and Gilchrest."[41] In Philadelphia in the summer of 1969, recipients won a struggle for credit at major department stores giving them "the same opportunities to shop economically that are afforded more affluent citizens."[42]

The language of equality was central to the welfare rights movement's campaign for credit. George Wiley explained that Sears "discriminates against welfare recipients in its credit policies and therefore, denies them access to the buying power that Sears has and for the inexpensive merchandise available at their stores."[43] While the movement's analysis was premised on recipients' unequal treatment in the marketplace, its strategy was intimately tied to building the organization because it extended credit only to its members. Nevertheless, the movement's rhetoric about equal opportunity for welfare recipients meshed with the larger dialogue about consumerism and raised awareness about recipients' particular problems as consumers. Moreover, they characterized credit—and consumption—as a basic right and entitlement. By claiming credit as a right of American citizenship, activists in NWRO helped expand the meaning of citizenship and the discourse of rights.[44]

Consumer Power

In their dialogue with department stores, welfare rights activists characterized credit agreements as beneficial to the companies as well. In a letter to the president of W.T. Grant, a department store in Washington, D.C., NWRO wrote, "We believe that these proposals offer your company a unique opportunity to penetrate a $10-billion market presently not significantly touched by W.T. Grant."[45] In a press release after reaching an agreement with Montgomery Ward, Etta Horn, welfare rights leader in Washington, D.C., expressed confidence that it would lead to "increased buying power and economic ability for poor people as well as increased sales for Montgomery Ward."[46] In the 1960s, American businesses saw dollar signs in catering to untapped consumer groups. Companies marketed products specifically to African Americans, feminists, young people, and other constituencies.[47] African Americans became an increasingly lucrative market for white- and black-owned companies because of migration, urbanization, and economic and educational gains.[48] In the 1960s, the black power movement called for black pride and renewed interest in black culture. Shedding the accouterments of the dominant white culture, African Americans began to connect politically and commercially with what they perceived as an authentic African or African American culture. They celebrated black holidays, such as Kwanzaa, tucked away the business suits and donned the dashikis, wore their hair naturally, and voraciously consumed black literature and music. While some companies—often black owned—had always served the cultural and economic needs of the black community, by the late 1960s this was becoming mainstreamed. In this period, major U.S. corporations took advantage of surging interest in black culture and marketed products such as African clothing, black hair and skin products, soul food, and soul music.[49] As one business magazine reported, "The Negro today is the last big uncommitted force in the battle for the consumer dollar. His $27 billion income is new wealth."[50] Most companies acted out of self-interest; as John Johnson of *Ebony* wrote:

> I asked corporate leaders to act not for blacks, not for civil rights, but for their corporations and themselves. For it was true then and it's true now that if you increase the income of blacks and Hispanics and poor Whites, you increase the profits of corporate America. And if you decrease the income of the disadvantaged, you decrease income and potential income of American corporations . . . What it all boiled down to was that equal opportunity was good business.[51]

Similar developments took place among other constituents. In order to appeal to the New Left, for example, some businesses appropriated ideas of the countercultural movement by redefining themselves as "hip." These companies saw financial gain in the commodification of "hip"—marketing material goods as symbolic of nonconformity, youth, and rebellion.[52] In addition, although middle-class women had long been targeted as a consumer group, the women's movement made feminists a prospective consumer outlet. Rather than promising them gadgets for more efficient housekeeping, advertising to this group of women spoke to their desire for liberation from traditional gender norms. The notorious Virginia Slims "You've Come a Long Way, Baby" cigarette ad is perhaps the most well-known example of how ideas of progressive movements became integrated into the dominant discourse. Advertising agencies turned goals of women's liberation into slogans to sell the products of companies that helped exploit women politically and economically.[53] In all of these cases, companies came to see economically disadvantaged communities as budding consumer markets. So, department stores extending credit to welfare recipients may have done so because it corresponded nicely with the aim of corporate profitability.

While welfare recipients were a potential consumer market, the amount of power welfare recipients had as consumers was questionable. Financially strapped welfare recipients had less economic clout than middle-class people. They exerted less influence as a consumer group than African Americans or women. Although the welfare rights movement pressured some companies to extend credit, give them coupons, or advertise in their conference program, they could not wield the same leverage as other consumer constituencies. Their vulnerability to arbitrary reductions in their welfare grant and removal from the welfare rolls increased their financial insecurity and weakness as consumers. Apart from recipients' limited economic power, as businesses pondered the demands of NWRO, they had to wrestle with the prejudices of other customers who believed welfare recipients did not deserve credit. The advantages of extending credit to recipients were tempered by a rash of negative reactions. After a few New York City department stores gave welfare recipients credit, they received a slew of angry letters and phone calls from people fearing that reliable customers would be charged higher prices if recipients failed to make their payments. Others were upset because many low-income working people did not qualify for credit.[54] In their view, the credit campaign granted women on welfare special treatment and rewarded them for their dependence. Recipients demanding new clothing and household items they could not pay for fueled hostility. The public image of welfare recipients as undeserving and dependent upon tax dollars undermined activists' claim that they were consumers just like other Americans. Rather than transforming the dominant image of welfare recipients, the credit campaign might have reinforced the widespread belief that people on welfare were living beyond their means and were ungrateful, to boot. It was one thing to say every child in the house needed his or her own bed, as they did during the special-grant campaign. It was quite another to say that everyone had the "right" to shop at Sears.

NWRO and Consumer Tactics

As with many of their campaigns, grassroots women welfare rights activists had a multifaceted view of access to credit, which encompassed their work as mothers, their desire for equality, their identity as welfare recipients, their monthly budget constraints, and their status as poor people in a wealthy country. Women in the welfare rights movement explained access to reasonable and reliable credit as mothers needing to feed, clothe, and provide a comfortable and nurturing environment for their children, thus employing a strategy historically used by women of different racial and class backgrounds.[55] By highlighting their status as mothers and consumers, welfare rights activists could remake their identity and circumvent the denigrating stigma that defined their status as welfare recipients. In the 1960s, consumerism was a core American identity, one denied to welfare recipients because they were not considered legitimate consumers.[56] Activists sought to recast this image. In this sense, welfare rights activists followed in political traditions of African Americans and women in the United States who relied on consumption to transform their political status. American women have historically been socialized to equate self-worth with personal appearance and, thus, consumption became a way to assert or reject gendered conventions.[57] In addition, for African Americans, consumption was a way "to separate themselves from a 'degraded past.'"[58] For all these groups, the culture of consumption promised to remake identity and minimize social divisions. For welfare recipients as well, consumption could narrow the class divisions between the wealthy and the poor. Equal access to material goods could blur the outward signs characterizing poverty in the United States. Welfare rights activists believed consumerism was an antidote to class oppression.

But, most importantly, credit provided women on welfare with a level of independence. The struggles over welfare budgets and consumer credit were partly about power. Who had the power to decide welfare recipients' consumption patterns or where they would shop? In setting up buying cooperatives, demanding credit, and coming to terms with their power as consumers, welfare recipients attempted to assert some economic control over their lives. They wanted the prerogative to choose where to shop and to have the convenience of credit to purchase items they otherwise could not afford. Even though buying on credit was more expensive than paying cash, it offered them flexibility to purchase pricey items.[59] Credit gave recipients a measure of freedom from the constraints of a meager monthly AFDC budget and unshackled them from the control of the caseworker.

Although activists justified the credit campaign in many ways, the NWRO staff and some recipient leaders were most interested in how it might strengthen the organization by increasing participation and membership in WROs. By persuading companies to give credit only to those recipients with a letter of recommendation from the welfare rights organization, they invested the heads of local WROs with the power to decide who did and did not qualify for credit. The national office instructed local leaders to base decisions, not on the financial security or responsibility of a member, but on her level of participation in the organization. After negotiating a national agreement with Montgomery Ward in 1969, NWRO explained to its local chapters, "Providing credit benefits to active WRO members can be an important tool in building your WRO. Getting benefits must be related to membership. If only WRO members can get credit other recipients will want to (and have to) join your WRO to get these benefits."[60] The credit protests, said Jennette Washington, an organizer of the campaign, "wasn't about getting clothing to dress up and suddenly sit on our tails and watch these stupid soap operas and become dull individuals. It was a means of motivating some of the people [to join the movement]." A New York City group encouraged clients to go to "ALL" welfare rights meeting to learn how they could buy clothes and toys for their children for Christmas on credit.[61] In Ohio, recipients, who wanted to "accumulate membership," asked people applying for credit to "be an active member for 3 months prior to applying for credit [and] have participate[d] in some action campaign around welfare."[62]

Building the organization was part of a larger strategy for NWRO organizers. Hulbert James explained how the credit campaign contributed to this: "How does Sears relate to the rhetoric of revolution? It relates because this organization has taken a conscious approach, which is that we are going to build power through organization . . . The Sears Campaign fits into that because our contention about that is that it is going to help build numbers."[63] George Wiley staunchly advocated the credit campaign, even when local organizers were reluctant.[64] His strategy was to create a power bloc of welfare recipients who could lobby on their behalf and defend their public and private interests. James elaborated that the demand for credit would "force organizations like P&G and Sears to recognize NWRO or the MWRO on a group basis . . . If we ever get a group contract from anyone . . . then we are going to be able to deal in a much more effective way with the whole private sector."[65] For Wiley and James, building the organization would enhance the political power of welfare recipients.

The allegiances of NWRO staff and national recipient leadership committed to building a membership base through the credit campaign were often confused. The agreements with the companies sometimes assumed an unparalleled level of importance, surpassing the relationship between the local and national WRO. The NWRO office warned local chapters that "if its delinquency rate is so high as to jeopardize the national agreement, [the] whole group's credit privileges could be terminated by the NWRO Ways and Means Committee."[66] Organizers wanting amicable relations with the retail companies sometimes prioritized building the organization over the goal of reforming the welfare system. In fact, requiring recipients to obtain a letter from a welfare rights organization meant that recipients not involved in the welfare rights movement did not have access to credit. Therefore, NWRO was not fighting for welfare recipients to have the same access to credit as other consumers, but for the privilege of credit for its members.

National leaders and staff believed that alliances with stores were an essential part of the consumer strategy and would benefit the movement in numerous ways—materially, in terms of stature, and to build its political power. They appealed to corporations by couching their goals in a language of moral values, common creed, and political priorities. NWRO promoted a partnership with big companies such as Proctor and Gamble, suggesting that coupons for recipients would help ameliorate poverty, benefit the company, and nurture values of individual initiative and democratic participation. In a letter signed by Tillmon and Wiley, but likely written by Wiley, he struck a note of conciliation, not confrontation:

> Since poor people do not have enough *money*, we ask that your company distribute a share of your great wealth to those poorest of the poor. This could be in the form of coupons distributed through NWRO, which are redeemable for your products. The value of the coupons distributed would be commensurate to your commitment to the eradication of poverty. Furthermore, distributing your contribution in this way would especially reward those people who had the initiative to develop their own independent organization in the democratic spirit of our country. This program would directly benefit your company by giving your company and your products high visibility in a market frequently missed by conventional advertising techniques. We plan to publish an honor role of participating companies and their products, so that our members, as well as friends of poor people everywhere may direct their dollars toward the products of [those] companies.[67]

Staff members in the national office also encouraged local groups to raise money by selling ads to big corporations for the program for the national convention. In a memo to local WROs, Wiley suggested targeting "big stores downtown where you have gotten credit" and reminded recipients "to ask your local Sears store for a full page ad."[68] They hoped companies with which they developed relationships would advertise in their national newsletter, thus defraying the costs of publication. One national staff member suggested, "There is a possibility that Montgomery Wards will advertise and this seems advisable in light of the prospective credit union with that company. It would also be advisable to solicit national concerns for adver-tisements (i.e. Coca-Cola, TWA, etc.)."[69]

Welfare rights activists, both staff and recipients, were so intently fo-cused on how pressuring or allying with corporate America could reap re-wards for NWRO and its members, they did not question the principle of interest charges, the way the system of credit exploited those unable to pay cash, or the pattern of consumption and materialism that had come to de-fine an American standard of living. Granted, this campaign emerged be-cause of the limited economic choices for poor women on welfare and it attempted to rectify a long history of discriminatory credit practices. But, ultimately, NWRO tried to devise ways for welfare recipients to have access to credit to integrate them more fully into the consumer culture.

The consumer strategies were rooted—as with the special-grant cam-paign—in the basic problem of an inadequate budget. But instead of look-ing to the public sector, they examined their place in the private sector as well and demanded equal treatment. These claims to equality were impor-tant because as consumers welfare recipients were stigmatized and faced discrimination in the private sector. In making claims for equality, welfare recipients wanted to be recognized as consumers with economic clout. In doing so, they challenged the one-dimensional public image of recipients as "dependents." They wanted their welfare benefits to be recognized not as charity from the state, but as legitimate income, upon which they could qualify for credit. And, through this process, they asserted their rights in the private sector as mothers, consumers, citizens, and welfare recipients.

Live on a Welfare Budget

Welfare rights activists also organized campaigns to demonstrate the detri-mental effects of poverty and highlight the difficulty of living on a small monthly AFDC allowance. The live-on-a-welfare budget campaign was de-signed to raise the monthly grant and direct public attention to the inade-quacy of the food budget. After the crackdown on special-grant protests in late 1968 and early 1969, welfare recipients hoped to shore up public sup-port and sympathy by pointing to the injustice of poverty amid affluence.

Welfare rights organizations launched live-on-a-welfare-budget cam-paigns, which recruited middle-class people, both well known and un-known, to live for one week on the welfare household allowance. Based on family size and ages of the children, the WRO calculated for each partici-pating family a budget, including all food, personal items, and household goods. In most cases this amounted to thirty to fifty cents per person per day. The Massachusetts WRO explained the purpose of the campaign: "to consciencize [sic] the participants—to sensitize them to some of the realities of the public welfare system."[70] According to Wiley, participants would "find out what the gnawing hunger of poverty mean[s] to welfare recipients who live on those inadequate budgets fifty-two weeks of the year."[71] First conducted in Boston in April 1969, the campaign was planned in conjunction with the Massachusetts Council of Churches, the Christian Family Movement, and several local Fair Housing and Human Rights Associations. In June 1969 the campaign went national cresting in a "week of welfare protests" organized by NWRO to coincide with the third anniversary of the first national welfare rights demonstration.

The project profoundly impacted participating families, who undoubtedly sympathized with the plight of welfare recipients before the campaign began. The campaign in Boston was the most well documented, with written evaluations from participants. The range of responses to the Massachusetts project provides insight into the effects on individual families, many of whom experienced deprivation for the first time: "We have never been so hungry in our lives . . . We left every meal hungry."[72] One family, unable to cope with the lack of choice and type of diet, explained, "We found the menu very monotonous. By the end of the week we craved sweets or something 'different' to eat. My children became sick of the same meats and vegetables and therefore didn't finish their meals. They then asked for food between meals, and I had only Saltines."[73] The campaign also compromised the emotional and physical well-being of participants: "The children complained and snitched food from the cupboards. I tried to make up for their over-eating by starving with the result that I felt guilty for denying them the food they wanted and at the same time resentful of their greediness."[74] A mother described her irritability and frustration with the constraints of a limited budget: "I was really cross one day when the baby spit up on a clean shirt—meaning I was going to have to do laundry sooner, which I couldn't afford. Normally this wouldn't have bothered me. It was really a problem to do laundry and eat too."[75]

The campaign generated extensive publicity in newspapers and national magazines such as *Newsweek*. Local papers sometimes adopted families that they closely followed. A suburban reporter from the *Boston Evening Globe* participated and wrote extensively about his family's experiences. NWRO and local groups also enticed several prominent politicians and policy makers to join the campaign. Between thirty and forty employees of the Department of Health, Education, and Welfare (HEW) participated, including Roy Morgan, president of the HEW employees' local union in Washington. His family reported, "He has lost two pounds, feels very tired and weak and says he is getting more and more irritable. He is having trouble working, even though he has a desk job that doesn't require much physical work."[76] In Syracuse, NY, a member of the State Board of Regents commented about his experiences: "While we were grumbling about the amount of starch we were eating, we were wondering what happens to the pre-natal mother who is not getting enough protein."[77]

Through the live-on-a-welfare-budget campaign organizers hoped to spark discussion about the meager monthly allowance for food and refute misconceptions and misunderstandings about both poverty and welfare. Participating families began to think and feel differently about welfare recipients. A family in Massachusetts wrote: "We definitely have different attitudes toward welfare now. First of all, we had only a superficial knowledge and very ambivalent feeling from the news media. But now we feel the beginnings of some intellectual and emotional understanding."[78] Hostile reactions from family and neighbors helped some participants understand the extent of antipathy toward welfare recipients: "I'm exhausted from battle fatigue, 5% of the people who called were sympathetic. The rest was ridicule, disgust, great hostility, and even strong, abusive language. We found out what we knew already—that for those on welfare it's rough—not only financially, but mostly because of the attitude of the rest of society."[79]

The live-on-a-welfare-budget campaign was directed primarily at middle-class people accustomed to a more comfortable standard of living. According to Andrea Jule Sachs, it helped build cross-class female solidarity around the "hallmarks of female domesticity," such as shopping, cooking, and meal planning. Sachs suggests, however, that it was a program in which middle-class women testifying about the inadequacy of the welfare budget authenticated the experience of poor women.[80] Nevertheless, the small number of people participating developed more sympathy and support for the goals of the welfare rights movement. The campaign drew attention to the enormous gulf between the lives of most welfare recipients and most middle-class people. Because the campaign identified the different standards of living of the poor and the middle-class, it was not just an attack on poverty, but a critique of inequality.

The Problem of Inequality

Through the special-grant, credit, and inadequate diet campaigns, welfare rights organizations addressed the fundamental problem of inequality: that they had so little while others had too much. Recipients' desires for new furniture, more household appliances, and credit at major department stores were a product of the ostentatious wealth and affluence surrounding them. They wanted to participate fully in the postwar consumer culture and be brought up to par with the American standard of living. They also believed that the nation was capable of providing a higher standard of living for them. As welfare recipients in Cleveland explained in 1966, "Nobody argues whether there is enough money in this nation to clothe and feed everyone decently. Everyone agrees that there is enough. If this is true, then WHO decides that some people get their share and other people don't? WHO makes the decisions that some people can have enough and others just can't?"[81]

Certainly many welfare recipients in the 1960s would have been defined as poor by objective as well as relative standards. In 1960, 28 percent of AFDC households had no flush toilets or hot water and 17 percent had no running water at all.[82] Most women on AFDC struggled to put food on the table and buy clothes for their children. Welfare recipient Esther Washington explained, "Sometimes a child only gets one meal a day. He usually has to go without breakfast because there's nothing available, he has to go without lunch because there's no money to pay for lunch at school, and the only meal he gets is dinner and that is often inadequate."[83] Recipients lucky enough to have a roof over their heads often lived in dilapidated and neglected spaces that fell far short of national standards of health and decency. In 1968, a hearing officer for the D.C. Department of Public Welfare confirmed "the inadequacy of the existing shelter and food allowances."[84]

Yet the definition of poverty in the 1960s was a relative and arbitrary concept, as it has always been. Since the late nineteenth century, officials defined poverty in relation to the general standard of living. In calculating a minimum standard of living, social scientists assumed that the poor needed less than middle- or working-class Americans. The standard of living for average Americans fluctuated as well. Thus, the criteria bringing a family above the poverty line changed over time, and might have included indoor plumbing, electricity, a refrigerator, a telephone, or two pairs of shoes for every child. This variability in the meaning of poverty and its relation to general living standards suggests that what constituted a minimum standard of living was open to interpretation.[85] Rather than an objective measurement, the term "poverty" described how the living conditions of people at the bottom of the economic ladder differed from those in the middle and on the top. Inherent in this analysis was the logic that efforts to eliminate poverty will make little headway, unless the problem of inequality is addressed. In addition to raising the standard of living of the poor, the gap between the rich and the poor had to be narrowed.

Welfare recipients, vocalizing the problems of lack of credit, an inadequate diet, and insufficient home furnishings, challenged the accepted definition of poverty and urged policy makers, social workers, and the public to raise the minimum standard of living. Based on their understanding of what constituted a modern-day level of health and decency, they argued that they needed specific items or services. They analyzed how a poor diet led to poor health, how improper clothing impeded their children's education, how the lack of a telephone could endanger their lives and safety. They argued that what the poor deserved depended on how society defined an adequate living. As Mothers for Adequate Welfare in Boston explained,

> The MAWs' view is that recipients need to live in a way which approaches the average for the society around them . . . A "revolution of rising expectations" has hit the underdeveloped parts of America . . . Frustrating the expectations of a good life—fairly or not—gives rise to bitterness and distrust. The resultant of these considerations is that the mere fact of being forced to live on an income which is sub-par—of having to bear the stigma of "'welfare" —may help cause demoralization in adults and life-defeating despair in children.[86]

Welfare recipients' inadequate monthly benefit became a central organizing issue for the welfare rights movement. Most recipients faced day-to-day hardship putting food on the table, clothing their children, paying the bills, and maintaining their household. The paltry monthly sum impinged not only on their ability to raise their children, but on their sense of dignity. They strove valiantly to improve the quality of life and expand opportunities for their children. In addition, because many poor people had little choice but to rely on credit, often with excessive interest charges, welfare rights organizers explored the best available options for welfare recipients. Giving recipients access to less exploitative forms of credit was an important stopgap measure. Through the special-grant, credit card, and food budget campaigns recipients won some concessions, materially improved their lives, and raised the minimum standard of living. Whether an additional fifteen cents a day for food or an extra blanket on a cold night, these concrete improvements meant a lot to people with very little.

More important, activists argued that because of its immense wealth, the country could afford to raise the living standard of the poor. Mildred Calvert, of the Milwaukee County WRO, explained the problem as one of distribution of resources:

> Poor people have a right to welfare . . . We have a right to live decently as dignified human beings today. When I see money being wasted—sending men to the moon to play golf, dumping nerve gas in the ocean, burning potatoes, killing off hogs . . . and then I see hungry and raggedy children running around, this is the kind of country that we live in, and this is what just burns me up. I feel

the only way changes will be made, especially in the welfare system, is through poor people, welfare people, organizing and raising a lot of hell.[87]

Welfare activists had good reason to believe that the nation could provide more for the needy. Economic growth, although somewhat slow in the 1950s, in 1966 was an astounding 7 percent and unemployment a low 3.8 percent.[88] Average personal income of families increased from $5,150 to $6,193 between 1946 and 1960, in constant 1954 dollars. In addition, the percentage of families officially living in poverty declined from 33 percent in 1940 to 27 percent in 1950 to 21 percent in 1960.[89] Despite these frequently cited indicators of economic progress, many families on AFDC still found themselves in dire circumstances.

Ultimately, welfare recipients wanted to share in the wealth that defined American society in the postwar period and decrease the inequality between rich and poor. Clarence Singleton, an NWRO member from Beaufort County, SC, testified before Congress in 1969: "We have been eating the crumbs from the rich man's table for too long, eating what the rich man don't want."[90] Explaining that hunger and want takes many different forms, welfare recipients in the Side Family Council in Columbus, OH, wrote in 1963, "People say to us, but you make out, don't you; nobody's starving in Columbus. Perhaps not—but there is hunger, all kinds of hunger, hunger for food, hunger for a girl's dress that fits or a boy's pants without holes in the patches, hunger for school shoes."[91]

Recipients' sense of entitlement and their expectations were shaped partly by the affluence surrounding them. Although they critiqued inequality, welfare recipients and their liberal allies firmly believed the poor could be provided for without taking away from the rich. They did not advocate redistribution of the nation's wealth as much as a reshuffling of government priorities to raise the standard of living of the poor. A radio commentator explained,

> The bounty and productive capability of America are so grand that we need not strip the rich to cover the poor; so lush is our promise, so vast our productive capacity that we can maintain individual wealth and still abolish poverty.[92]

Welfare rights activists believed the country could not only endure a redefinition of priorities, but would flourish because of the contributions of the well-educated and well-trained children of poor mothers and the purchasing power of recipients, which stimulated economic growth. The demand for a basic minimum income won some of the movement's earliest victories, catapulted the movement into the national spotlight, and laid the basis for a guaranteed annual income, which became the focus of welfare rights activity after 1969.

Both the campaign for dignity and representation and the campaign for minimum standards or "more money now" found sympathy within the liberal community. The black freedom movement and the antipoverty struggle created a climate in which certain ideas in the 1960s were enshrined in the political discourse and became essential to any conversation about eradicating poverty or achieving justice or equality. These ideas included: (1) protection of the basic civil rights of all Americans, whether on welfare or not; (2) participation as a central component of American democracy; and (3) a basic living standard, including such things as adequate shelter, medical care, education, and home furnishings, for all Americans. The welfare campaigns for dignity and for more money spoke to and emanated from these liberal sensibilities. Few liberal Americans in the 1960s disagreed with propositions that welfare recipients' basic right to privacy should be protected or that their children ought to have shoes that fit. Even the majority of Americans who may not have considered themselves liberal supported the idea that the federal government ought to guarantee the civil rights of its citizens. And, depending on how the question was worded, most also opposed poverty and believed that poor people ought to have certain guarantees of income security. NWRO's antipoverty strategies directed at the private sector and consumer practices were consistent with much of the conservative rhetoric of this period as well. This level of consensus among radicals, liberals, and some conservatives, was masked by bitter and divisive conflicts about how to define participation and income security. Thus, intense disagreement about a range of issues assumed center stage in the political debate. These disagreements emerged between the welfare rights movement and its allies and within the movement itself, wracking it with acrimonious conflict just as the movement reached its pinnacle.

Washington speaking at a rally. National Welfare Rights
Organization Records, Moorland-Spingarn Research
Center, Howard University.

Beulah Sanders speaking at a forum. National Welfare Rights Organization Records, Moorland-Spingarn Research Center, Howard University.

Johnnie Tillmon addressing a Mother's Day march in Washington. George Wiley sits directly behind her, on the left. Ethel Kennedy looks on from behind him, 1968. Image #8771, courtesy of Wisconsin Historical Society.

George Wiley speaking at a rally, 1972. Image #10937, courtesy of Wisconsin Historical Society.

Hulbert James, Beulah Sanders and George Wiley at a panel discussion. National Welfare Rights Organization Records, Moorland-Spingarn Research Center, Howard University.

Duncan, Ralph Abernathy, and George Wiley lead a march down the Las Vegas Strip. March 1972. From the papers of Frances Fox Piven. Sophia Smith Collection, Smith College.

The NWRO poster depicted Nixon's Family Assistance Plan as providing an inadequate standard of living, Image #12243, courtesy of Wisconsin Historical Society.

An NWRO pamphlet depicts the staff's primary concern that the WIN program would train women on welfare for low-paying, dead-end jobs, May 1969. From the Frances Fox Piven Papers. Sophia Smith Collection, Smith College.

The cover of a welfare rights handbook published by the Massachusetts Welfare Rights Organization in 1970. Sophia Smith Collection, Smith College.

CHAPTER 5

Internal Tensions

In the summer of 1969, the welfare rights movement reached its peak. It had initiated several successful campaigns to establish welfare recipients' civil rights, protect them as consumers, and insist that caseworkers treat them with dignity. Organizers won thousands of dollars in special grants for recipients and assisted countless women on AFDC in their day-to-day struggles with the welfare department. Welfare rights activists gained respect and standing within the world of social work, persuading social workers to recognize them as an essential part of the policy-making process and invite them to meetings and conferences. Amassing a respectable following, the national organization had a membership of 30,000, but, according to some estimates, participation in the movement reached 100,000.[1] The largest local chapters, Boston and New York City, counted 1,600[2] and 4,000 members, respectively.[3] Attendance at the annual convention in Detroit in 1969, the largest ever, drew between 3,000 and 5,000 people, exceeding by ten times the 350 people at the 1967 convention in Washington.[4] The number of affiliated locals increased as well, from 130 groups in December 1966 to 800 in 1971.[5]

While the Detroit Convention was a benchmark of successful organizing, it also revealed growing divisions within the movement, between staff and recipients, black and white participants, and men and women. Ostensibly about decision making and control of resources, in reality the divisions ran deeper, reflecting competing philosophies and organizing strategies. Many staff members advocated mobilization strategies to build the membership of the organization and gain political and electoral leverage for welfare recipients, measuring success by recipients' power to extract concessions from welfare officials. For welfare recipients, the stigma, political isolation, and mistreatment characterized the problem of welfare as much as political allocation of resources. An ideology of black mothers as undeserving of assistance, lazy, and promiscuous was embedded in the postwar AFDC program and justified cutbacks and other punitive welfare policies. Consequently, they worked not just to build the organization, but to transform public perceptions of welfare recipients by making claims as mothers. In addition, most welfare recipients valued the process of organizing as much as the result. They were interested not just in the victories, but in the decision making behind the victories. They had come to believe, as had many other political activists in the 1960s, that day-to-day interactions between people reinforced and recreated racism, sexism, and class oppression; patterns manifested in their own organization.[6] They believed that political organizing that led to incremental improvements in the welfare system would also empower welfare recipients, enabling them to overcome the stigma associated with AFDC. Although middle-class support aided the movement immensely by providing office space, money, or access to welfare manuals, many welfare recipients, ultimately, wanted to stand up for themselves.

These ideological camps were not rigid, however. Some recipients were more in tune with the politics of white staff members. And some staff members allied closely with recipients. Staff members in the national office often clashed, as did recipients on the national and local level. The conflicts were not consistent or predictable, but always in flux, with battle lines redrawn frequently and personal animosity sometimes overshadowing political differences. Nevertheless, some basic divisions emerged that seemed to have a long-standing impact on both the structure and politics of the movement.

Because most men and women in the organization had divergent goals and defined the problem of welfare differently, they disagreed about how to address the rise in single parenthood and respond to newly instituted work requirements. Race, class, and gender influenced staff members' and recipients' understanding of these issues and strategies they outlined. The three orientations converged to shape their political visions. The conflict within the organization indicated both a stronger racial consciousness among people of color and an emerging feminism among women in the organization, which would come to fruition a few years later.

Staff Versus Recipients

The predominantly white, middle-class male staff and the overwhelmingly poor black female constituency wrestled since the movement's inception about control of the organization and the strategies and goals of the movement. In 1966, when a white organizer in California called a statewide meeting of welfare activists, Johnnie Tillmon tore up the Constitution the organizer had written and pointedly instructed him, "You don't just come into somebody's neighborhood and run it."[7] Staff domination within the national organization and in local groups was an ongoing problem in the welfare rights movement. George Wiley hired and supervised the NWRO staff in Washington and field organizers working with state and local groups. In theory, the National Coordinating Committee (NCC) and the executive committee, both comprised of welfare recipients elected by the general membership at the annual conferences, were responsible for policy making. In practice, however, staff members wielded disproportionate power because they applied for grants, managed the budget, wrote the newsletter, maintained contact with local groups, and spoke for the organization. Middle-class organizers in Washington, not welfare recipients, mapped out many of the earliest national campaigns. George Wiley, Tim Sampson, Hulbert James, and other key staff members regularly attended executive committee meetings. While meeting minutes suggest that executive committee members participated actively in discussions, it also seems that staff members influenced the outcome of many decisions and often set the agenda.[8] More striking is the lack of substantive policy discussion within NCC meetings, which often focused on updates, workshops, details of membership, and upcoming meetings. Even when the NCC decided policy, staff members responsible for implementation rarely followed through. In 1970, for example, the NCC proposed a "Southern strategy" to counter welfare cuts in Louisiana and Arkansas, but nothing tangible came of this suggestion.[9]

Moreover, staff members, many of whom were white, college-educated, and had organizing experience, carried themselves with an immense amount of self-confidence. They devoted long hours to welfare rights activity, often sacrificing personal needs. They learned the intricacies of welfare policy, fund-raising, and organizing, becoming more confident about their abilities over time. Responding to criticism that she was dominating, a middle-class organizer in Detroit explained that she and other organizers were in the office every day: "It would probably be better if we made the decisions since we do all the work, instead of having to go through all kinds of people."[10] Staff members, frequently schooled in political theory and social change, formulated their own political strategy about how to transform the welfare system. Welfare recipients, on the other hand, had less formal training. They often had a history of political participation, but they also had the added responsibility of maintaining their home and caring for their children. Their theoretical understanding was rooted in their day-to-day experiences as poor black women. Their confidence was nurtured because of their intimate knowledge of how welfare functioned. As they became more self-assured over time, as the organization encountered more hurdles, and as staff control became more glaring, clashes with staff members became frequent and sometimes bitter.

A common source of tension for recipients was staff domination at meetings. In some cases, staff members designated leaders and set the agenda of the welfare rights organization. At a National Coordinating Committee meeting in Washington, D.C., in 1967, amid chaos and confusion, organizers, in the words of one staff member, "hand-picked" a recipient leader to "pull things together."[11] In another case, a black man at a Michigan Welfare Rights Organization meeting observed that staff members attempted to "impose their middle-class values" on the organization. Welfare recipient leaders, he said,

> were not in complete control of the meeting, as was indicated by the frequent interruption and take-over by non-public Assistance people. These persons, who were both Black and White, hold influencial [sic] positions with the Welfare Rights Organization, and made their presence felt by introducing several proposals which were passed by the mothers.[12]

He concluded that recipients seemed hesitant, looking to organizers for direction and leadership.

In another case, some Virginia WRO staff members controlled meetings and rigged an election in 1969. Wanting to elect Phil Perkins for executive director, and Andrew Bowler and Rafe Pomerance for other leadership positions, staff members did not notify local groups about the election or give them time to nominate candidates, completing the election with uncharacteristic speed. Recipients and other staff members objected vociferously, some even resigning. Dora Bonfanti, a recipient leader, labeled VWRO "a crooked organization."[13] Staff member Sally Ylitalo suggested in a six-page letter to Wiley that Virginia staff "do a great deal of manipulating and lying." According to Ylitalo, other organizers told her "'yes, this was a farce, yes, this was predetermined' but that 'these people *think* this is democracy, that this is the closest thing they have *seen* to democracy.'" Both Bonfanti and Ylitalo charged Perkins with bringing "weak" people from around the state to the meeting and telling them what to say. Perkins had apparently been nominated before the election and had suggested that if he was not elected "he would take away his money." When Ylitalo asked why recipients could not be nominated, she was told that they "did not have cars, that they had children, and that a community leader should not be an 'organizer' because it makes for personality conflicts and competition." Yet, she pointed out, "community leaders do as much as the organizers but get no money for it." Ylitalo denounced the paternalism practiced in the VWRO:

Does NWRO merely replace *one* system with *another*? Here in Virginia the organizers talk about the people as something less than them. The organizers are mainly middle class and live in the suburbs far away from the people. Some of the organizers write statements for the people to be made at city council and letters to be sent to the welfare department when the *people* are capable of doing this.

Pleading for a truly democratic organization, she suggested that only when middle-class domination has ended will recipients gain their rights, dignity, and equality.[14] Bonfanti and other recipient leaders with the backing of staff member Ylitalo ultimately appealed to Tillmon about their right to hire recipients as organizers.[15]

In Boston, white organizers rigidly controlled meetings and demonstrations and sometimes told recipient leaders what to say in meetings.[16] Bill Pastreich, organizer of the Massachusetts WRO, exemplified some organizers' sense of self-importance as well as their view of women in leadership. In a letter to the national office, Pastreich trivialized the needs and problems of the women by suggesting that the national office should guarantee organizers a car and insurance, whereas national officers (who were welfare recipients) "should be people who can take care of their own babysitting problems and they should look to neither their local WRO or [the] National [office] for babysitting money." Speaking to a student group, Pastreich said, "I would discourage their picking a lady [as an organizer], because she doesn't have the time to put in the hours on that kind of stuff. I also think that women in general are bad leaders. They have to take a week off to have emotions."[17]

In a few cases staff members deliberately disregarded the wishes of welfare recipient leaders. Debby Spider, a white staff person working in Rhode Island, Ohio, and Virginia, helped prepare NWRO's Guaranteed Adequate Income proposal. In a private letter to George Wiley, Spider explained how she would circumvent the executive committee, made up of mostly black women, if they disagreed with her plan of garnering support for the guaranteed income among NWRO friends. She wrote that because of "how important the NWRO Friends list was . . . The plan only called for stealing the list if we had trouble with the NWRO executive committee or the national office." She continued: "The list will never be used for any purpose without your *secret* approval. But only *you* will have any sayso [sic] in the matter and nobody need know that you participated."[18]

These staff members assumed black welfare recipients were politically incompetent and unable to make rational decisions or run their own organization. At a training session for VISTA volunteers, Hulbert James -

implied that he was far more sophisticated politically than the women recipients: "One of the greatest difficulties I have as an organizer is that often I recognize the gap between where I am politically . . . and where the ladies are. I think that your success as an organizer is to be able to live with that gap, and to some extent to help to close that gap."[19] These attitudes contributed to the marginalization of poor women on welfare, reinforcing the dominant idea that black women needed the guidance and supervision of the white middle class.

To counteract the problem of staff domination, women in the welfare rights movement repeatedly demanded that NWRO hire black AFDC recipients as organizers. The executive committee and staff members discussed in early 1969 the need to hire welfare recipients. The hiring didn't take place quickly enough, however, and Wiley, among others, were concerned about "jealousy" if some recipients got positions when others did not.[20] One of the most explosive situations occurred in Michigan where NWRO hired an organizer without the approval of recipients. One local leader explained, "We had already voted to have a welfare mother as the first choice for the job and the national office hired this student without clearing it with us . . . For a while, the national office wouldn't even accept phone calls from Detroit because of all the complaints."[21] In Massachusetts, ongoing conflict plagued relations between white organizers in the Massachusetts WRO and Mothers for Adequate Welfare (MAW), which was independent of NWRO. MAW members resented Bill Pastreich, hired by NWRO to work with Massachusetts WRO.[22] According to researcher Mary Davidson, MAW member Doris Bland criticized Pastreich because he "is a white organizer who was not invited, not wanted and who is using the mothers for his own ends."[23] She wanted, instead, "to reconstruct, reorient, and have welfare mothers themselves implement, the welfare system."[24] The recipient members of the South Boston committee of MWRO, however, defended Pastreich.

As the movement matured, welfare recipients more strenuously protested the control and domination by white middle-class staff. They, like other activists in the 1960s, made connections between the personal and the political. They examined how racial, gender, and class oppression permeated everyday interactions among individuals. They believed that patterns of structural discrimination were manifested in their day-to-day lives. Transforming these personal relations—or seeking autonomy—became one component of the agenda for social change.

Different Strategies

The goals, aspirations, and strategies devised by the black women were often at odds with those of the male staff. Some staff members followed political theorist Saul Alinsky, who argued that poor people only wielded power through mobilization. In this tradition, Wiley hoped to build a national organization of poor people, a union of welfare recipients, to enable them to bargain for higher welfare payments and a guaranteed income.[25] He believed that civil disorders, such as riots and rebellions, gave numerical minorities such as African Americans or welfare recipients "substantial . . . power" to "have a major impact on the country."[26] Consequently, he sought to build a mass base, exploiting the public fear of urban uprisings and threatening more such violence if NWRO's demands were not met.[27]

For this reason, many organizers advocated tactics such as the special-grant campaign, which promised an immediate material benefit to recipients who became members. This strategy was successful for a short period of time, but when the material rewards disappeared, membership rolls shrank. Organizers were less successful at developing long-term participation in the movement. A supporter of Columbus WRO explained: "The prime method for organizing [used by WRO staff] has been a union-type model in which benefits (or gains) are used as ways to draw people into the organization. The difficulty of such organizing is that goals and ideology are often ignored. Therefore people often fail to establish a commitment for ongoing change based on his understanding of social change."[28] A Michigan organizer reported similar problems. "There is a great deal of new life around the times for major campaigns, but then the groups fall back into nothingness. But there is no 'mortar' to hold things together between times, to deal with individual grievances."[29]

The staff eagerly planned protests and persuaded recipients to participate. Many organizers, like Pastreich, considered protests "radical" or "real organizing." He criticized recipients reluctant to take to the streets: "One problem is that people [on welfare] want to be reasonable . . . They want to be seen in a good light. They come to get their stuff, not for confrontation."[30] Organizers ultimately wanted to "radicalize" the oppressed. An SDS organizer explained how she and other students working with poor people had fixed notions about social change in their heads. Day-to-day organizing, however, dispelled these ideas.

> We started with personal senses of moral outrage against poverty and [racial] discrimination . . . We felt that if we simply talked to poor people, and got a few of them together, that their oppressed situation would become apparant [sic] to them. Through talk and confronting the city by fighting for reforms, they would become radical. This radical condition would spread from block to block, and we would have a community of "participating" people whose activity would change the state of affairs. This community would be a permanent radical base that we could leave after a year or two.[31]

She continued, "We found out that the only thing that neighbors on a [racially] mixed block could easily talk to each other about was garbage removal and the need for street lights. But we discovered that *we* did not consider garbage removal a radical thing."[32] As this student recognized, recipients often had competing goals and a different agenda from middle-class organizers. Something that seemed quite ordinary to other people might be viewed as radical by welfare recipients if it transformed their day-to-day lives. So, demands for garbage removal or safe play spaces for children or even the very act of speaking in a common voice could radically alter the situation for a group of people historically disempowered and silenced and might be the basis upon which they build their political analysis.

Staff and recipients also measured success differently. Many staff members counted the number of people joining welfare rights organizations while recipients gauged sustained involvement. These categories were fluid however. Some recipients, especially national leaders, were whole-heartedly committed to building a mass-based group, and some staff members, such as Rhoda Linton and Tim Sampson, valued individual empowerment. Nevertheless, a general thrust within NWRO shaped the contrasting views of many staff members and recipients. A member of a non-NWRO affiliated welfare rights organization in Chicago explained that NWRO's "crisis orientation works against a sustained organizing effort. With NWRO groups get started and are coordinated around local crises. There is no follow-up after the crisis is over—no real nitty-gritty organizing is done at all."[33] In another case, welfare recipients accused organizers in Michigan of protesting "in a vacuum" without a clear sense of goals.[34] Instead of relying solely on pressure tactics, women in the organization were also interested in education and politicization. They looked at long-term goals, not just short-term concessions. Alice Jackson and Roxanne Jones of Pennsylvania are a case in point. Jones, a mother of two surviving on a monthly AFDC check of $232, had led the Philadelphia WRO since 1968. Proud of the fact that it was a recipient-run organization, she wrote in 1969, "To me the obvious strength of the Philadelphia Welfare Rights Organization is that recipients have learned to organize and become organizers."[35]

The group disapproved of Wiley's confrontational tactics. At the assembly of the National Conference on Social Welfare in New York in 1969, Wiley locked the doors, took the microphone, and demanded a $35,000 contribution to NWRO as well as a $1 "surcharge" from individual social workers.[36] In a formal statement to "all persons attending the National Conference of Social Welfare" the Pennsylvania WRO labeled this "robbery." They said: "We question the National Welfare Rights Organization's Attack on Social Workers as the stereotype of the establishment of this country. National Welfare Rights Organization is as much a part of the establishment by accepting $434,930 from the U.S. Department of Labor." These welfare recipients opposed such strong-arm tactics to simply get a chunk of change. Instead, they favored educating social workers and welfare recipients to persuade them to work toward long-term goals of social justice: "education of social workers is essential—but it cannot be done through fear or intimidation."[37]

The NWRO executive committee, made up of national recipient leaders, criticized Dovie Coleman, a recipient organizer in Chicago, for not signing up enough members. Coleman moved in 1948 from St. Louis to Chicago, where she worked as a hairdresser until 1952 when a near-fatal auto accident left her paralyzed for several months. Unable to return to work, she applied for public assistance. She started working with the SDS-run Jobs or Income Now (JOIN) organization in Chicago in 1964.[38] Despite the protestations of white JOIN organizers, she and other recipients broke away from JOIN and formed Welfare Recipients Demand Action (WRDA) in 1967, an interracial group that included African Americans, poor whites, Puerto Ricans, and Native Americans. Run out of Coleman's apartment, WRDA was a resource-poor, but recipient-led organization that refused "outside" staff.[39] Coleman represented Illinois on the NCC and served as NWRO Financial Secretary. Reputedly an effective citywide organizer since 1968, according to the local Friends group, she "knows welfare regulations better than most caseworkers."[40] After criticism by NWRO Coleman resigned, explaining that numbers alone could not measure her organizing success. There was a difference, she argued, between "deeply organizing" people and simply "getting a lot of people together." She continued:

> People will give up easy unless they are really organized and determined to keep fighting; as soon as the system fights back or refuses to change they will give up. Then the movement will fall apart. We have to stop somewhere along the line to teach people what this system is all about. This is what I have done. This is what I think the key to organizing is.[41]

Sensitive to her role as a staff member, Coleman never intruded where she was not welcome or imposed her views on others. She always waited until invited to a meeting: "It takes a long time and the work is very slow to build up trust between you and other organizations." In a poem she expressed her feelings about working for the national office as well as her deep commitment to political work.

> I don't like those words and I can't stand those threats,
> Because it still reminds me I am in slave days yet,

I found freedom of mind in an organizing school
I accepted the salary because they owe me dues,
And that's the reason I'm trying so hard,
to open an organizing school
Because I want other people to feel the way I do.
So I'm going to keep on working and not give up
And have that school or bust a gut.
So I'm telling you the truth and I'm not lying,
I'm going to keep on organizing till the end of time.[42]

Many staff members believed that welfare recipients, incapable of developing an analysis of long-term social change, needed political guidance. They were wrong. Not formally educated in political theory and often unfamiliar with classic organizing texts, recipients such as Dovie Coleman developed a multilayered analysis of their situation: combining ideology, economics, and political power. They drew from their daily experience, from their involvement with the poor, a sensibility of how to empower and create a better society for the disenfranchised. It was a vision that rested on the slow and patient work of winning people over politically and ideologically—of empowering them to take control of their lives. Loretta Johnson of Richmond, the VA representative to the NCC, helped kick off a Hunger Campaign in 1970 to inform people of the food stamp program.[43] She eloquently explained her commitment to social justice:

WRO has been the backbone and the power I've needed to make my voice heard, to get action and bring to light the ill-treatment and lies the people in power have given the poor, voiceless, helpless, elderly, the blacks, and the oppressed people in this country . . . I will never, can never, shall never give up this fight for human dignity, equal rights plus Bread and Justice which will put an end to hunger in this country.[44]

Like many other recipients, Catherine Jermany, a member of the Los Angeles County WRO, NCC representative, and later Western Regional representative, addressed the stigma and stereotypes associated with receipt of welfare. Born and raised in Los Angeles, Jermany was an outspoken, confident, and articulate woman who questioned unfair policies and practices when employed by General Hospital and the Police Department in Los Angeles.[45] Jermany came from a politically active family, with one uncle who ran for governor of California in the 1960s, another uncle who worked with the Dodge Revolutionary Union Movement in Detroit, and a grandmother who was an activist. Jermany was involved with SCLC and Ron

Karenga's cultural nationalist U.S. organization in Southern California.[46] She went on welfare after the birth of her third child when the county refused to give her job back because she was "too heavy." She helped organize a citywide welfare rights group in L.A. long before the formation of NWRO and quickly rose up the ranks of welfare rights leadership.[47] In a speech before the State Welfare Finance Officers in Nevada in 1969, Jermany attempted to turn the notion of fraud on its head, by suggesting that welfare recipients rarely committed fraud. She argued that the inefficiency, inhumanity, and deception of welfare department administrators more often made recipients and taxpayers the victims of fraud. She debunked the popular stereotype that recipients cheated the system and attempted to expose the inconsistencies and unfairness of welfare policy and practices.[48] Welfare recipients such as Jermany and Coleman developed an independent political analysis and formulated their own methods of organizing.[49] And as the welfare rights movement progressed, the gulf between recipients and staff widened. It included not just organizing tactics but also political positions, perhaps the best example of which was their opposing views on employment of welfare recipients.

Employment and Welfare

In the 1960s, employment of welfare recipients became a permanent feature of federal welfare policy. Work incentives were first introduced in 1962 and in 1967 the Johnson administration mandated employment of women on AFDC. The new work rules shifted the focus of AFDC from counseling and rehabilitation to get people out of poverty toward job training and employment.[50] The 1967 Work Incentive Program (WIN) required women with school-age children receiving AFDC to accept either job training or employment. It also provided some funding for day care services for women on welfare and included a work incentive allowing working recipients to keep the first $30 of their monthly income and one-third of anything beyond that, without a reduction in monthly benefits. Recipients refusing to participate in work or training lost their benefits.

Congressional debate about the 1967 Social Security Amendments revealed the increasing association of welfare, illegitimacy, and employment of poor black women. The Amendments were a response to the heightened criticism of AFDC since the late 1950s and were designed to put women on welfare to work, reduce the welfare rolls, and limit federal support of out-of-wedlock births. In addition to implementing the WIN program, the bill also capped federal funding increases in AFDC because of parental absence from the home due to desertion, divorce, or illegitimacy at the 1968 level. Cases in which a father had died or a parent lost a job were exempt.

Repealed before it ever took effect, the inclusion of this clause was nonethe-less important.[51] The House Ways and Means Committee, for example, re-ported that it was "very concerned about the continued growth" of the ADC rolls due to "family breakup and illegitimacy."[52] In addition, during an NWRO protest of the 1967 Amendments, Senator Russell Long became en-raged at the black recipient protesters and referred to them, in a revealingly racial manner, as "brood mares."[53] Race laced the discussion and debate about the 1967 Social Security Amendments.

The new welfare proposals represented a widespread consensus in the 1960s that women on welfare should work. Liberals, conservatives, and many radicals concurred that jobs programs would solve the immediate problem of rising welfare rolls and the long-term problem of poverty.[54] Democrats and Republicans did not agree completely on all aspects of the WIN proposals. Johnson offered amendments for child care and a work in-centive allowing recipients to keep a portion of their earnings and sug-gested making mandatory the AFDC-Unemployed Parent program, which extended benefits to two-parent families. But even these proposals rein-forced the dominant view about the need to bolster the two-parent family and require recipients to work. Employment was the cornerstone of the War on Poverty, which emphasized job training and education over direct income support. Programs such as Head Start and Manpower Develop-ment gave people the necessary tools to compete in the labor market. Government bureaucrats also responded to rising welfare rolls by turning to work. For example, in a 1967 report, the mid-Atlantic regional office of the Bureau of Labor Statistics suggested "training and education of the un-employed who don't qualify for [existing] jobs and day-care for public as-sistance recipients" to enable them to enter the labor market.[55] The public also seemed to enthusiastically support employment of women on welfare. At a welfare rights protest for furniture and clothing guidelines in Boston, construction workers dropped lunch leftovers and containers of water on demonstrators and called out "We work, why don't you try it?!"[56]

In 1967 NWRO planned its first annual convention in Washington to coincide with the Congressional debates and lobby against the proposed work requirements for welfare recipients. NWRO wanted to solve the prob-lem of poverty through an adequate income, not employment. It argued that "having a job is no guarantee against poverty" and that the proposed federal program would create hardship for women on AFDC. In a pam-phlet called "Six Myths about Welfare" written a few years after passage of the bill, NWRO wrote that under WIN, the welfare department would force a mother "to take any job, even if it's not covered by minimum wage laws. In the South, especially, where cheap 'domestics' are in greatest demand, the WIN program can be tantamount to involuntary servitude."[57] They called the bill "a betrayal of the poor, a declaration of war upon our families, and a fraud on the future of our nation."[58]

To protest the welfare amendments, in 1967 NWRO held a public hearing in Washington and members spoke to a roaring crowd of several hundred, in the presence of what one reporter called an "unusual force" of police officers.[59] The delegates then adjourned to the Mall in downtown Washington for a "Mothers March," which drew 1,000 people, and later a picket at the Department of Health, Education and Welfare. At the rally, Margaret McCarty, welfare rights leader in Baltimore, invoked the historical oppression of African Americans as well as the racial pride of period, when she said, "Lousy, dirty, conniving brutes" devised the bill to "take us back to slavery . . . I'm black and I'm beautiful and they ain't going to take me back."[60]

The next month, NWRO testified before the Senate Finance Committee about the impending legislation. Fifty women attended, many with their children in tow. Welfare recipients with prepared testimony denounced the regulations as "disgraceful." Beulah Sanders explained the impact of the work requirements on their children: "When our children are picked up by the police, they'll ask them where their parents are. And we'll have to tell the police that we've been forced to let them roam the streets because the Government says we have to go to work."[61] Trying to strike a note of urgency, Etta Horn, of the Citywide Welfare Alliance in Washington, D.C., outlined potentially dire repercussions of the welfare bill. "The only time you listen to us is when the cities are burning and the people are dying. The time to listen is now."[62] Only two of the seventeen Senators were present to listen to them, however. In protest, the women staged a three-hour sit-in demanding that all seventeen members of the Senate Finance Committee appear. Committee Chairman Russell Long, Democrat from Louisiana, was so angry at the mothers' conduct that when adjourning the meeting he banged the gavel so hard its head flew off. The welfare recipients only left when the district police threatened to fine and arrest them for unlawful entry.[63] Despite NWRO's intense lobbying, WIN was enacted into law, becoming the first mandatory work requirement for AFDC recipients.

Although NWRO had opposed WIN since it was first debated, the national office, under Wiley's leadership, signed in December 1968 a $434,000 contract with the Department of Labor to educate and train participants in the WIN program.[64] Carl Rachlin, general counsel for NWRO, proposed the contract. He wrote in a letter to Wiley that the 1967 law was distasteful not because it encouraged employment but because it punitively required recipients to accept jobs. He suggested that NWRO devise its own voluntary work program, demonstrating that with training and support recipients were eager to work.[65] Run by Nashco, NWRO's nonprofit arm, the Citizen

Participation Project, as NWRO's proposal was called, informed "welfare recipients of opportunities avaliable (sic) in the WIN program while at the same time advising recipients of their rights and protections."[66] For Wiley and his staff, the Department of Labor contract was not inconsistent with their opposition to the Work Incentive Program. They wrote in the national newsletter:

> We are still opposed to forcing mothers to work and the other terrible features of the anti-welfare law. We have applied for and are operating this contract because we feel that since this law is on the books, we must see to it that the rights of recipients are protected.[67]

Thus, implicitly assuming that women on welfare should work, staff members believed that mitigating the punitive component of the law would make it palatable.

The national office staff signed the contract for two reasons. First, they believed the organization would benefit from the infusion of cash, permitting NWRO to hire more organizers, print more literature, and plan more campaigns. It would strengthen the organization, expand its base, and consequently contribute to the long-term goal of reforming the welfare system.[68] Second, the staff signed the Department of Labor contract because they differed with the women in the organization about work. Staff members opposed WIN and other work-related programs, arguing that recipients wanted to work but that jobs and training were in short supply. Tim Sampson explained that the government's unwillingness to create jobs justified NWRO's focus on a guaranteed income. But strategically, the organization favored employment: "Whenever we tried to figure out how to . . . [relate] . . . to the public obviously jobs, the work issue, was always a key issue around communication."[69] Wiley similarly felt that recipients, eager to work, did not have to be forced. He believed that emphasizing employment dispelled the racist stereotype that women on AFDC were lazy.[70] Staff members did not oppose the 1967 law because it required mothers to work, but opposed its punitive nature. NWRO's Department of Labor grant proposal stated that WIN "can provide new opportunities for training of welfare recipients for meaningful jobs which could lift them out of poverty."[71] Most of the NWRO staff concurred with the popular belief that employment was the best solution for poverty.[72]

Many female leaders of the organization, primarily black, did not see employment for women on AFDC as a prescription for poverty. Most recipients valued choice. The Department of Labor contract troubled many of them, especially at the grassroots level, precisely because of the lack of choice. Some bitterly opposed it as validating the 1967 work requirements.

The Philadelphia Welfare Rights Organization lambasted Wiley and the other staff in Washington for selling out to the establishment. To Roxanne Jones and Alice Jackson of Philadelphia, the national office's endorsement of the "WIP program," as they preferred to call it, would help implement "the most reactionary program in decades. It is designed to remove mothers from the home and place them into 'slave labor' jobs."[73] Opposing WIN because of its work requirement, a Massachusetts group argued, "This means that a mother with school-age children will be forced (if they do not volunteer) to accept the same old inferior training or jobs that have always been left for poor people."[74] They believed that mothers and poor people had a right to welfare, regardless of the availability of jobs, and that as mothers they *did* work. For the women in the movement, challenging society's assumptions about poor mothers, putting forth a morally defensible position, and protecting their dignity and worth as mothers was more important than the infusion of cash to build up the national organization.[75]

The Pennsylvania leadership was so disturbed by the WIN contract that in May 1969 they disrupted the NCC meeting in New York City and issued a press release outlining their grievances and threatening to secede from NWRO. When the national staff refused to return in a single check to PWRO the members' dues that went to the national office, the group decided to remain with NWRO until the organization's convention in Detroit in August. If they did not get a fair hearing then, they planned on establishing an autonomous state organization.[76]

The staff's response to the conflict with Pennsylvania was varied. Some staffers respected the position of the dissenting group and worked to retain them as part of the national organization. More commonly, however, staff members criticized recipients and assumed they did not understand the larger political goals of the movement. According to one national staff person, "Roxanne Jones was still 'turn-oriented' rather than 'change-oriented.' She was seeking, he thought, to retain a secure position of local domination to the detriment of the ideological goals of the movement."[77] After PWRO issued its press release, the national leadership of NWRO sent a memo signed by Johnnie Tillmon to PWRO members. A handwritten note at the top of the memo suggests it was never sent, but the document is revealing nevertheless. Calling the public attack on NWRO by the PWRO leadership divisive, it asked for a poll to see if the membership wanted to pull out of or remain with NWRO.[78] The national leadership's direct appeal to members was unusual. NWRO was not a membership organization, but a federation of local groups, and the staff and national officers rarely intervened in internal decision making of local groups.

Contrary to staff opinion, the women opposing the contract were not concerned primarily about "local domination" but had an ideological -

position rooted in their experiences and identity as mothers. Women in the welfare rights movement resisted WIN and the WIN contract because they valued motherhood and opposed forcing women into the workforce. Roxanne Jones suggested that the WIP program allowed the welfare department to "take mothers from their children."[79] Welfare rights activists often referred to themselves as "mothers" or "mother-recipients," and sought to bring dignity and respect to their work as mothers.[80] Welfare rights activists had long asserted the importance of motherhood. Ethel Dotson, participant in the Richmond, CA, WRO and Northern California representative to the NCC, explained her situation. Working until she became pregnant with her first child, she initially drew unemployment and then in 1965 started receiving welfare. She recounted:

> I had seen a lot of kids where the parents worked and they had babysitters and the kids would end up calling the babysitter "momma." And calling mother something else. And I stayed at home and made sure I did not work for at least two years, so that my son, you know, we had our time together with me raising him. So, he was calling me "momma" and not the babysitter momma.[81]

Welfare recipients challenged the artificial dichotomy between work and welfare, insisting that as mothers they did, in fact, work. In 1968 a Boston group said that "motherhood—whether the mother is married or not—is a role which should be fully supported, as fully rewarded, as fully honored, as any other."[82]

Welfare recipients' insistence that the work of mothering served an important function in society resonated with the maternalist movement of the early twentieth century. Maternalists pushing for mothers' pensions, the precursor of AFDC, justified assistance on similar grounds as women in the welfare rights movement.[83] But the maternalist movement of the progressive era differed qualitatively from the struggle of women in the welfare rights movement. Most maternalists were prosperous white women as concerned with social disorder as helping the poor and used class and cultural bias to force poor women to adapt to middle-class standards of respectability.[84] Their reforms reinforced women's socially defined role. Women in the welfare rights movement, on the other hand, ultimately sought to give women autonomy to make choices for themselves. They believed that black women, often expected to work, did not have the same social status or primary identity as mothers that white women had. Valuing black women's work as mothers challenged social norms. It did not conform to dominant expectations.[85]

The greater proportion of black women on the welfare rolls in the 1950s and 1960s prompted legislation requiring women on AFDC to enter the paid labor force. Although a minority of women on welfare, African Americans became the stereotypical recipient and AFDC identified as primarily a black program. In addition to changing perceptions, the practice and ideology of welfare also transformed. Linda Gordon and Nancy Fraser argue that ideological constructions of notions of dependency shaped the discourse around welfare, which considered women on AFDC undeserving. In contrast to recipients of Social Security and unemployment compensation, recipients of AFDC were considered "dependent." Originally defined by social relations, the term "dependency" did not necessarily have a negative connotation. They argue that in the postindustrial period notions of dependency changed, stigmatizing people on AFDC and defining social problems as individual and psychological.[86] However, it seems that in the postwar period as welfare increasingly came to be seen as a problem of race more than individual failure, dependency was defined culturally rather than psychologically. In the 1960s, the poor became a culturally distinct group and poverty was more closely identified with African Americans.[87] The changing views of AFDC reflected the emerging culture of poverty thesis and long-standing perceptions and stereotypes of black women. Concomitant was the expectation that women on welfare would be employed.

This view of black women on welfare contrasted sharply with the situation of white women, many of whom adamantly challenged the dominant assumption that employment would impair the emotional and psychological development of their children. Even into the early 1970s, no consensus existed that paid employment of middle-class women did not do damage to their children, let alone that such employment was positive. An official HEW publication exposed the disjuncture between what was considered appropriate for middle-class white women and what was considered appropriate for women on welfare. Concluding that children on AFDC have more behavioral problems than children of other poor families, a study found that problems worsened when the mother stayed at home with the children. Welfare children "seem to have a higher incidence of serious disorders such as psychosis and appear to be more isolated, mistrustful, and anxious than the nonwelfare children . . . The employment status of the welfare mothers also seems to affect impairment: children of working mothers have less impairment."[88]

Women in the welfare rights movement analyzed and scrutinized the different social expectations of white middle-class women and poor women of color, who had never been seen primarily as mothers and had never approximated the domestic ideal. One welfare recipient cleverly contrasted her situation with the reigning symbol of womanhood of the time when she asked, "Jackie Kennedy gets a government check. Is anyone making her go to work?"[89] Welfare activists insisted that society value their work as mothers, illustrating the very different perceptions and realities of gender across racial and class lines. For African American women, gender had not been shaped primarily by their roles as mothers and housewives, but instead by wage work. So, while middle-class white women in the 1960s sought to enter the world of paid employment, black women on welfare wanted to be recognized as mothers.[90] This ideological front constituted part of their struggle for welfare rights.

Although welfare rights activists valued motherhood, they did not encourage mothers to stay home with their children, believing that women should have the opportunity to choose whether to work outside the home or not. Some welfare recipients took jobs while on welfare and valued these experiences. Majorie Caesar, of the Pittsfield Association of Adequate Welfare in western Massachusetts, worked in a bar, as a nurse, in a bank, and as a bookkeeper: "I've always been a person, independent, very independent. And so I always looked for a job."[91] Catherine Jermany, as well, supported the work ethic and believed employment allowed recipients to reach their "maximum potential."[92] To assist mothers wanting paid employment, welfare recipients supported the creation of child care centers. This was "one of the first priorities" of Johnnie Tillmon's welfare rights organization in California.[93] Mothers entering the workforce needed child care, but recipients cautioned that poor women employed at day care centers might also be exploited. The image of the "Mammy" was a powerful one for African American women. Since slavery, black women had been forced, because of lack of options, to care for other people's children.[94] Usually paid meager sums, they left their own children to create a comfortable home and environment for middle-class or wealthy families. Therefore, day care centers freed some women from the constraints of child care, but could just as likely exploit other women.

Thus, men and women in the welfare rights movement made claims for public assistance and challenged work requirements differently. The male staff did not believe that welfare recipients should be forced to work. To counter racist images of black women as lazy, however, they publicly took a position that women on AFDC wanted to work, and given the opportunity, they would do so. On this, they were not that far from the women, who also believed that AFDC recipients should have the opportunity to work. But the female recipients justified public assistance by their work as mothers rather than simply the lack of employment opportunities. In doing so, they sought to transform not just the welfare system but the public's perception of black women as well. On the issue of single motherhood, however, the staff and recipients were even further apart.

Single Motherhood and the Black Family

Staff and recipients also grappled with the issue of single motherhood. Most people in the NWRO national office assumed that single motherhood was a social problem and, like many other black and white activists in the 1960s, ascribed to traditional notions of proper family forms. Richard Cloward, one of the most ardent defenders of the rights of welfare recipients, wrote in 1965:

> Men for whom there are no jobs will nevertheless mate like other men, but they are not so likely to marry. Our society has preferred to deal with the resulting female-headed families not by putting the men to work but by placing the unwed mothers and dependent children on public welfare—substituting check-writing machines for male wage earners. By this means we have robbed men of manhood, women of husbands, and children of fathers. To create a stable monogamous family, we need to provide men (especially Negro men) with the opportunity to be men, and that involves enabling them to perform occupationally.[95]

Male organizers within NWRO supported strategies reinforcing the traditional family. White male staff members at the national office wrote in the platform for the Poor People's Campaign in 1968 that "there is a desperate need for jobs in the ghettoes for men to permit them to assume normal roles as breadwinners and heads of families."[96] Dovetailing with mainstream policy analysts, many male leaders of NWRO agreed that single motherhood was a social pathology, every family needed a male breadwinner, and male employment was a long-term solution to poverty.[97]

In the 1960s, for the first time, black family policy became a subject of national interest and public concern. A plethora of articles, studies, and conferences examined the rising number of single parents, relations between black men and women, and cultural traits of African Americans. This focus on the black family, which eventually came to be defined as a "crisis," forged two major concerns on the domestic agenda—racism and poverty. The concentration of black poor in urban areas, the increasing number of black women on welfare, as well as protests and demonstrations by civil rights activists and welfare recipients highlighted the problem of black poverty. Politicians and policy makers explained the extent of poverty among African Americans by looking at characteristics and behavioral patterns of the black family. Many academics pointed to the rising number of black welfare recipients as one of the most reliable indicators of the widespread problems of poverty and racism.

The most well-known study to connect welfare, poverty, and race was *The Negro Family: A Case for National Action* by Daniel Patrick Moynihan, Assistant Secretary of Labor under President Lyndon Johnson. Published in 1965, the *Moynihan Report*, as it is more popularly known, addressed black urban poverty and the rising number of female-headed households. Moynihan argued that "at the heart of the deterioration of the fabric of Negro society is the deterioration of the Negro family. It is the fundamental source of the weakness of the Negro community." He attributed the disproportionate number of black single-parent families, which he called a "tangle of pathology," to the "matriarchal" black family structure. A long history of slavery, exploitation, racism, and unemployment had led to an increased divorce rate, a large number of illegitimate children, male desertion, and a rapid growth in AFDC families. The solution, Moynihan claimed, was to establish a stable black family structure.[98]

Echoing an argument made twenty-five years earlier by black sociologist Franklin Frazier, the *Moynihan Report* was nevertheless important because of its impact on welfare policy. In the mid-1960s social policy and urban politics were at a critical juncture, making the reception of Moynihan's report invaluable to critics and reformers of welfare policy. Strengthening age-old debates about why poor single mothers should not get government assistance, the *Report* cemented the issue of race to welfare and single-parent families in a way that made it difficult to talk about one without the others.[99] Moynihan's report helped shift the debate about urban poverty from structure and economics to culture and values. Although Moynihan suggested expanding employment opportunities for black men, his emphasis on black family cultural practices overshadowed his other points. The ensuing debate centered on changing the "domineering" position of black women, bringing black men back into the household, and ending the "cycle of poverty." Moynihan's report encouraged President Lyndon Johnson to make "Negro family stability" the focus of the 1965 White House Conference on Civil Rights. One participant of the Conference, Benjamin Payton, testified in 1965 that the *Moynihan Report* would profoundly shape future civil rights strategy.[100]

George Wiley, like most black leaders of the time, was outraged by the *Moynihan Report* and questioned whether the patterns of family breakdown that Moynihan identified pertained only to the black family. He argued that if AFDC statistics were broken down by race, the same trends could be applied to white families as well.[101] Like countless others, Wiley challenged Moynihan's focus on race rather than income to explain the deterioration of two-parent families. These critics objected to Moynihan's characterization of the black family as "matriarchal" rather than questioning the dubious link between matriarchy and social pathology.[102] The debate around the *Moynihan Report* demonstrated the widespread consensus among people on both the left and the right of the "problem" of single motherhood in the black community.[103]

Benjamin Payton was wrong that Moynihan's report would be instrumental in future Civil Rights strategy. Instead it had a lasting impact on welfare policy. Moynihan's theories undermined much of what the welfare rights movement struggled for and contributed to a backlash against welfare. His analysis that the "deteriorating" black family, i.e., single motherhood, was the source of many problems in the black community fueled criticism of AFDC, enabling conservative and liberal politicians and policy makers to demand a retrenchment in the welfare state. They argued that assistance from the government discourages two-parent families, promotes out-of-wedlock births, gives fathers little incentive to pay child support, and, according to Moynihan's logic, leads to an array of other social and economic problems. These critics concluded that poor women should not have access to a source of income independent of men.

While both liberals and conservatives wrestled with restoring the traditional two-parent family, women in the welfare rights movement attempted to debunk the notion that single motherhood signaled culture deficiency and challenged the assumption that poor single mothers needed a male breadwinner.[104] Welfare rights activists in West Virginia counseled recipients to get a "pauper's divorce" if the welfare department won't pay for a divorce, suggesting that women separate from their husbands and plead ignorance about their whereabouts.[105] When women did marry someone who was not the father of their children, they wanted to continue to receive welfare and maintain their economic independence. The Westside ADC Mothers of Detroit sought to overturn a policy making the new husband financially liable for the children of the recipient.[106]

Welfare rights activists criticized domestic relationships that oppressed women. According to reporter Gordon Brumm, MAW believed that marriage with its "fixed rules and obligations" was a "means for domination more than a means for expressing love."[107] Although they valued motherhood, they did not promote marriage or encourage women to accept a subordinate status as mother and homemaker. They believed women should have autonomy in choosing their partners and suggested alternative family and relationship models—where women had control in their personal lives and could strive for fulfilling relationships. MAW explained, "Instead [of institutional marriage], they favor love, . . . responsibility toward other persons, and freedom to whatever extent that responsibility allows."[108] Welfare rights activists asserted their right to date without negative repercussions from the welfare department. Welfare recipients in Morgantown, WV, wrote in a handbook that "an AFDC mother can have male visitors as often as she wants and go out on dates if she leaves her children in the care of a responsible person."[109]

In claiming public assistance as single mothers, women in the welfare rights movement tackled head-on criticisms that welfare recipients' "dependency" distinguished them from other women. MAW argued that women on AFDC, "supported out of public funds," were not much different from wives dependent on wages paid to men and also supported by public funds in the form of taxes or higher prices. The family-wage system assumed that men had families to sustain and justified paying them higher wages. Yet the same consideration was not given to women supporting their families. Working mothers "need nearly the same income as a family man, yet they are expected to take jobs ordinarily occupied by young unmarried women."[110] Welfare rights activists explored how the disparate realities of men and women caring for families were socially constructed. The critical factor determining their entitlements was not their familial responsibility, but their gender, race, and class status.

Women in the welfare rights movement attempted to legitimate their status as single parents and assert their right to marry or date on their own terms free of social stigma or repercussions from the welfare department. For them, an adequate income rather than a two-parent family was a sensible solution to the poverty of single-parent mothers. They defended their status as single mothers and disputed arguments vilifying them. For these welfare activists, liberation meant preserving their right to be women and mothers independent of men. Thus, men and women in the organization had very different analyses of employment and single motherhood. These issues, in combination with competing organizing strategies and the question of control, all came to a head in August 1969 as the group gathered in Detroit for their third annual convention.

Detroit

At the 1969 Detroit Conference local welfare leaders and black staff members working in the national office launched scathing attacks on Wiley and white national staffers, culminating a long period of brewing resentment. Welfare mothers charged the staff with rigidly controlling the organization. Although not always working in alliance, recipients and black staff members demanded a greater role for African Americans in the decision making and insisted that Wiley hire welfare recipients, rather than "outsiders." The conflict was so heated that by the end of the year a number of staff members had quit or were fired and several welfare rights organizations severed their ties with NWRO.

The tensions over control and decision making came to a head most overtly between black and white staff members in the national office several months earlier. Middle-class white men dominated the administrative and organizing positions. Most black staff members worked in the NWRO print shop. According to white organizer Rhoda Linton, who began working in the national office in 1968, "There were a lot of white people involved in making decisions about what the organization was going to do. And there were a lot of people of color doing the 'do,' doing the work."[111] By 1969 black staff members were very dissatisfied with white control within the organization. John Lewis, an African American who headed the printing division, wrote in an article in the *Washington Afro-American* that black staff members formed a caucus in June "to discuss the grievances they had as a people." Feeling "manipulated by white people," black staff members believed that "at national headquarters, professionals have a paternalistic frequently racist attitude about recipients, consistently making policy decisions the recipients themselves should have made."[112] Caucus members made no demands, yet "word got around that we had a black caucus and the whites became afraid and suspicious." The NWRO executive committee, attempting to maintain the interracial unity that had characterized NWRO since its inception, denounced the black caucus. In the words of one staff member, the executive committee argued that NWRO was about "poverty and poor people, not just black people."[113] According to Lewis, "We were accused of creating a racial issue. They refused to deal with the overwhelming number of white people directing NWRO."[114] The actions of the black caucus both reflected and reinforced the racial divide emerging among grassroots activists within the welfare rights movement.

By mid-1969 racial tension in the national office reached a breaking point. Black and white staff members became resentful, fearful, and at times violent. In one incident, Dave Fishloe, a white man hired by Wiley, fired a black staff person who he believed was incompetent. The staff person physically attacked Fishloe twice, once in the presence of John Lewis and Hulbert James, both African Americans, who did nothing to intervene. After hearing of this incident, a Massachusetts organizer reported that "Pastreich is seriously looking for a way to learn karate fast and cheap."[115]

Racial divisions also dominated a national staff meeting at Trinity College in Washington on August 1, a few weeks before the Detroit conference.[116] According to a white organizer in Boston, participants spent an entire day discussing "whether or not Tim Sampson was a white racist."[117]

Black staff members expressed concerns about racial tension and recipient control. John Lewis explained, "The main issue is—do the recipients control the organization. And they don't . . . As [the organization] grew, it became very clear that most of the policy-making positions were going to whites." They pointed out that only one recipient out of a total of forty staff members worked for NWRO. "Recipients should have been brought in from the beginning to learn the administrative jobs, but they weren't. The issue is not just race, but whether a recipient should be executive director . . . and have a person like Dr. Wiley to give him assistance if he needs it"[118] According to Lewis, midway through the Trinity retreat, "Dr. Wiley got out of a sickbed to come to the staff conference, but instead of criticizing the whites, accused the blacks of creating disunity."[119]

A few days after the Trinity meeting, in response to accusations of white control, Wiley reshuffled key staff positions, appointing Hulbert James director of operations and Tim Sampson director of research and development. He offered John Lewis a position in public relations, but Lewis refused.[120] After his appointment, James, with Wiley's approval, set out to downsize the publications department.[121] A majority of the black staff, nearly all members of the black caucus working in the publications office, were subsequently fired.[122]

The black staff members fired from the national office attended the Detroit conference armed with evidence of white domination and control in the organization. They circulated leaflets recounting the racial tension in the national office and lamenting that important staff and policy-making positions, such as executive director, were filled by "middle-class professionals"—clearly a swipe at Wiley. They also demanded that the staff "reflect the racial constituency of NWRO members."[123] The actions of the black caucus struck a cord with some recipients critical of staff domination and the operation of the national office; others simply wanted more information about the discontent. A white delegate from Milwaukee stood up during the opening session of the convention and asked Wiley to answer the accusations in the leaflet. When she didn't get a response, she went on stage and asked if other delegates wanted an explanation. Some audience members applauded approvingly while others demanded she sit down. Five or six members of the NCC forcibly escorted the woman off the stage and out of the auditorium.[124] While the national officers and staff prevented a debilitating disruption in this instance, in the long run their actions fostered unease and intensified concerns about democracy and dissent.

For most recipients the tensions within the organization were complicated. Many black recipients and staff members were undoubtedly influenced by the rising tide of black power in the late 1960s. Throughout much of the postwar period, black power had an undeniable presence in both northern and southern communities, operating, in the words of historian Timothy Tyson, "in tension and in tandem with legal efforts and nonviolent protest."[125] Similarly since the welfare rights movement's inception, activists had articulated a vision of racial empowerment concomitant with their struggle for welfare rights. But the persistent clashes between black and white participants in the welfare rights movement, combined with the greater visibility of black power as more black freedom activists were won over to this ideology, gave recipients a language and a framework to make a case that their movement should not only preach, but practice racial equality. As a result, many grassroots welfare recipients and black staff members developed a stronger racial identity in the late 1960s. This was, in part, an outgrowth of racial characterizations of welfare recipients. The public identified welfare as a disproportionately black program populated by people who were lazy and prone to "broken families."

Black welfare recipients saw the stereotypes of welfare recipients as a product of a racist society that marginalized and demeaned them. Welfare cutbacks in the late 1950s and early 1960s were often racist in nature and directed at regulating the lives of poor black women in particular, as the situation in Newburgh, NY and Louisiana indicate. In some cases, African Americans constituted 90 percent of the victims of repressive state welfare policies. In many northern communities punitive policies were designed to keep African Americans out of predominantly white areas. Many welfare recipients located their problems with the welfare program within the larger system of racism. Loretta Domencich, an Indian organizer in Milwaukee, explained, "I think Welfare Rights has also given me a clearer idea of racism. The Welfare Department has a way of lumping people together; whether you're black, white, red, or brown, you're all a bunch of niggers when you go into the Welfare Department."[126] These welfare recipients tried simultaneously to dispel the myth of welfare as a black problem and recognize the role of racism in their own experiences on welfare. Catherine Jermany of the L.A. County WRO acknowledged that most welfare recipients were white, yet underscored her own black identity as an organizer.[127] Speaking before the Association of Black Social Workers, she counseled them, "to think Black is revolutionary"—they should therefore "Think Black" and "Talk Black."[128] Using language that echoed Black Power slogans, she clearly hoped to build support for the welfare rights movement through an appeal to racial solidarity. Thus, racial politics were central to understanding the welfare system and over time became increasingly important in building a movement to change it. A MAW member explained at a training conference in 1969 that black communities in Boston did not want "to be involved with white organizers."[129] In Ohio, welfare recipients had a training session in 1968, run with the help of black cultural nationalist

Maulana Ron Karenga, "to wed the skills of massive community organization for self-determination to the black movement of self-identity."[130] In Denver, CO, the Eastside WRO entreated for an African American to be considered for the position of citywide organizer.[131] Many black staff members and welfare recipients both inside and outside NWRO had come to believe, as Doris Bland of MAW put it, that the organization was "not oriented to black people" because most of the staff and organizers were white.[132]

Despite the significance of race, many women welfare rights activists, concerned about recipient control and autonomy, did not simply want NWRO to hire more African Americans to work in the national office. They were as concerned about middle-class and male domination as they were about white domination. According to Tim Sampson, Wiley's policy of almost always hiring male organizers created a backlash.[133] The Pennsylvania contingent, led by Roxanne Jones of PWRO and Frankie Mae Jeter, chair of the Welfare Rights Organization of Allegheny County, pushed NWRO to "spend its money to hire welfare mothers to organize their own communities instead of professional organizers." They backed the reelection of Johnnie Tillmon for chairman, who they believed had an "excellent record" and had been supportive of the Pennsylvania groups.[134] The recipients' criticisms combined issues of race, gender, personal power, autonomy, respect, class privilege, and strategic differences. Not all recipients had the same positions. Some were dissatisfied with the political direction of the organization. Others opposed staff members' class privilege or craved personal power. Catherine Jermany, a black welfare recipient from Los Angeles, worked in the national office and recalled that the staff "questioned our decision-making ability . . . [They] placated the ladies. They would buy them a hamburger rather than taking into consideration what they had to say . . . The ladies felt that disrespect. And they made suggestions that never got acted on. And not only didn't they get acted on. They didn't even get discussed." However, "the women always tried to exert power inappropriately. They had power, but didn't know how to use it."

Tension also increased between black and white recipients. Many white welfare recipients had joined the movement as well because they saw welfare as a fundamentally economic problem. Moiece Palladino worked with the Sunnydale Projects Mothers Group, joined the San Francisco City Wide WRO, and became the first vice president of the statewide California WRO. She believed that "economic freedom is the only real freedom in this society." From a white working-class family in San Francisco, Palladino married young, divorced her husband because of physical abuse, and went on welfare to support herself and her three children. She attended her first welfare rights meeting "looking for . . . sociability." She worked for many years on welfare rights activity in her racially mixed neighborhood. Palladino remembers intense conflicts around race in the San Francisco City Wide group. "Whites" she said, "didn't want to be identified with the movement or with them blacks." And many African American activists discussed "white privilege," sometimes targeting Palladino, one of the few white people in the movement: "I understand why people would attack me because . . . they perceive me to be the representative of a majority class, culture for which they perceive got benefits they didn't get." She believed ultimately, however, that race was just an "excuse" and that the conflicts were at the core about economics.[135]

Jermany believed tension between the black and white recipients worked in two ways. She suggested that "the contributions" of white welfare recipients "wasn't recognized . . . It was viewed by many black welfare recipients that there was no reason for a person who was white to have to be on welfare because all the opportunities were for them." On the other hand, Jermany explained, white welfare recipients didn't "necessarily recognize their own racism."[136]

The conflicts over race notwithstanding, the vast majority of recipients were committed to interracial organizing, as long as NWRO was not dominated by whites or nonrecipients. Roxanne Jones, a vehement critic of staff control within NWRO, wrote in the PWRO newsletter in 1969:

> I am proud that our poor white brothers and sisters in other parts of Pennsylvania are requesting and getting their money and other benefits under welfare . . . We must never forget that until all poor people begin working together rather than fighting each other and hating each other we will never fully achieve our basic goals.[137]

The Kansas WRO wanted to hire a recipient and expressed its commitment to developing "alliances across barriers of race, neighborhood, and family income."[138] Similarly, the Baltimore Welfare Rights Organization (BWRO) actively recruited white recipients. According to BWRO activist Rudell Martin, "I don't care what color you are. Everybody gets treated the same way—nasty."[139] Mrs. Rosie Hudson of Milwaukee explained, "Too many people are saying welfare's a black problem, when it's really a green problem. Why don't we have decent food, clothing, or shelter? It's simple. We don't have enough money."[140] Tillmon also focused on welfare's impact on both black and white women. She explained in a 1971 interview: "NWRO is not a black organization, not a white organization . . . We are all here together and we are fighting the people who are responsible for our predicament . . . We can't afford racial separateness. I'm told by the poor white girls on welfare how they feel when they're hungry, and I feel the same way when I'm hungry."[141]

Nevertheless, conflict plagued the organization in 1969. Many recipients were also dissatisfied with the planning for the Detroit conference, the handling of finances, and the running of the national office. For example, the

Illinois delegation objected to being housed in the dormitory of a college several miles from the conference and having to rely on buses to take them back and forth to the sessions. They were particularly irate because nearly all of the national staff stayed at one of the best local hotels, across the street from the convention quarters. Members of a local Chicago group, Welfare Recipients Demand Action (WRDA), refused to stay in their assigned accommodations and checked into the hotel as well. The Chicago WRO chairman reported "they are mad as hell" and believe that "recipients are getting second-class treatment."[142] These and other recipients, feeling they had little input into decisions, questioned how money they had raised for the conference was spent. They believed that the staff exercised an enormous amount of control over the organization and were often privileged over recipients. Wiley and a national officer responded by telling the Illinois delegation that they had not sent in sufficient money to be housed closer and that the national office had covered most of their conference expenses.[143]

NWRO's finances aggravated the conflict. Although the organization's income, in the form of membership dues, grants, and donations, had increased dramatically by 1969, its operating expenses grew even faster. NWRO's annual budget increased from $200,000 in 1968 to $500,000 in 1969 to $900,000 in 1970. But in 1969, expenses exceeded income by more than $50,000. Two-thirds of the 1969 budget was allotted to staff salaries.[144] The organization's indebtedness became a source of criticism and exacerbated tensions.

But many recipients were less concerned about the amount of money in NWRO's coffers than the distribution of limited resources. The Illinois delegates, for example, questioned how NWRO paid for staff members' hotel rooms, yet could not afford reasonable accommodations for recipients. Similarly, John Lewis wrote in 1969 that "although we were told there was no money, many of these whites were brought in at substantial salaries."[145] The African American staff and grassroots recipients assumed that funds were improperly handled and that any disposable cash benefited the staff. John Lewis reflected a more widespread sentiment when he said, "NWRO . . . is virtually bankrupt, a condition due primarily to the inefficiency and laxness in the handling of the hundreds of thousands of dollars which came in from private foundations, gifts and government grants."[146] Despite repeated requests, the staff did not detail NWRO finances until the last day of the Detroit conference.[147]

After the Detroit convention, the organization was in disarray. Catherine Jermany feared "we didn't know whether the organization was going to die after that or what."[148] National leaders sought to remedy some of the problems that arose in Detroit. They designated regional representatives on the executive committee to facilitate communication between national officers, staff, and local groups.[149] They barred staff members from business meetings and divided national meetings into a conference for non-welfare recipient organizers and a convention for welfare recipient delegates to minimize control by the staff. In the summer of 1970 Wiley hired eight black field organizers as well as two recipients and a larger number of middle-class black men to work in the national office.[150] This, however, failed to address the fundamental problem of different organizing styles of recipients and their middle-class counterparts. Shortly thereafter, conflict reemerged between the recipients and middle-class staff members working in the national office. The two recipients attended to the individual problems of people calling the office and accused the staff of insensitivity toward the people they served. Middle-class staff members, interested in organizational issues, referred people with individual problems somewhere else. The two groups functioned together ineffectively.[151] Moreover, Wiley still retained power to hire and fire the staff, delegate responsibilities, and control the budget. Despite the token hiring of two recipients, the overwhelming power remained with the middle-class staff, black and white, most of whom were men. This began to change with the formation of a Personnel and Policy Committee, charged with hiring and evaluating national staff.[152] The National Office also responded to charges that NWRO was white-oriented by renaming the newsletter from *NOW!* to the more militant and less civil-rights-oriented *Welfare Fighter*. Wiley grew an Afro hairstyle, began to wear a dashiki, and emphasized his black background, clearly hoping to alter NWRO's image and ally the movement with militancy and black nationalism.[153]

Despite these changes, some of the divisions emerging in 1969 were debilitating. In December 1970 a member of the National Office in an "Evaluation of NWRO and Affiliates" pointed out persistent problems of staff domination: "The policies approved by the executive committee tend to be ignored or half heartedly carried out." The author was also skeptical about the "ability to recruit and train member [sic] of minority groups."[154] Thus, problems persisted a year and a half after the conflict in Detroit. In addition, a number of WROs, including WRDA, disaffiliated from the national group to pursue their own welfare agenda. In other cases, grassroots welfare rights activists wanted autonomy over the local organization and demanded that Wiley replace current NWRO field organizers with recipients. Other staff members resigned out of frustration or because they felt that ongoing recipient dissatisfaction would impair the goals of the movement.

One of the most rancorous conflicts took place in Michigan. In November 1969 Pamela Blair resigned as organizer because the state WRO wanted a recipient in the job. Hired by Wiley in June 1969, Blair had worked with

MWRO as a student volunteer since late 1967. Although Wiley notified the Michigan WRO of his decision to hire Blair and asked if they objected, he did not seek prior input.[155] The following month, with NCC delegate Mamie Blakely at the helm, MWRO, in a letter to Wiley, expressed un-equivocal opposition to the hiring of Blair. They had decided that only the State executive committee should hire staff, and that members and their children should fill jobs.[156] Recipients commonly complained that staff in Michigan held disproportionate power, pushed recipients to demonstrate when they weren't interested, kept speaking engagements away from moth-ers, and discredited recipient activists disagreeing with them.[157] But Michigan members who lived "out-state" and those in the Detroit area also clashed. Blair had a better relationship with out-state groups, which criti-cized Detroit members opposing Blair.[158] Attempts by the national office to resolve the crisis in Michigan, including a visit by Hulbert James, had little impact. Blair resigned because of the discontent and her conviction that the organization needed "a strong and *united* front against the terrible welfare system in Michigan."[159] Another Michigan organizer, Bill Buffum, upset that Wiley and the national office didn't support Blair more avidly, felt that Blair was qualified, committed, and had been unfairly pushed out of her job. He doubted that a recipient could replace Blair, writing to Wiley, "I am not aware of a recipient who could handle things statewide."[160] While pos-sibly reflecting Buffum's biases against recipient organizers, this statement might have simply been an astute observation, because the following year, the MWRO offered Buffum the permanent position of state director, which he declined.[161] Thus, the agitation around hiring a recipient in Michigan didn't pan out as expected. It is possible that full-time organizing work was too demanding for single mothers. Buffum, however, disappointed with the national office, wondered "if there are any competent organizers in the National Office. Either this is true or nobody there gives a damn about NWRO anymore; and that's the way I'm beginning to feel at times." Buffum's frustration exemplified how many people, black and white, recip-ient and staff, had come to feel about the internal politics of NWRO.

Internal tension plagued the welfare rights movement since its incep-tion, revolving around control of resources, decision making, and the structure of the organization. But the question of power and control only became important because of the substantive issues at stake. These in-cluded competing organizing strategies, different analyses of what was wrong with the welfare system, and sexism within NWRO. Recipients val-ued the process of organizing as much as the result. Wanting to politicize and empower welfare recipients, they sought not just to mobilize women on welfare to participate in demonstrations, but to educate them in the long-term goal of social change. They believed that reform of the welfare system required recipients to have confidence, skills, and political acumen. In most cases, this meant giving them the opportunity to run their own organization.

Women in the welfare rights movement also believed that transforming the welfare system involved changing the public's perception of black women as well as making demands on the state for more money or the elimination of specific regulations. For them, the "welfare problem" was complex and as much about ideology as facts and figures. By the 1960s the welfare system was dominated by myths and stereotypes. Perceptions about black women's sexuality and notions of the black family and the black work ethic justified cutbacks in assistance and provided grounds for work requirements. Ideology shaped public policy and, in this case, bolstered popular support for more punitive and repressive policies.[162] Countering some of the stereotypes of AFDC, women in the welfare rights movement demanded that their work as mothers be recognized and insisted that single motherhood was not a social pathology. They sought to increase their monthly benefits through pressure tactics, and to make a moral claim for assistance as mothers. Their analysis demonstrates how gender is mediated by race and class and the way in which race, gender, and class all shape the welfare system. Not all poor people or women were affected in the same way by welfare policies. Black women were treated differently by welfare officials and viewed differently by the public. This was all the more important in the 1960s when questions of illegitimacy, employment outside the home, and black cultural traits helped define welfare as a black issue.

Women in the welfare rights movement insisted that the battle for public assistance was only partly about power, making demands upon the state, holding demonstrations, and having sit-ins. They believed that an argument for a welfare state based on economic efficiency or self-interest—that everyone would benefit if no one lived in dire poverty—would not be longstanding. Once the costs outweighed the benefits, then concessions would be revoked. By making demands on the state as mothers, welfare rights activists questioned the popular belief that welfare recipients did not work, and the dominant assumption that black women were not primarily mothers. Their battles with the staff and their experiences in the welfare rights movement sowed the seeds of a nascent black feminist ideology, which would only sprout in the early 1970s. Rooted in their multiple identities— as mothers, poor people, women of color, welfare recipients, and community members—it was a distinctive ideology fertilized with their day-to-day experiences and nurtured through political struggle.

CHAPTER 6

The Guaranteed Annual Income and FAP

The most ubiquitous slogan of the welfare rights movement was "welfare is a right." T-shirts, banners, buttons, and posters were emblazoned with that short but provocative phrase. Welfare activists believed, as New York City welfare recipient Jennette Washington succinctly stated, that they "have a right to [welfare] because the Constitution says that everyone has a right to life. Life includes everything necessary to maintain life."[1] In the 1960s, welfare organizers sought to make the right to welfare available to everyone. The movement's early campaigns to bring AFDC under constitutional protection and raise the standard of living for welfare recipients contributed to this goal. The right to welfare, however, was most clearly embodied in the movement's demand for a guaranteed annual income, which would make economic status the only criteria for eligibility and sever the historic link between employment and income. Since the 1966 founding convention, a guaranteed income had been NWRO's long-term goal, but little had been done to explicitly plan or organize for it.

By 1969, NWRO made the guaranteed annual income its main strategy. In that year, the organization entered the national political debate about income maintenance when Richard Nixon proposed his own version of a guaranteed income, the Family Assistance Plan (FAP). The differences between Nixon's and NWRO's plan notwithstanding, the organization seized the moment to influence the direction of legislative reform and implement its dormant long-term goal. Welfare organizers demanded that the federal government replace the current welfare system with a guaranteed minimum income, which would bring all people who fell below that, working or not, up to a decent standard of living. They believed that the guaranteed annual income ought to be a targeted grant, with money going to the poor to lift them above the poverty line, rather than a universal grant given to everyone, regardless of income. This demand was in many ways a culmination of many of the earlier struggles of welfare recipients. A guaranteed minimum income for all poor people, regardless of sex, family status, personal behavior, or employment status, promised to eliminate casework and standardize and simplify the administration of welfare. Raising the living standard of all poor Americans to an adequate level could also ameliorate racial and economic inequality. In addition, divorcing wages from work challenged age-old American traditions, which tied economic well-being to employment.

Although men and women in NWRO had a different rationale for wanting a guaranteed income—the male staff emphasizing the lack of employment opportunities and the female constituency framing the guaranteed income as necessary because of their work as mothers—they united around this goal. The struggle for a guaranteed income revealed the organization's principal strength and prime weakness as a political movement. Nationwide debate about the merits of a guaranteed income enabled NWRO to push its agenda, bringing it to the zenith of its influence. Nixon introduced FAP in part because of NWRO's agitation and political pressure, which contributed to the momentum to reform the welfare system. In addition, NWRO leaders met frequently with members of the Nixon administration, introduced their own guaranteed income bill into Congress, and helped shape the debate about a guaranteed income. It was a moment when welfare recipients had unprecedented influence on legislative debate and policy discussions around welfare. However, over the course of the FAP debate, NWRO became more entrenched in political lobbying instead of organizing recipients and the source of its strength—the grassroots base—eroded. NWRO's attention to national lobbying came inevitably at the expense of the local chapters.

After pushing for a guaranteed income from 1969 to 1972, members of the welfare rights movement realized that revamping the welfare system was a bigger political battle than simply getting a place at the bargaining table. The guaranteed-income debates illustrated the degree of consensus among liberals and conservatives that the poor needed income support. Although they disagreed bitterly on where to establish the minimum income, the nature of the work requirement, and the expansiveness of the program, people across the political spectrum agreed on the need for an income floor. Ideologies of race and gender circumscribed this consensus, however. If the public believed that such support would benefit African American women on welfare, political resistance swelled. The racial and gender stereotypes long associated with AFDC doomed the passage of any guaranteed-income legislation. After FAP failed, many welfare rights activists maintained their commitment to a comprehensive system of economic support. But in the wake of FAP's defeat, NWRO turned its attention to an ideological battle to neutralize or dispel the stereotypes linked to AFDC.

NWRO Turns to the Guaranteed Income

Securing an adequate income for all poor Americans was the first basic principle of NWRO. In its early years, the organization demanded an increase in monthly welfare grants and campaigned for minimum standards to achieve an adequate income. These campaigns brought new clothes, furniture, and other household items to thousands of AFDC recipients in hopes of raising their standard of living. The 1935 Social Security Act measured "standard of need" by requiring states to determine how much money families on ADC needed to live in a healthy and decent way. It did not, however, mandate that they provide that level of support for recipients. Through the Social Security Act, the federal government regulated and set guidelines for ADC, but because it only provided matching funds to states, it could not dictate state benefit levels. Locally administered and controlled, welfare payments in many states fell far short of state-defined standards of "health and decency."

Many local welfare rights organizations demanded that states reassess the cost of living and that AFDC payments match the state-determined level of need. In Washington, D.C., members of the Barry Farms Welfare Movement wrote in a letter to the welfare commissioner that "it is our contention that the budget standards should be revised and raised from the 1957 levels to 1968 living standards. And the new standard must reflect the needs of the recipient."[2] In Ohio, activists waged the most sustained local campaign to bring recipients up to the standard of need. In 1966 members of the Ohio Steering Committee for Adequate Welfare (OSCAW) pressured the governor and legislature to bring AFDC benefits up to 100 percent of the standard of need, implement a yearly cost of living adjustment, issue clothing grants, and allow recipients to keep a portion of their earnings from employment.[3] They invited their state representatives and other concerned people to a mock Legislative Assembly for Adequate Welfare. Ohio Governor James Rhodes did not call a special session of the legislature to increase welfare grants for 1966, as OSCAW demanded, but he did promise to request 100 percent of the 1966 standard of living for the 1967 budget.[4] In January 1967, the organization went to Washington to persuade congressional representatives to raise the AFDC grant. Four years later, in 1971, recipients, social workers, and other supporters, still struggling for an adequate standard of living in Ohio, launched a letter-writing campaign urging the Governor to increase welfare benefits.[5]

The 1967 Amendments to the Social Security Act, which required states to adjust their standard of need by July 1, 1969 to reflect changes in the cost of living, invigorated struggles such as the one in Ohio. Local welfare officials argued that the new regulations required only that states reassess need, not that they pay recipients the new standard. Welfare rights activists, on the other hand, insisted that Congress intended for states to raise benefit levels. The Social Security Amendments provided welfare recipients with a legal argument for higher living standards. Local groups, including OSCAW and the Philadelphia WRO, sued their states for inadequate welfare benefits.[6] And, in 1969, NWRO and the Center on Social Welfare Policy and Law campaigned nationally to ensure enforcement of the 1967 Act, initiating law suits in several states where grant levels fell below the established standard of need.[7]

NWRO's legal test case to guarantee welfare recipients a basic minimum income originated with Governor Nelson Rockefeller's plan to tighten welfare eligibility and eliminate the special-grant system in New York in 1969. Shortly after the New York State legislature approved Rockefeller's reforms in March 1969, the Center on Social Welfare Policy and Law and NWRO filed a lawsuit charging that cuts in welfare benefits without regard to the needs of recipients violated the 1967 Social Security Act. The case, *Rosado v. Wyman*, sought to establish the right to live—that a basic minimum income was a protected right that could not be compromised or violated because of budgetary needs. The Center on Social Welfare Policy and Law argued before the U.S. Supreme Court that the reduction of benefits left recipients in a situation that fell far short of the "health and decency" required by the 1967 Social Security Amendments. Moreover, they claimed that the cuts violated the equal protection clause because a minimum income was necessary to exercise other constitutionally protected rights. That is, denial of basic human necessities, such as food and shelter, jeopardized freedom of speech or assembly since an individual consumed with the work of sheer survival could not effectively exercise these rights. The Supreme Court decided in April 1970 that the state had haphazardly eliminated special grants, but that after recomputing the standard of need, the state had the right to reduce grants to accommodate its budget.

In another case, *Dandridge v. Williams*, lawyers argued that Maryland's practice of setting maximum public assistance grants violated the equal protection clause because the state denied assistance to poor children in large families available to poor children in small families. In 1970, the Supreme Court upheld Maryland's right to set family maximum grants and decide how to distribute its scarce resources. In both cases, the court dismissed the notion that the equal protection clause guaranteed a minimum income or a "right to live" as the Center lawyers argued. Instead it dealt only with the procedural issues—that as long as everyone was treated equally, a state could limit grants.[8] Thus, NWRO was unable to constitutionally establish the right to a minimum welfare payment.[9]

In addition to a legal strategy to secure for AFDC recipients a basic standard of living, the organization also advocated a guaranteed annual income administered by the federal government. NWRO only turned to the guaranteed income in the late 1960s, when it demanded a yearly income of $5,500 for a family of four. This would have addressed problems with caseworkers making arbitrary decisions, variations in AFDC payments among states, and the susceptibility of welfare to the changing winds of local politics. The guaranteed annual income had the potential to radically transform not only welfare, but the meaning of citizenship and government responsibility. It would have established the principle of social citizenship —that everyone was entitled to a basic standard of living.

Citizenship in the United States has historically been tied to civil and political rights: freedom of mobility, the right to vote, the right to own property, freedom of speech, and the right to due process. The welfare rights movement's inclusion of economics as a "right" of citizenship was both radical and very much a product of its time. Numerous economists and scholars took similar positions in the 1960s. Sociologist T. H. Marshall, for example, made a case for expanding public services such as health care and education and implementing a guaranteed income to provide a "modicum of economic welfare and security." He argued that after granting political and civil rights, the state should extend social rights, which could ameliorate some differences in status and create a level of social stability. For him, citizenship also required duties and obligations such as work.[10]

In 1962 conservative economist Milton Friedman, who advised Barry Goldwater in the 1964 presidential campaign, proposed a negative income tax, in essence the same thing as a guaranteed annual income. He argued for "governmental action to alleviate poverty; to set, as it were a floor under the standard of life of every person in the community."[11] Friedman hoped to abolish the patchwork of government programs, such as public housing, agricultural subsidies, and social security, and replace them with a federal cash grant allowing individuals to purchase what they needed in the free market.[12] John Kenneth Galbraith, the liberal counterpoint to Friedman, also endorsed the idea of a negative income tax in his influential book *The Affluent Society*. He wrote,

> For those who are unemployable, employable only with difficulty
> or who should not be working, the immediate solution is a source

of income unrelated to production. In recent years, this has come extensively into discussion under various proposals for guaranteed income or a negative income tax. The principle common to these proposals is provision of a basic income as a matter of general right and related in amount to family size but not otherwise to need. If the individual cannot find (or does not seek) employment, he has this income on which to survive.[13]

Galbraith went on to say that "an affluent society" that is "compassionate and rational" would provide for all people a basic minimum income to ensure "decency and comfort."[14]

Economist Robert Theobald, author of *Free Men and Free Markets* (1965) and editor of the influential volume, *The Guaranteed Income: Next Step in Economic Revolution* (1966), also hailed the benefits of a guaranteed income. Suggesting that scientific and technological advancements necessitated a break in the link between jobs and income, he proposed a basic economic security of $1,000 per adult and $600 per child provided by the government as an "absolute constitutional right." He argued that the "extraordinary success" and "productive potential" of Western nations made it "possible to provide every individual in rich countries with a decent standard of living while requiring a decreasing amount of toil from the vast majority of the population."[15]

Theorists discussing social rights in the 1960s came to similar conclusions for different reasons. Their justifications varied from concerns about an inefficient government bureaucracy to problems of unemployment in an age of automation, but they all grappled with how the nation might provide a basic level of economic security for its citizens. The most radical economists proposed divorcing income from employment, past and present, and basing it only on need. They envisioned a future in which human labor was minimal or obsolete. The welfare rights movement found its niche in this mold, pushing the boundaries of the discussion by insisting that a guaranteed income provide a level of security without obligation to work outside the home. This position dovetailed with that of many economists in this period.

Although few welfare recipients had read the political theory about social citizenship, some expressed similar sentiments. Loretta Domencich, an Indian organizer of a WRO in Milwaukee, explained,

A lot of things that Welfare Rights is going after are Indian ideas—Guaranteed Adequate Income is really an Indian concept. It is the way the Indians themselves ran their early communities . . . The dignity of the individual says that no matter what a person's capabilities are, whether he is the leader or whether he is a person who is crippled or elderly or can't do anything, he still has a place in the tribe.[16]

Before mid-1969 Wiley and other movement participants spoke generally about how a guaranteed income could address inadequate benefit levels in the current welfare system, but support was inconsistent. As late as early 1969 George Wiley was skeptical about a guaranteed income:

The talk is going around in this country that welfare is very undignified, since poor people have welfare. We need to convert to a system that gives a nice, clean slice of money, call it a flat grant or a guaranteed income that gives you a certain amount of money and you can't get any more, they say. They are doing that because they want to close the door on the possibility of people getting their real needs met.[17]

Frances Fox Piven and Richard Cloward outlined in a 1966 article how welfare rights activists could achieve a guaranteed annual income. They encouraged welfare rights organizers to add to the welfare rolls people qualifying for, but not receiving, assistance. This would precipitate a "profound financial and political crisis," and city governments, unable to deal with the crisis, would pressure the national government to implement a guaranteed annual income.[18] Although NWRO never adopted Piven's and Cloward's crisis strategy, the organization designed campaigns to enhance its power to push for reforms such as a guaranteed income. Some local groups, such as the Pittsfield Association of Parents for Adequate Welfare in western Massachusetts, were unfamiliar with the concept of a guaranteed income. But as the movement evolved, most welfare rights activists came to see the guaranteed income as the most obvious solution to a system that not only provided inadequate money, but also demeaned its recipients.[19] The guaranteed annual income was, as the Philadelphia WRO explained in an internal document, "the out-growth of the concept of welfare as a right."[20]

For example, OSCAW did not advocate a guaranteed annual income during the 1966 Walk for Adequate Welfare, but proposed that the nation "study all possible alternatives to demoralizing public assistance programs."[21] In fact, some OSCAW members were initially wary of the guaranteed income proposal. One participant wrote,

I thought that the subject and the discussion on Guaranteed Annual Income was also very enlightening and interesting with respect to the clients reaction towards the program. They felt that

Guaranteed Annual Income would just be another hold-out and would keep the people on welfare really lazy and having no self-respect. The welfare recipients want to be able to work and earn up to poverty level.[22]

By 1968, however, OSCAW staunchly backed a guaranteed income, arguing,

The economic strength and growth of this nation make it not only possible but necessary that increases in our national wealth be invested in our human resources. A guaranteed annual income which becomes possible in the era of economic abundance could, for the first time, free man from the threat of starvation and other economic threats. Nobody would have to accept conditions of work merely because he would otherwise be afraid of starving; a talented or ambitious man or woman could learn new skills to prepare himself or herself for a different kind of occupation.[23]

The next year, after failing to raise AFDC benefits, OSCAW argued even more stridently:

Each person in this country has a right to life. Our society must *subsidize life*. We call upon this nation to eliminate the inadequate, humiliating hodge podge of programs like food stamps, welfare and the others that perpetuate poverty. This country must get down to business with a Guaranteed Adequate Income for all.[24]

Other organizations underwent similar transformations. Mothers for Adequate Welfare (MAW) in Massachusetts, hoping to "relieve those people who had real problems," lobbied to centralize welfare in the state, but noticed little improvement in the welfare system. Three years later, in 1969, a MAW member explained that they "are not interested in the public welfare system as it exists now" but instead worked toward "some kind of income maintenance program."[25] The Los Angeles County WRO, which called in 1966 for a "decent standard of living," demanded in 1969 a "guaranteed adequate income."[26]

The Citywide Coordinating Committee in New York hoped a guaranteed annual income would lead to greater client autonomy to decide what items to have in their homes, how to raise their children, and with whom to cohabitate. As the special-grant campaign came to a close in 1968 with the implementation of the flat grant, Hulbert James advocated "replacing the welfare system by some form of guaranteed annual income," which he believed should be "close to six thousand dollars a year for a family of four."[27]

Gender Differences and the Guaranteed Income

By 1969 most people in the welfare rights movement had coalesced around a guaranteed annual income, but their explanations for why one should be instituted varied. The main divide seemed to be between the predominantly middle-class male staff and the black female members. Staff members rationalized a guaranteed income in a number of different ways. The primary justification was the lack of available paid employment. George Wiley explained in 1970, "We agree that there must be an economic incentive to work. But we know there aren't enough jobs to go around *now*, that there is 5.5% unemployment. In New York 70% of the welfare recipients who answered a survey said they would rather work, but there were no jobs available to them at their skill level, or there was no day care for their children."[28] Wiley and many staff members did not challenge the traditional notion of the work ethic or the trend requiring welfare recipients to take paid employment. The guaranteed income was a practical solution to support people who could not find jobs. In addition, Wiley argued in an interview in 1970 that the guaranteed income could decrease racial inequality: "if we had an adequate income system it would raise the income of probably 75 to 80% of the black population in this country."[29] The national office produced a position paper characterizing the welfare system as an example of "institutionalized racism" because a disproportionate number of "black people fall into [AFDC, the category] that pays the lowest level of benefits and mistreat recipients most."[30] Wiley and other national office staff, promoting traditional nuclear families, also saw the guaranteed income reducing the number of female-headed families. They blamed the welfare system for the rise in single-parent families. One staff person said, AFDC "does undermine the family structure because in most states a family headed by an able-bodied man cannot get welfare no matter how poor it is. So to get help for his family the father has to leave."[31] The guaranteed income, available to two-parent and single-parent families, would resolve this problem.

Women in the welfare rights movement, on the other hand, believed that a guaranteed income would acknowledge and compensate them for the valuable work they performed as mothers. Johnnie Tillmon summarized the position formulated by many welfare rights activists at the grassroots level when she proposed in 1971 that we could resolve the "welfare crisis" and "go a long way toward liberating every woman" in the country if the President issued "a proclamation that women's work is *real* work" and paid women "a living wage for doing the work we are already doing—child raising and housekeeping."[32] A welfare rights group in Ohio advocating a guaranteed income argued that "raising five kids is a full time job" and mothers should have a choice about taking paid employment.[33] Cassie Downer, Chair of the Milwaukee County WRO, explained, "A guaranteed adequate income will recognize work that is not now paid for by society. I think that the greatest thing that a woman can do is to raise her own children, and our society should recognize it as a job. A person should be paid an adequate income to do that."[34] For women in the welfare rights movement the guaranteed annual income was both an avenue to achieve women's economic independence and compensation for their work as mothers, because, as an NWRO pamphlet read, "most welfare mothers are needed full-time by their own families."[35] Foreshadowing a key political position of black feminists, these women sought autonomy to decide whether to work inside or outside their home.

Many African American and women activists called for self-determination and personal autonomy in the 1960s. Women's liberationists, for example, touted women's right to choose to work or to have an abortion. But these demands rang hollow if a woman couldn't pay for an abortion or had to work out of necessity. Black community organizations demanded control over the schools in their neighborhood. But community control would only marginally improve the education of poor children in inner-city schools without the resources to purchase textbooks, pay teachers adequately, improve facilities, or decrease class size. Similarly, poor women needed financial support to allow them to make choices that middle-class and wealthy women could make. By advocating a guaranteed annual income, welfare rights activists hoped to eradicate the financial constraints restricting poor women's choices about work, motherhood, and personal relationships, and realize autonomy in less abstract and more concrete terms.

Like Wiley, many welfare recipients also identified labor market problems such as low wages and scarcity of jobs.[36] The Philadelphia WRO, in an undated analysis of a guaranteed-income plan entitled "A Federal Family Investment Program: The Basic Goal of the Philadelphia Welfare Rights Organization," argued that the welfare system kept "a cheap slave work force on hand . . . to collect its garbage, sweep its streets, harvest its crops, and fight its wars." The organization argued that by failing to provide adequate resources, the labor market and the welfare system relegated poor women and men to the most menial and lowest-paying jobs and denied them the opportunity to parent properly. The Philadelphia document continued:

> The federal government must now invest in families to assist them economically to raise their children. Families produce this country's most important natural resource: CHILDREN.[37]

Thus, women in the welfare rights movement explored the practical issue of availability of jobs but emphasized the ideology associated with AFDC. By redefining "work" to include mothering, or parenting, they hoped to remove the social stigma tied to the receipt of welfare, which assumed that mothers on welfare didn't work, were lazy, and contributed little to society. The Philadelphia WRO suggested that a guaranteed income "would eliminate the stigma of being a special class or more accurately caste within our society since it is for all families."[38]

For women in the welfare rights movement, a guaranteed annual income served several purposes at once. It forced the state to recognize housework and child care as legitimate work, freed women from dependence on men, debunked the racial characterizations of black women as lazy by acknowledging their work as mothers, and gave women a viable option to degrading labor market conditions. This analysis integrated their multiple realities and many social positions: as mothers, women, poor people, workers, African Americans, and welfare recipients. The guaranteed income would have a perceptible impact on how the poor related to the labor market and women's position in the family. It promised to reshuffle national interests, making women's and children's security a priority. It would improve the economic situation of poor people and women and thereby remedy, to a degree, racial and gender oppression.

Despite the differences between men and women in NWRO, they found common ground in the demand for a guaranteed annual income. In June 1969 the organization officially launched its campaign for a guaranteed income of $5,500 for a family of four without any other income.[39] To maintain a work incentive, it proposed a tax rate of 66 percent on the earned income of recipients. Under the plan a family of four would be entitled to some level of assistance until their income reached just under $10,000. An NWRO brochure outlined the proposal:

Earnings	Final Income Under the NWRO Adequate Income Plan	Final Income Under the 1966 Tax Law
$ 0	$5,500	$2,460 (Avg. AFDC grant)
$2,000	$6,166	$2,000
$3,000	$6,499	$3,000
$4,000	$6,832	$3,860
$5,000	$7,165	$4,710
$7,500	$7,998	$6,814
$8,246	$8,246	$7,432
$9,000	$8,497	$8,057
$9,887	$8,792	$8,792

NWRO's guaranteed income plan replaced all existing public assistance programs. Administered by a single federal agency, it determined eligibility based on a person's declaration of need, with spot checks. NWRO's plan offered fair hearings, free medical care, legal services, day care, as well as emergency grants to "take care of critical or unusual situations" and to bring recipients up to standard at the grant's inception.[40]

In establishing a minimum standard of living, NWRO rejected the federal government's official poverty line as an accurate assessment of the cost of living. Although social scientists had measured poverty since the turn of the century, in 1965, Mollie Orshanky of the Social Security Administration created the official poverty line, basing it on the Department of Agriculture's "economy food plan."[41] According to NWRO, the Department of Agriculture claimed that the poverty line "is not a reasonable measure of basic money needs for a good diet" and should only be used in emergencies.[42] NWRO reported, "Government surveys show that 70% of the families with food budgets equivalent to the [Department of Agriculture's] low cost food plan have nutritionally inadequate diets."[43] They believed that even if states raised welfare benefits to the official poverty level, recipients would still be mired in poverty. NWRO based its figure of $5,500 for a family of four on estimates by the Department of Labor's Bureau of Labor Statistics, which developed three budgets, low, moderate, and high, for an urban family of four. NWRO relied on the lower budget, which provided for "maintenance of health and social well being, the nurture of children, and participation in community activities."[44] Although NWRO's basic minimum income exceeded the poverty line, it did not provide for a "lavish" lifestyle and excluded money for items such as a car, cigarettes, out-of-town travel, use of a laundromat, long-distance phone calls, or life insurance.[45]

On June 30, 1969, the third anniversary of the Ohio march that launched NWRO, 20,000 people demonstrated nationwide in support of a $5,500 minimum income. NWRO renewed its interests in the guaranteed income in mid-1969 partly because of the movement's internal developments. But in addition, it supported more ardently the guaranteed income because of the larger political climate that increasingly focused on the merits of a basic minimum income. The national dialogue about a guaranteed income created a political opening and impelled the organization to more clearly define this aspect of its agenda. In effect, these larger developments pushed the guaranteed income to the forefront of the movement's agenda.

Consensus on Income Maintenance

People from vastly different political places supported one or another version of income maintenance plans in the 1960s. The plans varied by scope, administration, and level of assistance. The guaranteed income advocated by NWRO allocated direct cash assistance to any poor person whose income fell below a basic minimum. The Negative Income Tax, administered through the Internal Revenue Service (IRS), functioned in the same way to subsidize individuals whose income was too low to pay taxes. These IRS payments brought recipients up to a minimum standard and, as with the NWRO plan, payments decreased as income rose. Children's allowances subsidized families with children, regardless of family income, with cash payments. Other proponents linked a guaranteed income to employment through government job creation and wage subsidies. Despite the many differences, all of these plans established a basic minimum standard of living for recipients and simplified and standardized payments across the country.

Republicans, conservatives, liberals, and radicals proposed income maintenance plans. The Ripon Society, a Republican youth group, endorsed in 1967 the Negative Income Tax as a way "to help the poor." They urged the Republican Party to adopt the Negative Income Tax and make it the "cornerstone" of an alternative to the War on Poverty.[46] The National Council of Churches wanted to make a guaranteed income "available to all as a matter of right . . . with need as the only eligibility criterion and adequate standards of assistance."[47] In 1966 the Southern Christian Leadership Conference called for the government to "ensure all American families an income of at least $4000 a year."[48] The Black Panther Party's Ten Point Program demanded full employment or a guaranteed annual income. In 1968, 1,200 economists, including James Tobin, John Kenneth Galbraith, and Robert Lampman, lobbied Congress "to adopt this year a national system of income guarantees and supplements."[49] And in the same year, the National Association of Social Workers presented a petition to the Democratic and Republican Party Conventions "For the Elimination of Poverty in the U.S.A.," calling for "an assurance of job opportunity for those able to work and, for all Americans, a guaranteed minimum income."[50]

In the electoral arena, some Democrats steadfastly supported guaranteed income plans, while others vacillated. President Johnson never championed such a reform. The War on Poverty, his major antipoverty achievement, expanded social services and created avenues for the poor to organize. It relied most heavily on education and job training and provided people with opportunity, not cash, to get out of poverty. The slogan of the Office of Economic Opportunity was "a hand up not a hand out." Wilbur Cohen, Johnson's Secretary of Health, Education, and Welfare, backed a Negative Income Tax, but never endorsed it publicly because he felt it was not politically feasible.[51] In addition, liberal Democrat Robert F. Kennedy didn't advocate a guaranteed annual income, arguing during his 1968 presidential campaign that "the answer to the welfare crisis is work, jobs, self-sufficiency, and family integrity; not a massive new extension of welfare."[52]

Over time, many Democrats came to embrace a guaranteed income.[53] Sargent Shriver, head of the Office of Economic Opportunity, concluded in 1968, "We think that [the negative income tax, graduated work incentives program,] or some similar scheme is an ultimate necessity as part of the War on Poverty."[54] President Johnson formed several task forces and a Presidential Commission on Income Maintenance, made up of economists, community leaders, and businessmen, to study the benefits and viability of an income maintenance plan. In its final report, released in 1969 just two months after President Richard Nixon proposed his Family Assistance Plan, the Presidential Commission, also known as the Heineman Commission, endorsed a guaranteed-income system. Headed by Ben W. Heineman, president of North West Industries, the Commission characterized poverty as an economic, not a cultural problem, and proposed a guaranteed income with a floor of $2,400 a year for a family of four.

The relatively widespread support for the guaranteed income in the 1960s represented a common understanding among economists, policy makers, activists, and politicians about how best to address problems of poverty. Proposals to alleviate poverty varied, and included increasing production to stimulate growth, altering the behavior and characteristics of the poor through job training or consumer education, expanding opportunity for those "left out" of the widening prosperity, and instituting a guaranteed annual income to provide a safety net for the poor. Despite these differences, Democrats and Republicans, liberals, some conservatives, and some radicals in the 1960s converged on several points. First, they assumed that poverty and unemployment were anomalies in postwar America and needed to be explained, understood, and addressed. They argued that everyone could be brought up to a minimum standard of living through economic growth, training programs, or a more generous welfare state. Second, fewer people contended that giving money to the poor was detrimental to their character, a long-standing belief shaping the American welfare state from poorhouses to FDR's New Deal. Friedman saw cash assistance as a superior alternative to government-run services because it would shrink the bureaucracy of the federal government and strengthen the market economy. Similarly, Galbraith argued, "The corrupting effect on the human spirit of unearned revenue has unquestionably been exaggerated as, indeed, have the character-building values of hunger and privation."[55] Finally, many people addressing poverty in the 1960s proposed that the federal government actively work to stabilize the economy and meet the basic economic needs of its citizens. Liberal, conservative, and some radical promoters of a guaranteed annual income ultimately had faith that

American capitalism could create profit for the wealthy, satisfy the middle class, and ameliorate the problems of the poor at the same time.

Nixon and FAP

The policies of Richard Nixon, the first president to propose a guaranteed income, reflected most clearly the consensus around poverty and welfare in the 1960s. Elected in 1968, Nixon ran on a platform of law and order as well as his "secret plan" to end the war in Vietnam. During the campaign he distanced himself from the previous Democratic administration and catered to more conservative sectors of the population. The year 1968 seemed to be a moment of extreme crisis, testing the limits of U.S. international power and the strength of cherished American political and economic ideals. In response, Nixon crafted an image of someone who would clamp down on disruptive protests and advocate for the "silent majority," the large number of Americans disdainful of political activism. Nixon promised to restore order to a country shaken by urban rebellions, military setbacks in Vietnam, violent confrontations between demonstrators and police, assassinations of several national figures, and threats of violent insurrection, however feeble those threats might have been. He successfully associated his Democratic and liberal opponents with the dissenters and promised a different political course.

Upon taking office, however, Nixon's policies seemed to extend, rather than reverse, the Democratic liberal agenda. Nixon appointed both Democrats and Republicans to his administration, instituted cost-of-living adjustments for Social Security recipients, expanded the food stamp program, and excluded the poorest Americans from paying income tax. He repealed a freeze on federal AFDC payments to states for women who had children out of wedlock, which passed as part of the 1967 Social Security Amendments with President Johnson's support. He formed the Urban Affairs Council, a domestic counterpart to the National Security Council, making urban policy a priority in his administration. In addition, his choice of Democrat Daniel Patrick Moynihan to head the Council indicated his liberal orientation on some issues.[56]

Nixon's attempts to restructure welfare also belied his conservative rhetoric. In August 1969 he proposed replacing AFDC with a new federal program, the Family Assistance Plan (FAP). While nearly every politician and policy maker in the country wanted to reform welfare, the particular direction of Nixon's reforms is instructive. He sought to simplify the program, reinforce the work ethic, and provide a basic level of financial support for poor male- and female-headed families. Cost cutting was not his central goal. FAP assured a minimum annual income of $500 for the first two household members and $300 for each additional family member, which worked out to $1,600 for a family of four, plus $864 in food stamps. Nixon set his base income very low but even this amount significantly improved the living standard for families in the South, where both welfare payments and wages were lower than in the rest of the country. Mississippi, the state with the lowest benefits, paid the average AFDC family $396 per year in 1965.[57] FAP required states with higher welfare payments to supplement the federal income until recipients reached their current standard, ensuring no reduction in recipients' benefits. Designed to assist single-parent and two-parent families with children, whether working and not, FAP included both a work requirement and a work incentive. Able-bodied adults and parents of school-age children had to register for work or training. If they refused, their monthly allowance was withheld, but their children continued to receive assistance. Working heads of households could keep the first $60 a month they earned and anything beyond that was taxed at a rate of 50 percent. The federal subsidy, therefore, also brought working families up to a minimum standard. A working family of four received assistance until their total income reached $3,920. Nixon also allotted $600 million for job training and child care.[58] Under FAP, the federal government, not states, determined eligibility standards and spot-checked income to verify eligibility.[59] NWRO had demanded this kind of certification for many years. Whatever problems were inherent in FAP, it was a dramatic move for a Republican in the 1960s. As one HEW staff member explained: "I couldn't believe that I was sitting there talking to a Republican administration that seemed eager for this new solution [negative income tax] that six months before I hadn't been able to convince [Democrat] Wilbur Cohen it was the right thing to do."[60]

Although support for income maintenance plans crossed political boundaries, over the course of the decade, the term "guaranteed annual income" became associated with leftists and liberals. Indeed some historians have erroneously attributed income maintenance proposals exclusively to the Democratic Party.[61] Similarities in liberal and conservative proposals notwithstanding, partisan politics greatly influenced the contours of the debate. Democrats eagerly embraced phrases like income maintenance and guaranteed income to champion the needs of the poor and underprivileged. Conservatives framed their proposals differently, using terms and language such as work ethic and reducing the welfare rolls. In keeping with his conservative image, Nixon distanced himself, at least rhetorically, from those on the left and argued that his proposal was not a guaranteed income.[62]

Despite Nixon's insistence that FAP was not a guaranteed income, it looked very much like a guaranteed-income proposal. In his 1969 televised speech he proposed "that the Federal Government build a foundation under the income of every American family with dependent children that cannot care for itself."[63] FAP provided a minimum income for all American families and federalized and standardized welfare payments. Potentially costing the federal treasury between $4 billion and $6 billion a year, it extended benefits to more than 10 million people in poor working families with children and tripled the number of children aided by the federal government.[64] Nixon's welfare reform proposal reinforced the work ethic and attempted to placate the working poor, but his plan also spoke to the needs of the welfare poor. He justified his reforms by arguing that "the tragedy [of the current welfare system] is not only that it is bringing states and cities to the brink of financial disaster, but also that it is failing to meet the elementary human, social, and financial needs of the poor."[65]

So why did Nixon support a guaranteed annual income? The welfare system had been severely criticized since the early 1960s because of rising welfare costs, a political tug-of-war between federal and state officials, the perceived inefficiency of the system, ongoing political protest, and the belief that AFDC did little to bring people out of poverty. The racial and gender composition of the welfare rolls and assumptions about recipients' loose morals and lack of a work ethic undoubtedly contributed to negative characterizations of AFDC. The short of it is that by the end of the 1960s few people were happy with the welfare system. A scholar at the time noted that "general dissatisfaction with the failure of Public Welfare to deal adequately with the massive problems of poverty" resulted in "far-reaching proposals" by economists, social scientists, and politicians.[66] Many people believed that if poverty could be diminished, then other social problems would be alleviated as well. The National Advisory Commission on Civil Disorders, appointed by Johnson, traced urban unrest to the depths of poverty in northern ghettos and, in particular, the welfare system. "The Commission believes that our present system of public assistance contributes materially to the tension and social disorganization that have led to civil disorders."[67] Consequently, it urged establishing an income maintenance program.

The increases in the welfare rolls in the late 1960s fueled criticism. From 1960 to 1965 the number of families on AFDC increased by only 200,000. After that, however, the number rose dramatically from one million people in 1965 to over two and a half million in 1970.[68] Primarily a state-run program, to which the federal government contributed funds, AFDC and its escalating costs burdened state and local officials most heavily. In regions with high AFDC payments, such as the Northeast, state governments bore a greater portion of the AFDC budget. For example, in 1965 the federal government gave Alabama, Mississippi, Georgia, and South Carolina between 75 and 78 percent of their public assistance budgets. But California, New York, Massachusetts, and New Jersey received between 41 and 48 percent of their public assistance budgets from federal funds.[69] These states more acutely felt the burden of higher costs and experienced most of the increase in the welfare rolls. In New York, one of the hardest-hit states, the number of families on AFDC more than doubled from 133,000 to 272,000 between 1965 and 1969.[70]

The rising caseload and skyrocketing expense led to demands for greater federal funding and responsibility. New York Governor Nelson Rockefeller, for example, favored federalizing welfare to address the escalating costs.[71] In 1971 New York City Mayor John Lindsay filed suit in federal court contending that federal and state mandates of welfare payments were unconstitutional because of the city's ultimate responsibility for the expense. The court ruled against the city arguing that states opted to participate in the welfare system.[72] These examples illustrate that the issue of funding seemed to pivot on local versus federal responsibility rather than how to get people off the welfare rolls. Although some states attempted to remove recipients from the welfare rolls and cut benefits, in the late 1960s many local officials sought greater federal assistance to resolve the welfare crisis. The 1969 Supreme Court decision declaring residency requirements unconstitutional also increased pressure for a federalized system. Local officials feared that freedom of mobility would encourage welfare recipients to move from states with low monthly payments to states with higher monthly payments. Thus, the rising welfare rolls created a crisis of major proportions for local and state officials, particularly in a few key areas such as New York, increasing the momentum to replace AFDC with a new program such as FAP.

Nixon also faced growing pressure from grassroots groups, the inner-city poor, and African American activists.[73] The country had experienced massive unrest in urban centers, where local officials seemed unable to control looting, arson, and general mayhem. Urban rebellions such as those in Watts, Detroit, and Newark as well as political campaigns by SCLC, SDS, SNCC, and NWRO drew attention to black poverty. Radical groups, such as the Republic of New Afrika and the Black Panther Party, declared independence or threatened political instability, while also articulating a critique of the political and economic system. The Panthers, for example, organized free breakfast programs and SCLC launched "Operation Breadbasket" in Chicago to highlight problems of poverty and unemployment. The politically explosive climate and social disorder undoubtedly forced Nixon to consider addressing the inadequacies of the nation's economic policy. It led to pressure to dismantle an inefficient welfare system, and replace it with something that could provide basic support as a way to mollify the inner-city malcontents.

NWRO's protests and organizing helped push the Nixon administration and the public at large to a point of dealing seriously with welfare reform. Members of the welfare rights movement raised issues of minimum standards, discretionary power of caseworkers, the bureaucratic tangles of AFDC, and as well as other inadequacies. Explaining why the country needed a guaranteed income, the Heineman Commission, in 1969, echoed the welfare rights movement:

> This legislation meets some of the most serious gaps in our Public Assistance Programs; namely, the failure of many States to meet full need as defined by the States, the failure to update these standards to reflect changes in the costs of living, the absence of monetary incentive to work because of the 100 percent tax rate on the earnings of adults, and the failure to provide emergency assistance for needy children and their families.[74]

In the late 1960s, the specter of welfare mothers protesting and demanding more money and better treatment contributed to a sense of crisis of the welfare system, which was as much a political crisis as a fiscal crisis. Whether observers were sympathetic, scared, or fed up with the demonstrations, they nearly all concluded that something had to be done.

Taxpayer organizations, citizens groups, and political pundits similarly advocated reforming the welfare system because of concerns that tax dollars unwisely supported people capable of taking a job, but refusing to do so; that welfare eroded the work ethic; that the welfare system contributed to the rise in single-parent households; and that welfare simply cost too much. Nixon and his aides had little doubt about the need to completely revamp the current welfare system. At a private meeting on welfare reform, Nixon articulated the overwhelming pressure to reform AFDC: "We're doing it because we can't go on with the present system . . . I am not for improving the present system . . . We don't know whether [FAP] will work, but we can't go on with the present system."[75]

The needs of the working poor and apprehension about undermining the work ethic also guided welfare reform. Most proposals to revise AFDC expanded the welfare system to include two-parent families and the working poor, with the goals of encouraging employment and preventing fathers in poor families from leaving home so mother and children could qualify for assistance. Including the working poor in an assistance plan minimized the danger of eroding the work ethic, since people who worked also qualified for assistance. But expanding the program to include the working poor and two-parent families also greatly enlarged the number of people eligible for assistance and increased costs. Administration officials grappled with how to justify more people on welfare and keep costs low yet have an effective work incentive. Robert Finch, secretary of HEW, suggested constructing a conservative argument about the benefits of including the working poor in the proposal: "To include the working poor is not basically a 'leftish' or liberal initiative, but rather an essentially conservative move which, while appealing to liberals, is rooted in the concept of making work as rewarding as welfare in a system which in many cases has reversed the incentives."[76] The Nixon administration was less concerned about cost than reducing the number of single-parent families and reinforcing the work ethic. Although politicians preferred to contain the costs of any reform, most proposals, including FAP, would have cost more than the present AFDC program.

FAP seemed to address the concerns of people across the political spectrum: conservatives and liberals troubled about single parenthood, the working poor who felt left out of the Great Society, local politicians burdened with paying for welfare, taxpayers frustrated about supporting a system they believed was inefficient, free-market advocates who favored cash assistance over government services, and radicals demanding an end to poverty and discrimination. At a Cabinet meeting to discuss FAP, Nixon's Urban Affairs advisor, Moynihan, argued: "We now have terror in our cities . . . We've got to move on this issue or we will be recorded as the people who sat by." Budget Director Robert P. Mayo concurred with Moynihan on the necessity of radical reform: "I think what Pat [Moynihan] has said is almost gospel. I fear that we may have a revolution if we don't do some of these things."[77] Hoping to stave off political protest and pacify the inner-city poor, the Nixon administration intended to abolish welfare as they knew it and replace it with a system that more adequately met the needs of the poor. Moynihan outlined four reasons why the administration should support FAP.

(1) It will give money to women and children who desperately need it, mostly in the South . . . (2) It will give financial relief to large cities that are now providing decent enough welfare payments, but at great costs to their taxpayers. (3) It will help the Negro poor . . . (4) It will be received by the white middle and working classes as a measure that will impede northward migration. I have some doubts whether it actually will, but it will be taken as such, and that is a plus.[78]

There was no consensus within the administration about the guaranteed income. Commerce Secretary Maurice Stans, for example, opposed FAP and suggested in a memorandum to the President that instead of relying on federally supported income maintenance, the poor and unemployed "reduce their living costs by self-help means such as growing gardens, fishing and hunting."[79] Aside from the lone dissenters, however, the parameters of debate reveal an astonishing level of agreement among administration officials committed to expanding and raising welfare benefits and enlarging the role of the federal government. The central disagreement was whether to maintain the AFDC structure with national minimum standards fully paid by the federal government or replace AFDC with a federally run program with a basic minimum income. Both plans offered job training and placement. Whatever the differences, nearly everyone in the administration concurred on the need for national minimum standards for welfare recipients.[80]

Nixon's support for a guaranteed income was less an indication of his own political orientation—he was still to the right of most public figures of the time—than a reflection of the political climate. The political instability, widespread protests, and urban rebellion instilled fear in many Americans about the future of the nation. Nixon's far-reaching welfare proposal attempted to either placate the poor or co-opt radical protest. While heralding black capitalism as black power, Nixon at the same time felt pressure to offer palliatives to constituencies he likely perceived as his enemies. Political volatility in an era of expanding social programs led to an unlikely moment when Nixon and some radical groups spoke the same language and battled for control of the same playing field. People on both the right and left worked to establish new priorities and meet the needs of the underprivileged within the framework of the existing economic system, albeit they were motivated for different reasons and feuded fiercely about exactly how to define those priorities. In 1966 two researchers at Mobilization for Youth, a demonstration project in New York City, commented on the widespread support of guaranteed income proposals:

> Given [the economic and political] forces [of the postwar period], the proposition that there ought to be a federally guaranteed level of minimum income as a right was an inevitable outcome. This proposition has been stated with increasing frequency in recent years, and its sponsorship has ranged across the political spectrum, from right to left.[81]

Both liberals and conservatives lauded Nixon's Family Assistance Plan. Wilbur Cohen, Johnson's secretary of HEW, commented about FAP, "Yes, I think it's heading in the right direction because it's adopting most of the ideas that the Democrats have advocated for quite a number of years."[82] The weekend after the announcement of FAP, the White House was flooded with phone calls and telegrams, the overwhelming majority supporting the proposal.[83] In an October 1969 Harris Survey 47 percent of Americans favored FAP and only 17 percent opposed it.[84] James Reston, a columnist for the *New York Times*, wrote,

> A Republican President had condemned the word "welfare," emphasized "work" and "training" as conditions of public assistance . . . but still comes out in the end with a policy of spending more money for relief of more poor people than the welfare state Democrats ever dared to propose in the past . . . He has cloaked a remarkably progressive welfare policy in a conservative language . . . He has insisted that poverty in a prosperous country must be eliminated.[85]

The administration prided itself on the cross-section of support for FAP. Robert Finch, Secretary of HEW, believed this reflected "the fact that Family Assistance is a sensible though revolutionary plan—that it commends itself to persons of all persuasions who seek a workable solution to the crisis in our current welfare system."[86]

NWRO and FAP

NWRO saw Nixon's proposal as a window of opportunity for the welfare rights movement, a potential step toward a guaranteed income. Initially, rather than oppose FAP, NWRO sought to amend it to more closely resemble its own guaranteed-income proposal. Objecting vociferously to FAP's low monthly payment and the work requirement, NWRO also denounced FAP for its lack of provision for cost-of-living increases, emergency grants, Medicaid, guarantees of due process, or assistance to families without children.[87] The organization sought to influence the legislative outcome as well as the parameters of discussion about income maintenance. NWRO criticized Nixon's proposal and eventually launched a nationwide campaign to "ZAP FAP," submitting instead its own legislative bill for a guaranteed income.[88]

Criticisms of FAP reflected the divisions within NWRO between the middle-class male staff and female recipients about the guaranteed income.[89] Recipients opposed the work requirement because they believed it impeded women's ability to properly raise their children. In a 1969 statement to the House Ways and Means Committee, which was considering Nixon's proposal, Beulah Sanders explained:

> Surely the mother is in the best position to know what effect her taking a particular job would have on her young school child, but

now we are told that for welfare mothers the choice will be made for them, work for the mother, government centers for the children, the government decides.[90]

They adamantly believed a mother should choose whether or not to work. Sanders continued, "NWRO is for adequate jobs for all men who are able to work. We are for adequate jobs for all mothers who freely decide that it is in their own and their children's' best interest for them to work in addition to their primary job as mother and homemaker."[91]

The men in the movement did not object as staunchly to the work requirement as did the women. Wiley and other staff members opposed forcing mothers of small children to work, but as Nixon stated quite clearly in his speech proposing FAP before Congress in 1969: "It is not our intent that mothers of preschool children must accept work."[92] Wiley supported a work incentive, however, arguing that any guaranteed-income plan should have "a certain degree of reverence for the Protestant ethic, which infuses all of us in and out of the welfare system, and therefore should provide economic incentive so that recipients who try to improve their economic situation by work can actually do so, and hopefully work their way off the welfare system."[93] Moreover, Wiley advocated including the working poor, believing this would blunt the sharp distinction in the public mind between people on welfare and people who work. In other literature produced by the National Office, the staff wanted FAP to provide *"guaranteed adequate jobs!"* Further down the list, it stated, much less forthrightly, FAP should ensure "that no mother is forced to work at times when she is needed in the home to care for her children."[94] Wiley emphasized not the legitimacy of recipients working, since he "revered the Protestant work ethic," but the lack of jobs and methods of encouraging people to work. As with NWRO's own guaranteed-income proposal, women and men in the welfare rights movement had different approaches to the meaning of work. Women wanted their work as mothers to be recognized while men continued to speak primarily in terms of employment outside the home.

Despite their differences, both the men and women in the organization shared the view that FAP "fails to provide *adequate* income to meet basic human needs."[95] Arguing that $1,600 a year was simply not enough for a nutritionally adequate diet or a decent standard of living for a family of four, NWRO advocated a higher minimum income. Nixon and NWRO did not disagree about the principle of a minimum-income standard, but about where to set that standard.

In 1970, NWRO drafted its own guaranteed-income proposal for legislative debate in Congress.[96] Introduced by Senator Eugene McCarthy, Democrat from Minnesota, and endorsed by twenty-one members of the

House of Representatives, the Adequate Income Act of 1970 called for $5,500 for a family of four. The bill had no work requirement, but included a work incentive so recipients' earnings were not taxed at 100 percent. The basic minimum income for nonworking heads of households was $5,500, and the working poor received federal subsidies until their income reached $10,000. In February 1971, taking into account inflation, NWRO's National Coordinating Committee raised the minimum income to $6,500.[97]

NWRO, as always, combined a strategy of confrontational protest with peaceful negotiation and compromise. Organizers threatened disruption while working within the system to gain political influence. During the FAP debate, they attempted to build support among Congressional representatives. In October 1969 Beulah Sanders, George Wiley, and Carl Rachlin testified before the House Ways and Means Committee as it deliberated about FAP. NWRO members also developed position papers, met with elected officials, and encouraged local chapters to send letters to Washington.[98] Wiley outlined for congressmen his specific criticisms of FAP and asked them to support amendments.[99] After FAP passed the House of Representatives, NWRO lobbied the Senate in the spring of 1970, demanding that "the Senate Finance Committee hear from organized poor people."[100] During the Committee hearings on FAP, activists from the Greater Cleveland WRO, the Minnesota WRO, and Sanders and Wiley from the National Office all requested to testify about the bill.[101]

In addition to lobbying, NWRO organized militant actions. In one interview, Wiley threatened a "violent revolution" if the nation failed to respond to the needs of poor people.[102] Welfare rights activists planned demonstrations and marches across the country in the spring of 1970 as the Senate debated FAP. One hundred twenty-five people attended a rally in front of the White House. In May, Wiley and a group of NWRO members held a seven-and-a-half-hour sit-in at the office of Robert Finch, Secretary of HEW. The next day they seized an auditorium at HEW and held hearings on their adequate-income proposal. Calling FAP "an attack on poor people," on June 30, NWRO organized nationwide demonstrations in support of the $5,500 plan.[103] In the fall, it encouraged groups around the country to plan "People's Hearings" with social workers, politicians, labor unions, welfare recipients, welfare officials, and community leaders.[104]

By late 1970, NWRO opposed the passage of FAP, rather than working to amend it.[105] George Wiley explained: "We felt the bill was highly complicated, we thought in many cases, it was unworkable, we thought there were many things about it that were unfair . . . but at the same time there were certain features of it, up until that time, that caused us to feel, that perhaps could be modified into an acceptable instrument."[106] In November 1970, Senator Eugene McCarthy sponsored unofficial Senate hearings, attended by 350 NWRO members, twenty-three of whom spoke passionately about the drawbacks of FAP and called on the eleven Senators present to oppose it. Shortly after that, on November 20, 1970, the Senate Finance Committee voted down the first version of Nixon's Family Assistance Plan.

After the Senate Committee voted FAP down, a revised version, known as HR1, was introduced into the House of Representatives in early 1971. Even less acceptable to NWRO, HR1 guaranteed an annual income of $2,400, but eliminated food stamps, resulting in less money for families than under FAP. Unlike FAP, HR1 expected mothers with preschoolers to register for work and did not require states whose current benefit exceeded the minimum income to maintain benefit levels.[107] Throughout 1971 NWRO lobbied to defeat the new version of FAP. It held a two-day workshop, attended by WRO members from around the country, to coordinate strategy to oppose FAP. It encouraged local groups to meet with representatives, send telegrams, and write letters.[108] In September, groups across the country, in places as diverse as Maine, Nevada, Washington, Illinois, and Missouri, planned anti-FAP protests. Neil Downey, an NWRO volunteer, wrote a protest song to the tune of "Battle Hymn of the Republic":

> Oh, they've got a bill in Congress
> that they're calling H.R.1;
> And it's coming to destroy us,
> every single mother's son
> F-A-P is what they call it,
> and you'd better understand
> The letters stand for Family Annihilation Plan.
> Gory, gory, what a helluva way to die!
> Gory, gory, what a helluva way to die!
> Gory, gory, what a helluva way to die!
> Kill FAP instead of me![109]

HR1 passed the House of Representatives in June 1971, but the Senate voted it down in October 1972.[110] It failed, in part, because Nixon lost interest and did not actively back the legislation. Although Nixon publicly reaffirmed his support for FAP in 1972 and two years later promised to reform welfare, he no longer prioritized this kind of legislation. His 1974 message to Congress did not mention a basic minimum income.[111]

By 1972, NWRO attacked Nixon for FAP, as well as his appointments to the Supreme Court, his opposition to busing, and his position on Vietnam.[112] Wiley threatened "to organize the poor into a powerful political unit and . . . to see that the Richard Nixons of this country get voted out of office with their racist attacks on the poor."[113] The honeymoon was over.

Nixon had abandoned the strategy of placating the left and liberal community. Counseling a new political course, his chief of staff suggested there is a

> need to reexamine all our appointments and start to play to *our* group, without shame or concern or apology. Should feel our way, *appear* to be listening to critics, but we have now learned we have gained nothing by turning to the other side. [The President] has changed his mind, reached a new conclusion. Is convinced policy of sucking after left won't work, not only can't win them, can't even defuse them.[114]

During the 1972 election, NWRO and local welfare rights groups petitioned other presidential candidates, including Eugene McCarthy and George McGovern, to endorse the $6,500 guaranteed-annual-income proposal in exchange for the organization's support. The Omaha Welfare Rights Council promised to "leaflet and canvass in poor communities urging support for McGovern" because he backed NWRO's guaranteed-adequate-income proposal. Despite the persistence of NWRO, this last-ditch effort to push for its guaranteed-income proposal in the national electoral arena proved futile. Although NRWO participated in the welfare debate and influenced the political climate, its proposal stood little chance of being adopted.

NWRO's Influence

Assessing whether NWRO's opposition sealed the fate of FAP is difficult. Piven and Cloward argue that NWRO did not sway the decisions of Senate Finance Committee members who voted against FAP, attributing the plan's failure to southern resistance and wavering support by Nixon.[115] Gilbert Steiner similarly argues that the organization had minimal influence on the national level.[116] But even if the organization did not impact Congressional votes, its involvement on the national level, nevertheless, reveals the parameters of debate and points to some influence by NWRO. Both NWRO and Nixon concurred that the poor ought to participate in policy making. During the Nixon administration, NWRO had access to the most powerful political offices. Leaders of NWRO had faith that as representatives of the poor they could influence federal welfare policy. More strikingly, they relied on Nixon to provide them with the opportunity. Johnnie Tillmon and George Wiley wrote to Nixon during his first year in office: "When you were elected you promised to 'bring us all together.' You asked that we lower our voices and listen to one another. Poor people have tried to give you the chance to hear our concerns and to show that you respect our needs and want to include us *in—in* your new consensus, *in* this country."[117] NWRO members met regularly with administration officials, submitted proposals and recommendations, and were recognized as representatives of the poor. Nixon, for very different reasons, gave a voice to the poor and included them in policy discussions about welfare.

During the first month of Nixon's presidency, NWRO representatives met with members of the administration to discuss welfare reform. In January 1969 the NWRO Executive Committee met Moynihan, Nixon's Director of Urban Affairs, at the White House. According to Tim Sampson, NWRO staff member, the meeting indicated NWRO's rising stature: "Moynihan wanted to show George that he was interested in George's movement and that he was concerned." In February they met with Robert Finch, Secretary of HEW, to discuss state compliance with federal AFDC regulations. Members of the welfare rights movement also participated on the FAP recipients' advisory committee.[118] They contacted HEW officials several times about federal administration of AFDC and FAP.[119] In a 1969 press release, Wiley said, "The meetings represent a recognition by the Administration of the growing power of NWRO's grass-root membership which has more than doubled in the past 17 months and now includes more than 30,000 members in 250 local WROs in 100 cities."[120] The Nixon administration may or may not have recognized NWRO's "growing power"; it, nevertheless, maintained close contact with the organization.

When dissatisfied with the pace of change, NWRO submitted to HEW a list of grievances:

> NWRO began serious negotiations with HEW at the outset of your administration. We brought specific complaints of illegal practices and regulation counter to Federal Law to Secretary Finch's attention in February and March. There has been no forthright response to these complaints and although discussion has continued, HEW officials have not yet taken action to enforce federal welfare regulations guaranteeing due process to welfare recipients and those in need who apply for aid.[121]

In response, HEW presented to NWRO a seven-page, single-spaced letter addressing their list of demands.[122] Shortly after that, Elliot Richardson, the new Secretary of HEW, assured George Wiley in a telegram that "the department is eager to continue its discussion with the NWRO and other similar organizations."[123] The Nixon administration and NWRO fashioned together a democratic process that acknowledged poor people's participation in shaping policies affecting them. In one of the most important developments of the 1960s, poor people were considered an indispensable part of policy discussions about poverty. Input and dialogue were the catchwords cementing the new consensus on policy making and the new vision for democracy in America.

NWRO leaders' participation in the policy-making process—their frequent meetings with members of the Nixon administration, their representation on local welfare boards, the introduction of their proposal into Congress, and the legal struggles they waged—indicated a change in the role and status of NWRO. On one level, the organization reached its pinnacle of influence. NWRO had argued for many years to include the poor in the decision-making process. During the Nixon administration, for the first time, they had access to the highest echelons of power in the country. AFDC recipients discussed, debated, and voiced their opinions about social welfare policy on a national level. Although Nixon and NWRO differed on the meaning of representation, both agreed that input of the poor was imperative when reforming social and welfare policy. Rather than excluding poor people, Nixon presented himself as committed to open lines of communication, dialogue, and mutual decision making. It is unlikely that Nixon had truly been won over to this new vision of politics, as his abrupt reversal in 1972 indicates. He probably felt political pressure and saw few other avenues to defuse the protests and disruption. But this ostensible agreement, while falling short of full-fledged commitment, might make its mark on the historical record, as well. In other moments politicians would not hesitate to demonize and ostracize their opponents. These meetings between NWRO and federal officials reflected the administration's attempt, however meager, to pay lip service to needs of welfare recipients, and in the process it legitimated the articulated needs of people on welfare. Never before had the poor felt such entitlement to government assistance, or participation in the policy-making process. Never before or since has there been such consensus on including welfare recipients in the making of social policy.

It is unclear whether NWRO altered the policies and practices of HEW. In hindsight, looking at the administration's turn away from concern about the poor after 1972, it is doubtful that NWRO had any direct, lasting impact. But NWRO's influence on welfare policy has to be measured in broader terms than simply the failure or passage of a legislative bill or whether HEW implemented NWRO's suggestions. NWRO helped shape the political climate, making welfare a public issue and shifting the terms of the debate. It raised public awareness about the inadequacy of welfare benefits and the need to raise recipients' standard of living. Organizations otherwise unconcerned about welfare took positions because of NWRO. In the 1960s few elected officials or political organizations could stand on the sidelines as the debate about welfare raged around them.

NWRO's lobbying and mobilization presented an alternative and compelled many political organizations to take a position for or against FAP.[124] In 1970, the National Federation of Social Service Employees passed a resolution favoring an income floor of $5,500.[125] The National Association of Laymen, an organization of 12,000 Catholic laymen, officially endorsed NWRO's demand for a guaranteed income of $5,500.[126] In April 1971, twenty-one congressmen, including the Black Caucus, supported a welfare reform bill for $6,500 for a family of four. In May 1971 the National Women's Political Caucus endorsed the $6,500 plan.[127] Historians of FAP, Vincent and Vee Burke argue that NWRO mothers had political influence "far beyond their numbers" and that many liberals refused to support FAP "unless at the same time Congress acceded to the demands of leaders of the National Welfare Rights Organization."[128]

NWRO's exhibited its political influence in December 1969 when welfare rights members attended a White House Conference on Food, Nutrition, and Health. Through persuasive argument and political posturing NWRO convinced participants from across the political spectrum to endorse their $5,500 guaranteed-income plan. A reporter for the *Daily World* wrote, "The conference became a major embarrassment to the Administration precisely because of its representative character. How could Nixon ignore the demand for a $5,500 annual income, supported as it is by the National Council of Churches, the AFL-CIO, the United Auto Workers and others totaling a majority of the people."[129] Another commentator observed,

> In one way it is a miracle that this administration, whose constituency is the smug and comfortable, called a hunger conference at all . . . It was also a miracle that a conference which started out looking as if it were pre-packed with advertising men and food industry executives and programed [sic] to discuss "nutrition" instead of hunger should have been turned around by a handful of militants to the point where it voted $5,500 a year for a family of four. This was largely the triumph of those wonderful black welfare mothers who run the National Welfare Rights Organization and the skilful [sic] aid of George Wiley.[130]

NWRO's political positions also became a measure to judge other proposals. During the legislative debate, moderates in Congress formulated compromise bills between FAP and NWRO's Adequate Income Bill. Senator Abraham Ribicoff, in 1971, introduced amendments to FAP calling for a minimum income of $3,000 a year for a family of four, to be increased to $4,000 a year within three years. Congressman Donald Fraser proposed

$3,600 a year. These compromise bills suggest that NWRO's political posi-
tion, in effect helped set the terms of the debate. Their proposal of $5,500
made the Nixon proposal seem inadequate and prompted liberals and
moderates to search for a middle ground. Thus, Nixon and NWRO, in
effect, became the two poles of debate about welfare.

Race, Sex, and Social Policy

Despite the unprecedented level of consensus about the need for some kind
of income support, no minimum income proposal for AFDC recipients
passed in the 1960s or 1970s. That failure cannot be attributed solely to the
inflation and recession of the early 1970s or public clamoring to reduce the
size of the welfare state, as many historians have argued. Tight economic
circumstances decreased support for massive new federal outlays and the
public was increasingly reluctant to expand assistance to the poor. But simple ideological beliefs to expand or reduce the welfare state did not drive social reform in the 1960s. Examining the dialogue about social policy and
the passage of social programs suggests that the public and policy makers
did not oppose all assistance programs, only those colored by racial and
sexual stereotypes that branded recipients undeserving. For example,
Congress implemented in October 1972 Supplemental Security Income
(SSI), a need-based federal income guarantee for the elderly, blind, and disabled. SSI made old age assistance, aid to the blind, and aid to the disabled,
which were previously state-run programs and considered part of "public
assistance," federally funded and administered programs. SSI passed with
little discussion or fanfare and federalized part of the welfare state, leaving
the portion serving poor women and children—AFDC—in the hands of
state and local officials. In addition, unlike AFDC, SSI and Social Security
were pegged to inflation with automatic cost-of-living-adjustments
(COLAs). This meant that even if AFDC budgets remained constant the ac-
tual value of monthly benefits might decrease as inflation rose. In addition
to SSI, in December 1970 the federal government expanded the food stamp
program and raised benefits. And in 1972 it increased Social Security benefits across the board by 20 percent. Between 1969 and 1973 Social Security
benefits rose by 52 percent, adding $25 billion to the cost of welfare.[131] Thus,
the welfare state expanded for some people, but not for others. This legislation widened the gulf between the deserving and undeserving poor, further stigmatizing single mothers.

Political mobilization and electoral power might explain the expansion
of the welfare state for the elderly. Older citizens had pushed for government assistance as early as the New Deal. In the 1960s and 1970s, groups
such as the Gray Panthers and the National Council of Senior Citizens

(NCSC) formed. Started by Maggie Kuhn and other retirees, the Gray Panthers, an intergenerational, multi-issue group, tackled the war in Vietnam, health care, and racism. The NCSC, established in 1961, lobbied for expanded cash benefits, health care, and services for the elderly. With a dues-paying membership of around 250,000 in the mid-1970s, the NCSC more than likely had close to 3 million people in its senior citizen clubs nationwide.[132] This surely influenced the vote of some political officials. A staff member to Representative Wilbur Mills said of the 1972 Social Security bill: "Mills knew the increase was a good thing for the aged and, accordingly, a good thing for him at the polls . . . there are a lot of organized senior citizens in this country and their voting turnout is relatively high."[133] While important, this single factor of voting power cannot explain the complex unfolding of government policy and public opinion in the 1970s. It doesn't account for the expansion of benefits for the blind and disabled or the increases in funding for food stamps. Political mobilization, moreover, doesn't necessarily reap positive political results. Public perceptions that a politician caters to a particular constituency might hinder his or her chances of reelection. Had there been strong public sentiment opposing benefits for the elderly, politicians would have had to weigh the potential loss of those votes with the gain of elderly votes. Thus, while voting power might have influenced the allocation of resources in the early 1970s, more critical was the makeup of the constituency. Many Americans considered the elderly, disabled, and working poor worthy of assistance; and disproportionately black, poor, single mothers unworthy.[134]

The Talmadge Amendments, strengthening the coercive features of the Work Incentive Program, passed Congress unanimously in December 1971. Rather than allow states to determine which recipients to refer to the work program, the Talmadge Amendments required all recipients with school-age children to register for work. Recipients who did not register received no benefits and those states that did not refer at least 15 percent of their adult AFDC population to WIN lost federal funds. Recipients without jobs were placed in a public service employment program in exchange for their welfare check. Politicians passed SSI and the Talmadge amendments within a year of one another, demonstrating that as the welfare state expanded for certain sectors of the population in the 1960s, it became more constricted and punitive for one group in particular: poor women on AFDC. This indicates the influence of race on shaping social policy in U.S. history.[135] The merits of small government and the availability of funding seemed less important in guiding the reforms than racial/gendered assumptions about who deserves support and under what circumstances.[136]

The fate of income maintenance plans such as FAP also rested on assumptions of potential beneficiaries. Guaranteed-income proposals not tied to reform of AFDC and that did not see AFDC recipients as the primary beneficiaries received the most support. Negative Income Tax Experiments conducted by OEO and Friedman's and Galbraith's proposals relied on a model of a two-parent family with a working father. These economists and policy makers formulated a guaranteed income to benefit a typical two-parent, male-headed, and, implicitly, white, family; people they believed were poor because of circumstances beyond their control, such as regional economic depression, technological advancements, or low wages. OEO organized a controlled experiment of two-parent families with a working male in New Jersey to test the feasibility of a negative income tax. This and other similar experiments in the late 1960s and 1970s examined whether breadwinners would choose not to work and whether extra disposable income would be wasted if they were guaranteed an income. The study concluded that breadwinners reduced the number of average working hours by only a very small amount and that families spent additional income on housing and durable goods.[137]

Like these other proposals, some politicians packaged FAP as a plan with a strong work incentive to assist two-parent working households.[138] In his opening statement to Congress, Representative Wilbur Mills endorsed FAP as "a supplement to the income of the individual who is working and not making enough to supply his family with the ordinary needs of life, but who is not now on welfare." Furthermore, to disassociate FAP beneficiaries from the stereotypical welfare recipient, he claimed that over half the working poor lived in the South, many in rural areas, and 70 percent were white.[139] By and large, congressional conservatives who believed FAP contained an effective work incentive and would benefit the working poor supported it. But, in reality, FAP could not be disentangled from welfare or the politics of race. NWRO's activism helped identify the program in the public mind with welfare and with militant black women on AFDC. In addition, FAP was billed, in part, as welfare reform, as a solution to the multiple problems plaguing AFDC. In 1969 Nixon justified the Family Assistance Plan in this way: "Whether measured by the anguish of the poor themselves or by the drastically mounting burden on the taxpayer, the present welfare system has to be judged a colossal failure."[140] Liberals and conservatives, favoring or opposing FAP, connected FAP to AFDC. The debate, moreover, had obvious racial overtones. Welfare policy is often analyzed in class terms, but race and gender contributed to the failure of FAP.[141] Using scare tactics, conservatives charged that FAP would add millions to the welfare rolls.[142] In addition, many people were concerned that FAP—a guaranteed income—would discourage people (black women in particular) from paid employment. Senator Russell Long of Louisiana, powerful chair of the Senate Finance Committee, summed up his racially coded position clearly in a statement to Elliot Richardson, secretary of HEW, during FAP committee hearings: "I can't get anybody to iron my shirts!"[143] During the hearings Long also worried about the racially tainted issues of "illegitimacy and fraud."[144] Long's opinions dominated the Senate debate about FAP and, according to the *New York Times*, he served as a "one-man blockade" for FAP because he refused to report the bill out of committee.[145] The logic behind FAP had everything to do with the present welfare system.

The stereotypes and snapshot images of black single mothers on AFDC, who many assumed were lazy and promiscuous, dominated the FAP debate. Concern abounded that FAP would encourage the dependency that many people believed characterized the current welfare rolls. Russell Long argued that FAP's work incentive was ineffective because current work training programs gave mothers "absolute veto over whether she will agree to the provision of day care for her children."[146] Most important here is the use of the pronoun *she*. In his analysis of FAP, Long focused, not on two-parent families, but on single mothers, who he believed didn't want to work. The stereotypical African American woman on welfare had become the pivot around which the FAP debate revolved.

The guaranteed-income debate reflected a seldom acknowledged level of consensus in the late 1960s. People across the political spectrum, with exceptions such as Ronald Reagan and George Wallace, embraced the belief in a guaranteed minimum standard of living. Nixon's and NWRO's welfare reform proposals are the most striking examples of the level of consensus.[147] The unity in the political debate is obscured because Nixon and NWRO adopted militant postures and claimed to be public enemies on opposite sides of the battle lines. However, liberal ideas of government intervention in the economy, work opportunities as a strategy to end poverty, and political representation of the poor in the policy-making process informed Nixon's and NWRO's welfare reform proposals. There was also widespread support for a work incentive or requirement among many economists, the Nixon administration, and much of the NWRO staff. NWRO staff and progressives in Congress argued only for a work incentive, rather than a work requirement, because women on welfare, they suggested, were willing to work and they did not need to be forced. But they all believed in the principle of the work ethic. Finally, NWRO attended meetings with the administration and conferences about welfare reform, was recognized as a legitimate representative of the poor, and worked to influence the outcome of social policy. Nixon, NWRO, and other advocates of a guaranteed income operated under a set of assumptions that had come to define liberalism in this period.

The push for welfare reform by both the moderate right and the left, while radical in language and posture, was negotiated within a dominant liberal paradigm in the 1960s, which cannot be tied to the Democratic Party. As Nixon summed up,

> I realize that there is a ready disposition, whenever we confront an ill that is still uncorrected in America, to cry that "the system" is corrupt, or "the system" has failed . . . It is a system that embraces compassion and practicality; it has given us the abundance that allows us to consider ending hunger and malnutrition . . . It has a capacity for self-correction, for self-regeneration.[148]

This liberal paradigm was characterized by a faith that people at the time had in the American political system and their sense of the abundant wealth of the nation. Welfare recipients in Ohio explained:

> The economic strength and growth of this nation make it not only possible but necessary that increases in our national wealth be invested in our human resources. A guaranteed annual income which becomes possible in the era of economic abundance could, for the first time, free man from the threat of starvation and other economic threats.[149]

Women in the welfare rights movement were an exception to the consensus around the guaranteed income. Although they concurred on the need for a minimum standard of living and wanted the poor to be recognized as a political force, they differed with others about how to define work. They challenged the assumption by many on the right and the left that women at home with their children did not work and they wanted society to recognize women's work as mothers. Thus, men and women in the welfare rights movement disagreed, not about whether poor black women deserved assistance, but why they deserved assistance and the best way to enact a guaranteed income.

After Nixon took office in 1969, NWRO devoted its energies to national political reforms and lobbying. The rapid legislative changes on the national level and the possibility of input propelled NWRO onto the national stage. NWRO's demand for a guaranteed annual income addressed many problems with the current welfare system that the organization identified: the work disincentive, meager monthly grants, the discretionary power of caseworkers, and extensive application procedures. Ensuring everyone a basic minimum income, through either work, an allowance from the government, or a combination of the two, attained their goal that "welfare is a right." NWRO worked to enact its own legislation and influence policy, but did so at the expense of grassroots political organizing. As its political base dwindled, the public climate became more hostile, and it became increasingly clear that a guaranteed income would not be implemented legislatively, NWRO considered new political strategies. This transition in the welfare rights movement strengthened the movement in some ways, but also divided it irreparably.

CHAPTER 7
Decline of the Movement

In the early 1970s, the welfare rights movement reached a critical juncture. The struggle for a guaranteed income bill had consumed NWRO for several years, draining it of resources and detracting from grassroots organizing. Still, the struggle to implement such a bill legislatively seemed futile. At a crossroads, movement leaders contemplated a new strategy. Relentless internal debates about how to deal with these new obstacles brought to the fore the many undercurrents of tension and conflict. The most glaring division remained that between the mostly male staff and female constituency. NWRO leaders grappled with how to address the deep-seated negative popular attitudes, and, at times, downright hostility that the movement had encountered.

Keenly aware that the battle for welfare rights would have to be fought not just in welfare offices and the halls of Congress, but in the arena of public opinion as well, both staff and recipients took notice of the racist and sexist stereotypes of black women embedded in debates about welfare. Vocal, public demonstrations reaped fewer concessions from welfare officials because of the greater public hostility toward welfare recipients. Consequently, welfare rights activists pondered how to build popular support for their position. The staff wanted to expand the movement to include the working poor and men in order to minimize the focus on black women. The women, on the other hand, sought to demystify the stereotypes and misconceptions by remolding the image of AFDC recipients into one of women who worked and contributed to society. Drawing inspiration from the burgeoning women's movement, they increasingly identified as feminists. At the same time, an internal struggle for power and concern about control within NWRO heightened their consciousness as feminists. Women in the welfare rights movement who had articulated the elements of a feminist analysis since the mid-1960s became convinced, by the early 1970s, of the need for an organization run by and for welfare recipients. When they gained control in 1973 and pursued a feminist agenda, however, the movement had already begun its decline. Membership rolls shrank, the political climate became more hostile as the public and policy makers clamored for greater cutbacks in AFDC, and many staff members with fundraising skills left because of the internal conflict.

Public Hostility

Toward the end of the guaranteed-income struggle, NWRO was floundering. Tight finances, internal struggles, and a loss of direction compounded a less receptive political climate. State officials and welfare administrators, responding to and fueling a white backlash, reduced AFDC payments and winnowed down welfare rolls. Local welfare rights groups fought bitterly to avoid losing ground. Paid membership declined nationally from 22,500 in 1969 to 11,500 in 1971.[1] The future of the movement looked bleak.

Since the welfare rights movement's inception, it had encountered hostility from the white working class, which resented that its hard-earned tax dollars supported supposedly lazy and undeserving welfare mothers. Historians sometimes explain this hostility as a response to the expansion of social welfare programs in the 1960s: that the white working class became angered and disaffected by Great Society programs funded by their tax dollars to benefit the poor and people of color.[2] Indeed, antiwelfare sentiment abounded among sectors of the working and middle classes.

For example, a Pennsylvania woman wrote a letter to the Blair County WRO advocating public assistance for the elderly and disabled, but not for single mothers. The working class, she said, was "tired of seeing all of their hard earned money go to people who do not deserve it or who could be working and supporting their own families."[3] Families on welfare, she argued, received dental care, hospital care, food stamps, "yet, the working man has to pay taxes, which are increasing by leaps and bounds, in order to provide these 'poor' people with such privileges."[4] She contended that welfare programs "undermin[e] the very basis on which this country was founded—free enterprise and the right to work to obtain what you want."[5]

This woman's views were not out of the ordinary. Beginning in the late 1960s, local taxpayer groups emerged around the country and a National Taxpayers Union, founded in 1969, dedicated itself to "lower taxes, less wasteful spending, and the principles of rational and limited government."[6] Taxpayers' organizations crossed political boundaries and addressed such issues as property tax assessment, tax distribution, and government spending. In the early 1970s people on the left also mobilized around taxes, calling on corporations and the wealthy to bear a greater share of the tax burden. By the late 1970s, however, the antitax position had become a prime conservative issue.[7] One recurring theme among tax protesters throughout the 1970s was spending on welfare. Conservatives latched onto this issue to discredit AFDC and social welfare spending. In 1971, Roger Freeman of the Hoover Institution, for example, blamed the welfare state for "imposing an excessive and lopsided tax burden" and thus "sap[ping] the natural growth potential of our economy."[8] Conservatives successfully linked rising taxes and economic straits of the middle and working classes to the expansion of the welfare state by capitalizing on racist and sexist stereotypes about welfare recipients and beliefs about welfare spending.

These working-class views were based on a skewed perception of spending on social welfare. First, the defense budget, not social welfare spending, exacerbated the tax burden in the 1960s. In 1973, for example, national defense cost federal and state governments $79 billion, while public welfare totaled $27 billion.[9] Second, poor people of color were not the largest beneficiaries of the Great Society programs, if spending on education, social security, food stamps, and medical assistance is considered. According to historian Michael Katz, 75 percent of federal social welfare dollars between 1965 and 1971 went to the nonpoor. Statistical comparisons bear this out. In 1973, federal and state governments spent $27 billion on public welfare for the poor, and twice as much, $56 billion, on social security and disability insurance, neither of which is means-tested. In the same year, they spent $19 billion on highways and $7 billion on public housing and urban renewal.[10] In 1975, the federal government spent $13 billion on Medicare for the elderly and $6.5 billion on Medicaid for the poor.[11] In addition, the bulk of the increase in social welfare spending occurred in non-means tested programs. Between 1970 and 1973, the costs of public aid—which included Old Age Assistance, Aid to the Blind and Disabled, and AFDC—increased from $16.5 billion to $28.7 billion. Yet, during the same time period, social insurance—which included social security—increased from $54.7 billion to $86.1 billion. Even though public aid rose at a slightly faster rate than social insurance, it comprised a much smaller portion of the budget. In 1974 public aid comprised 13.9 percent of the total social welfare budget and social insurance 40.6 percent.[12]

Finally, the hostility toward AFDC predated the social spending of the 1960s and is rooted in social and political changes in the immediate postwar period. Welfare rights organizing, other militant protests, and a liberal social program did not generate negative public sentiment about welfare, although it may have aggravated it. Widespread disdain for women on

AFDC can be traced back to the late 1950s and preceded the social reform efforts by Democrats and dramatic increases in the welfare rolls that only occurred in the mid-1960s. It was rooted in the changing racial composition of the welfare rolls, black migration into predominantly white northern communities, and stereotypes about black women's sexual mores and work habits.[13]

Nevertheless, in the early 1970s these attitudes intensified, became more firmly implanted in the public mind, and laced the dialogue and discourse about welfare. Many working-class people had come to believe that welfare recipients were sexually promiscuous, could not control their childbearing, did not want to work, and collected hefty government checks enabling them to live a comfortable lifestyle on someone else's dime. Guy Drake's popular song "Welfare Cadillac," on the charts for six weeks in 1970, was emblematic of these stereotypes:

> Some folks say I'm crazy
> And I've even been called a fool
> But my kids get free books and
> All them there free lunches at school
> We get peanut butter and cheese
> And man, they give us flour by the sack
> 'Course them Welfare Checks
> They meet the payments on this new Cadillac.
> Now the way that I see it
> These other folk are the fools
> They're working and paying taxes
> Just to send my young'uns through school.[14]

The lyrics reflect a sentiment that the working class paid taxes and footed the bill for welfare recipients living the high life. People on welfare were characterized as irresponsible agents of self-inflicted poverty.

These perceptions intensified for many reasons. Historian Ricki Solinger suggests that the postwar discussion of reproductive rights framed as women's choice to bear children reinforced the notion of poor women on welfare as bad choice makers for having children they could not afford to raise, and perhaps made them more culpable for their situation.[15] Consequently, assertions of autonomy and individual self-control by the mainstream women's movement may have exacerbated the political fallout experienced by women on welfare. One woman from Flushing, NY, referring to herself as a "hardworking taxpayer," seemed to provide evidence for this view in a letter to the editor of the *New York Times*: "There is no longer any excuse for illegitimacy to be supported by our welfare laws. Now that we have effective birth control methods and legal abortion, no child should be born to become a burden to society."[16] In addition, images of angry welfare mothers demanding their rights rather loudly and without shame undoubtedly fueled the resentment toward welfare recipients brewing since the late 1950s.[17] The welfare protests may have reinforced the popular conception of the lazy, ungrateful woman on welfare looking for a handout. Opposition to welfare and the welfare rights movement encouraged people already disdainful of welfare to vocally oppose AFDC.

Anger about welfare also tapped into the economic hard times of working- and middle-class Americans. High unemployment, spiraling inflation, and a greater tax burden characterized the early 1970s. The overall unemployment rate increased from 3.5 percent in 1969 to 8.6 percent in 1975. For blue-collar workers, unemployment rose from 3.9 percent in 1969 to 13.4 percent in 1975.[18] At the same time, consumer food prices rose by 20 percent in 1973 and 12 percent in 1974, and fuel prices by 11 percent in 1973 and almost 17 percent in 1974.[19] These economic realities burst the bubble of prosperity and deflated the optimism of the 1960s. Many Americans caught in the quagmire of stagflation began to rethink their own, as well as their government's, political priorities. The 1970s ushered in a new political alignment and a new set of assumptions about political reform. Electoral power shifted from the rustbelt states of the Midwest to the sunbelt states of the Southwest. The strategies of expansive government—solving social problems of poverty, a weak economy, and housing shortages and as a regulatory state—faded quickly.[20] In this political climate welfare recipients became convenient scapegoats for economic distress and helped justify a conservative political turn.

Opposition to welfare often centered on assumptions about recipients' needs and values. Many people believed that a vast majority of welfare recipients could, but refused to, work and simply took advantage of government handouts. In a 1971 Gallup poll two-thirds of respondents supported a program requiring welfare recipients to take jobs in private industry with the government paying most of their salary for the first year.[21] In addition, in a 1972 Boston-area survey, people of all social classes believed that welfare recipients were idle and dishonest, and had more children than they actually did.[22] In most cases, the negative images were racially inscribed, portraying the "typical" welfare recipient as an African American woman. Much of the news coverage, for example, reinforced the connection between race and welfare. From 1972 to 1973, the peak years of discussion of the welfare controversy in popular newsmagazines, 75 percent of the photographs were of African Americans, even though they constituted only 46 percent of welfare recipients.[23] Both the racial- and gender-encoded images and the articulated concerns about tax dollars echoed the long-standing belief that

African American women, considered workers primarily and mothers only secondarily, should be employed—not on relief.

In addition, for a variety of reasons, including opportunism on the part of politicians and sensationalized news coverage, the public blamed increases in the welfare rolls to the liberal Democratic policies of the 1960s. Even though during the 1960s Democratic and Republican positions on welfare did not differ drastically, in the 1970s Republicans and conservatives successfully tied welfare to Great Society programs, and the Democratic Party became the culprit of the "welfare mess." Welfare, liberalism, and the Democratic Party converged in the popular discourse with the politics of race. Americans opposed welfare because of the racial images associated with it; and bolted the Democratic Party became of its association with welfare.[24] They correspondingly concluded that government bureaucracy was inefficient and wasteful. An article in *Newsweek* in 1972, for example, suggested that a bigger problem than individual cases of welfare fraud was the "ineptitude, sloth, mismanagement" by the "welfare establishment."[25] This dialogue laid the basis for a right-wing resurgence that differed from the solutions to the "welfare problem" in the late 1960s when policy makers sought to discipline welfare recipients through greater monitoring and work requirements, and more expensive programs that expanded the welfare bureaucracy. In the 1970s, charges of fraud and mismanagement suggested one conclusion: shrinking the public sector.

The welfare debate was dominated, not by facts, figures, and rational argument, but by stereotypes, snapshot images, and ideology. In the 1970s, journalistic accounts, government reports, political rhetoric, and academic studies highlighted cases of welfare fraud, portrayed recipients as lazy and dishonest, and characterized the welfare bureaucracy as inefficient. A 1975 *New Yorker* article by Susan Sheehan is a good example. Sheehan tells the tale of a Puerto Rican mother of nine on welfare, recounting multiple sexual partners, carefree men, out-of-wedlock births, poor housekeeping, drug use, and indifferent attitudes about paid employment, school, and personal morality.[26] The widely read article reinforced popular misconceptions of welfare recipients as irresponsible and lacking discipline. Sheehan depicted a welfare system supporting a dysfunctional, multigenerational culture of poverty and dishonest recipients who took advantage of the AFDC program. Based on anecdote, rather than scientific study or statistical analysis, studies such as Sheehan's created enduring images repeated and retold when convenient—images of a lazy recipient purchasing expensive items with little regard for money or budgeting. This type of coverage contradicted the notion that welfare recipients were truly poor and instead attributed any hardship to the lifestyle choices of recipients themselves, fostering negative public perceptions of people on AFDC. From the 1960s to the 1970s, the terms of the debate had shifted dramatically from concerns about establishing a basic minimum standard of living to an assessment that very few people on welfare deserved assistance, and that welfare, in fact, damaged recipients. It contributed to the reversal of many of the successes of the welfare rights movement in the early 1970s, putting welfare recipients and the welfare system on the defensive and providing a rationale for reducing the welfare rolls.

New Directions

The hardening political climate combined with the failure of the guaranteed income redirected welfare rights activists. Although implicit in their earlier work, in the early 1970s to counter the public hostility, welfare rights activists began to address more consistently the stereotypes of welfare recipients and the ideological components of the welfare system. A welfare recipient in Milwaukee said:

> Myths are needed to justify the welfare system, a system that cheats the very people it is supposed to help. Myths are needed to discourage eligible, low-paid workers from applying for aid. Myths are needed to divert taxpayer frustrations away from the country's big welfare recipients—the rich and the military—and onto the defenseless, powerless poor. In short, myths are needed to hide the real welfare crisis.[27]

Reflecting the new direction, in 1971 NWRO published a pamphlet, "The Six Myths About Welfare," to set the record straight and correct misconceptions about AFDC. It addressed recipients' childbearing rate, employment history, and benefit levels.

At a retreat in Romney, WV, in 1970, the staff contemplated two new strategies to address recipients' political isolation. George Wiley advocated an electoral strategy to change voting patterns, particularly "of those citizens whose income falls below the $10,000 level." Paralleling Wiley's earlier goal of creating a power bloc of welfare recipients, the new approach would establish a political association of poor people who could vote together to affect change. The other approach sought to ally the welfare rights movement with other oppressed people, a kind of poor people's united front, to bring about a rather undefined "revolutionary change." They would essentially create a grassroots poor people's movement, which would engage in militant actions. In both cases, the staff concluded it was absolutely necessary to expand NWRO's constituency to include others, especially low-income wage earners.[28]

At the Detroit convention in 1969 delegates voted to extend membership to any family earning less than $5,500 a year, a decision Wiley applauded.[29] The following year at the Pittsburgh conference, Wiley pushed to broaden NWRO's agenda to include health care, an issue, he argued, affecting all poor people, not just welfare recipients. He said in a speech: "We have got to get it together on health rights and medical care and with the people who don't make an adequate income but don't get welfare either, and with the aged, and with the disabled—all those people who don't know their rights yet."[30]

Wiley and other staff members hoped that inviting the working poor and unemployed fathers to join NWRO would revive the floundering organization. This strategy may have been, in part, because of organized labor's increased financial support of NWRO in the early 1970s.[31] But, in addition, including the working poor as members, the staff believed, would strengthen the movement, chart a new organizational strategy, and appease the backlash of the white working class against the "dependent" poor. Advocates of this strategy hoped to overcome public hostility. The racist and sexist attacks on the welfare rights movement could be neutralized, they argued, if the constituency encompassed more men and white families. In addition, recruiting the working poor into the movement as beneficiaries of government programs might blur the distinction between the "dependent" and "independent" poor and diminish the stigma of welfare, thus forging a real alliance between welfare recipients and the working poor.

On the grassroots level, staff members began to organize the working poor through wage supplements or home relief, a state-run program giving poor working people a government subsidy for work-related expenses and for dependents. Wage supplements in combination with wages, explained Hulbert James, enabled a working man to earn more than a welfare recipient. Predicting "this would start a whole new movement," he advised welfare organizers to recruit construction workers in unemployment centers because "the time may be coming in this movement when we will have to do some of our own labor organizing."[32] Organizing low-income and unemployed men also dovetailed nicely with their ultimate goal of reestablishing the traditional two-parent family. James explained that wage supplements would keep "men and women together with their families."[33] But the staff also subscribed to a romantic notion of union organizing with all of its gendered connotations. They pictured "workers" not as employed women, but as typical blue-collar, male-dominated, largely white construction workers. The AFDC recipient was a woman, the wage supplement recipient, a man. As one journalist reported, they sought "a new constituency of tough men to support the struggle of the ADC mothers."[34]

These staff members' idealization of masculinity was fed by a broader social trend. Both within popular culture and in activist circles, the macho character became one to which many people aspired or revered. Masculine images permeated radical groups such as the Black Panther Party and the Weathermen, both of which adopted strategies, attitudes, and attire reflecting their male-centered politics. The "blaxploitation" films of the early 1970s captured the sensibility that physical strength would ultimately subvert racism.[35] Even within more conservative and mainstream circles, traditional notions of manhood resurfaced in the early 1970s partly as a response to the perceived instability and erosion of traditional values. A reassertion of masculinity seemed both an antidote to racism and a cure for the popular protests that middle America hoped to quash.

Some welfare recipient leaders at the Pittsburgh Conference expressed doubts about an electoral strategy and resisted the move toward organizing the working poor. Jennette Washington, a New York City activist, explained: "I see that we can't get it through the vote, nothing has been gotten through the vote . . . We don't have political power and we have to keep up the [disruptive] pressure if we want to see our program, that we've been pushing since 1966, come through."[36] The staff believed that recipients resisted the working poor strategy because of self-interest and a desire to maintain power within the movement.[37] Some recipients may have been concerned about personal power, but others differed politically from the men in the movement. They feared the shift to the working poor would dilute the focus on the needs of women and children. Emphasizing rather than retreating from their agenda as poor black women, they countered the public sentiment that women on welfare were lazy and undeserving of support by arguing that as mothers they did work:

> The belief that welfare mothers can work assumes that they are not working now. The work of raising a family, of household tasks, is not considered worthy of even an unjust wage. Scrubbing floors, preparing meals, changing bed linens, sewing, caring for the sick, budgeting, and helping educate and discipline children—all this is very hard work, as every woman knows.[38]

Women in the welfare rights movement placed greater value on motherhood and worked to redefine welfare rights as women's rights. Redirecting the political attention to another constituency, they believed, would not debunk the popular racist and sexist stereotypes about them and thus would have minimal impact on the ideology of welfare.

Despite these differences, staff members pushed ahead with their agenda. They employed the working-poor strategy to reconstitute the organization and to challenge the power of recipient leaders. Wiley stated this explicitly: "The staff will have to organize groups like the working poor without much help from the mothers, and then bring the organized groups into NWRO to challenge the mothers. Through a challenge like this, some kind of accommodation will be worked out."[39]

In the early 1970s, several staff members around the country worked to expand the constituency of NWRO. Wilbur Colom, editor of the *Welfare Fighter*, proposed to the executive committee the creation of a new national newsletter, *Economic Justice*, to be jointly published with other poor people's organizations.[40] Although never approved by the Executive Committee, the proposal indicates the shifting focus of the national office. In Rhode Island, Massachusetts, and New York, welfare rights organizers recruited the unemployed and working poor.[41] In Massachusetts, Bill Pastreich formed a wage supplement organization independent of the WRO. In mid-1969, predating the official expansion of NWRO's membership, he made a case in a letter to Tim Sampson for NWRO to get involved in other issues besides welfare and urged visible demonstrations with working men and old-age-assistance recipients.[42] Frances Fox Piven and Richard Cloward originally outlined the wage supplement campaign, which they believed could build bridges between labor and the poor and could also be "a very handy strike fund."[43] Getting seed money from the two social scientists, Pastreich began door knocking in New Bedford, a mostly white mill town in Massachusetts where men worked in sweatshop conditions for minimum wage. Before the first meeting of the New Bedford Wage Supplement Organization (WSO) in August 1969, he worried the men would not show up. Revealing his interest in not just mobilizing masses, but in creating a new racial and gendered image of "the poor," he said, "A lot of guys will send their wives—we want the guys . . . I'll kill them if they send their wives."[44] More than a hundred people, mostly men, showed up to fill out forms for aid.[45] This laid the basis for a statewide wage supplement association affiliated with NWRO.[46] Just a few months later, however, in January 1970, Pastreich left Massachusetts to organize welfare rights groups in Ohio and Washington, D.C.

Pastreich left Wade Rathke in charge of MWRO. Hired by Pastreich in June 1969 to organize in Springfield, MA, Rathke also saw a need to broaden the movement's base beyond welfare recipients. After working with MWRO, he went to Arkansas in June 1970 on NWRO's payroll to organize the Arkansas Community Organizations for Reform Now (ACORN). Established with the goal of building a "mass-based, multi-issue, multitactical community organization," just seven years later ACORN had nearly 10,000 members nationwide.[47]

Operation Nevada

At the very moment when staff members launched efforts to broaden NWRO's base, the movement encountered dramatic local and state reductions in AFDC. In the early 1970s, staff members and recipients worked tenaciously to reverse state cutbacks in welfare. One of NWRO's most sustained and successful campaigns took place in Nevada. In September 1970, after a random sampling audit, the state of Nevada enacted massive cuts in welfare, claiming that one-half of all welfare recipients earned additional, unauthorized income. It reduced the budgets of 4,500 women and children and cut 3,000 recipients off welfare completely, eliminating nearly one-quarter of the caseload. The state did not give recipients prior notice of termination nor did it inform them of their right to a fair hearing. In one situation, a caseworker told a welfare recipient from Reno, Joanna "Cookie" Bustamonte, on three different occasions to work as a prostitute to support her children.[48] Democratic Governor Mike O'Callahan, who had won a narrow victory with poor and black support, enacted the Nevada cuts, the largest in the history of NWRO.

As with many of NWRO's national campaigns, the mobilization in response to the state cutbacks germinated on the local level. The Clark County Welfare Rights Organization, headed by Ruby Duncan, took the initiative to roll back the Nevada cuts. A group of women on welfare living in the Marble Manor housing project on the Westside of Las Vegas formed the WRO in 1969 and very soon after elected Ruby Duncan as president. Duncan was born in Tallulah, LA, her parents died when she was two-and-a-half years old, and by the age of 8 she plowed fields and chopped cotton. Like many of the African Americans living on the Westside of Las Vegas, she traveled from Louisiana to Nevada in the early 1950s at the age of 18, leaving behind the racial violence of the Ku Klux Klan and low wages in search of better job opportunities. A mother of seven, Duncan worked for nearly 15 years in hotels on the Las Vegas strip in the low-paying service sector, applying for welfare only after a debilitating work-related accident.[49]

When Duncan joined the WRO, she had little political experience. The first campaign sought increases in the shoes and clothing allowance for children on welfare. Despite her inexperience she spoke passionately before elected officials about the difficulties of single motherhood and living on a welfare budget. Inspired and emboldened by the example and contact with the men and women of NWRO, after the welfare cuts Duncan began to consider how to hit Las Vegas "in the pocketbook," a phrase she had heard women such as Johnnie Tillmon utter. Her idea to target on the Las Vegas Strip culminated in a national campaign by NWRO to roll back the Nevada cuts.[50]

George Wiley believed the Nevada cuts were a pivotal turning point in welfare history—a moment politicians might exploit to repeal the gains of the previous years. He urged NWRO to make Nevada an organizational and political priority. At a staff retreat in January 1971, participants adopted Wiley's suggestion to fight the cutbacks in Nevada, which they considered "a training ground for similar actions in other states."[51] The staff decided to launch the Nevada campaign without approval from the National Coordinating Committee. Although staff members polled the executive committee, it had little input in formulating the campaign.[52] In fact, it seemed that the opinions of the recipient leaders mattered little. During the retreat, Hulbert James said, "Whether NCC approves or not is inconsequential, because the action is on anyway. If field members don't approve, they shouldn't expect support from National on local actions, which don't relate to this National campaign."[53] Although the NCC met the following month in Nevada because of the planned campaign, it did not discuss Operation Nevada, focusing instead on FAP and the floor for an adequate income.[54] The planning of Operation Nevada illustrated staff use of the purse strings to push a particular political agenda, regardless of the views of grassroots members or leaders who differed with them.

NWRO designed Operation Nevada to "meet the repression head-on" and put other states on notice that it would not tolerate such illegal, arbitrary, and unjust actions. During the campaign, lawyers, national officers, organizers, recipients from the region, and other well-known personalities descended on Nevada to help recipients file fair hearings and mobilize for mass action to force the state of Nevada to reinstate recipients cut off welfare. A contingent of welfare recipients from Northern California spent two weeks in Nevada organizing and demonstrating against the cuts.[55] NWRO demanded restoration of benefits and removal of the head of the state welfare department.[56] After several failed attempts to meet with welfare officials, the organization planned demonstrations at the welfare department and marches down the central casino and entertainment strip in Las Vegas.[57] At one demonstration in mid-March, 1,000 welfare recipients and supporters, including Dave Dellinger, Jane Fonda, George Wiley, and Ralph Abernathy, marched into the world-famous Caesar's Palace Hotel. As gamblers and tourists stopped to watch, incredulous, protestors singing "we are into Ceasar's Palace; we shall not be moved" paraded into the hotel lobby, downstairs to the casino, and then back out onto the street.[58] The following week, another march down the Las Vegas Strip drew 250 demonstrators. During this protest, in typical fashion combining militance, political accommodation, and the uncanny attempt to creatively raise money, Wiley threatened civil disobedience, but exempted those hotels pledging financial support to NWRO. When security guards blocked entrances to the Sands

Hotel, protestors sat down in the middle of the street and impeded traffic for a half an hour before police arrested those refusing to disperse.[59] Just a few short weeks after NWRO began Operation Nevada, a federal district judge ordered Nevada to reinstate all recipients cut off welfare, arguing that welfare benefits were a statutory right, as ruled in the 1969 Supreme Court Goldberg decision, and that the state's action violated the constitutional rights of recipients.[60]

The welfare rights movement's success in Nevada did not stop the overall trend toward more punitive and repressive welfare policies. Between 1970 and 1980, the median monthly AFDC benefit for a family of four fell from $739 to $552 in constant 1990 dollars. In addition, states employed a number of alternate, albeit legal, strategies, including a cumbersome application process and higher rejection rates, to discourage recipients from applying for or continuing to receive welfare.[61] Nor did Operation Nevada diminish the negative sentiment and public hostility toward welfare recipients. In fact, unfavorable and irresponsible news coverage of the campaign may have encouraged such attitudes. The *Las Vegas Sun* reported in large headlines that Ruby Duncan, a leader of the Clark County WRO and organizer of the Nevada protests, had put her license plates, registered to a 1968 Chevrolet, on a 1971 Cadillac Eldorado. This report undoubtedly nourished the popular misconception that recipients lived "high on the hog" and rode around in Cadillacs. Two days later the newspaper printed in a small article that their earlier report about Duncan was unsubstantiated and, in fact, incorrect.[62] Thus, the victory in Nevada proved to be bittersweet. Self-congratulatory celebration aside, Nevada was a harbinger of more punitive welfare measures, as the staff originally predicted, but one they had little power to thwart. Despite their success, welfare rights activists still faced the fundamental problems of a repressive welfare state and a hostile public.

The Children's March

Consistent with their strategy to deflect the spotlight from black women on welfare and shore up public support, the NWRO staff planned a Children's March on Washington. Although Wiley believed that the March might be "the beginning of a grassroots movement . . . around issues affecting children," in reality, it was NWRO's last attempt at mass mobilization.[63] The staff hoped that the March would put the National Office "back meaningfully in touch with local WRO's,"[64] but, instead, it exposed more vividly differences between staff and recipients, and local and national activists. Designed by the male staff in part to protest Nixon's welfare agenda and to pressure Congress to defeat the Family Assistance Plan, both the planning and the organizing for the march was a top-down affair. Staff members clearly stated, "There is neither the time, nor interest on NWRO's part to develop, at this time, a truly participatory structure of supporting organization."[65] But equally important, as with organizing the working poor, staff member Bert DeLeeuw outlined the campaign with the hope that the march would "change the focus away from welfare moms, work, etc . . . to a much more politically and emotionally acceptable group, i.e., children."[66]

Women in the welfare rights movement refused to shift their focus or redefine their goals because they encountered public opposition. Soliciting charity or cultivating sympathy by relying on images of children was not an adequate response to welfare cutbacks, they argued, particularly when the reason for the cutbacks was the perceived inadequacies of the women. Although they had often made claims for assistance as mothers and asked for items to benefit their children, they always emphasized the work they performed as mothers. Moreover, over time they came to view their struggle as one to assert their rights as women, not just as mothers. Minimizing the attention on women and focusing exclusively on children, they believed, could serve to further circumscribe women's rights. The internal conflict around the Children's March reinforced the belief among women in the welfare rights movement that welfare was a women's issue. It hardened the different visions and strategies of Wiley and the female leadership and ultimately contributed to the resignation of Wiley and many other staff members.

The Children's March on March 25, 1972 drew close to 40,000 people to the Washington Monument. A large proportion of participants were children from the Washington, D.C. area, who attended after the District school board, in a much-criticized decision, endorsed the march and encouraged students to attend. In a carnival-like atmosphere with games and activities for children, protesters chanted opposition to Nixon's FAP. They carried signs reading "Nixon Doesn't Care," and highlighted the particular problems of children in poverty. The speakers list included Ralph Abernathy, Jesse Jackson, Coretta Scott King, Eugene McCarthy, Shirley McClaine, and Gloria Steinem.[67] Despite the large turnout the march garnered little support from grassroots welfare recipients from around the country. Moreover, it gained little publicity, drained NWRO of much-needed resources, and strained internal politics in the organization. The *New York Times* called the protest a "dubious venture on every ground."[68]

The conflict within the welfare rights movement—of whether or not to focus on the pariah class of recipients of government assistance—is indicative of a broader political tension between people supporting targeted programs and those supporting universal programs. Some scholars have argued that in the United States, social programs serving "targeted" and politically unpopular groups, like African Americans, are susceptible to cutbacks and repressive policies. They argue that policy makers should instead develop universal programs, such as social security, benefiting everyone and, in the process, those needing help the most will be assisted.[69]

But only some, not all, targeted programs encountered problems of public support. Historically, popular sentiment considered some targeted groups, such as the elderly, blind, disabled, and students, more worthy and deserving than other groups. Initially, single mothers were deemed worthy of financial assistance. Assistance programs for mothers prior to World War II were restrictive and hardly generous, but not controversial.[70] When black women became overrepresented in mothers' assistance programs, those programs became less popular and even despised. During the 1960s when the United States expanded programs for the poor and increased social spending, AFDC came under severe attack, with benefit reductions, stricter eligibility standards, and the implementation of work requirements. Moreover, retrenchment of AFDC always had bipartisan support.

Within the United States welfare state African Americans have always been categorized as undeserving. Regardless of the type of program, when the constituency of a program shifts from predominantly white to predominantly nonwhite, the program also shifts from popular to despised. The real problem, therefore, is the way in which racism and sexism are embedded in American culture and reflected in the politics of welfare. Instead of camouflaging the truly needy in universal programs that give handouts to those who don't need help, perhaps a better solution would be to make a convincing political and moral claim for those needing assistance. Such an approach would challenge popular myths and stereotypes and may eliminate the stigma associated with particular groups. It will help to create a welfare state serving people unable to support themselves, regardless of societal prejudices, and will begin to close the racial and gender gap. Universal programs, benefiting everyone regardless of need, would not address the fundamental problem of inequality in society or in the welfare state. In addition, they would do little to present a moral case that some people need and should be given assistance because of structural inequalities.

The Children's March heightened tension within the welfare rights movement. Staff and recipients disagreed on whether to deal with the racism and sexism directed at welfare recipients by trying to dispel the myths or by shifting attention away from recipients altogether. Operation Nevada and the Children's March were such top-down affairs, however, that in both cases, professional organizers and celebrities subsumed the voices of local welfare recipients or erased the women's presence altogether.[71] The March sharpened differences between staff and recipients and laid bare the core conflicts about the future direction of the movement. In combination with other factors, it led to a permanent split and ultimate control of the organization by welfare recipients.

The Breaking Point

Tight finances and rocky personal relations compounded the crisis of direction in the welfare rights movement. In 1972, NWRO's financial situation became acute. Wiley estimated the organizational debt at about $150,000. At the same time, important funding sources began to dry up. Support from Protestant churches, the "largest private source" of funding for NWRO, contributing close to half of its 1968 budget, had nearly vanished by 1973 because of a more general decline in funding of social protest.[72] In a letter to supporters, Wiley wrote: "Most of you are probably aware that NWRO has been going through one of the most serious financial crisises [sic] in our history. We had invested every last nickel we could beg or borrow into the Children's March for Survival, the Democratic Convention platform fight and fight against FAP."[73] At the NCC meeting in October 1972, Wiley warned that the lack of funds may force him to close the national office.[74] Questions about bookkeeping procedures and the handling of national finances also plagued NWRO. The organization's accountant wrote to Wiley in September 1971 that they were "dissatified [sic] with the reliability of the internal control . . . lack of written procedures in the fiscal department and the high turn-over of fiscal personnel."[75]

Despite attempts at leadership training since 1969, conflicts between staff and recipients and among recipients on the local level persisted.[76] Organizers had problems communicating, became burned out, and exhibited domineering behavior. Recipient members also criticized recipient leaders for inefficiency and power-hungry behavior. In New Jersey, NCC representative Corethea Saxon expressed dissatisfaction with nonrecipient VISTA workers in New Jersey and asked that they be removed because she found "our groups falling apart due to the workers, seemingly trying to take over rather than help strengthen."[77] Recipient members also complained about New Jersey WRO Chairwoman Barbara Brown. In 1971 Saxon wrote a letter explaining that Brown was not passing along information about meetings or actions.[78] A few months later several New Jersey WRO members wrote letters calling for the resignation of Brown. Jacquline Pierce labeled her "very power hungry." Karen Lewis instructed Brown to "be more for the people and not just for your own ego." The correspondence suggested that, despite her frequent speaking engagements, Brown was out of touch with her membership, had not met many of the people whom she purportedly represented, and communicated poorly with the group.[79]

In Ohio, internal conflict wracked the Ashtabula County WRO. Organizer Fred Barrick, who had worked with a welfare rights groups in Cleveland, went to Ashtabula County to help organize. According to a member of Ashtabula County WRO, Barrick said the group was not organized correctly and would never be recognized by NWRO: "He claimed to have voting power to exclude us from NWRO and also bring charges against the county group for using the WRO name illegally." Several recipient members wrote to Johnnie Tillmon asking how they can be recognized but also expressed concern that Barrick simply wanted to get rid of the executive director of the group and "us[e] WRO to serve his own purposes."[80] Barrick developed a base of support with the Geneva WRO, which eventually broke away from the county organization. Both Barrick and the Geneva WRO wanted the National Office to give Barrick a green light for his organizing efforts.[81] In a letter to Mel Turner of NWRO, Barrick specifically requested "a free hand in organizing Ashtabula County WRO without the interferrence [sic] of the County and Local Chairmen."[82] In this case, a middle-class organizer, concerned about maintaining exclusive control, fostered a split in the local welfare rights group and disregarded the wishes and needs of some welfare recipients. These struggles over power, recognition, and control of organizing regions differed little from the problems that plagued NWRO since 1969.

These power struggles did not reflect the politics of all welfare rights organizations around the country, however. Many local groups had little contact with the national office and few had professional organizers hired by NWRO. During the Washington-centered FAP struggle the local groups that remained active tended to devote their energies to immediate and local issues. They organized around welfare, food, education, and housing.[83] Although rhetorically supporting NWRO's struggle for a guaranteed income, the FAP campaign may have been somewhat abstract and distant. Welfare rights groups in Delaware County, PA, for example, had only marginal contact with the national office. According to Jon Van Til, who worked with three organizations there, two of which were not affiliated with NWRO: "The issues . . . were largely focused around their own very small communities. And a lot of this had to do with, you know, these women that were under a lot of pressure and stress in their own lives finding the organization as a really important support group for themselves." This emphasis on local needs characterized many groups throughout the FAP debate.[84]

Tension among people working in the national office also reached a breaking point. Backstabbing, manipulation, threats, gossip, and overt hostility became commonplace. Some of the tension revolved around race, which continued to divide black and white activists. A white welfare recipient working in the national office resigned toward the end of 1970 because she was "so discouraged at the way in which people in this organization deal with each other." She could not continue to work for NWRO or with "the racist people I have met here, who despite the fact that poor white people are just as oppressed as poor black people and are greater in number, still feel that white people don't belong here."[85] Some staff members criticized other staff members for an inability to work cooperatively, communicate well, or set priorities.[86] In addition, communication between the NCC and the executive committee broke down in 1972 and resentment built among NCC members. They believed that the executive committee, charged only with carrying out NCC policy, had overstepped its bounds by nullifying NCC decisions.[87]

The situation of James Evans exemplifies the personal conflicts plaguing the national office. An older black man with a long history of organizing experience, Evans began volunteering with NWRO in June 1970. The executive committee hired him, over the wishes of George Wiley, as executive director of the Misseduc Foundation. Although Evans had a good relationship with and unwavering loyalty to the executive committee, Wiley and other staff members disliked him, in part, because he laid off a number of staff members in an attempt to make the national office more efficient and balance the budget. He criticized the way Wiley ran the national office, the ongoing racial tension, his lack of autonomy, and the disdain the staff expressed for executive committee decisions.[88] Citing his "mediocre" job performance as Misseduc executive director, and the discontent of several staff members, Wiley eventually fired Evans.[89] In another case, Chuck Hodden, an organizer in South Carolina, had a personal falling out with Mel Turner and George Wiley. According to Hodden, Wiley believed he "had problems relating to people in the National Office so it was in the best interest of the organization maybe I should quit."[90] Essentially fired, Hodden got caught up in personality conflicts. While job performance may have been an issue, in many cases perceptions of staff competence rested on one's loyalty to Wiley or the recipient leadership. In this way political differences translated into day-to-day control of the national office. As the direction, sense of unity, and political victories diminished, internal tension became more pronounced. Because many of the problems centered on the national office, some people attributed this to Wiley's leadership and his lack of availability. He became a target of criticism.[91] Andrea Kydd, one of Wiley's most loyal supporters in the national office, wrote him a lengthy letter discussing the staff and programmatic problems in the national office: "The [National Office] is floundering cause there is no direction—no vision. You could provide it but you don't and you're never there and when you are there you talk to no one about anything except FAP and you only talk to 2 or 3 people out of 25 about that."[92]

In addition to personal tensions in the national office, sexism in the movement also became a source of conflict between men and women in NWRO. Male organizers and staff exhibiting paternalistic and condescending attitudes had wielded power through their positions as organizers, fund-raisers, lawyers, and directors, becoming, in effect, the informal leaders. As an internal report documented in 1972:

> Attitudes of sexism on every level affect the way that programs are implemented. Major decision-making comes out of the national offices which is controlled by men. Because of this, membership at local, state and regional levels do not have the opportunity to participate in any meaningful way in their organization, and every time they attempt to participate they are ignored or regarded as emotional women. The problem then becomes not "how do we have an effective program guided by the membership," but "what do we do about the ladies" . . . Further, the program areas cannot be implemented properly as long as there is such wide range sexism. This is evidenced by the predominance of paid male organizers and how male staff dominate decision-making of a women's organization on every level. [93]

The subtle and not-so-subtle racism and sexism of mostly white, male organizers in NWRO reinforced the feminist orientation of women in the struggle for welfare rights. As women in the organization became increasingly aware of the sexism of staff members, they asserted their right to control their own organization and determine its political direction. Paralleling the experiences of some women in the Student Non-Violent Coordinating Committee (SNCC), Students for a Democratic Society (SDS), and the Black Panther Party, who encountered sexism when expected to perform menial tasks or excluded from decision making of the group, the day-to-day practices of sexism encouraged women in the welfare rights movement to question their marginalization within NWRO.

A number of welfare recipients also began to express concern about the funding of the organization. Catering to financial supporters, they believed, led to misguided priorities for the organization and concentrated power in those people in the national office with the skills and contacts to raise money. Relying on foundation money and grant writing, in effect, excluded poor women from control of the organization. A member of Mothers for Adequate Welfare (MAW) commented in 1969 about George Wiley's "relationship to the power structure. If he was an uneducated type of guy, how much would he really do? How many friends could he really get?" She believed that the work of MAW was far more important "because it was done on the local level with a handful of mothers, with the median education being the eight grade . . . NWRO had money, people with doctorates."[94]

Although some recipients had been hired to work in the national office, the question of employing mothers lingered. Many recipients believed that middle-class organizers and staff members still wielded disproportionate power. The Philadelphia WRO lobbied to hire mothers as organizers, hoping this would alleviate some of the tension between organizers and local groups.[95] Faith Evans, Associate Director under Tillmon, wanted all jobs in the national office to be filled by welfare mothers.[96] A single father unable to find work as a machine tool operator, Evans raised his four children on AFDC. He eventually took a job with the Community Action Program in New York and became involved in welfare rights. A firm advocate of recipient control, after joining the NWRO executive committee in 1971 he came in direct conflict with George Wiley.[97]

The internal tensions solidified the sentiment among welfare recipients that NWRO was a black women's organization. The ongoing political differences between staff and recipients—evident since the mid-1960s—had flared up at particular moments and was subsumed at others. Whether it pertained to decision making, how to frame particular campaigns, how to justify welfare and counter public hostility, or who would be hired to organize, the movement for much of its history was able to unite around specific goals, while continuing to struggle internally. By the early 1970s, the convergence of internal and external difficulties and the political evolution of recipient leaders led them to assert their independence. Many recipient leaders argued that the means of organizing and the process of politicization, empowering one of the most oppressed sectors of society, was as important as demanding adequate state assistance for the poor. Within any cross-race, cross-class, and cross-gender organization, the issues of racism, sexism, and classism operate both between the organization and society and within the organization itself—on both a personal and a public level. The welfare rights movement was not sheltered from the politics of the dominant culture but recreated those politics in the constant battles over goals, aspirations, and organizational style. Whatever good intentions motivated the staff, through their sexist and racist behavior, they ended up replicating the very power relations they sought to eradicate. The popular perception of welfare recipients as unworthy and undeserving was only reinforced when the central organization formed to remedy their situation continued to marginalize recipients and belittle their ideas and input. Thus, black women on welfare waged a struggle not only against mainstream American society, but their radical allies as well. This process of seeking empowerment within their organization helped crystallize their feminist outlook.

NWRO Is a Woman's Organization

The various crises of the movement came together in 1972 and led to a change in leadership. The instances of racism and sexism, control wielded by the predominantly middle-class staff, and conflicts over the direction of the organization prompted welfare recipients to look more critically at middle-class participation in NWRO. Consistent with the rhetoric of self-determination, both nationally and internationally in this period, Johnnie Tillmon argued that the nonpoor should serve only in supportive, not leadership, roles. She proposed that women on welfare "try and do something for ourselves and by ourselves to the extent that we could." By the early 1970s Tillmon and many other welfare rights activists wanted autonomy and self-sufficiency and, consequently, they sought control of NWRO.

Welfare recipients' demands for input in decision making and differences over the direction of the organization contributed to George Wiley's resignation from NWRO in late 1972. Subsequently, he launched the Movement for Economic Justice, enabling him to pursue unhindered his objective of developing a broader movement that included the working poor.[98] When Wiley resigned, Johnnie Tillmon replaced him as executive director and moved to Washington to take charge of the national office. Despite the tension surrounding Wiley's departure, Tillmon tried to strike a conciliatory note: "George Wiley is not the problem of NWRO. We all played a major part in creating the present situation . . . " Yet, she hoped he would "leave in a way that whatever he would be doing that it would not be detrimental to the organization."[99]

Although the organization remained interracial and open to men, with Wiley's resignation black women took complete command of NWRO, both formally and informally. Shortly after assuming her new position, Tillmon outlined to the Executive Board her goals, most importantly recommitting NWRO to its grass1roots base. She wanted to help "folks out there that are steadily organizing and sending in their memberships . . . They need to be assured that we have on-going programs and something worthwhile for them to give to."[100] She pledged to make the organization self-supporting through membership dues, rather than relying on outside funding. In response to the long-standing criticisms of staff domination, she promised to eliminate conflict between the staff and the Executive Board by respecting and following the policies outlined by the Board. The next year, at the 1973 convention, delegates decentralized the functions of the national office by creating regional representatives who would have more say in the programs of NWRO and communicate better with the local and state offices. In addition, "there was a mandate put on the National Office by the delegates at the Convention for us to reorient our priorities and begin redeveloping our field operation, so that we can provide continuing build-up and support to local organizing groups."[101] In July 1974, delegates voted to replace Beulah Sanders as national chairperson with Frankie Jeter as part of their effort to reorganize and change "its heavy emphasis on lobbying in Washington." They also pledged to organize the aged and working poor through the development of "bread and butter" issues.[102]

With black women more firmly in control of NWRO, the elements of feminism that had taken root several years earlier cohered more visibly into an analysis that saw NWRO as part of the larger women's movement. Because of NWRO's internal conflict and the greater visibility of women's liberation in the larger political discourse, women in the welfare rights movement more overtly, and with greater frequency, spoke of themselves as a part of the women's movement. Tillmon wrote in a 1971 article that women in the welfare rights movement believed they were "the front line troops of women's freedom" and their primary aim to ensure the right to a living wage for women's work concerned all women.[103] Even women who did not explicitly characterize their organization as part of the women's movement, clearly identified as women and attempted to ally with other women's organizations. Rather than eclipsing their struggle for economic justice, their identity as a women's group was firmly rooted in their struggle to mitigate the effects of poverty. Far from being contradictory, the various goals of the movement lent strength and support to their agenda.

Upon assuming control of the organization, recipient leaders immediately issued a "Women's Agenda," defining poverty and welfare as women's issues. A press release in July 1973 stated that "since the departure of founding executive director George Wiley, the women's leadership of NWRO has been considering radical revisions of the organization; prime among these consideration [sic] was a closer association with the women's movement." In the same press release, Tillmon asserted: "NWRO is primarily a women's organization in membership."[104] Reflecting the official shift in focus, recipient leaders began to refer to the convention chair as chairwoman rather than chairman.[105] Chairwoman Beulah Sanders expressed "whole-hearted" support for the National Women's Political Caucus and its goals.[106] At the 1974 national convention, the organization offered a panel on feminist politics at which Margaret Sloan of the newly organized National Black Feminist Organization spoke.[107] Women in the welfare rights movement also endorsed the Equal Rights Amendment and, at one point, the executive committee considered changing the name of the organization to the

National Women's Rights Organization.[108] Welfare rights organizers developed alliances with women's organizations, sent special appeals to women, and coordinated campaigns with women's groups. Jennette Washington, a prominent welfare rights leader in New York City, wrote,

> We women must stay together on this issue and not let anyone divide us. We can do this first by challenging the male power-holding groups of this nation. We must make them remember that we, as mothers and as women, are concerned about the survival of our children, of all human life. We women have to organize, agitate, pressure and demand; not beg. You see, in the past, women have always been told that they should stay behind their men and be nice and cool and don't rock the boat. Well, I just don't want to rock one boat, I want to rock all boats—the big boats. And I want all women to help me.[109]

The feminism of women in the welfare rights movement was also apparent in their attention to reproductive rights. The introduction of the birth control pill, advancements in other forms of contraception, and more liberal attitudes about sexuality promoted greater sexual freedom, especially for women, in the 1960s. Welfare recipients, as well, wanted to choose for themselves, whether or not and under what circumstances to have a child or have sex. Tillmon argued in 1971: "Nobody realizes more than poor women that all women should have the right to control their own reproduction."[110] Some handbooks and manuals created by local welfare organizations to educate recipients about their rights informed them of birth control. While providing information on birth control, they stressed that "this is your choice."[111] Recipient Evelyn Sims supported family planning because she believed that it would have provided her and her children a better quality of life.[112] Catherine Boddie, chairwoman of the Upstate New York WRO, similarly had a positive view of family planning, on condition there was "community control of the family planning money."[113] Olive Franklin, chair of the St. Louis City-Wide WRO, put it more bluntly:

> Planned Parenthood should firstly be planned by the parent. No one from outside should be able to tell a parent when they may or may not, should or should not have a child. Just because a person happens to be poor and black and unmarried, uneducated, etc., does not in my opinion give some capitalistic pig the authority to set up genocidal clinics with some false façade that this is one of the answers to the many welfare related crises in this country.[114]

She, like Tillmon, wanted poor women to control their own reproduction. Welfare recipients, as concerned with the right to bear children as access to contraception, framed the issue as one of personal choice rather than simply access to birth control. Many middle-class white feminists cast motherhood and the home as the cornerstone of their oppression and saw birth control their ticket to freedom. Efforts to limit childbearing, such as contraception and abortion, dominated the agenda of the mainstream women's movement. Many women of color, on the other hand, had for generations struggled for the right to raise their own children. Under slavery, slave masters often forcibly separated black children from their parents. At the turn of the century, social reformers launched campaigns to limit the fertility of the so-called "lower-races." As a result, many African American men and women had historically identified birth control with the eugenics movement. Attempts in the 1930s and 1940s to introduce birth control in the black community were unsuccessful because of fears that such methods would be used as a form of genocide.[115]

Welfare rights activists also opposed coerced sterilization, practiced on poor, nonwhite, and so-called "feeble-minded" women since the Progressive Era.[116] Welfare recipients, in particular, were sometimes sterilized under the threat of losing their welfare payments.[117] In the early 1970s, in a notorious case, doctors sterilized two black teenagers in Alabama without their consent. A lawsuit was brought on their behalf and a federal district court found "uncontroverted evidence in the record that minors and other incompetents have been sterilized with federal funds and that an indefinite number of poor people have been improperly coerced into accepting a sterilization operation under the threat that various federally supported welfare benefits would be withdrawn unless they submitted to irreversible sterilization."[118] In the mid-1970s, women on public assistance with three children had a sterilization rate 67 percent higher than women with the same number of children but not on public assistance.[119]

Coerced sterilization of poor women and women on welfare was sometimes blatant, as in the case above. But the federal government also found less overt ways to encourage sterilization of poor women to keep them from having children. Since 1975, for example, Medicaid has covered 90 percent of costs of sterilization, but only 50 percent of cost of abortion. "Enacted in a time of rising inflation, swelling unemployment, reduced standards of living, and political retrenchment, the 1975 revisions give health-care agencies economic incentive to persuade Medicaid patients to choose sterilization."[120] Hardly an accident, increases in sterilization represented a strategy on the part of federal officials. According to one scholar: "The editors of

Family Planning Digest, the official HEW family planning publication, prophetically hoped in 1972 to 'see sterilization become as important in family planning in the fifty states as it already is in Puerto Rico.'"[121] Some policy analysts, such as Phillips Cutright and Frederick Jaffe, argue for the cost-effectiveness of family planning and have estimated how much money is saved on welfare, social services, and medical care when social workers rely on family planning or sterilization.[122] Thus, it seems that for some policy makers, sterilization might be used as a budgetary measure to reduce the childbearing of poor women and women on welfare.

Consequently, welfare recipients, both locally and nationally, defined sexual freedom not only as access to birth control, but complete control over one's reproduction, including the right to oppose sterilization and bear children.[123] Formed in the early 1960s, the Black Women's Liberation Group in Mount Vernon, NY actively supported the birth control pill by 1968.[124] Members wrote in an essay in the landmark 1970 anthology *Sisterhood is Powerful*: "Poor black sisters decide for themselves whether to have a baby or not to have a baby . . . Black women are able to decide for themselves, like poor people all over the world, whether they will submit to genocide. For us, birth control is the freedom to *fight* genocide of black women and children" [original italics].[125] Johnnie Tillmon explained NWRO's position on the issue. "We know how easily the lobby for birth control can be perverted into a weapon against poor women. The word is choice. Birth control is a right, not an obligation. A personal decision, not a condition of a welfare check."[126] The 1971 NWRO national convention had a panel on abortion and two years later Tillmon issued a statement jointly with Charles Fanueff, executive director of the Association for Voluntary Sterilization, opposing forced sterilization of welfare recipients.[127] In February 1974 NWRO's newsletter, the *Welfare Fighter*, outlined problems of forced sterilizations of "minority groups" and welfare recipients. It stated: "Human reproduction should be entirely voluntary and the government has no right to force men or women to be sterilized . . . It is NWRO's contention that all methods of birth control, including sterilization, be available for poor people as they are for all others."[128]

Although NWRO expanded the meaning of reproductive rights, the language of choice was a double-edged sword for welfare recipients. Arguing that women should have control over their reproduction could also hold them accountable for any children they chose to bear, helping construct the gendered myth of the "welfare queen" and reinforcing the notion that poor women should simply use birth control, have abortions, or abstain from sex if they could not afford to raise their children.[129] Personal responsibility might serve as a substitute for public support. In this way, the politics of choice both provided an important opening for the welfare rights movement and worked against its long-term goals. Indeed, for a complex set of reasons, perhaps the discourse of choice among them, the 1970s witnessed an intensification of antiwelfare hostility. Nevertheless, NWRO's approach to reproductive rights provided meaningful choices for poor women and sought to remake the image of the welfare recipient by casting their lot with the burgeoning women's movement.

NWRO's position on reproductive rights resonated with that of many black women at the time, including the National Black Feminist Organization, but it preceded mass movements of white and black women around this issue. As early as 1969, the Citywide Welfare Alliance in Washington, D.C., challenged restrictive eligibility policies for free abortions at the city's only public hospital. They argued that limiting access to free abortions disadvantaged low-income women, since these women would most likely resort to an illegal abortion or attempt to self-induce, putting themselves in grave danger. After welfare activists picketed and filed a lawsuit, administrators appointed them to a committee to review the hospital's abortion policy.[130] For these activists, access to abortion meant not just demanding its legality, but assuring public funding for poor women who otherwise would not be able to afford these services. The concerns of welfare recipients with reproductive rights soon developed into a more widespread political movement. In the mid- and late-1970s feminists formed several local organizations to end sterilization abuse and protect women's right to abortion, including the Committee for Abortion Rights and Against Sterilization Abuse (CARASA), an interracial group in New York City. In 1981 a group of mostly white socialist-feminists formed the Reproductive Rights National Network, embodying NWRO's goals for both abortion rights and prevention of sterilization abuse.

In her 1971 article, Johnnie Tillmon articulated most clearly the movement's position of welfare as a women's issue:

> The truth is that AFDC is like a super-sexist marriage. You trade in *a* man for *the* man. But you can't divorce him if he treats you bad. He can divorce you, of course, cut you off anytime he wants. *The* man runs everything. In ordinary marriage sex is supposed to be for your husband. On AFDC you're not supposed to have any sex at all. You give up control of your own body. It's a condition of aid. You may even have to agree to get your tubes tied so you can never have more children just to avoid being cut off welfare. *The* man, the welfare system, controls your money. He tells you what to buy, what not to buy, where to buy it, and how much things cost. If

things—rent, for instance—really cost more than he says they do, it's just too bad for you. He's always right. Everything is budgeted down to the last penny and you've got to make your money stretch. *The* man can break into your house anytime he wants to and poke into your things. You've got no right to protest. You've got no right to privacy when you go on welfare. Like I said. Welfare's a super-sexist marriage."[131]

For Tillmon, "the man" was a metaphor for both the welfare system and in-stitutionalized white racism. Her analysis combined racial, class, and gen-der oppressions, laying the basis for an argument that welfare should be defined as a feminist issue. She put forth an insightful critique of the wel-fare system and the ways in which it controlled and regulated the sexuality and lives of women. First published in *Ms. Magazine*, the preeminent fem-inist magazine of the time, Tillmon's article symbolized in many ways the culmination of a long struggle within the welfare rights movement to de-fine welfare as a women's issue and the welfare rights movement as a part of the larger women's movement. Its publication in *Ms.* signaled the women's movement's willingness, however limited, to address issues of concern to poor women and women of color.

In the early 1970s mainstream feminist organizations took a greater in-terest in poverty and welfare. The National Organization for Women (NOW), which had its founding meeting on June 30, 1966, the same day as the first national welfare rights demonstration, developed a closer alliance with NWRO.[132] In 1970, NOW passed a resolution supporting NWRO and recognizing poverty as a woman's issue,

> The poor in the United States are predominantly women . . . NOW must, therefore, work particularly hard to free our sisters in poverty from the intolerable burdens which have been placed on them. The system must work for the most oppressed if it is to suc-ceed. The National Organization for Women, therefore, proposes to establish at the national level immediate and continuing liaison with the National Welfare Rights Organization and similar groups and urges each chapter to do the same at the local level in order to keep us currently briefed on matters of federal or state legislation and public policy which call for NOW action in support of our sis-ters in poverty.[133]

The following year, NOW endorsed the guaranteed income, which, Merrille Dolan, Chair of Task Force for Women in Poverty, said, "is *the* most important women's issue for which we should be fighting."[134]

Similarly, the National Women's Political Caucus (NWPC) supported NWRO's proposal for a guaranteed annual income and formed a Welfare Reform Task Force.[135]

The resolutions and symbolic actions by NOW and other feminist organizations demonstrated the impact of the welfare rights movement on the priorities of more mainstream feminist groups.[136] Scholar Martha Davis suggests that NOW's relationship with NWRO encouraged feminists to recognize poverty as "inextricably linked to common barriers faced by women in society, such as violence, wage discrimination, and disproportionate family responsibilities" and that poor women needed "social supports to redress these burdens."[137] By the early 1970s welfare had become clearly identified as a women's issue. Both NOW and the NWPC built on the activities and analyses offered first by welfare rights activists.

This success, however, was both temporary and superficial. Although NOW officially expressed support for NWRO, little came of this relationship. Welfare rights organizations and middle-class white feminist organizations interacted very little, largely because of their divergent views about work, family, and independence.[138] Frances Fox Piven remembered: "Representatives from NWRO went to NOW meetings and they felt that they were treated very badly. And they came to the conclusion that the class divide was really searing and permanent."[139] In addition, some welfare recipients couldn't relate to the views of feminists within NOW. At the 1971 NWRO conference at Brown University, Gloria Steinem gave a speech that "turned the welfare mothers off totally because it was anti-men."[140] Welfare rights activists, for the most part, felt little alliance with the mainstream feminist movement. Moiece Palladino, a white welfare recipient working with NWRO in San Francisco, recalled: "The women's movement has never, never, since it has started, ever given welfare mothers the due that they were entitled. They have always been a middle-class movement. They have no interest, though they may mouth the interest of working class women. When push comes to shove to the needs of poor women, their interests are not at all conceived."[141]

Once the welfare rights movement folded, mainstream women's organizations like NOW took little action for the next two decades on behalf of women on welfare. Both their ideological orientation and political platform continued to marginalize the concerns of poor women and women of color. The efforts within NOW to address poverty originated mainly with the leadership, while the middle-class membership remained "fixed on formal, legal equality for those already in the workplace as the proper instrument for addressing women's poverty."[142] Women on welfare fighting for the right to stay home and care for their children did not find this strategy useful or appealing. In addition to competing strategies, philosophical differences inhibited a working relationship between NWRO and NOW. Feminist groups like NOW, committed to assuring women's economic independence from both the state and men, wanted to liberate women from their homemaker status, not reinforce it.[143] Catherine Jermany, of the Los Angeles County WRO, summed up the welfare rights position succinctly, "We thought white women were crazy to want to give up their cushiony Miss Cleaver life . . . We thought that was a good life."[144] A common interest in empowering women brought NWRO and NOW together in the late 1960s and early 1970s, but the boundaries of class, race, and politics hindered a long-term alliance as black welfare activists and white middle-class NOW activists pursued different strategies to address their own particular experiences of sexism.

In contrast to feminist groups, the League of Women's Voters, a predominantly white middle-class woman's organization, had been involved in issues of welfare and poverty for many years. Although not an explicitly feminist organization, the League advocated for a more generous welfare state. It had few formal ties with NWRO, but it did lobby legislators, hold conferences and workshops, and work with local welfare rights organizations. Its support for higher welfare benefits was coupled with a commitment to the family wage ideal, which reinforced women's traditional role as homemakers and sought to provide them assistance in that role. The League opposed work requirements, supported the guaranteed annual income, and believed a mother should decide what was in the best interests of her children.[145]

As the welfare rights movement waned, the concerns of welfare recipients seemed to be more adequately addressed by emerging socialist-feminist groups than by NOW. Socialist-feminists made poverty a central component of their analysis of women's oppression. Many of the local groups opposing coerced sterilization, for example, grew out of a socialist-feminist conference in Yellow Springs, OH in 1975.[146] Socialist-feminists also addressed women's unequal wages in the workplace, and how women's reproductive labor in the home helped sustain capitalism by raising the next generation of workers and providing for the current generation. This translated, in the mid-1970s, into the wages for housework movement, in which socialist-feminists demanded pay for women's work in the household. The movement saw itself linked to both the welfare rights movement and the women's liberation movement. In England, wages for housework advocates suggested that "welfare mothers . . . not only spoke to the needs of all women but were in fact a public crescendo to the massive *rebellion of women* that had been going on behind closed doors" (original italics).[147] A more direct connection between welfare rights and socialist-feminism was evident in 1974, when a group of self-proclaimed socialist-feminists - renewed welfare activism in New York City by forming the Downtown

Welfare Advocate Center.[148] By combining an analysis of class and gender, socialist-feminists more effectively reached out to working-class women and tackled issues of poverty and reproductive rights. However, these groups were, for the most part, predominantly white and did not see race and racism as a core concern. Consequently, they, too, were unable to cross the racial divide.

Although NWRO and NOW never developed a successful long-term relationship and most socialist-feminist initiatives were short-lived, the attempts at cooperation reveal the possibilities for alliances across race and class among women. The gestures by NOW and other organizations symbolized the impact of the welfare rights movement on other organizations, encouraging them to define "welfare as a women's issue."[149] Because of the agitation by welfare recipients and mainstream women's organizations' interest in poverty, by the early 1970s welfare had become clearly identified as a women's issue.

Poor black welfare recipients' position at the bottom of the social hierarchy may have inspired their efforts to recruit allies of different class, race, and gender backgrounds. An alliance with white, middle-class women during a moment of heightened feminist activity brought rewards to a struggling, demonized group of poor black women. Similarly, welfare activists could work with men committed in a practical way to the eradication of poverty—so long as this did not impede their goal of autonomy. And they identified with and reached out to the ongoing movement for black liberation—so long as this did not subsume their concerns as women. They had simultaneous goals of personal autonomy, community empowerment, ideological transformation, and practical change. Their institutional powerlessness encouraged them to collaborate with and appeal to others who might respond to them. Indeed, from their vantage point, they needed such alliances to wage a successful struggle. But at the same time, they took care to ensure that their relationships with non-recipients did not compromise their integrity and political vision.

The End of NWRO

Once black welfare recipients held the reigns of power, most of the white organizers and volunteers loyal to Wiley also quit or resigned. Many chose to get involved in multi-issue community organizations such as the Movement for Economic Justice (MEJ) and ACORN. A group of organizers who had worked with the Massachusetts WRO, for example, took positions with the Workers' Alliance to Guarantee Employment, an outgrowth of a MEJ campaign.[150] Many staff members who left NWRO had become convinced that in order to be effective, the antipoverty movement needed to broaden its base to include men and the working poor.

The departure of Wiley and much of the middle-class staff, the primary fundraisers for NWRO, exacerbated financial constraints. When they left, 80 percent of the donations and pledges "went out the door," according to one observer.[151] This, in combination with the changing political climate, crippled NWRO.[152] Contributions from white churches and liberal groups stopped coming in and, at Wiley's resignation, NWRO was $100,000 in debt.[153] Moreover, the unexpected and tragic death of George Wiley in August 1973 shook up the members and staff of NWRO, making organizing more difficult. Efforts to raise money, even among former supporters, were unsuccessful and the organization never funded its 1973 budget. In 1974 Johnnie Tillmon organized what she called the "Half-A-Chance" campaign. With a goal of making NWRO self-supporting, the campaign appealed to poor people nationwide to give 50 cents each to the organization. According to Tillmon:

> Organizations like ours could not continue to depend on grants and other resources from foundations at a time when everyone is caught us [sic] in the economic squeeze and governmental repression that exists in this nation today. The types of organizing the action campaigns that NWRO continues to wage against the nation's oppressive institutions almost requires us to be self-sufficient because too many of those foundations and funding groups are running scared—too scared to deal with us.[154]

Little came of the campaign, however.[155] At the moment when African-American women were firmly in control, there was little left to control and the future of the organization looked bleak.

In July 1973 the IRS, after an audit, threatened to close down NWRO unless it paid back taxes of $20,000.[156] Along with other debts, this catapulted the organization into a period of severe financial difficulty, consuming time, energy, and resources to stay solvent. Through fund-raising events, appeals to middle-class liberals, and support from members, Tillmon and other staff in the national office eventually paid off the IRS and brought down NWRO's debt from $100,000 in 1972 to $20,000 in 1975.[157] Despite this achievement, NWRO found it difficult to function effectively without operating funds. In August 1973, the national staff shrank to eight, including four recipients working without pay. They published the newsletter and sent out mailings only intermittently.[158] Raising money to reduce the debt, rather than planning new campaigns, consumed the staff and, consequently, the organization's base of support continued to dwindle. In March 1975, NWRO declared bankruptcy and closed its doors.

After NWRO folded, Tillmon returned to California. She bought a house with her new husband, Harvey Blackston, just a few blocks from Nickerson Gardens, where she first began organizing welfare recipients. She continued to work with the local welfare rights chapter and got a job as a legislative aide on welfare issues for City Councilman Robert Farrell. She later served on a welfare advisory committee under Gov. Jerry Brown and subsequently under the administration of Republican Gov. George Deukmejian. She died of diabetes in 1995 at the age of 69.[159]

New Community Activism

The closing of the NWRO national office did not signal the end of welfare rights activity. The more conservative and restrictive political climate of the mid-1970s, however, did change the character of the welfare debate and welfare activism, making it more difficult to speak openly of a "right" to welfare or a guaranteed income for poor mothers. The stereotypes and negative images permeated popular culture. According to recipient Moiece Palladino, "More than anything [else] . . . the fact that nobody wanted to be identified publicly as being on the grant . . . contributed to [the movement's] demise."[160] Even long-time opponents of work requirements, such as the League of Women Voters, had come by the mid-1970s to discuss employment as a solution to women's poverty.[161] The shift palpably affected local welfare rights organizations, as well, leading many affiliated with NWRO to fold. Others continued to operate, but did so around a different set of issues, often locally based. In the mid-1970s, the Los Angeles County WRO refocused its energies on the local level and remained active until the 1990s. Similarly, in the late 1970s, the Baltimore Welfare Rights Organization (BWRO) maintained an exclusively local focus. Although formally headed by a man, Bobby Cheeks, women, like Annie Chambers, chair of the Board of Directors, ran the organization. In 1978 the BWRO launched a rent strike in the O'Donnell Heights housing project to protest plumbing problems, dangerous electrical wiring, rodent infestation, and generally poor maintenance and construction of the building. While a large number of residents wanted improvements in the housing complex, only a minority withheld their rent. A series of repairs by the housing authority to placate protesters and fear on the part of residents hampered full-fledged participation in the strike. BWRO found limited support for its more militant strategies. Its politics centered on quality-of-life issues, shying away from the more broadly based theme of economic justice that informed the welfare rights movement at its height.[162]

In many cases, welfare rights groups became less confrontational and more interested in social services and legal tactics. For example, the Clark County WRO in Las Vegas, in 1974, just two years after the struggle to roll back the state welfare reductions, adopted a helping-hand approach to poverty. With the aid of Legal Services and the League of Women Voters, the WRO, headed by Ruby Duncan and Mary Wesley, formed a nonprofit organization called Operation Life. The group leased a dilapidated hotel in a neglected neighborhood, renovated it, and turned it into a community center. Operation Life provided the black community an opportunity for "full participation in the economy—in the ownership and savings and the self-sufficiency which the more fortunate in our Nation already take for granted." The community center provided services for the needy, including a home for the elderly, a food commodity program, drug counseling and tutoring programs, vocational training for youth, aid to black-owned businesses, a public swimming pool, a child care center, a community-run press, and a youth-run restaurant, which also served as a training ground for food handling and preparation and restaurant management.[163] At the end of 1973, it opened a health center, the first medical facility on the Westside of Las Vegas. In 1974, Operation Life won a federal grant to operate a Women and Infant Child nutrition program. Its slogan was "We can do it and do it better." Despite continual harassment by local officials, in 1978 Operation Life became a Community Development Corporation, running several low-income housing units, and by 1981 was the largest property owner in the community. In the late 1980s, the federal government pulled funding from Operation Life and subsequently many of its programs and services were either forced to shut down or handed over to another, more conservative community group.

Similarly, welfare recipients in Mud Creek, KY formed the East Kentucky WRO (EKWRO). Organizing since 1969, the EKWRO never affiliated with NWRO, but worked to make government services available and more responsive to the needs of the poor. In 1973, members of EKWRO formed a free, community-run health care clinic, the Mud Creek Citizens Health Project. While providing a much-needed service for residents of East Kentucky, they were consumed with the bureaucratic details of running a clinic: hiring a doctor, staff salaries, Medicaid reimbursement, state licensing procedures, purchasing medical supplies.[164] A northern California group evolved in a parallel direction in the mid-1970s. Ethel Dotson, head of the Richmond, CA WRO, had served on the NCC and continued her involvement well after the national office closed its doors. In 1974 the group received a federal contract to run the Women, Infant, and Children (WIC) program, to provide adequate nutrition for pregnant women and children. Dotson didn't see a distinction between social services and political organizing. She believed servicing the community created avenues to become educated and engaged in political activity. The organization was on the verge of becoming a holistic health clinic, when the federal government revoked its grants in 1980.[165]

In another case, the Philadelphia WRO provided social services and pursued a legal struggle for equal education throughout the 1970s. It opened a tenement office, helping fifty to seventy-five people a day with problems related to housing, school, welfare, or police. Adopting the slogan "Welfare a Right; Education a Must," members, led by recipient Viola Sanders, had come to believe that social mobility required access to quality education for their children. In the summer of 1973 the PWRO sued the Pennsylvania State Department of Welfare because it believed the department did not spend enough money from Title I of the Elementary and Secondary Education Act of 1965 on educationally deprived children. With the help of lawyers, they succeeded by 1975 in getting more money from the city for new teachers, reading programs, clothing allowances, and free breakfasts for their children.[166] PWRO's history illustrates how welfare rights strategy shifted from the late 1960s to the early 1970s. In the late 1960s, PWRO called for a federal guaranteed annual income. By the early 1970s, it fought for access to education to enable poor people to help themselves become self-sufficient.

While these examples demonstrate the fortitude and vigilance of welfare recipients in the face of enormous obstacles, they also mark a new phase in the welfare rights movement. The community activism of the 1970s tended to be atomized reforms, rooted in the politics of representation and individualism. The tactics usually revolved around self-help or participation in formulating social policy, defined as civic action or community organizing, rather than the broad-based social changes that challenged the basic assumptions guiding the welfare system. Whatever particular path they chose, welfare rights activists found a way to adapt to the new climate and push for welfare reform and the empowerment of women on welfare. Catherine Jermany, who worked with the Los Angeles County WRO, dedicated herself to educating the poor "to help people help themselves." As the national movement faded, Jermany gave legal aid and assistance to poor people, and eventually became executive director of the National Self-Help Law Project in northern California.[167] Welfare recipients found community work empowering and an avenue to personal success, some gaining full-time, meaningful employment. Moiece Palladino, for example, landed a job with legal services as a "professional welfare mother" and worked her way through college and law school.[168] Many women for the first time sent their children to college. Others engaged in local and state politics. Former welfare recipients elected to public office or influential in public policy arenas often became advocates for the poor, consulting with nonprofit groups, foundations, or state and local agencies. They continued in the tradition of earlier welfare rights struggles, providing an alternative voice in policy discussions and working to achieve a more just public assistance program. The protracted activity of welfare recipients suggests that welfare politics were not transitory, even if they did diminish after the late 1960s. These local movements demonstrate the tenacity of welfare recipients and chart the changing nature of political organizing in the 1970s.[169] These successes should not be underestimated, given the history and marginalization of women on welfare. But equally revealing was the circumscribed nature of their struggle. Gone was the language of a right to a basic standard of living. Gone was the language of entitlement.

This transition in the welfare rights movement presaged and helped lay the basis for the community activism and civic action of the 1980s and 1990s. Community organizing appealed to groups with little access to formal channels of power—low-income people, women, people of color. Rather than relying on broad appeals, huge cash reserves, or formal membership affiliation, it depended more on one-to-one contact. In some ways, the welfare rights movement's evolution in this direction was logical. "Community issues" had always been central to the welfare rights movement. Distinct from traditional workplace organizing, community organizing more readily brought together the multiple issues with which women on welfare and poor people generally dealt. It had the potential to combine parenting, housing, education, health care, environmental, consumer, as well as employment issues. More important, the seeds for radical change could indeed be fertilized in the politics of community activism. This kind of civic participation finds an issue "close to home" and politicizes individuals one at a time, demonstrating how they can make a difference. It fosters a sense of identity and community, cultivating in poor people self-confidence, leadership abilities, and basic skills and training.[170]

Nevertheless, community activism absent a critique of political and economic structures could also retard long-term social change. Welfare rights activists turned to social service in the 1970s because of the retreat of state responsibility and ongoing state repression. Many of the campaigns revolved around basic survival—health care, food programs, and education. On the one hand, the response of activists represented grassroots resistance to neglect of their communities. At the same time, they often become embroiled in the day-to-day requirements of running and maintaining a complex social service agency. This immersion in bureaucratic details sometimes came at the expense of discussion of how change occurs and how to transform a political system that so inadequately meets the needs of its residents. In addition, many of the community groups were without a mass base or an independent source of political power and relied on funding from outside sources, often federal, state, or local governments. Thus, the Richmond WRO operated the food stamp and the WIC programs in California until an auditor shut them down in 1980. Ethel Dotson, head of the local group, maintains they were "clean as a whistle," but that politicians, threatened by welfare rights, audited them to pave the way for "welfare reform." She explains: "We was telling people, those mothers that need to stay at home should raise their kids. Stay at home and raise your children properly. Those that want to work, you know, develop your own self, jobs, etc. . . . [These politicians thought] the only way that welfare rights can exist is through food stamp outreach and the WIC program. If we take [these] away, they will cease to exist." In Las Vegas, as well, decisions at the Department of Health and Human Services effectively wiped out Operation Life's programs, transferring their contracts to a more conservative local group. This undercut the many years of organizing by welfare mothers in Nevada. Renee Diamond, who worked with Operation Life, believes that federal agencies deliberately took "funding out of the hands of militant community groups, particularly black organizations, and [gave] what little federal money there was in the eighties to more conservative groups."[171]

The precipitous decline in the welfare rights movement was not the end of welfare rights activity. In some cases, welfare rights organizations formed in the late and mid-1970s. In 1975, the state of Georgia reduced AFDC benefits and thousands of working people who previously qualified for assistance became ineligible. The welfare rolls plummeted from 360,000 in 1975 to 200,000 three years later. In response, a group called the Public Assistance Coalition lobbied, planned a public education campaign, and, by 1979, succeeded in raising the AFDC grant.[172] In another case, in 1974, welfare recipients in New York City started the Downtown Welfare Advocate Center (DWAC), which saw welfare as specifically a concern of poor women. Under the leadership of Theresa Funicello, DWAC planned public actions to draw attention to tax breaks for the wealthy, materially improve the lives of welfare recipients, and eliminate the stigma associated with receipt of welfare. Echoing the politics of many local welfare rights organizations in the 1960s and early 1970s, DWAC highlighted the contributions of poor women as mothers and insisted that they deserved compensation for their work.[173] In this way, NWRO left the footprints of its legacy.

Although not founded specifically as a women's organization, by the early 1970s, NWRO had been transformed into an organization controlled by women speaking in a distinctly feminist voice. In the process of building a movement, women activists challenged prescribed gender roles, attempted to legitimate their status as single mothers, and sought to ensure that women on welfare had greater control over their lives. In the struggle for welfare rights, motherhood and reproduction became a site of contestation for poor black women. Welfare rights activists demanded that society recognize and respect their work as mothers, that they have reproductive control over their bodies, and that the women in the organization determine its political direction. Even as they cultivated relationships with other women's organization and wrote platforms appealing to all women, their feminist agenda was influenced, not just by the political climate of the day, but by their class and racial background. Their experiences with poverty and racism shaped both their understanding of gender and their platform for addressing gender oppression.

Some members believed adamantly that they were a women's organization at the forefront of the struggle for women's liberation. While others may have been more reluctant to identify as women liberationists or feminists, through the struggle to improve their economic situation, they nevertheless articulated a program of economic demands that increasingly asserted a critique of gender roles, patriarchy, and proscribed sexuality. Despite differences among the women in the organization, in comparison to the men in the movement, who were resistant to the idea of women's empowerment or autonomy, the women seemed unified. Although members may not have explicitly pushed for gender equality, in essence they advocated women's liberation: liberation from poverty and reproductive control. They tied their campaigns for economic security to their desire for autonomy as women. Overall, their struggle represented a unique brand of feminism emerging in the 1960s, one that contributed to and expanded the boundaries of the existing women's movement.

Women in the welfare rights movement formulated a black feminist analysis integrating race, class, and gender. It included aspects of class empowerment, racial liberation, and a gender analysis.[174] While they understood the importance of gender in shaping their lives and attempted to connect with other women, they also realized that all women were not treated equally. Thus, their conceptualization of womanhood was dialectical rather than one-dimensional. They did not see their oppression through the additive components of race, class, and gender. Their analysis was more accurately one of "multiple jeopardy, multiple consciousness."[175] They believed that their treatment as women was determined not just by their status as women, but as poor black women. Racism and poverty influenced their opportunities and day-to-day experiences as women.

Using this analytical framework, women in the welfare rights movement critiqued the welfare system and the ways in which it controlled and regulated the sexuality and lives of women. Many welfare recipients were not self-avowed feminists and most cannot be called intellectuals, in the traditional sense of the word.[176] Nevertheless, they forged an analysis and voiced a world view on their own terms. The material reality of their lives and the culture surrounding them shaped their notions of gender politics and their identity as women. Through their struggle for economic security and welfare rights, they expressed many of the basic tenets of black feminist ideology.

Understanding the welfare rights movement as a part of the struggle for women's liberation in the 1960s enables us to rethink our definition of what constitutes "women's issues." As a movement dedicated to women's liberation, in fact if not in word, the struggle for welfare rights leaves little doubt as to how to redraw the map of feminism in the 1960s. The welfare rights movement expanded the notion of feminism by defining welfare and poverty as women's issues. This gave them a springboard to explore in a more sophisticated way how race and class relate to gender. They did not separate their oppression as women from their oppression as poor black people. As Patricia Hill Collins says, black feminists often reject the oppositional, dichotomized model.[177] These black women worked simultaneously on issues of race, class, and gender. They organized for their own benefit, while also improving their community. They attempted to make the system work for them as well as to challenge it. And in the process, they created a movement that was as much a feminist movement as a movement for racial equality and economic justice.

Conclusion

Through their struggle in the welfare rights movement, welfare recipients left a permanent mark on the history and politics of the 1960s. They gave a voice to one of the most disenfranchised sectors of American society—a voice that articulated a politics of black liberation, feminism, and economic justice. In doing so, the welfare rights movement reshaped the political landscape. Its most obvious impact was on welfare policy, both locally and nationally.

There is a rich history of poor people's movements, but the specter of single mothers militantly demanding state assistance to raise their children was rare prior to the emergence of the welfare rights movement in the 1960s. The struggle for welfare rights more often than not emanated from recipients' battles with their caseworkers, and often found its first site of contestation in local welfare offices. Nevertheless, the movement quickly expanded its range of targets to include department stores, policy makers, journalists, federal legislators, and popular culture. It became evident to welfare recipients that the power to which they were subject was not concentrated in the hands of welfare administrators, but was diffuse, reaching far and wide through myriad institutions in American society.

Welfare rights activists in the 1960s won concrete reforms such as higher monthly benefits and special grants for items they did not have. They pursued legislation, including the right to a fair hearing to appeal welfare department decisions, an end to residency laws denying assistance to recent migrants, and constitutional protection for recipients' right to due process. They challenged the basic tenets of the welfare system, which placed discretionary power in the hands of caseworkers and discouraged poor women from seeking assistance. They also attempted to influence public opinion by recasting their identities in ways that might complicate their unidimensional status as welfare recipients. Their goal of a guaranteed annual income redefined the relationship of the state to poor black women (as well as other poor people) across the country. It eliminated casework investigations into recipients' moral, sexual, and employment patterns. And, although it would not have eliminated disparities, a guaranteed annual income, to some degree, would have uplifted the poorest of the poor, many of whom were African-American women. The movement's proposal for $5,500 a year for a family of four, although never passed by Congress, became one measure by which policy makers judged other legislative proposals. The welfare rights movement, thus, influenced welfare policy and helped shape the debate about welfare in the 1960s.

The welfare rights movement provides a window into what welfare meant to the poor. In making claims upon the state for higher monthly benefits and a guaranteed annual income, activists essentially asserted their right to food, shelter, and basic subsistence. They justified welfare assistance as mothers caring for and rearing their children, and as citizens entitled to the same benefits and opportunities as all other Americans. The language of citizenship and rights is laced throughout the campaigns waged by the welfare rights movement. Recipients suggested that citizenship ought to guarantee them a basic standard of living, access to credit, and other social and economic opportunities. In making these claims, they built upon the work of economists and policy makers, who in an era of abundance had moved beyond a discussion of basic human survival to broach topics such as quality of life and emotional and psychological well-being. But welfare recipients went further than that and attempted to expand the definition of "rights" as it was used in the 1960s to demand economic resources independent of the market or their status as workers.[1] They also advanced the notion that domestic work, traditional women's work, had a value that society should recognize and even compensate. Later, a handful of feminists would advocate wages for housework as a spin-off of this idea. Welfare recipients suggested that mothers contributed to society even if they were not wage earners or producers of commodities. They also demanded privacy as an individual right, while simultaneously challenging the notion of child-rearing as the sole financial responsibility of individual parents. That is, child maintenance was not accepted as a wholly private affair that the government could rid itself of.

As the movement's position on women's labor demonstrates, the welfare rights movement was politically and intellectually sophisticated. Like other movements of the late 1960s, it had a richer and more complicated political terrain from which to draw lessons. Many in the welfare rights movement had observed or participated in consciousness raising, had come to view government bureaucracy with a critical eye, recognized the way in which individuals wielded racial power, and learned to speak the language of women's rights. The tactics, strategies, and array of protest options they employed were impressive, as were the discourses and dialogues in which they were engaged. It was a movement that overlapped with and was organically linked to many other reform efforts.

The welfare rights movement has to be viewed as an integral part of the black freedom movement. It teaches us, however, that the "typical" story of the emergence of black radicalism is a distortion of the historical record. That story depicts the early 1960s as the heyday of black freedom, a time when the movement was united and had a clear agenda and widespread political support. Although the historiography of the 1960s is hotly contested, most recent studies have argued against a particular master narrative, which itself is confining and circumscribed and doesn't make room for activists like those who led the welfare rights movement. Earlier scholars focused on the North-South divide, on the evolution from non-violence to self-defense, inter-racialism to nationalism.[2] All of these questions relate to the path by which the welfare rights movement evolved, but none are central defining features.

The welfare rights movement disrupts the conventional periodization of the black freedom movement and the false North-South dichotomy. It was not a northern movement but a national one, with chapters all across the country. Moreover, the welfare rights movement did not have its roots in the transition of 1964.[3] It did not emerge simply as a frustrated response to the loss of direction by black activists and a desire to focus more attention on economic issues. Nor did it result primarily from the organizing efforts of middle-class activists on behalf of the poor. Women on welfare had organized around economic issues such as urban renewal, fair housing, and neighborhood neglect as early as the late 1950s. Although support from middle-class activists—both before and after 1964—aided tremendously in the formation of a national movement, the impetus for organizing came from the women themselves and was rooted in their experiences.

By examining how welfare rights related to other discourses and political movements, we can develop a more nuanced analysis of liberalism, conservatism, and radicalism in the 1960s. Some scholars within the field of critical legal studies have labeled the welfare rights movement a liberal reform movement. They suggest that by focusing on civil rights, legal protections, and electoral politics, and relying on consumer and market strategies, the movement did little to challenge the underlying assumptions of liberal economic and political policy.[4] On the other side, some scholars have called welfare rights a militant movement, one that strayed far from mainstream liberal values by demanding material assistance apart from market employment. Its radicalism, according to this argument, contributed to the weakening of the Democratic Party by pushing many working-class white Americans into Republican hands.[5] I argue that neither of these approaches captures the essence of the movement; instead, we need to rethink the meaning of these political categories. Many scholars argue that by 1965 the political consensus characterizing the early 1960s had frayed, the political center was undermined, and support for both the left and right increased. It was, they suggest, a period of polarization. "Ordinary" white Americans, the so-called silent majority, had to choose between the increasingly militant voices of students, the poor, and people of color, on the one hand, and the appeals on the right for law and order, on the other. They ultimately chose stability and the status quo, as was symbolized most clearly in the election of Richard Nixon in 1968.[6]

I contend that the history of reform in the 1960s is more complicated than the ultimate victory of conservatism. Historians of the 1960s have tended to conflate liberalism with the Democratic Party and radical politics with total transformation. Many of the political movements of the late 1960s self-consciously placed themselves outside the mainstream of American politics and proudly adopted an image of rebelliousness. These movements, as the welfare rights movement shows us, drew upon a radical tradition as well as ostensibly core American beliefs and the values of mainstream society. This story helps us to understand how such movements were entangled with the dominant discourse of the period, and how they came to their own sense of radicalism, blurring the boundaries among radical, liberal, and even conservative ideas.

In some ways, the welfare rights movement clearly put forth alternatives to the dominant liberal ideology and patriarchal norms. It challenged the ostensible truism that the two-parent family should be the ideal, questioned the belief that employment outside the home was the only valuable work for women of color, and asserted that welfare and a basic subsistence income were rights, rather than privileges. While in these respects the movement departed from popularly accepted wisdom or mainstream ideas, in other ways, it did not. For example, not only Democrats, but many Republicans and some radicals subscribed to dominant New Deal liberal ideas, such as an activist federal government, commitment to an income floor, the politics of representation, and protection of civil rights. On certain topics, there was more consensus than conflict, with some Republicans advocating more government intervention. Both Richard Nixon and the National Welfare Rights Organization, for example, agreed on the need for an income floor, although they differed on where that floor should be set. Activists on the right and the left supported government action to alleviate poverty. In addition, the welfare rights movement incorporated into its rhetoric and policy platforms some key ideas that had come to define liberalism in the 1960s. Welfare rights activists fought for representation both in welfare departments and within the electoral and policy making arenas. They waged a political and legal struggle to ensure protection of their civil rights. They did not demand a different kind of economic system, but wanted to share in the prosperity that had come to define post-war America. The movement, therefore, borrowed rhetoric and concepts most closely associated with "Western" liberal values and made them its own.

The movement's rhetoric of inclusion and liberal reform was in part a strategic attempt to speak in a commonly acceptable language. In the process, they expanded and revised the liberal discourse of the day. But, in addition, by demanding that society give them their due, they defined radicalism on their own terms. Most of the "liberal" reforms the welfare rights movement struggled for—more formalized welfare procedures, protection of their civil rights, the right to stay home and care for their children, and representation in policy-making bodies—challenged the status quo for poor black women on welfare. Their status quo included arbitrary and demeaning treatment by caseworkers, requirements to work outside their home and find day care for their children, routine violations of their civil rights, and silencing and marginalization. By insisting that they had the same rights and privileges as other people, women on welfare questioned the boundaries that had come to circumscribe and control their lives. They formulated a politics that drew upon radical, conservative, and liberal discourses as it suited their needs. The moderate or radical nature of a demand or movement is not determined by some intrinsic ahistorical quality of the demand itself but by historical context and the actors involved. For poor women on welfare, these reforms had a tangible—and liberating—impact on their lives. Moreover, by vocalizing their interests and insisting on their rights, poor women on welfare altered the balance of power. The real victory was not that poor people were given a few more crumbs but the concession that they had a right to demand those crumbs for themselves. That scenario flew in the face of both liberal and conservative views about the role of the black poor, especially poor black women. So, not the demands but the process of demanding gave the welfare rights movement its radical edge.

By suggesting that a certain level of consensus characterized welfare politics in the late 1960s, I do not mean to gloss over the many differences among these ideologies. This was a period of profound conflict and hostility, when people from competing political factions rarely felt common cause with one another. However, precisely because of the intensity of disagreement it is important to recognize how the larger political dialogue and economic and political context influenced people across the spectrum. New Deal liberalism had such a powerful presence in the 1960s (in large part because of grassroots activism and reform movements) that even self-avowed conservatives like Nixon found it hard to reject wholesale certain basic liberal premises. This is not to say that either radicals or conservatives mindlessly absorbed the messages penetrating their society. Clearly the activism, initiative, and willingness to tackle difficult problems on both the left and the right is a testament that they did not. But the level of consensus many activists did reach—albeit strategic rather than "real" agreement —is instructive for political struggles today. Conservative politicians' conciliatory approach to political protest differed from earlier and later responses to similar problems. A mere twenty-five years later, both Democrats and Republicans would not only distance themselves from groups like NWRO, but would establish their reputation by denouncing them. The ongoing dialogue between the left and the right in the 1960s and the pressure on the right to ingratiate protesters suggests that the militant movements of the late 1960s and early 1970s should not be assessed in terms of failure or success of particular programs. Because "winning" and "losing" are never absolutes, we should instead look at their impact and influence on American culture.

During the 1960s, like all historical periods, there were multiple levels of political discourse. The dominant discourses of welfare exerted widespread influence and found outlets in policy, the press, and popular culture. Welfare recipients constructed alternative narratives about the politics of welfare. But they were never as influential, didn't have access to the same channels of information as the social workers or politicians, and had far fewer resources and less legitimacy than those with competing discourses. Even within the welfare rights movement, conflicting interpretations between staff and recipients and among recipients were characterized by differences in resources and political clout.

As the movement grew, the central conflict was that between the predominantly male, middle-class staff in the national office and the black women on welfare, most of whom worked on the grassroots level. Stereotypes about black women's promiscuity, dishonesty, and laziness dominated public perceptions about welfare. To counter this, the middle-class staff questioned the stereotypes by asserting that black women did, in fact, want to work, but that the lack of jobs and problems of day care prevented them from seeking paid employment. When public hostility did not subside, the staff considered ways to divert attention from black women and shift the movement's political focus by organizing poor working men, who they believed would draw more sympathy as recipients of public assistance.

The black women on welfare in the organization had a different approach. Since the movement's inception, they had put forth a critique of the way in which the AFDC program controlled the lives of poor women and articulated their concerns as mothers. They justified welfare assistance by arguing that as mothers, they *were* working and, therefore, contributing to society. Few black women had the "luxury" of being full-time mothers. Wage work for poor women and most black women was more often a source of oppression than a means for empowerment and had most often meant long hours, drudgery, and meager rewards, not a fulfilling career. Family often provided some of the few comforts poor and working class black families could enjoy.[7] For poor or low-income black women, their struggle to preserve the right to be mothers was a long-standing one and, historically, has been viewed as a challenge to the subordination of African Americans.[8]

Through the process of organizing, a core group of women in the welfare rights movement began to see themselves not just as mothers working to improve their children's lives, but as women struggling for autonomy and self-determination. Their political struggles with welfare officials as well as internal conflicts between the staff and the recipients over organizational platforms, fund-raising, and leadership pushed the women leaders toward advocating independence. These internal tensions led female welfare rights activists to become more aware of sexism in the organization, which in turn influenced their political development and thinking about feminism. By the time the welfare rights movement began to wane, they had formulated a full-fledged feminist agenda advocating autonomy and self-determination, and assumed control over their own organization.

So, where does this story leave us? There is certainly cause to celebrate a group of poor, stigmatized, and relatively powerless women who finally achieved the autonomy they so long desired—at least within the welfare rights movement. But that is not the whole story. Many years ago, when I started this project, I would have wanted to end there. Indeed my profound admiration for these women's achievements, given their limited resources and opportunities, initially motivated me to write about the welfare rights movement. While my respect for them has not diminished, I now view their actions and programs as having both strengths and weaknesses.

Women in the welfare rights movement made some headway on economic and social issues, including temporary access to decision-making processes within the welfare system and the larger progressive movement. Because of the movement's achievements, women on welfare participated in certain formal political processes; they won basic guarantees of their civil rights. They were accorded stature within policy-making circles that had, until then, not been granted to poor single mothers. They participated in and influenced the dialogue about poverty. They challenged the discretionary power of caseworkers. They won special grants and the right to fair hearings. They questioned unexamined assumptions about the political role of the poor, and they worked to refashion the nature of public assistance. These were enormous accomplishments. After the decline of the welfare rights movement, however, old stereotypes resurfaced with a vengeance at a time when neoliberals were employing austerity measures and neoconservatives were on the rampage against immorality; welfare recipients and single-parent families were their worst nightmare. The characterization of welfare recipients as undeserving, lazy, freeloading, promiscuous, and morally bankrupt still carried clout and found receptive audiences. The lives of the poor in this country, especially poor women and children, worsened in the years after NWRO folded. Welfare recipients were still on the margins.

In the 1980s, Democrats and Republicans found common ground in the racialized and gendered characterizations of recipients, portraying poor black women as unworthy of assistance. Politicians suggested that recipients' economic independence from men and the labor market, via the welfare system, was detrimental and threatened the stability of the black family and the viability of urban centers, where African Americans were concentrated. As Bill Moyers depicted so vividly in his 1980s documentary, *The Vanishing Family*, an entire generation of poor African Americans were ostensibly at risk because welfare bred teenage pregnancy, male irresponsibility, crime, drug use, and the unraveling of the fabric of home and community life. And in the post-Civil Rights era the voices of a new generation of black neoconservatives were added to the chorus, giving legitimacy to a racist argument against the black poor.

Moreover, as many ordinary Americans not on welfare feared—and as conservative Charles Murray explained—the black community was not the only one in jeopardy. Welfare, they argued, endangered core American values of the work ethic and family values. If working people subsidized the promiscuity, laziness, debauchery, and irresponsibility of some people, critics asked, then what will become of American society and its economic vitality? In the 1980s and 1990s, welfare became a touchstone for a general anti-social program position, a mantra for people calling for fewer taxes, smaller government, and an end to handouts for the poor. The ideology and rhetoric surrounding AFDC and the structure of the program helped to define appropriate and inappropriate behavior, shaped notions of government responsibility and the role of the state, and contributed to the restructuring of social hierarchies. Welfare also became even more closely associated with nonwhites, especially African Americans and Latinos. Stereotypes and mythologies emanated from the press, politicians, popular culture, and ordinary working-class Americans—black and white. They targeted welfare recipients as the root of many evils: from the tax burden, to the decline of family values, to the rise in drug use.[9]

Welfare came to represent all that had gone wrong with 1960s liberalism (despite the fact that most Republicans and Democrats concurred on many issues). Its failures cast a dark shadow on many public welfare programs and bolstered the individualist ethos and the work ethic. Welfare was used as a metaphor for race to discredit much of the liberal agenda of the postwar period. Few Republicans or Democrats found it politically feasible to publicly support welfare programs for fear of being labeled beholden to special interests. Kenneth Neubeck and Noel Cazenave in their important book, *Welfare Racism*, argue that the backlash of the 1960s brought welfare into the national spotlight.[10] In response to broader social and political changes, they suggest, welfare politics became a way to reestablish racial control.

In this way, welfare was essential to the dominant political discourse and served as a launching pad for a whole host of other issues. By the 1980s, the rhetoric and discourse around welfare were more virulent and less tolerant than they had been in the early 1960s. This discourse laid the basis for passage of the Personal Responsibility and Work Opportunity Act in 1996, which dismantled AFDC, our only guaranteed system of support for poor women.[11] Consequently, the trajectory of the welfare rights movement is also about the persistence and deep-seated nature of racism and sexism experienced by poor black women on AFDC. Welfare is not an isolated issue. As long as black women are not legitimately considered mothers, as long as the work of mothering is devalued, as long as independent women raising children apart from men threatens the patriarchal norm, as long as black women are characterized by a racial/class/sexual stereotype that not only stigmatizes welfare, but places them at the bottom of the social and economic hierarchy, then the forces that make the welfare system politically unpopular will remain. As many welfare recipients so clearly understood in the 1960s, overcoming the problems inherent in our system of public assistance requires that we address the broader problems of racism, sexism, and class bias.

African-American women in the welfare rights movement waged an admirable battle to better their own and their children's lives, despite encountering problems of minimal resources, personal shame, and public hostility. Their momentary victories of engaging the public dialogue and reforming the welfare system are important, particularly in light of the powerful and enduring forces arrayed against them. Their personal journeys from silent, marginalized welfare recipient to political and/or community leader testify to the strength of who they are and what they achieved. Their efforts were individual and collective. Their sustained commitment to a more just society, to helping those less fortunate than them, and to dismantling the racial/sexual structures that continue to silence many poor women, are an inspiration for anyone committed to social justice. The life of

Roxanne Jones appropriately illustrates the enormous accomplishments the movement achieved. Jones led the Philadelphia WRO since its inception in 1968. A relentless proponent of recipient leadership, she influenced developments within NWRO. After the movement declined, Jones served as a member of the Pennsylvania state senate from 1984 until 1996—the first black woman elected to that position. She became a role model and advocate for poor African Americans in North Philadelphia. In a period of renewed welfare rights activism in the mid-1990s, Jones inspired and extended practical support to welfare rights groups in Philadelphia.[12] She worked with the Kensington Welfare Rights Union and other welfare rights groups in Pennsylvania, providing assistance to individuals, speaking at rallies, attending demonstrations, and lobbying on their behalf in the state senate. Her status as a former welfare recipient and activist proved important to these modern day welfare activists. Roxanne Jones died on May 19, 1996, two months before President Clinton signed the Personal Responsibility and Work Opportunity Act.

Women like Jones don't provide a blueprint for the political struggles of the poor, but they are part of an organizing tradition that has profoundly shaped and attempted to redefine what our society stands for. While they didn't achieve everything they hoped to, their campaigns were a critical part of the push and pull of history: to reframe political debates, to think about what we value as a society, to demand more equitable and just social programs. The most powerful component of the welfare rights movement was the way in which poor women of color, battling social and economic exclusion, stood up and articulated their needs and desires. Their struggles with the welfare department and their political allies suggest that social movements and political reform cannot filter down from the top. Instead the poor and disenfranchised need to be empowered to act on their own behalf, to think and speak for themselves. This process of empowerment is an essential part of restructuring and envisioning a different kind of society. Black women on welfare in the 1960s created a political space to challenge their marginalization and modeled an alternative black female identity, one predicated on autonomy and self-determination. They formulated a theoretical position that addressed simultaneously the many levels of oppression they experienced. In the face of daunting odds, they spoke on behalf of a different set of economic values and worked to establish new racial and gendered images of poor women of color. The welfare rights movement provides a window into the organizing tradition of a group of people from whom there is much to learn. We can learn from the obstacles it encountered as well as the victories it achieved; from its contradictions and its moments of consensus.

Over the past 20 years, welfare recipients have been speaking out and acting out to halt the deliberate and dramatic moves that have shredded the safety net for poor women. Groups like the National Welfare Rights Union (NWRU), Welfare Warriors, the Kensington Welfare Rights Union in Philadelphia, the New York-based Community Voices Heard, the Contact Center in Cincinnati, People Organized to Win Employment Rights (POWER) in San Francisco, as well as countless other groups of women in local settings have staged massive protests and have resisted in many ways to express their dismay at these developments. Two recently formed coalitions, Grass Roots Organizing for Welfare Leadership (GROWL) and the National Campaign for Jobs and Income Support, have attempted to coordinate activity on a national scale. Some activists have invoked the 1948 United Nations Universal Declaration of Human Rights to insist on a basic minimum standard of living. There is also a hopeful sign for future coalition work. The dismantling of AFDC and implementation of draconian work requirements has forged a tenuous, but symbolically important, alliance between labor and welfare constituencies. Workfare programs throughout the country often require welfare recipients to work in unsafe and unhealthy environments for nothing more than their welfare check (which falls well below minimum wage). The mutual interests of unions representing workers in these occupations and welfare advocates have converged to demand that municipalities extend labor standards and union membership to workfare workers. Living-wage campaigns also draw from the ranks of labor and welfare. These campaigns seek not just wages that correlate to the cost of living, but also push for child care and health insurance. The rationale is that if the state requires work, then the state must ensure that jobs are available and well paid and that supports are in place to enable recipients to work. While these strategies have the potential to develop a broad-based movement, some of the campaigns have not gone far enough to challenge the assumptions of work or to address the particular problems of women, especially women of color, or to place value on the work of parenting. Nevertheless, taken together, these campaigns are an important intervention that can reconfigure a new progressive coalition.

Although the agenda of the renewed movement is different from that of the 1960s and the political landscape is drastically different, it is nevertheless a part of a continuity of activism that has its peaks and troughs. People like Marion Kramer, chair of NWRU, and Roxanne Jones of Philadelphia bridge the two periods of struggle. But, in addition, many contemporary activists know about the earlier struggles for welfare and draw inspiration and strength from the women who came before them. The recent activism reminds us that in a period when only a few lone voices in the public arena defend the rights, integrity, and interests of the poor, welfare rights activists make an invaluable contribution to destabilizing assumptions about poverty, welfare, and the state. As welfare recipients and their allies organize, agitate, and mobilize, they will hopefully draw on the lessons of the past to help them chart a course for future struggles for justice and equality.

Notes

Introduction

1. By welfare I am referring specifically to Aid to Families with Dependent Children (AFDC), which in 1996 was revamped and became Temporary Assistance to Needy Families (TANF).
2. Katz (1989).
3. Piven and Cloward (1977), West (1981), Bailis (1972), Deneke (1991), Gelb and Sardell (1975), Hertz (1981), Jackson and Johnson (1974), Kotz and Kotz (1977), Martin (1972), Pope (1989), Rose (1988), Whitaker (1970), More recent scholarship includes, Chappell (2002), Davis (1993), Kornbluh (1997), Kornbluh (2000), Kornbluh (2003), Orleck, "Political Education of Las Vegas Welfare Mothers," (1997), Sachs (2001), Sparks (1999), Valk (2000), White (1999), White (1990), Williams (1998).
4. See Neubeck and Cazenave (2001), Piven and Cloward (1971), Zylan (1995).
5. See, for example, King (1988), Zinn and Dill (1996), Collins (1990), Umansky (1994), Samantrai (2002), White (2001), Mullings (1997), hooks (1981), Springer (1999), Anzaldúa and Moraga (1981).
6. Mohanty (1991); Stone-Mediatore (1998).
7. Although I use the term black feminism, my understanding of black feminism is very similar to what other authors have called womanism and multicultural feminism. In my view, the term is less significant than the substantive position and set of politics that the term defines.
8. Gilroy (1987) suggests that we cannot look at class only in terms of one's relation to the means of production and that economic classes, such as "the working class" has multiple identities, including race and community. Sacks (1988) explores the connections among work, family, culture, class, and race in her study of health care organizing at the Duke Medical Center.
9. For more on the multiple versions of feminism in the 1960s and 1970s, see Gluck (1998), Springer (1999), and Roth (2004).
10. See, for example, Friedan (1963), Firestone (1970).

Chapter 1

1. Colleen Agnew. Eyewitness Walk Report. n.d. Whitaker Papers, box 1, folder 22.
2. This was called the standard of need. The 1935 Social Security Act allowed each state to set its own standard of need, but did not require it to actually pay recipients this amount.
3. OSCAW leaflet, 1966. Rally for Decent Welfare. 30 June, Whitaker Papers, box 1, folder 22. NASW. 1966. Leaflet. Ohio Walk for Decent Welfare. 30 June. Whitaker Papers, box 1, folder 22.

4. After 1962, the program was extended in some states to two-parent families in which both parents were unemployed.
5. Frost (1996: 507).
6. *New York Times.* 1 July 1966.
7. Men who received Aid to Families with Dependent Children for Unemployed Parents (AFDC-UP), which extended benefits to poor two-parent families, were also eligible to join NWRO, although few actually did.
8. Seymour M. Hersh. 1966. Seek Welfare Power Bloc. *National Catholic Reporter.* 29 June. Wiley Papers, box 27, folder 7.
9. George Wiley. 1968. The Challenge of the Powerless. Presentation at Consultation on Economic Power and Responsibility, 29 March. Wiley Papers, box 36, folder 5.
10. I distinguish between the NWRO, a national organization comprised of local groups, and the welfare rights movement more broadly, which included organizations not affiliated with NWRO.
11. See West (1981) and Bailis (1974).
12. Quadagno (1988), Abramovitz (1989), Kessler-Harris (2001), Foner (1998).
13. Nelson (1990).
14. For a fuller discussion of the impact of the institutional structure on ADC, see Lieberman (1998).
15. Winifred Bell suggests that between 1937 and 1940 African Americans made up 14 to 17 percent of the ADC caseload. Bell (1965: 34).
16. See Mink (1995).
17. See Gordon (1994), Gordon (1990), Nelson (1990), Mink (1995), Skocpol (1992), Abramovitz (1989).
18. For a discussion of wage earning and welfare, see Goodwin (1995).
19. Gordon (1994: 48–49).
20. Number of families from Abramovitz (1989: 319), Percent African American from Bell (1965: 34).
21. For more on patterns of discrimination in the early years of ADC, see Neubeck and Cazenave (2001: Ch. 3).
22. Bell (1965: Ch. 3).
23. Middlestadt (2000).
24. Bell (1965: 62).
25. Piven and Cloward (1972), Bell (1965), Zylan (1995), Abramovitz (1989), Brown (1999: Ch. 5).
26. Bell (1965: 87).
27. Piven and Cloward (1972: 244).
28. Piven and Cloward (1972), Trattner (1974: 310–311).
29. *Statistical Abstract,* (1959, 1960, 1961, 1962, 1963, 1964, 1965).
30. See Rose (1988).
31. South Side Family Council, n.d., Whitaker Papers, box 2, folder 30.
32. *Statistical Abstracts.* 1970. Table no. 428. Public Assistance—Recipients and Payments by Program: 1950–1965.
33. U.S. Advisory Council on Social Security, 1938 Final Report, pp. 17–19, in Bremner (1974) p. 535, cited in Abramovitz (1989: 321).
34. U.S. Congress, House Ways and Means Committee, Background Material and Data on Programs Within the Jurisdiction of the Committee on Ways and Means, 1986 Edition, (Washington, D.C. Government Printing Office, 1986) p. 392. Quoted in Abramovitz (1989).
35. *Historical Statistics.* Series D 87–101. Unemployment Rates for Selected Groups in the Labor Force: 1947–1970. (1975: 135).
36. *Vital Statistics.* Table 29 Ratios of Illegitimate Live Births by Color. (1968: 185).
37. *Vital Statistics.* Table 29 Ratios of Illegitimate Live Births by Color. (1968: 185).
38. See Solinger (1992) and Kunzel (1994).
39. According to a HEW report, 4.5 percent of the nation's children in 1961 were illegitimate, but only 0.5 percent were illegitimate and on ADC. U.S. Department of Health, Education and Welfare, *Public Assistance 1961, reprinted from the Annual Report 1961* (Washington), p. 31. Cited in Steiner (1966: 125).

40. This conclusion is based on an extensive review of the popular press from 1945 to 1967. The review includes coverage about welfare in *Time, U. S. News and World Report, New York Times Magazine, Saturday Evening Post, Nation's Business, Atlantic Monthly*, and *Business Week*. See, for example, *New York Times Magazine* 17 December 1961, *U. S. News and World Report* 24 July 1961, *Saturday Evening Post* 11 May 1963, *Business Week* 22 July 1961.

41. *U.S. News and World Report*. 1965. The Mystery of Rising Relief Costs., 8 March.

42. Mary S. Larabee, "Unmarried Parenthood Under the Social Security Act," *Proceedings of the National Conference of Social Work, 1939* (New York: Columbia University Press, 1939), p. 449. Quoted in Bell (1965: 34–35).

43. Piven and Cloward (1971) and Zylan (1995: 104).

44. See, for example, Jones (1985) and Boris (1993).

45. Louisiana Revised Statutes, Title 46, Section 233 (D). Quoted in "Memorandum of the ACLU Filed with the Department of Health, Education, and Welfare with Reference to the Louisiana Plan for ADC" 22 November 1960, ACLU Archives, boxes 1134–1136.

46. African American children comprised 66 percent of the caseload. Bell (1965: 138).

47. Bell (1965: 140).

48. U.S. Department of Health, Education, and Welfare (HEW), Social Security Administration (SSA), Bureau of Public Assistance (BPA). Review of Practice under the Suitability of Home Policy in Aid to Dependent Children in Louisiana. June-October, 1960. Quoted in Bell (1965: 141).

49. Jack Brady to the ACLU, 16 June 1960, ACLU Archives, boxes 1134–1136.

50. Memorandum of the ACLU Filed with the Department of Health, Education, and Welfare with Reference to the Louisiana Plan for ADC, 22 November 1960, ACLU Archives, boxes 1134–1136.

51. Bell (1965: 42).

52. Bell (1965: 100).

53. Bell (1965: Ch. 9).

54. A. H. Raskin. *New York Times Magazine*. 1961. Newburgh's Lessons for the Nation. 17 December.

55. *County and City Data Book, 1962* (1967). See also 1967 book.

56. Bell (1965: 65).

57. See Jackson (1985) and Sugrue (1996).

58. *County and City Data Book*, 1962 (1967).

59. Gallup (1972: 1961 poll, p. 1731).

60. Lisa Levenstein fleshes out this issue more fully. See Levenstein (2000) and Mittlestadt (2000).

61. For more on this transition, see Mittlestadt (2000).

62. Mink (1995) discusses how maternalists of the early twentieth century used welfare policy to Americanize and improve—through cultural reform—the mothering of ethnic white Americans.

63. Patterson (1981: 107–109).

64. For an extended discussion, see Bell (1965).

65. O'Connor (2001) traces how certain social science news of poverty achieved dominance.

66. See Patterson (1981).

67. For a discussion of race and social science theory, see Scott (1997: Chs. 5 and 6); and O'Connor (1991: Ch. 4).

68. Scott (1997).

69. Welfare Recipients in Action's Organization History. N.d., Wiley Papers, box 26. *New York Amsterdam News*, 23 July 1966.

70. Hettie Jones. Neighborhood Service Center. In Weissman, *Individual and Group Services* (1969: 38–39).

71. Milwaukee County WRO (1972: 25).

72. President's Commission on Income Maintenance Programs, 1969, *Poverty amid Plenty: The American Paradox* (Washington, D.C. 1969) p. 87, 220. Cited in Patterson (1981: 106).

73. Hettie Jones. Neighborhood Service Center. In Weissman, *Individual and Group Services* (1969: 39).

74. Loretta Johnson, Virginia Welfare Rights Organization Proposal, December 1970, Wiley Papers, box 27, folder 3.

75. Rose (1988: 168).

76. *Statistical Abstract.*, Table no. 404. Public Assistance: Payments to Recipients, by Program, by States and Other Areas. (1962: 299).
77. U.S. Commission on Civil Rights (1966).
78. *County and City Data Book*, 1967 (1967).
79. *County and City Data Book*, 1967 (1967).
80. Rose (1988: 168–170).
81. Rose (1988: 175).
82. South Side Family Council, n.d., Whitaker Papers, box 2, folder 30.
83. South Side Family Council, n.d., Whitaker Papers, box 2, folder 30.
84. For more on early organizing in Cleveland, see Rose (1988).
85. South Side Family Council, n.d., Whitaker Papers, box 2, folder 30.
86. MAW Member, Speech to VISTA Training Conference, Boston, 31 May 1969, Whitaker Papers, box 3, folder 4.
87. MAW Member, Speech to VISTA Training Conference, Boston, 31 May 1969, Whitaker Papers, box 3, folder 4.
88. Westside Mothers (ADC). The Challenge. Newsletter, 21 January 1968, Wiley Papers, box 25.
89. Burch (1971: 14).
90. *New York Times,* 21 November 1995.
91. Jermany (2003).
92. Burch (1971: 16).
93. Minneapolis Community Union Project Welfare Committee, Status Report, Late Summer 1968, Wiley Papers, box 25, folder 6.
94. Lawrence Witmer and Gibson Winter. The Problem of Power in Community Organization. (Paper presented at Conference on Community Organization, University of Chicago, 12 April 1968) p. 11, MFY Papers, box 27.
95. Lawrence Witmer and Gibson Winter. The Problem of Power in Community Organization. (Paper presented at Conference on Community Organization, University of Chicago, 12 April 1968) p. 11, MFY Papers, box 27.
96. Guaranteed Annual Income Newsletter, (August 1966: 3–5), MFY Papers, box 14.
97. Birnbaum and Rabagliati (1969: 107).
98. Birnbaum and Rabagliati (1969: 107).
99. H. Lawrence Lack. People on Welfare Form Union. *Los Angeles Free Press,* 28 April 1967, Whitaker Papers, box 1, folder 19.
100. Dorothy Moore, quoted in H. Lawrence Lack. People on Welfare Form Union. *Los Angeles Free Press,* 28 April 1967, Whitaker Papers, box 1, folder 19.
101. Citywide Welfare Alliance. Newsletter. The Recipients Speak. 12 August 1968. Wiley Papers, box 24, folder 11.
102. For a discussion of the black freedom movement outside the south, see Theoharis and Woodard (2003), Biondi (2003), Self (2003).
103. Brush (1999). Carby (1987) argues that historical subjects can only draw on available discourse. Also see Fraser (1989: Ch. 8).
104. Human Resources Administration. Department of Social Services. *Monthly New York City Public Assistance Summary Data 1960–73.* (1974). *New York Times,* 27 October 1966. Lawson (1986).
105. See Gittell (1970: Ch. 2).
106. Frost (1996: 203).
107. Mobilization for Youth. Community Development. 1965, MFY Papers, box 7.
108. George Wiley. Round-Up of June 30th Welfare Demonstrations. 28 June 1966, Whitaker Papers, box 1, folder 22.
109. MAW, Press Release, 13 May 1968, Whitaker Papers, box 3, folder 8.
110. Sanders (1983).
111. Interview with Jennette Washington. Profile of a Welfare Fighter. March 1971, MSRC, box 2165, Washington (1981). Citywide Executive Board to Commissioner Jack Goldberg, 3 December 1968, and Minutes of the Executive Board Meeting, 21 November 1971, Wiley Papers, box 8. She was on the Board during these years, but she may also have been involved during an earlier and later period.
112. Espada (2003).
113. Birnbaum and Rabagliati (1969: 103–104).

114. Birnbaum and Rabagliati (104–106). *New York Amsterdam News*, 2 April 1966.
115. Espada (2003).
116. Lawrence Witmer and Gibson Winter. The Problem of Power in Community Organization. (paper presented at the Conference on Community Organization at the University of Chicago, 12 April 1968), p. 12, MFY Papers, box 27.
117. Guaranteed Annual Income Newsletter, June 1966, MFY Papers, box 14.
118. Pat Wagner. Bread and Justice. *Voice of the West End Community Council*, 14 June 1967, Wiley Papers, box 14, folder 9.
119. OSCAW. Ohio Adequate Welfare News. Newsletter, 8 March 1968, Whitaker Papers, box 1, folder 18.
120. See, for example, Theoharis and Woodard (2003), Biondi, (2003), Self (2003).
121. Englewood WRO, Report, 16 August 1968, Wiley Papers, box 25, folder 6.
122. Chommie (1969).
123. According to Ehrenreich (1985: 149–150), in the postwar period, African Americans "went through a process of demographic concentration" and "concentration meant politicization."
124. *Historical Statistics*, Series A 83–81. Population by Type of Residence, Sex, and Race: 1880 to 1970. (1975: 12).
125. See Jackson (1985: Ch. 12).
126. Statistical Abstract (1965).
127. Williams (1998: 146–148).
128. Dotson (1997).
129. David Street, George T. Martin, Jr., and Laura Kramer Gordon, *The Welfare Industry: Functionaries and Recipients of Public Aid* (Beverly Hills, CA: Sage, 1979) p. 124. Quoted in West (1981: 45).
130. Brumm (1968: 9).
131. See Piven and Cloward (1971), Bell (1965).
132. Ritz (1966).
133. Charles Sutton. *Independent Press Telegram*. 26 May 1968, Wiley Papers, box 24, folder 13.
134. Biondi (2003), Self (2003).
135. Cloward (1997).
136. Legal Defense Fund, Pamphlet. n.d. Whitaker Papers, box 1, folder 35.
137. Milwaukee County WRO (1972: 25–26).
138. Milwaukee County WRO (1972: 68).
139. H. Lawrence Lack. People on Welfare Form Union. *Los Angeles Free Press*, 28 April 1967, Whitaker Papers, box 1, file 19.
140. Joseph E. Paull. 1967. Recipients Aroused: The New Welfare Rights Movement. *Social Work*. Wiley Papers, box 27, folder 7. Also see no author. 1965. Northern Colorado: AFDC Mothers Clubs. News from the Chapters, NASW News. 10: 11.
141. Minnie Bradford, President of North Branch AFDC League. Letter to George Wiley. January 7, 1967, MSRC, box 1998.
142. OSCAW. Ohio Adequate Welfare News. Newsletter, 13 June 1966. Whitaker Papers, box 1, folder 17.
143. Birnbaum and Rabagliati (1969: 117).
144. Lois Walker. Virginia Welfare Rights Organization Proposal. December 1970, Wiley Papers, box 27, folder 3.
145. Nancy Naples coined the phrase "activist mothering" to refer to women whose activism grew out of struggles on behalf of their children. See Naples (1992). See also Jetter, Orleck, and Taylor (1997).
146. Tyson (1999), Umoja (1996), Lee (1999), Ransby (2003).
147. Harrington (1962: 1).
148. *Historical Statistics*, Series G 16–30, Family and Individual Income, (1975: 291).
149. See Biondi (2003) Theoharis and Woodard (2003) and Self (2003) on political struggles in the North. Marchevsky and Theoharris (2000: 235–265) critique underclass theory.
150. Burch (1971: 18). Tillmon's understanding of how this phrase could be used by the poor points to the divergence between those who inserted the phrase in the Economic Opportunity Act and those who sought to put it into practice. See, for example, Moynihan (1970).

151. Hulbert James. Statement to VISTA Training Institute, Boston. 1 June 1969. Whitaker Papers, box 3, folder 4. Piven and Cloward (1997).
152. WROAC. Welfare Righter. newsletter, 7 May 1970. Wiley Papers, box 27, folder 1.
153. Weissman (1969: 106). *New York Amsterdam News*, 2 April 1966.
154. Birnbaum and Rabagliati (1969: 122, 126).
155. WRO Columbus. Welfare Rights Organization. Whitaker Papers, box 1, folder 22.
156. People's Poverty Board. An Informal Statement of its Development and Purpose. Whitaker Papers, box 2, folder 18.
157. Frost (1996).
158. Brumm (1968:2).
159. Anne Whitaker. Contacting People—Notes. 31 May 1968. Whitaker Papers, box 3, folder 8.
160. Anne Whitaker. Contacting People—Notes. 31 May 1968. Whitaker Papers, box 3, folder 8.
161. OSCAW. Ohio Adequate Welfare News. Newsletter. 30 June 1970. Whitaker Papers, box 1, folder 17. Also see Rose (1988).
162. Ehrenreich (1985: Ch. 7).
163. Cloward (1997).
164. The union formed in 1959. Freeman (2000: Ch. 12).
165. Reeser and Epstein (1990).
166. Milwaukee County WRO (1972: 41).
167. MAW. Press Release. 13 May 1968. Whitaker Papers, box 3, folder 8.
168. West (1981: Chs. 2 and 4).
169. Myles Horton. 1973. Efforts to Bring About Radical Change in Education. In *Cutting Edge*, 4: 10 Highlander Collection, box 24.
170. Birnbaum and Rabagliati (1969: 106).
171. Birnbaum and Rabagliati (1969: 106).
172. Birnbaum and Rabagliati (1969: 134).
173. Farmer (1986: 302–303).
174. For more details on Wiley's life, see Kotz and Kotz (1977).
175. Cloward and Piven (1966: 510–517).
176. Barbara Schmoll. 1967. Center Set up for War on Guaranteed Poverty. *The Milwaukee Journal*, 3 March. Wiley Papers, box 27, folder 7.
177. For more on the disagreement between Wiley and Piven and Cloward, see Piven and Cloward (1977).
178. Piven and Cloward (1997).
179. Sampson (1997).
180. Huldschiner (1968). Barbara Schmoll, *The Milwaukee Journal*, 3 March 1967, Wiley Papers, box 27, folder 7.
181. The conference, on May 21, 1966, was also attended by Richard Cloward and seventy welfare recipients and welfare rights organizers.
182. P/RAC. Summary Report of Welfare Action Meeting May 21, 1966. May 27, 1966, MSRC, box 1998.
183. Espada (2003).
184. P/RAC. Summary Report of Welfare Action Meeting May 21, 1966. May 27, 1966, MSRC, box 1998
185. Alex Efthim to Val Coleman. 23 May 1966. The Chicago Conference. MFY Papers, box 14.
186. Kotz and Kotz (1977: 188).
187. P/RAC. Notes of Fund Raising Meeting. June 8, 1966, MSRC, box 2185.
188. Seymour M. Hersh. 1966. Seek Welfare Power Bloc. *National Catholic Reporter,* 29 June. Wiley Papers, box 27, folder 7.
189. James (1981).
190. Burch (1970: 8).
191. Sanders (1983). Citywide Prospectus, 1968, Wiley Papers, box 26.
192. Jermany (2003).
193. Piven (1997).
194. NWRO. Meeting Minutes for Poverty Line Discussion. February 1967. MSRC, box 1998. They defined poverty according to the Bureau of Labor Statistics figures rather than the official poverty line set by the Department of Agriculture.
195. West (1981: 54–55).

196. At the founding of NWRO, the women adopted the title chairman. In the early 1970s, when they articulated feminist goals, they changed the title to chairwoman.

Chapter 2

1. *New York Times*, 1 July 1966.
2. Rosenblatt (1982). Others have argued that the welfare rights movement was too radical. See, for example, Edsall and Edsall (1992), Moynihan (1973), Burke and Burke (1974).
3. Jennette Washington. I Challenge. published article, source unknown, n.d., Wiley Papers, box 28, folder 1.
4. William Engelhardt (Director of the Training Program in Community Development at the Penn Center) quoted in Tom Peck, Jr. 58 Welfare Applicants Appeal Decisions. *The (Charleston) News and Courier.* 3 August 1968, Wiley Papers, box 27, folder 2.
5. Etta Horn. Speech before Congress. 20 May 1969. Wiley Papers, box 24, folder 11.
6. Birnbaum and Rabagliati (1969: 133).
7. See, for example, Katz (1986), Mink (1995), Gordon (1994).
8. Caesar (1996).
9. Marie Childress. Chairwoman Cuyahoga County WRM. Letter to George Wiley. 14 September 1967. MSRC, box 1998. Cuyahoga County WRM. Newsletter. November 1967. MSRC, box 2139.
10. See Lipsky (1984).
11. Abramontz (1988): 337–338.
12. Citywide Welfare Alliance. The Recipients Speak. Newsletter. 12 August 1968. Wiley Papers, box 24, folder 11.
13. Joy Stanley. President L.A. County WRO. Speech at Public Forum. Citizens Committee for a Decent Welfare System. 5 September 1966, MSRC, box 1998.
14. See Ehrenreich (1985) and Trattner (1974).
15. Birnbaum and Rabagliati (1969: 133).
16. *New York Times*, 22 July 1967.
17. Milwaukee County WRO (1972: 132).
18. Joy Stanley. President L.A. County WRO. Speech at Public Forum. Citizens Committee for a Decent Welfare System. 5 September 1966. MSRC, box 1998.
19. PAPAW: How It Started, What It's Hoping to Do. *Berkshire Eagle,* 30 June 1967.
20. Englewood WRO. Report. 16 August 1968. Wiley Papers, box 25, folder 6.
21. Philadelphia WRO. Petition for Rights and Respect to Chairman and Executive Director of County Board of Assistance. 30 June 1967. MSRC, box 1998.
22. Philadelphia WRO. Petition for Rights and Respect to Chairman and Executive Director of County Board of Assistance. 30 June 1967. MSRC, box 1998.
23. Jennette Washington. I Challenge. published article. source unknown. n.d.. Wiley Papers, box 28, folder 1.
24. William Engelhardt (Director of the Training Program in Community Development at the Penn Center) quoted in Tom Peck, Jr. 58 Welfare Applicants Appeal Decisions. *The (Charleston) News and Courier.* 3 August 1968. Wiley Papers, box 27, folder 2.
25. Anna Marie LeClaire (Co-Chair of Massachusetts WRO). Speech at Rally, Boston. 30 June 1969. Whitaker Papers, box 3, folder 6.
26. Johnnie Tillmon and George Wiley to Wilbur Cohen (Secretary of Health, Education and Welfare). 8 January 1969. Wiley Papers, box 23, folder 3.
27. Johnnie Tillmon and George Wiley to Wilbur Cohen (Secretary of Health, Education and Welfare). 8 January 1969. Wiley Papers, box 23, folder 3.
28. Brumm (1968).
29. Minneapolis Community Union Project Welfare Committee. Status Report. Late Summer 1968. Wiley Papers, box 25, folder 6.
30. Englewood WRO. Report. 16 August 1968. Wiley Papers, box 25, folder 6.
31. Center on Social Welfare Policy and Law. Guidelines for the Preparation of Welfare Rights Handbooks. n.d.. Wiley Papers, box 15, folder 1.
32. Eleanor Norton. Memo to ACLU Foundation Board Regarding Proposed Welfare Civil Liberties Project. 11 November 1969. ACLU Papers, boxes 1134–1136.
33. Kornbluh (2000).

34. Shreshinsky (1970: 103).
35. Collection of WRO Handbooks. Whitaker Papers, box 3, file 17.
36. Charles Sutton. Newspaper Article. *Independent Press Telegram*. 26 May 1968. Wiley Papers, box 24, folder 13.
37. Brumm (1968).
38. Hinds County Welfare Rights Movement. Your Welfare Rights. Handbooks. July 1967 and March 1968. ACLU Archives, boxes 1134–1136.
39. Hinds County Welfare Rights Movement. Your Welfare Rights. Handbooks. July 1967 and March 1968. ACLU Archives, boxes 1134–1136.
40. *Beckley Post Herald*. 25 February 1971. Wiley Papers, box 27, folder 3.
41. L.A. County WRO. Newsletter. 1 November 1968. Wiley Papers, box 24, folder 13.
42. Andrew Bowler III (Executive Director of VWRO). Proposal. December 1970. Wiley Papers, box 27, folder 3.
43. Center on Social Welfare Policy and Law, A Project in Lay Advocacy, July 1967, Wiley Papers, box 14.
44. Nashco. Proposal for a One-Year Demonstration Grant to Train Welfare Recipients as Lay Advocates in the Legal Field. 14 June 1968. Wiley Papers, box 30, folder 1.
45. Myles Horton. 1973. Efforts to Bring About Radical Change in Education. In *Cutting Edge*, 4: 10. Highlander Collection, box 24.
46. Ehrenreich (1985: 176).
47. *New York Times*, 22 July 1967.
48. No author (probably NWRO staff). Project in Lay Advocacy. 1967. Wiley Papers, box 14. *New York Times*, 15 July 1968. Ginger (1970: 111) no. 673.
49. OSCAW. Press Release. 22 November 1967. Whitaker Papers, box 1, folder 16.
50. MAW member. Speech to VISTA Training Conference, Boston. 31 May 1969. Whitaker Papers, box 3, folder 4.
51. Brumm (1968: 8). Massachusetts WRO. The Adequate Income Times. Newsletter. 7 January 1969. Whitaker Papers, box 3, folder 5.
52. Englewood WRO. Report. 16 August 1968. Wiley Papers, box 25, folder 6.
53. NWRO. Report on Welfare Rights Organization Conference on Minimum Standards Campaigns. 12, 13 January, 1968, MSRC, box 1998.
54. For an extended discussion of the fair hearing process, see Kornbluh (2000: Chs. 6 and 7).
55. D.C. Citywide WRO. We Rap. Newsletter. 10 June 1969. Wiley Papers, box 24, folder 11.
56. Robert Maier. Field Notes. 8 April 1968. Whitaker Papers, box 3, folder 3.
57. Minneapolis Community Union Project Welfare Committee. Status Report. Late Summer 1968. Wiley Papers, box 25, folder 6.
58. Streshinsky (1970: 115).
59. Erie WRO. History. n.d. (probably August 1968). Wiley Papers, box 27, folder 1.
60. Mobilization for Youth. Meeting Minutes for the Committee on Individual, Family, and Group Services. 2 February 1966. MFY Papers, box 8.
61. Andrew Bowler III. Executive Director of VWRO. Proposal: Virginia WRO. December 1970. Wiley Papers, box 27, folder 3.
62. Lois Walker. VWRO Proposal. December 1970. Wiley Papers, box 27, folder 3.
63. Eleanor Norton. Memo to ACLU Foundation Board Regarding Proposed Welfare Civil Liberties Project. 11 November 1969. ACLU Archives, boxes 1134–1136.
64. See Davis (1993: Chs. 2 and 3).
65. Author unknown. Rights of Welfare Recipients. Weekly Bulletin. 16 October 1967. ACLU Archives, boxes 1134–1136.
66. Citywide Coordinating Committee of Welfare Rights Groups. Tell it Like it is. Newsletter. 22 May 1968. Wiley Papers, box 26. Ginger (1970: 110–111, 115–116) no. 673. *New York Times*, 30 January 1968, 27 November 1968. Davis (1993).
67. See Reich (1964) and Reich (1965).
68. OSCAW. Ohio Adequate Welfare News. Newsletter. 21 October 1968. Whitaker Papers, box 1, folder 17.
69. See Davis (1993: Ch. 8) and Bussiere (1989).
70. Jermany (2003).

71. For the relationship between the legal struggle and the social movement, see White (1990), Davis (1993). Lim (1991).
72. *New York Times*, 5 March 1968.
73. George Wiley to Hannah Weinstein (Emergency Committee for Action Against Poverty and Hunger). n.d. (probably 1967 or 1968). Wiley Papers, box 21, folder 3.
74. See, for example, Lewis (1966) and Harrington (1962). Some of this history is also covered in Ehrenreich (1985: Ch. 6).
75. Walter Heller. Memo to Council of Economic Advisers. 5 November 1963. Legislative History of the Economic Opportunity Act of 1964. Johnson Papers, box 1.
76. Administrative History of the Office of Economic Opportunity. Vol. 1:164–165, Johnson Papers.
77. Adam Yarmolinsky cited in Administrative History of the Office of Economic Opportunity. Vol. 1, p. 185. Johnson Papers.
78. NWRO Workshop Report. Negotiating with the Welfare Department. 27 August 1967. Whitaker Papers, box 1, folder 27.
79. Administrative History of the Office of Economic Opportunity. Vol. 1, p. 208–209. Johnson Papers.
80. H. Lawrence Lack. People on Welfare Form Union. *Los Angeles Free Press*. 28 April 1967. Whitaker Papers, box 1, folder 19.
81. See Sparks (1999).
82. See Carson (1981), Gitlin (1987), Payne (1995), Students for a Democratic Society (1990).
83. Bouchier (1987: 63–99).
84. George Wiley and Beulah Sanders. Draft of Letter to Larry O'Brien. n.d. Wiley Papers, box 32, folder 6.
85. Burch (1971).
86. OSCAW to President Lyndon Johnson. 30 January 1968. Whitaker Papers, box 1, folder 7. National Coordinating Committee, Minutes. 4 February 1968. Wiley Papers, box 7, folder 11.
87. Beulah Sanders. Statement Before the Presidential Commission on Income Maintenance. 5 June 1969. Wiley Papers, box 22, folder 4.
88. *Boston Globe*, 18 August 1968. Massachusetts WRO. Welfare Rights Handbook. n.d. Whitaker Papers, box 3, folder 5.
89. Mary Davidson. Interviews. October 1968. Whitaker Papers, box 3, folder 6.
90. Philadelphia WRO. History of Roxanne Jones' Involvement with Welfare Rights. n.d. (probably 1971). Wiley Papers, box 27, folder 1.
91. Joe McDermott. *Congressional Record*. 3 April 1969. Wiley Papers, box 21, folder 2.
92. Carmichael and Hamilton (1967), Lawson (1986), Self (2003).
93. Brenda Fisher. Indians Ask Control of Reservation Aid. *The (Kansas City) Star*. n.d. (possibly 1969). Wiley Papers, box 30, folder 4.
94. Brooklyn Welfare Action Council. Newsletter. 24 January 1969. Wiley Papers, box 26, folder 3.
95. See Gilbert (1983:118).
96. Ohlin and Cloward (1960) argued that institutions serving the poor would best be reformed by the poor.
97. Van Til (2003).
98. A similar policy about decision making guided the United Auto Workers in the 1960s. See Boyle (1995: Ch. 8).
99. See Hooks (1989).
100. See Fraser (1989) and Spivak (1988).
101. OSCAW. Ohio Adequate Welfare News. Newsletter. 14 March 1967. Whitaker Papers, box 1, folder 17.
102. Minutes of Meeting between Columbus WRO and Franklin County Welfare Department. 3 March 1967. Whitaker Papers, box 2, folder 3.
103. Mary Davidson. Interviews. October 1968. Whitaker Papers, box 3, folder 6.
104. *New York Times*, 1 July 1966, 16 July 1966. Birnbaum and Rabagliati (1969: 105).
105. Gilbert (1983).
106. Stanley Kravitz quoted in Administrative History of the Office of Economic Opportunity, Vol. 1, p. 19, 166–167, Johnson Papers.

107. Fraser (1989: 161) suggests that the negotiation takes place in the "social" which she defines as a sphere of public discourse that cuts across economic, political, and domestic arenas.

108. OSCAW. Press Release. 13 January 1967. Whitaker Papers, box 1, folder 16.

109. Massachusetts WRO. Legislative Alert. 26 May 1969. Whitaker Papers, box 2, folder 38.

110. Des Moines WRO. Report. August 1968. Wiley Papers, box 25, folder 2.

111. Brooklyn Welfare Action Council. Newsletter. 24 January 1969. Wiley Papers, box 26, folder 3.

112. Huldschiner (1968).

113. Minneapolis Community Union Project Welfare Committee. Status Report. Late Summer 1968. Wiley Papers, box 25, folder 6.

114. West Center City Welfare Rights Committee. Progress Report. 1968. Wiley Papers, box 25, folder 1.

115. MAW Member. Speech to VISTA Training Conference, Boston. 31 May 1969. Whitaker Papers, box 3, folder 4.

116. Wiley had written a letter to King in October 1966, urging King, in his campaign for poor people's rights and a guaranteed income, to take into account the "emerging local movements of welfare recipient groups in cities across the country." But King didn't meet with them for more than a year. George Wiley to Martin Luther King, 15 October 1966. Reprinted in the Poverty/Rights Action Center. Letter to Welfare Rights Leaders and Organizers. 31 October 1966. Wiley Papers, box 9.

117. *New York Times*, 9 July 1995, Sampson (1997).

118. Ruth Wootten. Do You Recognize These People? Leaflet. July 1968. Wiley Papers, box 24, folder 12.

119. Ralph Huitt (Asst Secretary for Legislation) to Mary Switzer (Administrator of SRS). 14 June 1968. Records of the Dept. of HEW, box 12, folder: Poor People's Campaign, Johnson Papers.

120. Office of the Administrator, Memo to State Administrators Regarding Response to Demands of the Poor People's Campaign. 31 May 1968. Records of the Dept. of HEW, box 12, folder: Poor People's Campaign, Johnson Papers.

121. Mary Switzer (Administrator of SRS). Memo to all SRS Employees. 10 May 1968. Records of the Dept. of HEW, box 12, folder: Poor Peoples Campaign, Johnson Papers.

122. HEW. Chart of Poor People's Campaign Demands. n.d. Records of the Dept. of HEW, box 46, folder: Poor Peoples Campaign, Johnson Papers.

123. Milton L. Shurr. Memo to Members of the SRS Committee on the Poor People's Campaign. 19 June 1968. Records of the Dept. of HEW, box 12, folder: Poor Peoples Campaign, Johnson Papers.

124. Fred Steininger (Asst Administrator of States Relations). Memo to Margaret Emery (SRS Policy Coordinator). 24 August 1968. Records of the Dept. of HEW, box 12, folder: Poor Peoples Campaign, Johnson Papers.

125. Fred Steininger. Memo to Regional Directors. 29 August 1968. Records of the Dept. of HEW, box 12, folder: Poor Peoples Campaign, Johnson Papers.

126. Neil Fallon (Regional Commissioner of HEW) to George Wiley. 23 August 1968. Wiley Papers box 23, folder 2.

127. For more on the broader definition of the black freedom movement, see Marable (1991), Ransby (2003), Tyson (1998).

128. Carmichael and Hamilton (1967: 173).

129. White (1990: 870).

130. White (1990: 884).

131. Bill Pastreich. Speech to the Student Health Organization. June 1969. Whitaker Papers, box 3, folder 10.

132. Maya Miller (League of Women Voters) to Paul Leonard. Wiley Papers, box 32, folder 1.

133. Hancock (2000) explores how the public identity of the welfare queen limits citizen participation.

134. Williams (1991: 153).

135. Lim (1991: 73).

136. This is very similar to a development in the labor movement in the 1930s when unions shattered management's arbitrary power over labor. Brody (1993) calls the new system of procedures "workplace contractualism."

137. Williams (1991: 159).

Chapter 3

1. Organizer Tim Sampson, who worked in the national office, came up with this slogan. Sampson (1997).
2. Graham (1990).
3. Espada (2003).
4. Minutes of the Committee on Individual, Group, and Family Services. 2 February 1966. MFY Papers, box 8, and Birnbaum and Rabagliati (1969: 112).
5. The Welfare Marches. *Trans-Action* 4 (2) (December 1966) Wiley Papers, box 27, folder 7. Brooklyn Welfare Action Council. A Description of the Birth and Growth of the Brooklyn Welfare Action Council. Wiley Papers, box 26. *New York Times*, 19 January 1968. *New York Times*, 20 November 1966. *New York Times*, 5 November 1966.
6. Welfare Grievance Committee, Newsletter, 28 June 1966, Whitaker Papers, box 1, folder 18.
7. OSCAW, Telegram to Governor Rhodes, 26 October 1966, Whitaker Papers, box 1, folder 1.
8. Judy Rensberger, *Detroit's Daily Express*, 9 December 1967, Wiley Papers, box 25.
9. *New York Times*, 30 May 1968, 31 May 1968, 1 June 1968.
10. *New York Times*, 16 July 1968, 31 August 1968.
11. Citywide Coordinating Committee of Welfare Rights Groups, Tell It Like It Is, Newsletter, 22 May 1968, Wiley Papers, box 26. *New York Times*, 30 May 1968.
12. "Citywide Demands," 28 June 1968, Wiley Papers, box 26, folder 1.
13. "Tell It Like It Is," Citywide Newsletter, 19 July 1968, Wiley Papers, box 26. *New York Times*, 4 July 1968, 17 July 1968, 15 July 1968, 14 August 1968. Beulah Sanders, Press Statement, 3 July 1968, Wiley Papers, box 26. and "Citywide Demands," 28 June 1968, Wiley Papers, box 26.
14. Sampson (1997).
15. *New York Times*, 20 September 1966. Ginger (1970: 110–111, 114–116).
16. "Ohio Adequate Welfare News" OSCAW Newsletter, 23 January 1969, Whitaker Papers, box 1, folder 17.
17. Gloria Brown, Report to NWRO, Before 2 January 1969, Wiley Papers, box 25, folder 4. Westside Mothers ADC, Report to NWRO, 30 December 1968, Wiley Papers, box 25, folder 4.
18. "NWRO in Action" Booklet, Welfare Rights Collection, Lehman Library.
19. Sampson (1997).
20. Kansas City Welfare Rights Training Project, "Background Information on Welfare Rights Mothers' Attempt to Secure School Clothing in Wyandotte County" 11 September 1968. Rev. Carl Crider, untitled article, *Community Now*, 15 November 1968, Wiley Papers, box 25, folder 2.
21. Linton (2003).
22. West (1981: 50).
23. *Boston Globe*, 18 August 1968, Welfare Rights Handbook, Whitaker Papers, box 3, folder 5.
24. "History of MWRO," 10 June 1969, Whitaker Papers, box 2, folder 38.
25. MacDonald (1969).
26. MacDonald (1969).
27. Friends of MWRO, Newsletter, 15 February 1969, Whitaker Papers, box 2, folder 40.
28. *Boston Globe*, 29 September 1968, Welfare Rights Handbook, Whitaker Papers, box 3, folder 5.
29. Alinsky (1969: xiv) quoted in Bailis (1972: 95).
30. Bill Pastreich, Quoted in *Boston Globe*, 29 September 1968, Welfare Rights Handbook, Whitaker Papers, box 3, folder 5.
31. See Finks (1984), Horwitt (1989).
32. Bailis (1972: 87).
33. Sampson (1997).
34. Linton (2003).
35. For more on the Boston model, see Bailis (1972).
36. MacDonald (1969).
37. Bailis (1972: 2).
38. MacDonald (1969).
39. Massachusetts WRO, "The Adequate Income Times," 31 October 1968, Whitaker Papers, box 3, folder 5.

40. NWRO, "Report on Welfare Rights Organization Conference on Minimum Standards Campaigns," 12–13 January 1968, MSRC, box 1998.
41. NWRO, NWRO Winter Action Campaign Ideas, Fall 1968, MSRC, box 2024.
42. Birnbaum and Rabagliati (1969: 135).
43. Andrew Bowler III, Executive Director of VWRO, "Proposal: Virginia WRO" December 1970, Wiley Papers, box 27, folder 3.
44. Andrew Bowler III, Executive Director of VWRO, "Proposal: Virginia WRO" December 1970, Wiley Papers, box 27, folder 3.
45. Lewis (1968).
46. Columbus WRO, flier, n.d., Whitaker Papers, box 1, folder 12.
47. *Evening Gazette*, 14 August 1968, Welfare Rights Handbook, Whitaker Papers, box 3, folder 5.
48. OSCAW, "Ohio Adequate Welfare News" Newsletter, 9 January 1967, Whitaker Papers, box 1, folder 17.
49. See, for example, Williams (1998) and Higginbotham (1993).
50. "Welfare Parents Group to Submit 16 Demands," *Berkshire Eagle*, 29 June 1967 and 8 July 1967.
51. Philadelphia WRO, "A Study Document on Welfare Rights Goals," n.d., Wiley Papers, box 27, folder 1.
52. Mary Wallace, "Welfare Mothers Seek Clothing Funds" *Ann Arbor News*, 4 September 1968, Wiley Papers, box 25.
53. Mary Wallace, "Mothers Reject Offer" *Ann Arbor News*, 6 September 1968, Wiley Papers, box 25.
54. Mary Wallace, "$60 ADC Grants to be Ready Monday" *Ann Arbor News*, 7 September 1968. Wiley Papers, box 25.
55. Birnbaum and Rabagliati (1969: 110).
56. Rhode Island Fair Welfare, Flier, "Experimental Title I Clothing Proposal," 30 July 1970, Wiley Papers, box 27, folder 2.
57. Philadelphia WRO, "A Study Document on Welfare Rights Goals," n.d., Wiley Papers, box 27, folder 1.
58. See Bell (1956) and Friedan (1963).
59. The Clarks found similar results for black children in the North. In addition, their research did not address the specific issue of school segregation, rather segregation, or racism, generally. See Kluger (1976) and Markowitz and Rosner (1996).
60. For a discussion of the evolution of social science and liberal racial ideology, see Scott (1997). For more on the Brown decision, see Kluger (1976).
61. May (1988) and Feldstein (2000).
62. Palladino (1997).
63. *New York Times*, 30 August 1968.
64. Massachusetts Department of Public Welfare, Memo to Regional Administrators, 11 March 1969, MSRC, box 2139.
65. MWRO, "Summary of Actions and News Coverage," 26 March 1969, Whitaker Papers, box 2, folder 37.
66. *Record American*, 30 November 1968, Welfare Rights Booklet, Whitaker Papers, box 3, folder 5.
67. Zala Forizs (Scholarship, Education, and Defense Fund for Racial Equality), "Letter to Tim Sampson," 4 December 1968, Wiley Papers, box 26, folder 6.
68. OSCAW, "Ohio Adequate Welfare News," Newsletter, 8 October 1967, Whitaker Papers, box 1, folder 17.
69. U.S. Riot Commission (1968: 299–318). Also see O'Reilly (1989) and Churchill and Vander Wall (1988).
70. *New York Times*, 17 July 1968, 15 July 1968. *New York Daily News*, 4 July 1968.
71. *New York Times*, 26 June 1968, 27 August 1968.
72. *Boston Globe*, 20 April 1969, Welfare Rights Handbook, Whitaker Papers, box 3, folder 5.
73. Citizens Committee to Change Welfare, Newsletter, 21 June 1970, Whitaker Papers, box 3, folder 5. Date of proposed change was August 15, 1970.
74. *New York Times*, 6 September 1968.
75. "Fact Sheet for Welfare Clients on Goldberg's Increase," 1968, Wiley Papers, box 26.

76. *New York Times*, 24 July 1968.
77. *New York Times*, 31 August 1968.
78. Crisis in Welfare in Cleveland (1969: 4).
79. Meeting of MWRO Organizers, 13 April 1969, Whitaker Papers, box 2, folder 38.
80. According to Bobby Seale of the Black Panther Party, in 1969 women made up two-thirds of the nationwide membership. Cleaver (2001: 125). Umoja (1996) argues that in Mississippi women were actively involved in armed resistance in the early 1960s.
81. U.S. Riot Commission (1968).
82. "Tell It Like It Is," Citywide Newsletter, 16 August 1968, Wiley Papers, box 26.
83. Sanders (1983). *New York Times*, 28 August 1968, 29 August 1968. *New York Amsterdam News*, 7 September 1968.
84. *New York Times*, 30 August 1968, 31 August 1968, 4 September 1968, 5 September 1968, 6 September 1968. *New York Amsterdam News*, 7 September 1968.
85. Piven and Cloward, (1967). *New York Times*, 26 October 1968.
86. *New York Times*, 24 September 1968.
87. *New York Times*, 26 October 1968, 8 November 1968.
88. Milton Berliner, "Welfare Voice: We Are Living Like Dogs" *The Daily News*, 27 April 1966, Whitaker Papers, box 3, folder 14.

Chapter 4

1. Cohen (2003: 11) argues that there was a "complex shared commitment on the part of policymakers, business and labor leaders, and civic groups to put mass consumption at the center of their plans for a prosperous postwar America."
2. In the 1930s trickle-down economics referred to Hoover's policy of tax cuts for the rich. For more on liberal economic policy in the 1960s, see Matusow (1984), Galbraith (1958).
3. Vivian Henderson (President of Clark College), "Jobs, Job Training, Economic Security and National Economic Policies" (paper presented at White House Conference on Civil Rights, Washington, D.C., 1965),Wiley Papers, box 7, folder 1.
4. Brinkley (1989).
5. OEO, "Statement of OEO Before Consumer Subcommittee of House Government Operations Committee," 12 October 1967, MFY Papers, box 23.
6. Benson (1996: 229).
7. George Katona et al., *1969 Survey of Consumer Finances* (Ann Arbor: Survey Research Center, Institute for Social Research, University of Michigan, 1970), 25, Cited in Andreasen (1975: 34).
8. See Caplovitz (1963), Andreasen (1975), and Aaker and Day, (1971).
9. Caplovitz (1963).
10. Federal Trade Commission *Economic Report on Installment Credit and Retail Sales Practices of District of Columbia Retailers* (Washington, D.C.: GPO, 1968) Cited in Andreasen (1975: 192–195).
11. Caplovitz (1963). See also Andreasen (1975) on black consumers and credit.
12. Lyndon B. Johnson, "Message to Committee on Consumer Interest," 5 February 1964, Johnson (1968).
13. OEO, "Statement of OEO Before the Subcommittee on Consumer Affairs of the House Committee on Banking and Currency on H.R. 11601," 9 August 1967, MFY Papers, box 23.
14. Ownby (1999).
15. Hine (1994).
16. For a fuller discussion, see de Grazia (1996).
17. Frank (1991) suggests this was the case in her study of the Seattle labor movement.
18. For more on the "third-wave" consumer movement and a general history of postwar consumerism, see Cohen (2003: Ch. 8).
19. David B. McCalmong, "Franklin County Welfare Information: Sales Impact of Welfare Expenditures", 1969, Whitaker Papers, box 2, folder 12.
20. George Wiley, "Letter to the Coca-Cola Company," 22 January 1969, Wiley Papers, box 7, folder 8.

21. MFY, Community Development Division, "Proposal for a Community Program in Consumer Affairs," June 1966, MFY Papers, box 20A.
22. D.C. Citywide Welfare Rights Organization, "We Rap" Newsletter, 10 June 1969, Wiley Papers, box 24, folder 11.
23. Ohio Steering Committee for Adequate Welfare, "Ohio Adequate Welfare News" newsletter, 14 June 1967, Whitaker Papers, box 1, folder 17.
24. Peggy Terry, "JOIN Community Union Newsletter" 1 March 1967, Whitaker Papers, box 3.
25. Hill Resident Welfare Moms, "Hill Residents: Save Money," n.d., Wiley Papers, box 25, folder 1.
26. Des Moines WRO, Report, August 1968, Wiley Papers, box 25, folder 2.
27. Hulbert James, Speech to VISTA Training Institute, Boston, 1 June 1969, Whitaker Papers, box 3, folder 4.
28. Kotz and Kotz (1977: 235–6).
29. *New York Times*, 22 November 1968, 23 November 1968, 7 February 1969. Citywide Coordinating Committee of Welfare Rights Groups, Newsletter, "Tell It Like It Is," 7 November 1968, Wiley Papers, box 26. NWRO, Booklet, "NWRO in Action," Welfare Rights Collection, Lehman Library.
30. Bob Agard, "Welfare Rights Group Seeks Charge Accounts," 6 December 1968, Wiley Papers, box 25, folder 2. "NWRO in Action," Lehman Library.
31. *New York Times*, 9 December 1968, Wiley Papers, box 25, folder 2.
32. Michigan WRO, Newsletter, "Mother Power," April 1969, Wiley Papers, box 25, folder 5.
33. George Wiley, Press Release, 27 March 1969, Wiley Papers, box 15, folder 2.
34. NWRO, "Ways and Means Committee Meeting Minutes," 24 March 1969, MSRC, box 2247. NWRO, "Ways and Means Committee Meeting Minutes," 25 March 1969, MSRC, box 2247. OSCAW, Flier, "Ohio's Continuing Welfare Disgrace," n.d., Wiley Papers, box 1, folder 1.
35. NWRO, "Sears Boycott Action List," 9 April 1969, Wiley Papers, box 15, folder 2.
36. Michigan WRO, Newsletter, "Mother Power," April 1969, Wiley Papers, box 25, folder 5.
37. Bailis (1974: 62–63).
38. Claradine James, "A Report on the National Coordinating Committee," June 1969, MSRC, box 2139. *New York Times*, 28 May 1969.
39. John Lewis (Director of Career Development, Klein Co.), "Letter to George Wiley," 17 October 1969, Wiley Papers, box 15, folder 2.
40. *New York Times*, 15 July 1969.
41. Author Unknown, Description of Massachusetts WRO, 10 June 1969, Whitaker Papers, box 2, folder 38.
42. Philadelphia WRO, History of Roxanne Jones Involvement, n.d. (probably 1971), Wiley Papers, box 27, folder 1.
43. George Wiley, Speech at MWRO Rally, Boston, 30 June 1969, Whitaker Papers, box 3, folder 6.
44. Kornbluh (1997, 2000, 2003) has elaborated on this point.
45. George Wiley and Etta Horn, "Letter to R.W. Mayer, President of W.T. Grant Co.," 12 September 1969, Wiley Papers, box 15, folder 2.
46. Etta Horn, Joint Press Release by Bert DeLeeuw of NWRO and Hugh Tassey of Montgomery Ward, 8 December 1969, Wiley Papers, box 15, folder 2.
47. For more on market segmentation, see Cohen (2003) Ch. 7.
48. For a fuller discussion, see Weems (1998).
49. See Van Deburg (1992: Ch. 5), Fergus (2002).
50. *Sponsor*, October 1962, quoted in Weems (1994: 96).
51. John Johnson, *Succeeding Against the Odds*: quoted in Weems (1994: 100).
52. See Frank (1997).
53. Douglas (2000) argues that corporations appropriated women's liberation and transformed it into personal private desires (p. 267). Indulging and pampering oneself became the way feminism was redefined by corporate America, which promised women products that made them feel more successful, more worthy, and that they have greater control over their lives, suggesting women's power comes from looking and feeling beautiful, thus reinforcing basic tenets of antifeminism.
54. Isadore Barmash, *New York Times*, 20 July 1969, Wiley Papers, box 15, folder 2.
55. Abramovitz (1995). Kornbluh (1997) also suggests that looking at NWRO's consumer strategies can help us rethink the wage-work philosophies of protest.

56. Solinger (2001: 179–182).
57. Kathy Peiss, "Making Faces: The Cosmetics Industry and the Cultural Construction of Gender, 1890–1930" cited in Weems, (2000: 172).
58. Weems (2000: 166).
59. Kornbluh (2000: Ch. 9) discusses the discretionary nature of the welfare budget as a basis for recipients' struggles.
60. NWRO, "Using Group Credit to Strengthen Your WRO," Fall 1969, Wiley Papers, box 15, folder 2.
61. Washington (1981). Citywide Coordinating Committee of Welfare Rights Groups, Leaflet, n.d., Wiley Papers, box 26.
62. OSCAW, Steering Committee Minutes, 25 October 1969, Whitaker Papers, box 1, folder 15.
63. Hulbert James, Speech to VISTA Training Institute, Boston, 1 June 1969, Whitaker Papers, box 3, folder 4.
64. Meeting of MWRO Organizers, 13 April 1969, Whitaker Papers, box 2, folder 38.
65. Hulbert, James, Speech to VISTA Training Institute, Boston, 1 June 1969, Whitaker Papers, box 3, folder 4.
66. NWRO Group Credit Guidelines, Fall 1969, Wiley Papers, box 15, folder 2.
67. Johnnie Tillmon and George Wiley, Letter to H.J. Morgans, President, Proctor and Gamble, 16 December 1968, Wiley Papers, box 16, folder 5.
68. Wiley, "Memo to all Local WRO's," 17 August 1969, Wiley Papers, box 7, folder 8.
69. William Procter, "Memo to George Wiley and Hulbert James," 21 October 1969, Wiley Papers, box 14, folder 4.
70. MWRO, Welfare Food Budget Project Report, April 1969, Wiley Papers, box 24, folder 9.
71. George Wiley, Speech at MWRO Rally, Boston, 30 June 1969, Whitaker Papers, box 3, folder 6.
72. MWRO, Welfare Food Budget Project Report, April 1969, Wiley Papers, box 24, folder 9.
73. MWRO, Welfare Food Budget Project Report, April 1969, Wiley Papers, box 24, folder 9.
74. MWRO, Welfare Food Budget Project Report, April 1969, Wiley Papers, box 24, folder 9.
75. Anonymous Letter, MWRO Welfare Food Budget Project Report, 10 April 1969, Wiley Papers, box 24, folder 9.
76. Marilyn Salzman Webb, "Week of Welfare Protests," The Guardian, 5 July 1969 Wiley Papers, box 24, folder 9.
77. Eleanor RoseBrugh, The Syracuse Post-Standard, 8 December 1969, Wiley Papers, box 26, folder 5.
78. MWRO, Welfare Food Budget Project Report, April 1969, Wiley Papers, box 24, folder 9.
79. MWRO, Welfare Food Budget Project Report, April 1969, Wiley Papers, box 24, folder 9.
80. Sachs (2001: Ch. 4).
81. Welfare Grievance Committee (Cleveland), Leaflet, "Something Is Wrong," August 1966, Whitaker Papers, box 1, folder 35.
82. Patterson (1981: 86).
83. Joseph McCarthy, Sun-Telegram, n.d., Wiley Papers, box 14, folder 9.
84. Laurens Silver (Deputy Director, Law Reform and Education), Letter to Wylie [sic], 9 October 1968, Wiley Papers, box 24, folder 11.
85. Appelbaum (1977). Duncan (1984). Patterson (1981).
86. Brumm (1968).
87. Milwaukee County WRO (1972: 29–30).
88. Matusow (1984: 160).
89. Patterson (1981: 79).
90. Clarence Singleton, Congressional Record, 3 April 1969, Wiley Papers, box 21, folder 2.
91. South Side Family Council, "Letter to the City-County Relief Committee" 16 August 1963, Whitaker Papers, box 2, folder 10.
92. Dave Hess, "They Walked and they Talked . . . 1" in WRFD Commentator, July 1966, Whitaker Papers, box 1, folder 22.

Chapter 5

1. West (1981: 50). Bailis (1972) writes that NWRO claimed a membership of between 75,000 and 125,000.
2. Bailis (1972: 55).

3. West (1981: 51).
4. West (1981: 52).
5. West (1981: 51).
6. See Evans (1979).
7. West (1981: 84).
8. Minutes of NWRO Executive Committee Meeting, 24–27 January 1969, MSRC, box 2024. NWRO Executive Committee with Betty Younger and Helen Williams, 2 May 1969, MSRC, box 2193. Executive Committee Meeting, 30 October 1969, MSRC, box 2193. "Executive Committee," 5 December 1970, MSRC, box 2193.
9. "NWRO National Coordinating Committee Meeting," 5–8 February 1970, MSRC, box 2165; "NCC Meeting" 29 May 1970, MSRC, box 2165.
10. Quoted in Martin (1972: 146).
11. Martin (1972: 94).
12. "Observation of Michigan Welfare Rights Organization Meeting," Early 1969, no author, Wiley Papers, box 25, folder 5.
13. Dora Bonfanti, Letter to George Wiley, 15 May 1969, MSRC, box 2211.
14. Sally Ylitalo, Letter to George Wiley, 14 May 1969, MSRC, box 2211.
15. Dora Bonfanti and other recipients, Letter to Johnny Tillman, 26 May 1969, MSRC, box 2211.
16. Bailis (1972).
17. Bill Pastreich to Tim Sampson, 26 July 1969, Wiley Papers, box 25. Bill Pastreich, Speech to the Student Health Organization, June 1969, Whitaker Papers, box 3.
18. Author unknown (possibly Andrew Bowler), Letter to George Wiley, n.d., Wiley Papers, box 27, folder 2.
19. Hulbert James, Speech to VISTA Training Institute, Boston, 1 June 1969, Whitaker Papers, box 3, folder 4.
20. Minutes of NWRO Executive Committee Meeting, 24–27 January 1969, MSRC, box 2024.
21. Martin (1972: 95).
22. *Record American*, 27 August 1968, in Welfare Rights Handbook, Whitaker Papers, box 3, folder 5.
23. Mary Davidson, "Interviews," October 1968, Whitaker Papers, box 3, folder 6, 3.
24. Mary Davidson, "Interviews," October 1968, Whitaker Papers, box 3, folder 6, 3.
25. *Washington Post*, 27 August 1967.
26. George Wiley, "The Challenge of the Powerless," Speech at Consultation of Economic Power and Responsibility Meeting, 29 March 1968, Wiley Papers, box 36, folder 5.
27. *Evening Star*, 29 August 1967.
28. "Log of Columbus WRO Activities," 8 December 1968, Whitaker Papers, box 2 folder 1.
29. Bill Buffum to George Wiley, 24 November 1969, Wiley Papers, box 25, folder 5.
30. Minutes of the MWRO Organizers Meeting, 2 August 1969, Whitaker Papers, box 2, folder 38.
31. Marya Levenson, "Local Organizing and the Democratic Convention," *The Paper Tiger*, (May 1968):7, Whitaker Papers, box 3.
32. Marya Levenson, "Local Organizing and the Democratic Convention," *The Paper Tiger*, (May 1968):7, Whitaker Papers, box 3.
33. Anonymous Welfare Recipient from Chicago, August 1969, quoted in Martin (1972: 148).
34. Anonymous Welfare Recipient from Detroit, August 1969, quoted in Martin (1972: 146).
35. Roxanne Jones, "Report of the Chairman" in Straight Talk, Newsletter of the PWRO, 11 June 1969, MSRC, box 2139.
36. Virginia Snead, NCC Representative, Report from NCC Meeting in New York 23–28 May, May 1969, MSRC, box 2139.
37. Philadelphia Welfare Rights Organization, "To: All Persons Attending the National Conference of Social Welfare," May 1969, MSRC, box 2211. *New York Times*, 29 May 1969.
38. The Chicago Friends of Welfare Rights Organization, "To the 'Concerned': An Invitation to Help Welfare Clients Help Themselves," 25 May 1968, MSRC, box 2139.
39. Anonymous (probably Dovie Coleman), "Resignation Letter to Executive Committee," possibly February 1969, Wiley Papers, box 25, folder 1. Author unknown, "Some Facts on Chicago Welfare Unions," 1967? MSRC, 2139. Martin (1972: 141).

40. The Chicago Friends of Welfare Rights Organization, "To the 'Concerned': An Invitation to Help Welfare Clients Help Themselves," 25 May 1968, MSRC, box 2139.
41. Anonymous (probably Dovie Coleman), "Resignation Letter to Executive Committee," possibly February 1969, Wiley Papers, box 25, folder 1.
42. Dovie Coleman, "Self-Explanation on an Over-All Thing, That's Pressure," Memo, Wiley Papers, box 25, folder 1.
43. Virginia WRO, "Newsheet: What's Been Happening Around the State," Early 1970, MSRC, box 2139.
44. Loretta Johnson, quoted in "Proposal: Virginia WRO," December 1970, Wiley Papers, box 27, folder 3.
45. Huldschiner (1968).
46. Jermany (2003). For more on U.S., see Brown (2003).
47. Huldschiner (1968).
48. Catherine Jermany, "Testimony Presented by Catherine Jermany Before the Annual Conference of State Welfare Finance Officers," 24 September 1969, MSRC, box 2080.
49. Hogan (2000) discusses a similar division within SNCC.
50. Mittlestadt (2000).
51. Abramovitz (1988: Ch. 10).
52. Congressional Quarterly Almanac, 1967, pp. 902–903. Quoted in Spitzer (2000: 126).
53. Sampson (1997).
54. For a discussion of civil rights organizations positions, see Hamilton and Hamilton (1997).
55. Bureau of Labor Statistics, Middle Atlantic Regional Office, "Press Release: Employment Rises and Unemployment Declines While Public Assistance Rolls Increase in NYC During the Past Three Years," 13 June 1967, MFY Papers, box 23.
56. *Record American*, 27 August 1968, in Welfare Rights Handbook, Whitaker Papers, box 3, folder 5. Chappell (2002) suggests that most people in the 1960s supported the family-wage ideal and few considered jobs and self-sufficiency a viable alternative for women on welfare. I think she is correct that many policy advocates, liberal, conservative, and radical, ideally wanted to "restore" the two-parent black family. Given the small chance that would happen, however, their solution was to put women on welfare to work. The push to force women on welfare to work, moreover, was influenced not just by discussions of the family wage, but also by the fact that black women had historically served as laborers.
57. "Six Myths About Welfare," NWRO pamphlet, 1971, Welfare Rights Collection, Lehman Library.
58. *Washington Daily News*, 20 September 1967.
59. *Washington Post*, 29 August 1967.
60. *Washington Post*, 29 August 1967.
61. *Washington Daily News*, 20 September 1967.
62. *Washington Post*, 20 September 1967.
63. *Washington Post*, 20 September 1967 and *Washington Daily News*, 20 September 1967.
64. U.S. Dept of Labor, Contract with the National Welfare Rights Organization, 24 December 1968, Wiley Papers, box 30, folder 3.
65. Davis (1993: 121).
66. U.S. Dept of Labor, Contract with the National Welfare Rights Organization, 24 December 1968, Wiley Papers, box 30, folder 3.
67. NWRO, NOW!, Newsletter, July 1969.
68. Minutes of NWRO Executive Committee Meeting, 24–27 January 1969, MSRC, box 2024.
69. Sampson (1997).
70. George Wiley, quoted in *Washington Post*, 29 August 1967.
71. NashCo, "Contract Proposal for a Technical Assistance and Citizen Participation Project to the Bureau of Work Training Programs, U.S. Department of Labor," October 1969, Wiley Papers, box 30, folder 3.
72. The professional staff of MFY who worked with the Committee of Welfare Families took a similar position. In 1966 they wrote a proposal to OEO for a summer training program to help women get jobs and get off the welfare rolls. They were granted $19,000, which was used to hire four professionals to train thirty recipients "to interview, . . . fill out questionnaires . . . do elementary filing, and . . . deal with unexpected situations during work with other people." Birnbaum and Rabagliati (1969: 119).

73. Philadelphia Welfare Rights Organization, "To: All Persons Attending the National Conference of Social Welfare," May 1969, MSRC, box 2211. *New York Times*, 29 May 1969.
74. Massachusetts Welfare Information Center Newsletter, 7 April 1969, Whitaker Papers, box 2, folder 38.
75. Sachs (2001: Ch. 3) also deals with the differences between staff and recipients on this point.
76. Virginia Snead, NCC Representative, "Report from NCC Meeting in New York, May 23–28" May 1969, MSRC, box 2024. NCC Meeting, 28 May 1969, MSRC, box 2024.
77. Van Til (1970: 211–213).
78. Johnnie Tillmon, Memo to NWRO Members of Philadelphia, PA, 27 June 1969, MSRC, box 2211.
79. Roxanne Jones, "Report of the Chairman" in Straight Talk, Newsletter of the PWRO, 11 June 1969, MSRC, box 2139.
80. Massachusetts Welfare Information Center Newsletter, 7 April 1969, Whitaker Papers, box 2, folder 38.
81. Dotson (1997).
82. Brumm (1968: 11).
83. Skocpol (1992), Gordon (1994).
84. Gordon (1994), Mink (1995).
85. Boris (1993) looks at strategies used by women during the Progressive Era and similarly concludes that black defense of motherhood challenged subordination of African Americans.
86. Fraser and Gordon (1994).
87. O'Connor (2001).
88. *Welfare in Review* (1969), quoted in Moynihan (1973: 89–91).
89. "Ohio Adequate Welfare News," 18 April 1968, Whitaker Papers, box 1.
90. For more on ideological differences between black and white activists in the 1960s, see Polatnick (1996: 679–706).
91. Caesar (1996).
92. Jermany (2003).
93. West (1981: 253).
94. Hunter (1997), Clark-Lewis (1994).
95. Cloward (1965).
96. West (1981: 86).
97. Chappell (2002: Ch. 1) makes a similar argument about the political consensus on the family-wage system.
98. Moynihan (1965), Matusow (1984).
99. Spitzer (2000) makes a similar argument that race and welfare became inseparable in the mid-1960s. He ties this development, however, more to the passage of the 1967 Social Security Amendments.
100. Benjamin Payton, "The President, the Social Experts, and the Ghetto: An Analysis of an Emerging Strategy in Civil Rights" (paper presented at White House Conference on Civil Rights, Washington, D.C., 1965), Wiley Papers, box 7.
101. George Wiley to Daniel P. Moynihan, n.d., Wiley papers, box 29.
102. Staples (1970).
103. See, for example, Taylor (2003) and Woodward (1999).
104. In 1972, Daphne Busby formed the Sisterhood of Black Single Mothers. This organization, much like welfare rights organizing, navigated the path between feminism and nationalism and defended black single motherhood. See Omolade (1986: Ch. 11).
105. Welfare Rights Committee, Mohongalia County, WV, "Your Welfare Rights" Handbook, n.d., Whitaker Papers, box 3.
106. Allan Becker, Robert Daniels, and Susan Wender, "Proposed Action: Public Assistance" (paper submitted to Metropolitan Detroit Branch, ACLU), 17 November 1968, ACLU Archives, boxes 1134–1136.
107. Brumm (1968).
108. Brumm (1968).
109. Welfare Rights Committee, Mohongalia County, WV, "Your Welfare Rights" Handbook, n.d., Whitaker Papers, box 3.
110. Brumm (1968).
111. Linton (2003).

112. Lewis (1969).
113. Martin (1972: 98).
114. Lewis (1969).
115. Minutes of the MWRO Organizers Meeting, 2 August 1969, Whitaker Papers, box 2, folder 38.
116. Lewis (1969).
117. Minutes of the MWRO Organizers Meeting, 2 August 1969, Whitaker Papers, box 2, folder 38.
118. Lewis (1969).
119. Lewis (1969), Sampson (1997).
120. Lewis (1969).
121. Lewis (1969) explained that James "had been with the black caucus at the beginning, but he disassociated himself from us after the executive committee said 'no more black caucuses.'"
122. The exact figures are unclear. Some sources say nineteen, others say seventeen, out of the twenty members of the publication department were black.
123. Martin (1972: 99).
124. Martin (1972: 100).
125. Tyson (1998: 541). Also see Self (2001) and Biondi (2001).
126. Loretta Domencich, quoted in Milwaukee County WRO (1972: 59).
127. Huldschiner (1968).
128. Los Angeles County WRO, Newsletter, 1 November 1968, Wiley Papers, box 24, folder 13.
129. MAW member, Speech to VISTA Training Conference, Boston, 31 May 1969, Whitaker Papers, box 3, folder 4.
130. Meeting Minutes of the Ohio Training Steering Committee, 3 April 1968, Whitaker Papers, box 2, folder 17.
131. Kathamay Hart, Letter to Tim Sampson, 7 July 1969, MSRC, box 2080.
132. Mary Davidson, "Interviews," October 1968, Whitaker Papers, box 3, folder 6, 4.
133. Sampson (1997).
134. WRO Allegheny County, "Welfare Righter," September 1969, MSRC, box 2139.
135. Palladino (1997).
136. Jermany (2003).
137. Roxanne Jones, PWRO, "Report of the Chairman" in Straight Talk Newsletter, 11 June 1969, MSRC, box 2139.
138. Kansas WRO, "A Proposal to Help Ghetto Families Help Themselves," 12 January 1970, MSRC, box 2024.
139. Rudell Martin quoted in Williams (1998: 283).
140. Rosie Hudson, quoted in Milwaukee Country WRO (1972: 81).
141. Burch (1971). Tillmon actively recruited white recipients and wanted to dispel the myth that most recipients were black. When some members dressed up in African garb for a press conference, she urged them to change. *New York Times*, 9 July 1995.
142. Martin (1972: 102–103).
143. Martin (1972: 104).
144. West (1981: 28–30).
145. Lewis (1969).
146. Lewis (1969).
147. Martin (1972: 107).
148. Jermany (2003).
149. NWRO Executive Committee Meeting, 30 October 1969, MSRC, box 2193.
150. Delgado (1986).
151. Martin (1972).
152. NWRO Personnel and Policy Committee, 16–17 October 1970, MSRC, box 2213.
153. West (1981: 109).
154. Author unknown, "Evaluation of NWRO and Affiliates," 22 December 1970, MSRC, box 2247.
155. George Wiley to Michigan WRO, 4 June 1969, MSRC, box 2080.
156. Members of MWRO to George Wiley, 17 July 1969, MSRC, box 2080.
157. Martin (1972).
158. Mamie Blakely to George Wiley, 17 July 1969, MSRC, box 2080.

159. Pamela Blair, "Memo to the Executive Committee of Michigan WRO," 11 November 1969, Wiley Papers, box 25, folder 5.
160. Bill Buffum to George Wiley, 24 November 1969, Wiley Papers, box 25, folder 5.
161. Louise Bryant, Chairman of MWRO, to Jerry Shea, NWRO Office Manager, 14 July 1970, MSRC, box 2080.
162. For more on racial stereotypes and welfare policy, see Jewell (1993), Gilens (1999), and Neubeck and Cazenave (2001).

Chapter 6

1. Jennette Washington, "I Challenge" published article, source unknown, n.d., Wiley Papers, box 28.
2. Etta Horn and Patricia Velentine, "Letter to Commissioner, Chairman of the Council of D.C., and Vice Chairman of the Council of D.C.," 25 April 1968, Wiley Papers, box 24, folder 11.
3. OSCAW, "Ohio Adequate Welfare News" Newsletter, October 1966, November 1966 and January 1967, Whitaker Papers, box 1, folder 17.
4. James A. Rhodes, "Press Release," 1966, Whitaker Papers, box 1, folder 16.
5. No author, "Letters," Spring 1971, Whitaker Papers, box 2, folder 25.
6. OSCAW, Memo, 1 October 1968, Whitaker Papers, box 1, folder 1.
7. NWRO, "402(a) (23): A New Weapon to Fight for More Money Now" 18 April 1969, Wiley Papers box 23, folder 3. National Organization for Women, Newsletter, 7 August 1969, Wiley Papers, box 23, folder 3.
8. For more details, see Davis (1993: Ch. 9).
9. Mink (1998) discusses the vulnerability of legislated social rights compared to rights derived from the Constitution.
10. Marshall (1964: 72).
11. Friedman (1962: 191).
12. Friedman (1962: 192).
13. Galbraith (1958: 266).
14. Galbraith (1958: 292).
15. Theobald (1966: 83). See also Theobald (1965).
16. Loretta Domencich, quoted in Milwaukee County WRO (1972: 59).
17. George Wiley, Speech at MWRO Conference, 8 February 1969, Whitaker Papers, box 2, folder 37.
18. Cloward and Piven (1966: 510–517).
19. Grier Horner, "PAPAW: How It Started, What It's Hoping to Do" *Berkshire Eagle*, 30 June 1967.
20. Philadelphia WRO, "A Study Document on Welfare Rights Goals," n.d., Wiley Papers, box 27, folder 1.
21. OSCAW, "Ohio Adequate Welfare News," Newsletter, 13 June 1966, Whitaker Papers, box 1, folder 17.
22. OSCAW, "Ohio Adequate Welfare News," Newsletter, 14 February 1967, Whitaker Papers, box 1, folder 17.
23. OSCAW, "Ohio Adequate Welfare News," Newsletter, 27 November 1968, Whitaker, box 1, folder 17.
24. OSCAW, "Ohio's Continuing Welfare Disgrace," flier, 1969, Whitaker Papers, box 1, folder 1.
25. MAW member, Speech to VISTA Training Conference, Boston, 31 May 1969, Whitaker Papers, box 3, folder 4.
26. Joy Stanley, President L.A. County WRO, Speech before the Public Forum, Citizens Committee for a Decent Welfare System, 5 September 1966, MSRC, box 1998. L.A. County WRO, Press Release, 30 June 1969, MSRC, box 2238.
27. Citywide Coordinating Committee of Welfare Rights Groups, "Fact Sheet For Welfare Clients on Goldberg's Increase," 1968, Wiley Papers, box 26. *New York Times*, 4 July 1968. The United Welfare League, in Harlem, researched the cost of living for a family of four on the Upper West Side and concluded that a family would need $6,566 to live modestly. This figure was very conservative compared to the Department of Labor's estimate that a family of four would need $10,195 to live decently in New York.
28. Burch (1970: 10).

29. Burch (1970: 5).
30. "FAP and Welfare—Racist Institutions," NWRO Leaflet, 11 May 1971, Wiley Papers, box 17, folder 5.
31. "Welfare Reform Called Repression of the Poor," *Greensboro Daily News*, 15 November 1970.
32. Tillmon (1971: 115).
33. OSCAW, "Ohio Adequate Welfare News," Newsletter, 18 April 1968, Whitaker Papers, box 1.
34. Cassie B. Downer, quoted in Milwaukee County WRO (1972: 135–136).
35. "Six Myths About Welfare," NWRO pamphlet, 1971, Welfare Rights Collection, Lehman Library.
36. For references to the problem of full employment, see Brumm (1968:8).
37. Philadelphia WRO, "A Federal Family Investment Program: The Basic Goal of the Philadelphia WRO," n.d., Wiley Papers, box 27, folder 1.
38. Philadelphia WRO, "A Federal Family Investment Program: The Basic Goal of the Philadelphia WRO," n.d., Wiley Papers, box 27, folder 1.
39. MWRO Chair, Speech at MWRO Rally, Boston, 30 June 1969, Whitaker Papers, box 3, folder 6.
40. NWRO, "Adequate Income Plan: $5500 or Fight," pamphlet, April 1970, Welfare Rights Collection, Lehman Library.
41. Orshansky (1965).
42. NWRO, Adequate Income Plan, 25 June 1971, Lehman Library.
43. NWRO, Adequate Income Plan, 25 June 1971, Lehman Library.
44. U.S. Department of Labor, "Three Standards of Living for an Urban Family of Four Persons," Bulletin No. 1570–5, quoted in NWRO, Adequate Income Plan, 25 June 1971, Lehman Library.
45. NWRO, Adequate Income Plan, 25 June 1971, Lehman Library.
46. Burke and Burke (1974: 49–50).
47. National Council of Churches, "Proposed Policy Statement on Guaranteed Income," 10 June 1967, ACLU Archives, boxes 1134–1136.
48. *Providence Evening Bulletin*, 17 August 1966, Wiley Papers, box 27, folder 7.
49. Moynihan (1973: 126).
50. National Association of Social Workers, Press Release, 11 June 1968, ACLU Archives, boxes 1134–1136.
51. Burke and Burke (1974: 37). For more on conservatism in the Johnson administration, see Spitzer (2000: Ch. 5).
52. Moynihan (1973: 61–62), Lemann (1991: 195).
53. Davies (1996) looks at Democrats who came to support a guaranteed income. But he ties this trend only to the Democratic Party and fails to acknowledge the extent to which conservatives also embraced income maintenance.
54. *Administrative History of the OEO*, vol. 1, p. 625. Johnson Papers.
55. Galbraith (1958: 292).
56. For more on the liberal orientation of Nixon, see Hoff (1994). Spitzer (2000: Ch. 5) similarly argues that, despite his conservative rhetoric, Nixon was liberal on welfare policy.
57. *Statistical Abstracts*, Table No. 431, "Public Assistance—Expenditures, by Source of Funds, and Monthly Payments to Recipients, by Program, States and Other Areas: 1965."
58. Richard Nixon, "Welfare Reform Message to Congress," 11 August 1969 in *Nixon: The First Year*.
59. "Welfare Reform Message to the Congress of the United States, 8/11/69," *Nixon: The First Year*.
60. For more on what motivated Nixon, see Spitzer (2000: Ch. 7) and Burke and Burke (1974: 39).
61. See, for example, Davies (1996).
62. "Text of President's Welfare–Workfare Speech, 8/8/69," *Nixon: The First Year*.
63. "Text of President's Welfare–Workfare Speech, 8/8/69," *Nixon: The First Year*.
64. Burke and Burke (1974: 5).
65. "Text of President's Welfare–Workfare Speech, 8/8/69," *Nixon: The First Year*.
66. David G. Gil, "Mothers' Wages or Social Security for Mothers: An Alternative Approach to Attack Poverty" (Paper Presented at Brandeis University, 23 July 1968), ACLU Archives, boxes 1134–1136.

67. U.S. Riot Commission (1968: 34–35, 37–38).
68. *Historical Statistics* (1975: 346–367).
69. *Statistical Abstracts*, Table 431, "Public Assistance—Expenditures, by Source of Funds, and Monthly Payments to Recipients, by Program, States and Other Areas: 1965."
70. *Statistical Abstracts 1970*, Table 453, "Public Assistance—Recipients of Money Payments, States, and Other Areas, 1969" and *Statistical Abstracts 1966*, Table 429, "Public Assistance—Recipients By Program, States and Other Areas, 1965."
71. Kotz and Kotz (1977: 260).
72. Moynihan (1973: 27–28).
73. For more on the impact of political protest on pushing politics to the left, see Davies (1996: Ch. 6).
74. "Program Memorandum on Income Maintenance and Social Services Programs of Department of HEW, Fiscal Years 1969–1973," Records of the Department of HEW, box 11, Johnson Papers.
75. Richard Nixon, quoted in Burke and Burke (1974: 106).
76. Robert Finch, "Memo to the President: Response to Arthur Burns Welfare Proposal," 30 April 1969, quoted in Burke and Burke (1974: 75).
77. Burke and Burke (1974: 77).
78. Daniel Patrick Moynihan, "Memorandum for the President on the New York City Welfare Situation," 31 January 1969, quoted in Burke and Burke (1974: 47–48).
79. Burke and Burke (1974: 78).
80. For more on internal discussion about the guaranteed income, see Burke and Burke (1974) and Moynihan (1973).
81. Bertram Beck and Jesse Gordon, "Research Proposal to Evaluate the Impact of Certain Forms of Guaranteed Income," October 1966, MFY Papers, box 14.
82. Wilbur Cohen on NBC, 8 August 1969, quoted in Burke and Burke (1974: 123).
83. Burke and Burke (1974: 126) and Moynihan (1973: 251).
84. Steiner (1971: 77).
85. Burke and Burke (1974: 127).
86. Robert Finch, "Statement Before the Senate Finance Committee on Family Assistance Act of 1970, HR16311," Hearings Before the Committee on Finance, United States Senate, 91st Congress, 2nd session, *Congressional Record*, 29 April 1970.
87. NWRO, "NWRO Position on the Nixon Welfare Plan," 25 July 1970, Wiley Papers, box 17, folder 4.
88. NWRO, fliers and position papers, 1969–1972, Wiley Papers, boxes 17 and 18.
89. Chappell (2002: Ch. 2) suggests that NWRO framed its criticism of FAP in racial terms and thus may have reinforced the image of black welfare recipients. This was true of certain prominent leaders such as Wiley, but Chappell fails to take into account the differences within the welfare rights movement. Nevertheless, her point about the images emanating from the debate is a good one.
90. Beulah Sanders, George Wiley, and Carl Rachlin, "Statement to the House Ways and Means Committee," 27 October 1969, Wiley Papers, box 17, folder 3.
91. Beulah Sanders, George Wiley, and Carl Rachlin, "Statement to the House Ways and Means Committee," 27 October 1969, Wiley Papers, box 17, folder 3.
92. Richard Nixon, "Welfare Reform Message to Congress," 11 August 1969 in *Nixon: The First Year*.
93. Statement by George A. Wiley at the Institute for Black Elected Officials, 13 September 1969, NOW!, NWRO Newsletter, Wiley Papers, box 17, folder 3. George Wiley, Untitled Speech, 1973, Wiley Papers, box 17, folder 3.
94. NWRO, "Fact Sheet on the New Nixon Welfare Plan," n.d. (fall 1969?), Lehman Library.
95. Statement by George A. Wiley at the Institute for Black Elected Officials, 13 September 1969, NOW!, NWRO Newsletter, Wiley Papers, box 17, folder 3. See also Beulah Sanders, George Wiley, and Carl Rachlin, "Statement to the House Ways and Means Committee," 27 October 1969, Wiley Papers, box 17, folder 3.
96. Jon Kaufman, "Memo to NWRO Research Staff," 18 March 1970, Wiley Papers, box 22, folder 4.
97. Congressman George McGovern introduced this as a bill into Congress in July 1971.
98. NWRO, fliers and position papers, 1969–1972, Wiley Papers, boxes 17 and 18.

99. George Wiley, untitled document, 16 March 1971, Wiley Papers, box 17, folder 5.
100. George Wiley, Packet for Welfare Rights Leaders and Friends, September 1970 and September 1971, Wiley Papers, box 17, folder 4.
101. George Wiley to Senator Russell Long, 30 March 1970, Wiley Papers, box 20, folder 16.
102. "Welfare Reform Called Repression of the Poor," *Greensboro Daily News*, 15 November 1970.
103. "Welfare Unit Blasts Nixon Reform Plan," *The Pittsburgh Press*, 23 July 1970, Wiley Papers, box 26, folder 2.
104. George Wiley, Packet for Welfare Rights Leaders and Friends, September 1970 and September 1971, Wiley Papers, box 17, folder 4.
105. Eliza Williams, "Report of the Committee on Legislation," 24 July 1970, MSRC, box 2185.
106. George Wiley, untitled speech, 1973, Wiley Papers, box 17, folder 3.
107. NWRO, "The Gaps in Fap: Ways and Means Welfare Bill, HR1," 18 November 1971. MSRC, box 1963.
108. NWRO, "What Your Group Can Do," 21 May 1971, MSRC, box 1963.
109. Burke and Burke (1974: 173).
110. The vote was 234–187 in the House and 52–34 in the Senate.
111. "Special Message to Congress on Welfare Reform," 27 March 1972 and "State of the Union Address," 1 January 1974, *Richard Nixon: Public Papers*.
112. "Does President Nixon Care About Children?" NWRO Flier, 1972, Wiley Papers, folder 15, box 6.
113. "Nixon Called 'Racist' by WRO President," *Albany Times-Union*, 25 August 1972, Wiley Papers, box 26, folder 5.
114. Haldeman (1994: Entry 187).
115. Piven and Cloward (1977: 335–349).
116. Steiner (1971).
117. Johnnie Tillmon and George Wiley to Richard Nixon, 5 August 1969, Wiley Papers, box 17, folder 4.
118. Brian Jeffrey and Tom Glynn, "Notes from Meeting with John Price, Assistant to Moynihan," 28 July 1969, Wiley Papers, box 18, folder 1.
119. Elliot Richardson (Secretary of HEW), "Telegram to Wiley," 19 November 1970, Wiley Papers, box 19, folder 11. NWRO Legislation Committee, "Meeting with John Montgomery, Family Assistance Plan," 4 September 1970, MSRC, box 2185.
120. NWRO, Press Release, 20 February 1969, Wiley Papers, folder 7, box 11.
121. Johnnie Tillmon and George Wiley to Richard Nixon, 5 August 1969, Wiley Papers, box 17, folder 4.
122. John Montgomery (Department of HEW), "Evaluation of NWRO Demands," 25 September 1970, Wiley Papers, box 17, folder 11.
123. Elliot Richardson, "Telegram to George Wiley," 19 November 1970, Wiley Papers, box 19, folder 11.
124. Davies (1996) recounts some liberals who were influenced by NWRO.
125. National Federation of Social Service Employees, "Resolutions Adopted at the 1970 Annual Convention," Wiley Papers, box 20, folder 7.
126. National Association of Laymen, "Convention Resolution," 11 July 1970, Wiley Papers, box 20, folder 4.
127. Bella Abzug, "Speech to NWRO Convention in Miami Beach," 9 July 1972, Wiley Papers, box 19, folder 1.
128. Burke and Burke (1974: 136–137, 173).
129. Tim Wheeler, *Daily World*, 11 December 1969, Wiley Papers, box 27, folder 7.
130. "I.F. Stone's Weekly," 15 December 1969, Wiley Papers, box 34, folder 12. See also *Washington Post*, 4 December 1969.
131. Pratt (1976: Ch. 11).
132. Pratt (1976: 88–89). The American Association of Retired Persons, chartered in 1958, had a membership of 9 million in 1975. But the AARP was more of a service and business association than a lobbyist.
133. Pratt (1976: 167–168).
134. Gilens (1999) makes a similar argument. He suggests that Americans are generally not opposed to government programs aiding the poor, except when recipients are considered undeserving, a perception colored by race.

135. See Iton (2000: Ch. 5) for influence of race on public policy.
136. For more on the relationship between liberal policy and race, see Spitzer (2000).
137. See Pechman and Timpane (1975), Ross and Lyall (1976).
138. For more on the racial politics of Nixon's FAP strategy, see Spitzer (2000).
139. *Congressional Record*, 15 April 1970.
140. "Text of President's Welfare–Workfare Speech, 8/8/69," *Nixon: The First Year*.
141. Quadagno (1990) suggests that the work requirement in FAP was directed primarily at men. I believe it was directed at both women and men.
142. James Welsh, "Welfare Reform: Born Aug. 8, 1969; died, Oct. 4, 1972: A Sad Case Study of the American Political Process," *New York Times Magazine*, 7 January 1973.
143. James Welsh, "Welfare Reform: Born Aug. 8, 1969; died, Oct. 4, 1972: A Sad Case Study of the American Political Process," *New York Times Magazine*, 7 January 1973.
144. "Work and Welfare," *New Republic*, 15 January 1972.
145. *New York Times*, 25 October 1971.
146. Russell Long, Hearings Before the Committee on Finance, United States Senate, 91st Congress, 2nd Session, *Congressional Record*, 29 April 1970.
147. Hoff (1994) and Brown (1999). Brown also points to Nixon's dismantling of Great Society programs and implementation of revenue sharing.
148. Nixon, "Hunger Must Be Banished: Remarks of the President at the White House Conference on Food, Nutrition, and Health, 2 December 1969" (1970).
149. Ohio Steering Committee for Adequate Welfare, "Ohio Adequate Welfare News," Newsletter, 27 November 1968, Whitaker Paper, box 1, folder 17.

Chapter 7

1. West (1981: 50).
2. See, for example, Quadagno (1994), Edsall and Edsall (1992).
3. Mrs. Anna Marie Mullen to Phillip E. George (Director, Blair County WRO), 28 June 1972, Wiley Papers, box 27, folder 1.
4. Mrs. Anna Marie Mullen to Phillip E. George (Director, Blair County WRO), 28 June 1972, Wiley Papers, box 27, folder 1.
5. Mrs. Anna Marie Mullen to Phillip E. George (Director, Blair County WRO), 28 June 1972, Wiley Papers, box 27, folder 1.
6. www.ntu.org
7. Self (2003).
8. Roger A. Freeman, "Wayward Ambitions of the Welfare State," *New York Times*, 4 December 1971, 31. Quoted in Chappell (2002: 180).
9. Table No. 418, "Total Governmental Expenditure, by Function: 1950–1973," *Statistical Abstract* (1975).
10. Table No. 418, "Total Governmental Expenditure, by Function: 1950–1973," *Statistical Abstract* (1975).
11. Table No. 377, "Federal Domestic Transfer Payments and Grants-In-Aid, by Function: 1965 to 1975," *Statistical Abstract* (1975).
12. Public Aid includes AFDC, Medicaid, Old Age Assistance, Aid to the Disabled, and Supplemental Security Income. Social Insurance includes Social Security, Medicare, Unemployment Insurance, Workers Compensation, Disability Insurance. Table No. 446, "Social Welfare Expenditures Under Public Programs: 1950–1974," *Statistical Abstract* (1975: 280).
13. See Zylan (1994). Abramovitz (1988). Brown (1999). Iton (2000) also argues that the "white backlash" predated the CRM. For other roots of white hostility, see Sugrue (1996).
14. http://www.allcountry.ed/Songbook/Texte_W/Welfare_Cadillac/body_welfare _cadillac.html
15. Solinger (2001).
16. Doris Lurie, Letter to the Editor, *New York Times*, 1 April 1971.
17. As a result of special grant protests in Massachusetts, the furniture guidelines, explaining recipients' entitlements, were publicized and caused some anger. see *Boston Globe*, 9 September 1968, in Welfare Rights Booklet, Whitaker Papers, box 3, folder 5.

18. Table No. 571, "Unemployed and Unemployment Insurance—Summary: 1960–1975," *Statistical Abstract* (1975).
19. Table 679, "Percent Change Per Year in Selected Price Indexes: 1961–1974," *Statistical Abstract* (1975).
20. Schulman (2001).
21. Gallup (1972).
22. Williamson (1973).
23. Gilens (1999: 122–23). For extended discussion, see Ch. 5 of Gilens. Wright (1976).
24. Neubeck and Cazenave (2001: Ch. 5).
25. "Welfare Fraud: The Backlash," *Newsweek*, 31 January 1972.
26. Sheehan (1975).
27. Milwaukee County WRO (1972: 72).
28. "Romney," Summary of Staff Retreat, 1970, Wiley Papers, box 8, folder 1.
29. Martin (1972: 128).
30. Martin (1972: 130).
31. AFSCME, "Letter to George Wiley," 8 April 1970, Wiley Papers, box 24, folder 7. Walter Reuther (Co-Chairman of Alliance for Labor Action), "Letter to George Wiley," 8 April 1970, Wiley Papers, box 24, folder 7.
32. Hulbert James, Speech to VISTA Training Institute, Boston, 1 June 1969, Whitaker Papers, box 3, folder 4.
33. Hulbert James, Speech to VISTA Training Institute, Boston, 1 June 1969, Whitaker Papers, box 3, folder 4.
34. Macdonald (1969).
35. For more on black popular culture, see Van Deburg (1992).
36. Interview with Jennette Washington, "Profile of a Welfare Fighter," March 1971, MSRC, box 2165.
37. Martin (1972: 132).
38. Milwaukee County WRO (1972: 77).
39. Martin (1972: 132).
40. Wilbur Colom, "New Direction for Fighter: Submitted to the Executive Committee," December 3, 1971, MSRC, box 2247.
41. Brooklyn Welfare Action Committee, flier, n.d., Wiley Papers, box 26, folder 4. Citywide Coordinating Committee of Welfare Rights Groups, flier, n.d., Wiley Papers, box 26, folder 4. Unemployed Workers Union, flier, possibly early 1971, Wiley Papers, box 27, folder 2.
42. Bill Pastreich to Tim Sampson, 26 July 1969, Wiley Papers, box 25, folder 3.
43. Frances Fox Piven and Richard Cloward, quoted in Macdonald (1969).
44. Macdonald (1969).
45. Macdonald (1969).
46. Massachusetts Wage Supplement Organization, flier, after 6 August 1969, Wiley Papers, box 25, folder 3.
47. Delgado (1986).
48. *Review Journal*, 15 March, 1971, Wiley Papers, box 32, folder 1. Also see Orleck, "If It Wasn't For You" (1997: 109).
49. Duncan (1997).
50. Duncan (1997).
51. "Staff Retreat," NWRO report, 29–31 January 1971, Wiley Papers, box 8, folder 1.
52. James Evans to George Wiley, 24 March 1971, Wiley Papers, box 8, folder 8.
53. "Staff Retreat," NWRO report, 29–31 January 1971, Wiley Papers, box 8, folder 1.
54. NCC Meeting, Las Vegas, Nevada, February 1971, MSRC, box 2193.
55. Palladino (1997).
56. *Las Vegas Voice*, 11 February 1971, v. 8 (22) Wiley Papers, box 32, folder 1.
57. NWRO, News Release, 21 February 1971, Wiley Papers, box 32, folder 1.
58. *Washington Post*, 7 March 1971, Wiley Papers, box 32, folder 1. Also see Orleck, "If It Wasn't For You" (1997: 109).
59. *Los Angeles Times*, 14 March 1971, Wiley Papers, box 32, folder 1. *Las Vegas Sun*, 14 March 1971, Wiley Papers, box 32, folder 1. *Las Vegas Sun*, 13 March 1971, Wiley Papers, box 32, folder 1.

60. *Las Vegas Sun*, 20 March 1971, Wiley Papers, box 31, folder 1. *New York Times*, 21 March 1971, Wiley Papers, box 32, folder 1.
61. Piven and Cloward (1971: 373–381).
62. *Las Vegas Sun*, 16 March 1971 and *Las Vegas Sun*, 18 March 1971, Wiley Papers, box 32, folder 1.
63. George Wiley, "Memorandum to WRO Leaders, Staff, and Friends Re: Children's March for Survival," 12 April 1972, Wiley Papers, box 15, folder 5.
64. Bert DeLeeuw, "Memo to NWRO Department Heads, Re: Draft for Internal Use Only of Proposed NWRO Spring Campaign," 22 January 1972, Wiley Papers, box 15, folder 5.
65. George Wiley, "Memorandum to WRO Leaders, Staff, and Friends Re: Children's March for Survival," 12 April 1972, Wiley Papers, box 15, folder 5.
66. Bert DeLeeuw, "Memo to NWRO Department Heads, Re: Draft for Internal Use Only of Proposed NWRO Spring Campaign," 22 January 1972, Wiley Papers, box 15, folder 5.
67. *New York Times*, 26 March 1972, p. 20.
68. *New York Times*, 28 March 1972, p. 42.
69. See Wilson (1987), Quadagno (1994).
70. Cohen and Hanagan (1991: 475) argue that programs relying on women's role as childbearer were appealing.
71. Sachs (2001: Ch. 6).
72. West (1981: 30–35).
73. George Wiley, "Letter to Welfare Rights Leaders, Members, Friends, and Supporters, Re: Resignation," 15 December 1972, Wiley Papers, box 36, folder 6.
74. NCC, "General Session," October 1972, MSRC, box 2193.
75. Bert N. Mitchell to George Wiley, 2 September 1971, Wiley Papers, box 9, folder 4.
76. NWRO, Summer Quarter (June-August) Summary, 30 September 1973, MSRC, box 2238.
77. Corethea Saxon, New Jersey NCC, "Letter to NWRO," 8 September 1971, MSRC, box 2238.
78. Corethea Saxon, NJ State Representative, "Letter to Barbara Brown," September 7, 1971, MSRC, box 2238, and Mrs. Norma Randolph, "Letter to Corethea Saxon," November 1971, MSRC, box 2238.
79. Jacquline Pierce, "Letter to Barbara Brown," 22 March 1971, MSRC, , box 2238, Karen Lewis, "Letter to Barbara Brown," 21 March 1972, MSRC, box 2238, and Mary Laws, "Letter to Barbara Brown," 22 March 1972, MSRC, box 2238.
80. Dianne Solembrina, Letter to Johnnie Tillmon, January or February 1972, MSRC, box 2238.
81. Fred E. Barrick, "Letter to Whom It May Concern (NWRO?)," March 1972? MSRC, box 2238, Bertha Lopez, "Letter to Whom It May Concern (NWRO?)," March 1972? MSRC, box 2238, Fred E. Barrick, "Letter to Whom It May Concern (NWRO?)," March 1972?, MSRC, box 2238, Fred E. Barrick, Memo to All Welfare Rights Organization Local Chairmen in Ashtabula County, March 1972? MSRC, box 2238.
82. Fred E. Barrick, "Letter to Melvin Turner," March 1972? MSRC, box 2238.
83. Linton (2003).
84. Van Til (2003).
85. Marie Ratagick to George Wiley, possibly November 1970, Wiley Papers, box 8, folder 8.
86. Andrea Kydd to George Wiley, 15 November 1970, Wiley Papers, box 8, folder 8.
87. Audrey Williams, NWRO Recording Secretary, NCC Minutes, 4 February 1972, MSRC, box 2193.
88. Jim Evans to George Wiley, 24 March 1971, Wiley Papers, box 8, folder 8.
89. George Wiley to James Evans, Jr., n.d., Wiley Papers, box 36, folder 6. James Evans to the Staff of the Misseduc Foundation and NWRO, n.d., Wiley Papers, box 36, folder 6.
90. Chuck Hodden, "Letter to Johnnie Tillmon," n.d., MSRC, box 2209.
91. James Evans, "Memorandum to the Staff of the Misseduc Foundation and NWRO," n.d., Wiley Papers, box 36, folder 6.
92. Andrea Kydd to George Wiley, 15 November 1970, Wiley Papers, box 8, folder 8.
93. "Report of Program Services Task Force," 22 August 1972, Wiley Papers, box 14. "Romney: Staff Meeting and Training Conference," 1970, Wiley Papers, box 8, folder 1. "Staff Retreat," January 1971, Wiley Papers, box 8.
94. MAW Member, Speech to VISTA Training Conference, Boston, 31 May 1969, Whitaker Papers, box 3, folder 4.

95. Audrey Williams, NWRO Recording Secretary, NCC Minutes, 4 February 1972, MSRC, box 2193.
96. Minutes of NCC Meeting, 7, 15 October 1971, MSRC, box 2193.
97. West (1981: 118–119).
98. Chappell (2002: Ch. 3) explains this development to address broader issues of economic justice as one that characterized the left more generally in the 1970s.
99. Johnnie Tillmon, "Memorandum to the Executive Board," 8 December 1972, Wiley Papers, box 36, folder 6.
100. Johnnie Tillmon, "Memorandum to the Executive Board," 8 December 1972, Wiley Papers, box 36, folder 6.
101. "NWRO 1973 Convention Report," July 1973, Welfare Rights Collection, Lehman Library.
102. NWRO Press Release, 18 July 1974, MSRC, box 2208.
103. Tillmon (1972).
104. NWRO Press Release, "Women's Rights to Be a Major Topic at NWRO Convention," 9 July 1973, MSRC, box 2193.
105. "Strategies for Survival," NWRO pamphlet, 1973, Wiley Papers, box 7.
106. West (1981: 254).
107. West (1981: 243).
108. West (1981: 49).
109. Jennette Washington, "I Challenge," published article, source unknown, n.d., Wiley Papers, box 28.
110. Tillmon (1972).
111. Chicago Welfare Rights Organization, Handbook, June 1968, Whitaker Papers, box 3. and Mothers for Adequate Welfare "Your Welfare Rights Manual," n.d., Whitaker Papers, box 3.
112. Evelyn Sims, Chairman of State Organization and local MCWRO, "My Conception of Family Planning," n.d., MSRC, box 2209.
113. Catherine Boddie, "Letter to Johnnie Tillman," 13 September 1972, MSRC, box 2209.
114. Olive Franklin, Chair of the St. Louis City-Wide WRO, "Letter to Johnnie Tillmon," 13 September 1972, MSRC, box 2209.
115. Gordon (1974).
116. Roberts (1997: Ch. 2) and Gordon (1974: Ch. 14).
117. Hartmann (1995: 255).
118. This was known as the Relf case. Rosalind Petchesky "Reproductive Ethics and Public Policy" (Hastings Center Report, October 1979), quoted in Hartmann (1995: 255).
119. Shapiro (1985: 103–104).
120. Shapiro (1985: 124).
121. *Family Planning Digest* (1972), quoted in Shapiro (1985: 124).
122. Cutright and Jaffe (1976).
123. Cade (1970).
124. Polatnick (1996).
125. Black Women's Liberation Group (1970).
126. Tillmon (1972).
127. "Strategies for Survival," NWRO pamphlet, 1973, Wiley Papers, box 7. The Association for Voluntary Sterilization had its roots in the eugenics movement, but was moving toward a position of voluntary sterilization.
128. NWRO, "Forced Sterilization: Threat to Poor," The Welfare Fighter 4 (February 1974), MSRC, box 2043.
129. Solinger (2001: Ch. 5).
130. Valk (2000: 41–42).
131. Tillmon (1972).
132. See Davis (1996).
133. "Women in Poverty" Statement Adopted by the NOW Executive Committee, 29 November 1970, Wiley Papers, box 21.
134. Merrillee Dolan (Chair of Task Force for Women in Poverty), "Letter to George Wiley," 1 October 1971, Wiley Papers, box 36.
135. West (1981: 254).
136. See West (1981: Ch. 5).

137. Davis (1996: 145).
138. West (1981: 248–55). Sachs (2001: Ch. 7) does a good job of analyzing differences between NWRO and NOW. My only disagreement with her is that I think by the early 1970s many welfare rights activists had begun to identify as feminists and did not just see themselves as "ambassadors" to feminist organizations, as Sachs suggests.
139. Piven (1997).
140. Cloward (1997).
141. Palladino (1997).
142. Davis (1996: 157).
143. Chappell, "Rethinking Women's Politics" (2002). See also West (1981: 249–250).
144. Jermany (2003).
145. Chappell, "Rethinking Women's Politics " (2002). See also West (1981: 249–250).
146. Rosen (2000: 180).
147. Edmond and Fleming (1975: 9).
148. Morrissey (1990).
149. Jo Freeman, conversation with Guida West, New Brunswick, NJ, 12 June 1975. Quoted in West (1981: 260).
150. Delgado (1986: 112–113).
151. Taped Interview 151. Quoted in West (1981: 35).
152. Personnel Committee, "Recommendations to the N.W.R.O. Executive Board," n.d., Wiley Papers, box 8. "Executive Directors Report," 17 May 1972, Wiley Papers, box 8.
153. West (1981: 36).
154. NWRO Press Release, 18 July 1974, MSRC, box 2208.
155. NWRO, *Welfare Fighter*, 4 (February 1974) MSRC, box 2043, NWRO Press Release, 18 July 1974, MSRC, box 2208.
156. Washington, D.C. Government, "Letter to NWRO" Wiley Papers, box 9, folder 10. Johnnie Tillmon and Faith Evans, "Letter to all WRO's and Friends from Tillmon and Evans" July 1973, Wiley Papers, box 9, folder 10.
157. West (1981: 36).
158. Johnnie Tillmon and Faith Evans, "Memo to All WRO's and Friends," 16 August 1973, MSRC, box 2209.
159. *New York Times*, 9 July 1995 and *New York Times*, 21 November 1995.
160. Palladino (1997).
161. Chappell, "Rethinking Women's Politics" (2002).
162. Williams (1998: Ch. 7).
163. Bill Vincent, "Operation Life Has Brought Hope," *The Nevadan*, 28 January 1973, Wiley Papers, box 25, folder 6. See also Orleck, "If It Wasn't for You" (1997: 109).
164. Couto (1978).
165. Dotson (1997).
166. Goldberg (1977).
167. Jermany (2003).
168. Palladino (1997).
169. Orleck, "If It Wasn't for You," (1997: 115) looks at the evolution in political consciousness of welfare rights activists.
170. There is a voluminous literature on women's community activism. See, for example, Naples, *Community Activism and Feminist Politics* (1998), esp. Naples, "Women's Community Activism" and Feldman, Stall, and Wright, who argue in their study of organizing in Chicago public housing that involvement in economic development builds that sense of community, self-confidence, and skills of women activists. Also see Abrahams (1996) on how community organizing helps develop sense of identity.
171. Annelise Orleck interviews with Renee Diamond, September 5, 1992 and December 9, 1994. Quoted in Orleck, "If It Wasn't for You" (1997: 114).
172. Levinson (1980).
173. Morrissey (1990).
174. Springer (1999) argues that black feminist organizations in this period did not take into account class or sexuality. The welfare rights movement did take into account class, but did not specifically address sexuality.

175. King (1988), Higginbotham (1992: 254).
176. See Said (1994).
177. Collins (1990: 69–70).

Conclusion

1. Kornbluh (2000) makes a persuasive case for the way in which NWRO's made a claim for credit as a right of American citizenship and how this emphasis on consumerism departed from traditional work-oriented strategies.
2. See, for example, Weisbrot (1990), Williams (1987), Sitkoff (1981), Matusow (1984), Carson (1981). There is much important scholarship that has already challenged the standard narrative. Theoharis and Woodard (2003), Biondi (2003), Self (2003), Tyson (1999), Payne (1995), Umoja (1996), Lee (1999).
3. This is probably true of other radical movements of the late 1960s as well. Biondi (2003), in her study of the Civil Rights Movement in New York City, and Self (2003), in his work on Oakland, both look at the roots of northern movements and suggest these were not simply outgrowths of the Southern struggle.
4. Rosenblatt (1982).
5. See Davies (1996). Edsall and Edsall (1992).
6. For the standard interpretation of the decline of liberalism see Matusow (1984) See also Edsall and Edsall (1992), Weisbrot (1990) and Quadagno (1994).
7. Hunter (1997). Collins (1990). Gutman (1976). Jones (1985).
8. Jones (1985), Boris (1993).
9. For a discussion of stereotypes associated with welfare, see Neubeck and Cazenave (2001), Gilens (1999), Jewell (1993) Sheared (1998). Hancock (2000).
10. Neubeck and Cazenave (2001: Ch. 5).
11. For a good discussion of welfare reform in this period, see Mink (1998).
12. See Zucchino (1997).

Bibliography

Primary Sources

Manuscript Collections

American Civil Liberties Union National Archives. Mudd Library, Princeton University.
Wiley, George Alvin. Papers. State Historical Society of Wisconsin.
Welfare Rights Collection. Lehman Library, Columbia University.
Highlander Research and Education Center Collection. State Historical Society of Wisconsin.
Johnson, Lyndon Baines. Presidential Papers. Lyndon B. Johnson Library, Austin.
Mobilization for Youth. Papers. Rare Book and Manuscript Library. Columbia University.
National Welfare Rights Organization. Papers. Moorland-Spingarn Research Center (MSRC). Howard University.
Whitaker, William Howard. Papers. Ohio Historical Society, Columbus.

Periodicals and Newspapers

Atlantic Monthly
Berkshire Eagle
Business Week
Congressional Record
The Nation
Nation's Business
New Republic
New York Amsterdam News
New York Daily News
New York Times
New Yorker
Newsweek
NOW!
Time
Saturday Evening Post
U.S. News and World Report
Washington Daily News
Washington Post
Welfare Fighter

Publications

Birnbaum, Ezra, and Mary Rabagliati. 1969. Organizations of Welfare Clients. In *Community Development in the MFY Experience*, ed. Harold H. Weissman. New York: Association Press.

Brumm, Gordon. 1968. Mothers for Adequate Welfare—AFDC from the Underside. In *Dialogues Boston*, January: 1–12. Whitaker Papers, box 3, folder 3.

Burch, Hobart A. 1970. A Conversation with George Wiley. *The Journal*, Nov-Dec, 2–12. Wiley Papers, box 27.

Burch, Hobart A. 1971. Insights of a Welfare Mother: A Conversation with Johnnie Tillmon. *The Journal*, Jan-Feb., 13–24. Box 27.

The Crisis in Welfare in Cleveland: Report of the Mayor's Commission. 1969. ed. Herbert D. Stein. Cleveland: Case Western Reserve University.

The Gallup Poll, 1959–1971. Wilmington, DE: Scholarly Resources.

Grove, Robert, and Alice Hetzel. 1968. *Vital Statistics Rates in the United States, 1940–1960*, Washington, D.C.: U.S. Department of Health, Education and Welfare.

Haldeman, H. R. 1994. *The Haldeman Diaries: Inside the Nixon White House*. New York: GP Putnam's Sons.

Huldschiner, Robert E. 1968. Fighting Catherine Gets Welfare Mothers Together. *Lutheran Women*, October. Wiley Papers, box 27, folder 7.

Johnson, Lyndon. 1968. *Public Papers of the Presidents of the United States*. Washington: GPO.

Lewis, John. 1968. Black Voices. *Washington Afro-American*, 14 September. Wiley Papers, box 27.

Lewis, John. 1969. Black Voices. *Washington Afro-American*, 19 August. Wiley Papers, box 27.

Macdonald, Michael C. C. 1969. Organizing for Welfare: Knock on any Door. *The Village Voice*, 4 September. Wiley Papers, box 25, folder 3.

Milwaukee County Welfare Rights Organization. 1972. *Welfare Mothers Speak Out: We Ain't Gonna Shuffle Anymore*. New York: Norton.

Moynihan, Daniel Patrick. Office of Policy Planning and Research, U.S. Dept. of Labor. 1965. *The Negro Family: A Case for National Action*. Washington, D.C.

New York Department of Social Services. 1974. *Monthly New York City Public Assistance Summary Data 1960–73*. New York: Dept. of Social Services.

Nixon, Richard. 1970. *Setting the Course, The First Year: Major Policy Statements by President Richard Nixon*. New York: Funk and Wagnalls.

Nixon, Richard. 1970. *Nixon: The First Year of His Presidency*, Congressional Quarterly, Washington, D.C.

Nixon, Richard. *Richard Nixon: Public Papers of the President*. Washington: GPO.

Students for a Democratic Society. 1990. *The Port Huron Statement (1962)*. Chicago: Charles H. Kerr Publishing.

Tillmon, Johnnie. 1972. Welfare Is a Woman's Issue. *Ms. Magazine* 1: 111–116.

U.S. Bureau of the Census. 1967. *County and City Data Book, 1962 (A Statistical Abstract Supplement)*.Washington, D.C.: GPO.

U. S. Bureau of the Census. 1975. *Historical Statistics of the United States: Colonial Times to 1970*. Washington, D.C.: GPO.

U.S. Bureau of the Census. *Statistical Abstracts of the United States*. Washington, D.C.: GPO.

U.S. Commission on Civil Rights. 1966. Children in Need: A Study of a Federally Assisted Program of Aid to Needy Families with Children in Cleveland and Cuyahoga County, Ohio. Washington, D.C.: GPO.

U.S. Riot Commission. 1968. *Report of the National Advisory Commission on Civil Disorders*. New York: Bantam Books.

Weissman, Harold H., ed. 1969. *Community Development in the Mobilization For Youth Experience*. New York: Association Press.

Weissman, Harold H., ed. 1969. *Individual and Group Services in the Mobilization For Youth Experience*. New York: Association Press.

Oral Sources

Interviews by Author:
Edwin Day, 31 October 2003.

Catherine Jermany, 11 October 2003.
Frank Espada, 9 October 2003.
Jon Van Til, 6 October 2003.
Rhoda Linton, 4 October 2003.
Richard Cloward, 19 June 1997.
Frances Fox Piven, 19 June 1997.
Tim Sampson, 21 April 1997.
Ethel Dotson, 27 April 1997.
Moiece Palladino, 27 April 1997.
Marjorie Caesar, 4 March1996.
Interviews by Guida West:
Hulbert James, 6 February1981, New York, NY.
Jeanette Washington, 25 September 1981, New York, NY.
Beulah Sanders, 7 July 1983, New York, NY.

Secondary Sources

Books

Aaker, David A., and George S. Day, eds. 1971. *Consumerism: Search for the Consumer Interest.* New York: Free Press.

Abramovitz, Mimi. 1988. *Regulating the Lives of Women: Social Welfare Policy from the Colonial Times to the Present.* Boston: South End Press.

Abramovitz, Mimi. 1995. *Under Attack, Fighting Back: Women and Welfare in the US.* New York: Monthly Review.

Alinsky, Saul. 1969. *Reveille for Radicals.* New York: Vintage.

Allen, Robert. 1990. *Black Awakening in Capitalist America.* Trenton: Africa World Press.

Andreasen, Alan R. 1975. *The Disadvantaged Consumer.* New York: The Free Press.

Bailis, Lawrence. 1972. *Bread or Justice: Grassroots Organizing in the Welfare Rights Movement.* Lexington, MA: Lexington Books.

Balogh, Brian, ed. 1996. *Integrating the Sixties: The Origins, Structures, and Legitimacy of Public Policy in a Turbulent Decade.* University Park, PA: Pennsylvania State University Press.

Bane, Mary Jo, and David T. Ellwood. 1994. *Welfare Realities: From Rhetoric to Reform.* Cambridge: Harvard University Press.

Bell, Daniel. 1956. *Work and Its Discontents.* Boston: Beacon Press.

Bell, Winifred. 1965. *Aid to Dependent Children.* New York: Columbia University Press.

Biondi, Martha. 2003. *To Stand and Fight: The Struggle for African American Rights in Postwar New York City.* Cambridge: Harvard University Press.

Block, Fred, ed. 1987. *The Mean Season: The Attack on the Welfare State.* New York: Pantheon.

Blum, John Morton. 1991. *Years of Discord: American Politics and Society, 1961–1974.* New York: W.W. Norton.

Boris, Eileen. 1994. *Home to Work: Motherhood and the Politics of Industrial Homework in the United States.* New York: Cambridge University Press.

Bouchier, David. 1987. *Radical Citizenship: The New American Activism.* New York: Schocken Books.

Boyle, Kevin. 1995. *The UAW and the Heyday of American Liberalism 1945–1968.* Ithaca: Cornell University Press.

Bracey, John H., August Meier, and Elliot Rudwick, eds. 1971. *Black Matriarchy: Myth or Reality.* California: Wadsworth Publishing Company.

Bremner, Robert. 1956. *From the Depths: The Discovery of Poverty in the U.S.* New York: New York University Press.

Brinkley, Alan. 1995. *The End of Reform: New Deal Liberalism in Recession and War.* New York: Knopf.

Brown, Elaine. 1992. *A Taste of Power: A Black Woman's Story.* New York: Pantheon Books.

Brown, Michael K. 1999. *Race, Money, and the American Welfare State.* Ithaca, NY: Cornell University Press.

Burke, Vincent J., and Vee Burke. 1974. *Nixon's Good Deed: Welfare Reform*. New York: Columbia University Press.

Butler, Judith. 1997. *Excitable Speech: A Politics of the Performative*. New York: Routledge.

Cantarow, Ellen. 1980. *Moving the Mountain: Women Working for Social Change*. New York: The Feminist Press.

Caplovitz, David. 1963. *The Poor Pay More: Consumer Practices of Low-Income Families*. New York: The Free Press.

Caraway, Nancie. 1991. *Segregated Sisterhood: Racism and the Politics of American Feminism*. Knoxville: University of Tennessee Press.

Carby, Hazel. 1987. *Reconstructing Womanhood: The Emergence of the Afro-American Woman Novelist*. New York: Oxford University Press.

Carmichael, Stokely, and Charles V. Hamilton. 1967. *Black Power: The Politics of Liberation in America*. New York: Vintage Books.

Carson, Clay. 1981. *In Struggle: SNCC and the Black Awakening of the 1960s*. Cambridge: Harvard University Press.

Chafe, William. 1980. *Civilities and Civil Rights: Greensboro, North Carolina and the Black Struggle for Freedom*. New York, Oxford University Press.

Churchill, Ward, and Jim Vander Wall. 1988. *Agents of Repression: The Secret Wars Against the Black Panther Party and the American Indian Movement*. Boston: South End Press.

Clark-Lewis, Elizabeth. 1994. *Living In, Living Out: African American Domestics in Washington, D.C., 1910–1940*. Washington: Smithsonian Institution Press.

Cohen, Lizabeth. 2003. *A Consumers' Republic: The Politics of Mass Consumption in Postwar America*. New York: Alfred A. Knopf.

Collins, Patricia Hill. 1990. *Black Feminist Thought: Knowledge, Consciousness, and the Politics of Empowerment*. New York: Routledge.

Cott, Nancy F. 1987. *The Grounding of Modern Feminism*. New Haven: Yale University Press.

Crawford, Vicki L., Jacqueline Anne Rouse, and Barabara Woods. 1990. *Women in the Civil Rights Movement: Trailblazers and Torchbearers, 1941–1965*. Bloomington: Indiana University Press.

Cutright, Phillips, and Fredrick Jaffe. 1976. *The Impact of Family Planning Programs on Fertility: The U.S. Experience*. New York: Praeger.

Danziger, Sheldon, and Daniel Weinberg. 1986. *Fighting Poverty: What Works and What Doesn't*. Cambridge: Harvard University Press.

Davies, Gareth. 1996. *From Opportunity to Entitlement: The Transformation and Decline of Great Society Liberalism*. Lawrence: University Press of Kansas.

Davis, Angela. 1981. *Women, Race, and Class*. New York: Random House.

Davis, Martha. 1993. *Brutal Need, Lawyers and the Welfare Rights Movement, 1960–1973*. New Haven: Yale University Press.

De Grazia, Victoria, ed. 1996. *The Sex of Things: Gender and Consumption in Historical Perspective*. Berkeley: University of California Press.

Delgado, Gary. 1986. *Organizing the Movement: The Roots and Growth of the Association of Community Organizations for Reform Now (ACORN)*. Philadelphia: Temple University Press.

Dittmer, John. 1994. *Local People: The Struggle for Civil Rights in Mississippi*. Urbana: University of Illinois Press.

Duncan, Greg. 1984. *Years of Poverty, Years of Plenty: The Changing Economic Fortunes of American Workers and Families*. Ann Arbor: Institute for Social Research, University of Michigan.

Eagles, Charles, ed. 1986. *The Civil Rights Movement In America*. Jackson: University Press of Mississippi.

Echols, Alice. 1989. *Daring to be Bad: Radical Feminism in America 1967–1975*. Minneapolis: University of Minnesota Press.

Edmond, Wendy, and Suzie Fleming, eds. 1975. *All Work and No Pay: Women, Housework and the Wages Due*. London: Power of Women Collective and Falling Wall Press.

Edsall, Thomas Byrne, and Mary Edsall. 1992. *Chain Reaction: The Impact of Race, Rights and Taxes on American Politics*. New York: W.W. Norton.

Egerton, John. 1994. *Speak Now Against the Day: The Generation Before the Civil Rights Movement in the South*. New York: Knopf.

Ehrenreich, John H. 1985. *The Altruistic Imagination: A History of Social Work and Social Policy in the United States*. Ithaca: Cornell University Press.

Evans, Sara. 1979. *Personal Politics: The Roots of Women's Liberation in the Civil Rights Movement and the New Left*. New York: Vintage.

Farmer, James. 1986. *Lay Bare the Heart: An Autobiography of the Civil Rights Movement*. New York: Plume.

Feldstein, Ruth. 2000. *Motherhood in Black and White: Race and Sex in American Liberalism, 1930–1965*. Ithaca: Cornell University Press.

Finks, P. David. 1984. *The Radical Vision of Saul Alinsky*. New York: Paulist Press.

Firestone, Shulamith. 1970. *The Dialectic of Sex: The Case for Feminist Revolution*. New York: William Morrow.

Foner, Eric. 1988. *The Story of American Freedom*. New York: W.W. Norton.

Frank, Thomas. 1997. *The Conquest of Cool: Business Culture, Counterculture and the Rise of Hip Consumerism*. Chicago: University of Chicago Press.

Fraser, Nancy. 1989. *Unruly Practices: Power, Discourse, and Gender in Contemporary Social Theory*. Minneapolis: University of Minnesota Press.

Fraser, Steve, and Gary Gerstle, eds. 1989. *Rise and Fall of the New Deal Order, 1930–1980*. Princeton, NJ: Princeton University Press.

Frazier, E. Franklin. 1939. *The Negro Family in the United States*. Chicago: University of Chicago Press.

Freeman, Jo. 1975. *The Politics of Women's Liberation: A Case Study of an Emerging Social Movement and its Relation to the Policy Process*. New York: David McKay.

Freeman, Joshua. 2000. *Working-Class New York: Life and Labor Since World War II*. New York: New Press.

Friedan, Betty. 1963. *The Feminine Mystique*. New York: Norton.

Friedman, Milton. 1962. *Capitalism and Freedom*. Chicago: University of Chicago Press.

Funicello, Theresa. 1993. *Tyranny of Kindness: Dismantling the Welfare System to End Poverty in America*. New York: Atlantic Monthly Press.

Galbraith, John Kenneth. 1958. *The Affluent Society*. Boston: Houghton Mifflin.

Gans, Herbert. 1962. *The Urban Villagers*. New York: Free Press of Glencoe.

Georgakas, Dan, and Marvin Surkin. 1975. *Detroit: I Do Mind Dying: A Study in Urban Revolution*. New York: St. Martins Press.

Giddings, Paula. 1984. *When and Where I Enter: The Impact of Black Women on Race and Sex on America*. New York: Bantam.

Gilbert, Neil. 1983. *Capitalism and the Welfare State: Dilemmas of Social Benevolence*. New Haven: Yale University Press.

Gilens, Martin. 1999. *Why Americans Hate Welfare: Race, Media and the Politics of Antipoverty Policy*. Chicago: University of Chicago Press.

Gilroy, Paul. 1987. *There Ain't No Black in the Union Jack: The Cultural Politics of Race and Nation*. Chicago: University of Chicago Press.

Ginger, Ann Fagan, ed. 1970. *Civil Liberties Docket*. no. 673: 110–111, 114–116. Meiklejohn Civil Liberties Libraries, Oakland, CA.

Gitlin, Todd. 1987. *The Sixties: Years of Hope, Days of Rage*. New York: Bantam.

Gittell, Marilyn. 1970. *Community Control and the Urban School*. New York: Praeger.

Gordon, Linda. 1988. *Heroes of Their Own Lives: The Politics and History of Family Violence, Boston, 1880–1960*. New York: Viking.

———. 1994. *Pitied but Not Entitled: Single Mothers and the History of Welfare*. New York: The Free Press.

———. 1974. *Woman's Body, Woman's Right: Birth Control in America*. New York: Penguin.

———, ed. 1990. *Women, the State and Welfare*. Madison: University of Wisconsin Press.

Graham, Hugh Davis. 1990. *The Civil Rights Era: Origins and Development of National Policy, 1960–1972*. New York: Oxford University Press.

Gramsci, Antonio. 1971. *Selections from the Prison Notebooks*. New York: International Publishers.

Gutman, Herbert. 1976. *The Black Family in Slavery and Freedom*. New York: Vintage Books.

Hamilton, Dona Cooper, and Charles Hamilton. 1997. *The Dual Agenda: Race and Social Welfare Policies of Civil Rights Organizations*. New York: Columbia University Press.

Handler, Joel. 1991. *Moral Construction of Poverty: Welfare Reform in America*. Newbury Park, CA: Sage.

Harrington, Michael. 1962. *The Other America: Poverty in the United States.* New York: MacMillan.

Hartmann, Betsy. 1995. *Reproductive Rights and Wrongs: The Global Politics of Population Control and Contraceptive Choice.* New York: Harper and Row.

Hartz, Louis. 1955. *The Liberal Tradition in America.* New York: Harcourt, Brace and World.

Helfgot, Joseph. 1981. *Professional Reforming: Mobilization for Youth and the Failure of Social Science.* Lexington, MA: Lexington Books.

Hertz, Susan Handley. 1981. *The Welfare Mothers Movement: A Decade of Change for Poor Women?* Washington, D.C.: University Press of America.

Higginbotham, Evelyn Brooks. 1993. *Righteous Discontent: The Women's Movement in the Black Baptist Church, 1880–1920.* Cambridge: Harvard University Press.

Hill, Robert, ed. 1993. *Research on the African-American Family: A Holistic Perspective.* Westport: Auburn House.

Hoff, Joan. 1994. *Nixon Reconsidered.* New York: Basic Books.

hooks, bell. 1981. *Ain't I a Woman: Black Women and Feminism.* Boston: South End Press.

_____. 1984. *Feminist Theory: From Margin to Center.* Boston: South End Press.

_____. 1989. *Talking Back: Thinking Feminist, Thinking Black.* Boston: South End Press.

Horwitt, Sanford. 1989. *Let Them Call Me Rebel: Saul Alinsky, His Life and Legacy.* New York: Alfred A. Knopf.

Hull, Gloria T., Patricia Bell Scott, and Barbara Smith, eds. 1982. *All The Women Are White, All the Blacks Are Men, But Some of Us Are Brave: Black Women's Studies.* Old Westbury, NY: Feminist Press.

Hunter, Tera. 1997. *To Joy My Freedom: Southern Black Women's Lives and Labors After the Civil War.* Cambridge: Harvard University Press.

Isserman, Maurice. 1987. *If I Had a Hammer: The Death of the Old Left and Birth of the New Left.* New York: Basic Books.

Iton, Richard. 2000. *Solidarity Blues: Race, Culture, and the American Left.* Chapel Hill: University of North Carolina Press.

Jackson, Kenneth. 1985. *Crabgrass Frontier: The Suburbanization of the United States.* New York: Oxford University Press.

Jackson, Larry R., and William A. Johnson. 1974. *Protest by the Poor: The Welfare Rights Movement in New York City.* Lexington, MA: Lexington Books.

Jacobs, Lesley. 1993. *Rights and Deprivation.* New York: Oxford University Press.

Jansson, Bruce. 1988. *The Reluctant Welfare State: A History of American Social Welfare Policies.* Belmont: Wadsworth.

Jetter, Alexis, Annelise Orleck, and Diana Taylor, eds. 1997. *The Politics of Motherhood: Activist Voices From Left to Right.* Hanover: University Press of New England.

Jewell, K. Sue. 1993. *From Mammy to Miss American and Beyond: Cultural Images and the Shaping of US Social Policy.* New York: Routledge.

Jones, Jacqueline. 1992. *The Dispossessed: America's Underclass From the Civil War to the Present.* New York: Basic Books.

_____. 1985. *Labor of Love, Labor of Sorrow: Black Women, Work, and the Family from Slavery to the Present.* New York: Vintage Books.

Katz, Michael. 1986. *In the Shadow of the Poorhouse: A Social History of Welfare in America.* New York: Basic Books.

_____. 1989. *The Undeserving Poor: From the War on Poverty to the War on Welfare.* New York: Pantheon.

Keller, Kathryn. 1994. *Mothers and Work in Popular American Magazines.* Westport, CT: Greenwood Press.

Kelley, Robin D. G. 1994. *Race Rebels: Culture, Politics, and the Black Working Class.* New York: Free Press.

Kessler-Harris, Alice. 2001. *In Pursuit of Equity: Women, Men, and the Quest for Economic Citizenship in 20th Century America.* New York: Oxford University Press.

Kluger, Richard. 1976. *Simple Justice: The History of Brown v. Board of Education and Black America's Struggle for Equality.* New York: Knopf.

Kotz, Nick, and Mary Lynn Kotz. 1977. *A Passion for Equality: George A. Wiley and the Movement.* New York: W. W. Norton & Co.

Koven, Seth, and Sonya Michel, eds. 1993. *Mothers of a New World: Maternalist Politics and the Origins of the Welfare States.* New York: Routledge.

Kunzel, Regina. 1993. *Fallen Women, Problem Girls: Unmarried Mothers and the Professionalization of Social Work 1890–1945.* New Haven: Yale University Press.

Ladner, Joyce. 1971. *Tomorrow's Tomorrow: The Black Woman.* Garden City, NY: Doubleday.

Lawson, Ronald. 1986. *The Tenant Movement in New York City, 1904–1984.* New Brunswick: Rutgers University Press.

Lee, Chana Kai. 1999. *For Freedom's Sake: The Life of Fannie Lou Hamer.* Urbana: University of Illinois Press.

Lemann, Nicholas. 1991. *The Promised Land: The Great Migration and How It Changed America.* New York: Alfred A Knopf.

Lewis, Oscar. 1966. *La Vida: A Puerto Rican Family in the Culture of Poverty—San Juan and New York.* New York: Random House.

Lieberman, Robert. 1998. *Shifting the Color Line: Race and the American Welfare State.* Cambridge: Harvard University Press.

Linden-War, Blanche, and Carol Hurd Green. 1993. *American Women in the 1960s: Changing the Future.* New York: Twayne.

Luker, Kristen. 1996. *Dubious Conceptions: the Politics of Teenage Pregnancy.* Cambridge: Harvard University Press.

Marable, Manning. 1983. *How Capitalism Underdeveloped Black America.* Boston: South End Press.

_____. 1991. *Race, Reform and Rebellion: The Second Reconstruction in Black America, 1945–1990.* Jackson: University Press of Mississippi.

Markowitz, Gerald, and David Rosner. 1996. *Children, Race, and Power: Kenneth and Mamie Clark's Northside Center.* Charlottesville, VA: University Press of Virginia.

Marshall, T. H. 1964. *Class, Citizenship and Social Development: Essays by T. H. Marshall.* Garden City: NY, Doubleday and Co.

Matusow, Allan. 1984. *The Unraveling of America: A History of Liberalism in the 1960's.* New York: Harper and Row.

May, Elaine Tyler. 1988. *Homeward Bound: American Families in the Cold War Era.* New York: Basic Books.

Mead, Lawrence. 1986. *Beyond Entitlement: The Social Obligations of Citizenship.* New York: Free Press.

Miller, James. 1987. *Democracy Is in the Streets: From Port Huron to the Siege of Chicago.* New York: Simon and Schuster.

Mink, Gwendolyn. 1995. *The Wages of Motherhood, Inequality in the Welfare State, 1917–1942.* Ithaca: Cornell University Press.

_____. 1998. *Welfare's End.* Ithaca: Cornell University Press.

Minow, Martha. 1990. *Making All the Difference: Inclusion, Exclusion, and American Law.* Itacha: Cornell University Press.

Moraga, Cherrie, and Gloria Anzaldua. 1981. *This Bridge Called My Back: Writing by Radical Women of Color.* New York: Kitchen Table Press.

Morgan, Robin, ed. 1970. *Sisterhood is Powerful: An Anthology of Writings From the Women's Liberation Movement.* New York: Vintage Books.

Morris, Aldon. 1984. *Origins of the Civil Rights Movement: Black Communities Organizing for Change.* New York: Free Press.

Moynihan, Daniel Patrick. 1970. *Maximum Feasible Misunderstanding.* New York: Free Press.

_____. 1973. *Politics of Guaranteed Income: The Nixon Administration and the Family Assistance Plan.* New York: Random House.

Mullings, Leith. 1997. *On Our Own Terms: Race, Class, and Gender in the Lives of African American Women.* New York: Routledge.

Muncy, Robyn. 1991. *Creating A Female Domain in American Reform, 1890–1935.* New York: Oxford.

Murray, Charles. 1984. *Losing Ground: American Social Policy, 1950–1980.* New York: Basic Books.

Naples, Nancy A. ed. 1998. *Community Activism and Feminist Politics: Organizing Across Race, Class, and Gender.* New York: Routledge.

Neubeck, Kenneth, and Noel A. Cazenave. 2001. *Welfare Racism: Playing the Race Card Against America's Poor*. New York: Routledge.

O'Connor, Alice. 2001. *Poverty Knowledge: Social Science, Social Policy, and the Poor in Twentieth-Century U.S. History*. Princeton: Princeton University Press.

Offe, Claus. 1984. *Contradictions of the Welfare State*. Cambridge: MIT Press.

Ohlin, Lloyd, and Richard Cloward. 1960. *Delinquency and Opportunity: A Theory of Delinquent Gangs*. Glencoe, IL: Free Press.

Omi, Michael, and Howard Winant. 1986. *Racial Formation in the United States: From the 1960s to the 1980s*. New York: Routledge.

Omolade, Barbara. 1986. *It's a Family Affair: The Real Lives of Black Single Mothers*. Albany: Kitchen Table Press.

_____. 1994. *Rising Song of African-American Women*. New York: Routledge.

O'Reilly, Kenneth. 1989. *"Racial Matters": The FBI's Secret File on Black America, 1960–1972*. New York: Free Press.

Ownby, Ted. 1999. *American Dreams in Mississippi: Consumers, Poverty, and Culture, 1830–1998*. Chapel Hill: University of North Carolina Press.

Patterson, James T. 1981. *America's Struggle Against Poverty, 1900–1980*. Cambridge: Harvard University Press.

Payne, Charles. 1995. *I've Got the Light of Freedom: The Organizing Tradition and the Mississippi Freedom Struggle*. Berkeley: University of California Press.

Pechman, Joseph, and Michael Timpane, eds. 1975. *Work Incentives and Income Guarantees: The New Jersey Experiment*. Washington, D.C.: The Brookings Institution.

Piven, Frances Fox, and Richard Cloward. 1977. *Poor People's Movements: How They Succeed, Why They Fail*. New York: Pantheon.

_____. 1971. *Regulating the Poor: The Functions of Public Welfare*. New York: Pantheon Books.

Pope, Jacqueline. 1989. *Biting the Hand that Feeds Them: Organizing Women on Welfare at the Grass Roots Level*. New York: Praeger.

Pratt, Henry J. 1976. *The Gray Lobby*. Chicago: University of Chicago Press.

Quadagno, Jill. 1994. *The Color of Welfare: How Racism Undermined the War on Poverty*. New York: Oxford University Press.

_____. 1988. *Transformation of Old Age Security: Class and Politics in the American Welfare State*. Chicago: University of Chicago Press.

Rainwater, Lee, and William Yancey. 1967. *The Moynihan Report and the Politics of Controversy*. Cambridge: MIT Press.

Ralph, James. 1993. *Northern Protest: MLK, Chicago and CRM*. Cambridge: Harvard University Press.

Ransby, Barbara. 2003. *Ella Baker and the Black Freedom Movement: A Radical Democratic Vision*. Chapel Hill: University of North Carolina Press.

Reeser, Linda Cherrey, and Irwin Epstein. 1990. *Professionalization and Activism in Social Work: The Sixties, Eighties, and the Future*. New York: Columbia University Press.

Reilly, Philip. 1991. *The Surgical Solution: History of Involuntary Sterilization in the US*. Baltimore: Johns Hopkins University Press.

Ritz, Joseph P. 1966. *The Despised Poor: Newburgh's War on Welfare*. Boston: Beacon Press.

Roberts, Dorothy. 1997. *Killing the Black Body: Race, Reproduction, and the Meaning of Liberty*. New York: Pantheon Books.

Robnett, Belinda. 1997. *How Long? How Long? African American Women in the Struggle for Civil Rights*. New York: Oxford University Press.

Rosen, Ruth. 2000. *The World Split Open: How the Modern Women's Movement Changed America*. New York: Viking.

Ross, Peter H., and Katherine C. Lyall. 1976. *Reforming Public Welfare: A Critique of the Negative Income Tax Experiment*. New York: Russel Sage.

Roth, Berita. 2004. *Separate Roads to Freedom: Black, Chicana, and White Feminist Movements in America's Second Wave*. Cambridge, U.K.: Cambridge University Press.

Ryan, William. 1971. *Blaming the Victim*. New York: Vintage Books.

Sacks, Karen Brodkin. 1988. *Caring by the Hour: Women, Work and Organizing at Duke Medical Center*. Urbana: University of Illinois Press.

Said, Edward. 1994. *Representations of the Intellectual: The Reith Lectures*. New York: Pantheon.

Samantrai, Ranu. 2002. *AlterNatives: Black Feminism in the Postimperial Nation*. Stanford: Stanford University Press.

Schram, Sanford F., Joe Soss, and Richard C. Fording, eds. 2003. *Race and the Politics of Welfare Reform*. Ann Arbor: University of Michigan Press.

Schulman, Bruce. 2001. *The Seventies: The Great Shift in American Culture, Society and Politics*. Cambridge: Da Capo Press.

Scott, Daryl Michael. 1997. *Contempt and Pity: Social Policy and the Image of the Damaged Black Psyche, 1880–1996*. University of North Carolina Press: Chapel Hill.

Scott, Joan Wallach. 1988. *Gender and the Politics of History*. New York: Columbia University Press.

Self, Robert. 2003. *American Babylon: Class, Race, and Power in Oakland and the East Bay, 1945–1978*. Princeton: Princeton University Press.

Shapiro, Thomas. 1985. *Population Control Politics: Women, Sterilization and Reproductive Choice*. Philadelphia: Temple University Press.

Sheahen, Allan. 1983. *Guaranteed Income: The Right to Economic Security*. Los Angeles: Gain.

Sheared, Vanessa. 1998. *Race, Gender, and Welfare Reform: The Elusive Quest for Self-Determination*. New York: Garland Publishing.

Sheehan, Susan. 1976. *A Welfare Mother*. Boston: Houghton-Mifflin.

Sitkoff, Harvard. 1981. *Struggle for Black Equality, 1954–1980*. New York: Hill and Wang.

Skocpol, Theda. 1992. *Protecting Soldiers and Mothers: The Origins of Social Policy in the United States*. Cambridge: Harvard University Press.

Sleeper, Jim. 1990. *The Closet of Strangers: Liberalism and the Politics of Race in New York*. New York: W. W. Norton.

Solinger, Rickie. 2001. *Beggars and Choosers: How the Politics of Choice Shapes Adoption, Abortion, and Welfare in the United States*. New York: Hill and Wang.

Solinger, Rickie. 1992. *Wake up Little Susie: Single Pregnancy and Race Before Roe v. Wade*. New York: Routledge.

Stack, Carol. 1974. *All Our Kin: Strategies for Survival in a Black Community*. New York: Harper and Row.

Starr, Roger. 1985. *The Rise and Fall of New York City*. New York: Basic Books.

Steiner, Gilbert. 1971. *The State of Welfare*. Washington, D.C.: Brookings Institution.

_____. 1966. *Social Insecurity: The Politics of Welfare*. Chicago: Rand McNally & Co.

Sugrue, Thomas. 1996. *The Origins of the Urban Crisis: Race and Inequality in Postwar Detroit*. Princeton, NJ: Princeton University Press.

Theobald, Robert. 1965. *Free Men and Free Markets*. Garden City, NY: Doubleday and Co.

_____. 1966. *The Guaranteed Income: The Next Step in Economic Evolution?* New York: Doubleday.

Theoharis, Jeanne, and Komozi Woodard, eds. 2003. *Freedom North: Black Freedom Struggles Outside the South, 1940–1980*. New York: Palgrave.

Trattner, Walter. 1974. *From Poor Law to Welfare State: A History of Social Welfare in America*. New York: Free Press.

Trotter, Joe. 1985. *Black Milwaukee: The Making of an Industrial Proletariat, 1915–45*. Urbana: University of Illinois Press.

Tyson, Timothy. 1999. *Radio Free Dixie: Robert F. Williams and the Roots of Black Power*. Chapel Hill: University of North Carolina Press.

Van Deburg, William. 1992. *New Day in Babylon: The Black Power Movement and American Culture, 1965–1975*. Chicago: University of Chicago Press.

Wallace, Michelle. 1979. *Black Macho and the Myth of the Superwoman*. New York: Dial Press.

Weems, Robert E. Jr. 1998. *Desegregating the Dollar: African American Consumerism in the Twentieth Century*. New York: New York University Press.

Weisbrot, Robert. 1990. *Freedom Bound: A History of the Civil Rights Movement*. New York: W.W. Norton.

West, Guida. 1981. *The National Welfare Rights Organization: The Social Protest of Poor Women*. New York: Praeger.

White, Deborah Gray. 1985. *Arn't I A Woman: Female Slaves in the Plantation South*. New York: W.W. Norton and Company.

_____. 1999. *Too Heavy a Load: Black Women in Defense of Themselves 1894–1994*. New York: W. W. Norton.

White, E. Francis. 2001. *Dark Continent of Our Bodies: Black Feminism and the Politics of Respectability*. Philadelphia: Temple University Press.

Wilensky, Harold. 1975. *The Welfare State and Equality*. Berkeley: University of California Press.

Williams, Juan. 1987. *Eyes on the Prize: America's Civil Rights Years, 1954–1965*. New York: Penguin.

Williams, Patricia. 1991. *The Alchemy of Race and Rights*. Cambridge: Harvard University Press.

Wilson, William J. 1980. *The Declining Significance of Race: Blacks and Changing American Institutions*. Chicago: University of Chicago Press.

_____. 1987. *The Truly Disadvantaged: The Inner City, The Underclass, and Public Policy*. Chicago: University of Chicago Press.

Woodward, Komozi. 1999. *A Nation Within a Nation: Amiri Baraka (LeRoi Jones) & Black Power Politics*. Chapel Hill: University of North Carolina Press.

Zucchino, David. 1997. *Myth of the Welfare Queen*. New York: Simon and Schuster.

Articles

Abrahams, Naomi. 1996. Negotiating Power, Identity, Family, and Community: Women's Community Participation. *Gender and Society* 10: 768–796.

Appelbaum, Diane Karter. 1977. The Level of the Poverty Line: A Historical Survey. *Social Service Review* 51: 514–523.

Baron, Harold. 1985. Racism Transformed: Implications of the 60s. *Review of Radical Political Economics* 17: 10–33.

Benson, Susan Porter. 1996. Living on the Margin: Working-Class Marriages and Family Survival Strategies in the United States, 1919–1941. In *The Sex of Things: Gender and Consumption in Historical Perspective*, ed. Victoria de Grazia, 212–243. Berkeley: University of California Press.

Bernstein, Blanche. 1984. Since the Moynihan Report. *New Perspectives* 16.

Blau, Joel. 1989. Theories of the Welfare State. *Social Science Review* 63: 26–38.

Boris, Eileen. 1993. The Power of Motherhood: Black and White Activist Women Redefine the Political. In *Mothers of a New World: Maternalist Politics and the Origins of the Welfare States*, ed. Seth Koven and Sonya Michel, 214–245. New York: Routledge.

Brauer, Carl. 1982. JFK, LBJ, and the War on Poverty. *Journal of American History* 69: 98–119.

Breines, Wini. 1996. Sixties Stories' Silences: White Feminism, Black Feminism, Black Power. *NWSA Journal* 8: 101–121.

Brewer, Rose. 1988. Black Women in Poverty: Some Comments on Female-Headed Families. *Signs* 13.

Brinkley, Alan. 1989. The New Deal and the Idea of the State. In *The Rise and Fall of the New Deal Order, 1930–1980*, ed. Steve Fraser and Gary Gerstle, 85–121. Princeton: Princeton University Press.

Brody, David. 1993. Workplace Contractualism in Comparative Perspective. In *Industrial Democracy in America: The Ambiguous Promise*, ed. Nelson Lichtenstein and Howell Harris. Boston: Cambridge University Press.

Brown, Scot. 2003. The Politics of Culture: The US Organization and the Quest for Black "Unity." In *Freedom North: Black Freedom Struggles Outside the South, 1940–1980*, ed. Jeanne Theoharis and Komozi Woodard, 223–253. New York: Palgrave.

Brush, Paula Stewart. 1999. Influence of Social Movements on Articulations of Race and Gender in Black Women's Autobiographies. *Gender and Society* 13: 120–137.

Cade, Toni. 1970. The Pill: Genocide or Liberation. In *The Black Woman: An Anthology*, ed. Toni Cade Bambara, 162–169. New York: New American Library.

Chambers, Clarke. 1986. Towards a Redefinition of Welfare History. *Journal of American History* 73: 407–433.

Chappell, Marisa. 2002. Rethinking Women's Politics in the 1970s: The League of Women's Voters and the National Organization for Women Confront Poverty. *Journal of Women's History* 13: 155–179.

Cleaver, Kathleen. 2001. Women, Power, and Revolution. In *Liberation, Imagination, and the Black Panther Party: A New Look at the Panthers and Their Legacy*, ed. Kathleen Cleaver and George Katsiaficas, 123–127. New York: Routledge.

Cloward, Richard. 1965. The War on Poverty. *The Nation*, 2 August.

Cloward, Richard, and Frances Fox Piven. 1967. Rent Strike: Disrupting the Slum System. *The New Republic*, December 2 December: 11–15.

_____. 1966. A Strategy to End Poverty. *The Nation*, 2 May: 510–517.

_____. 1967. The Weapon of Poverty. *The Nation*, 8 May.

Cohen, Miriam, and Michael Hanagan. 1991. The Politics of Gender and the Making of the Welfare State, 1900–1940: A Comparative Perspective. *Journal of Social History* 24: 469–484.

Collins, Pat Hill. 1989. Comparison of Two Works on Black Family Life. *Signs* 14: 875–884.

Couto, Richard. 1978. Mud Creed, Kentucky: Sick for Clinics. *Southern Exposure* 6: 76–79.

Davis, Angela. 1986. The Black Family and the Crisis of Capitalism. *The Black Scholar* 17.

Davis, Martha. 1996. Welfare Rights and Women's Rights in the 1960s. *Journal of Policy History* 8: 144–165.

Douglas, Susan J. 2000. Narcissism as Liberation. In *The Gender and Consumer Culture Reader*, ed. Jennifer Scanlon, 267–282. New York: New York University Press.

Duncan, Ruby. 1997. "I Got to Dreamin'": An Interview with Ruby Duncan, conducted and edited by Annelise Orleck. In *The Politics of Motherhood: Activist Voices From Left to Right*, ed. Alexis Jetter, Annelise Orleck, and Diana Taylor, 119–126. Hanover, NH: University Press of New England.

Feldman, Roberta M., Susan Stall, and Patricia A. Wright. 1998. The Community Needs to be Built by Us: Women Organizing in Chicago Public Housing. In *Community Activism and Feminist Politics: Organizing Across Race, Class, and Gender*, ed. Nancy A. Naples, 257–274. New York: Routledge.

Fields, Barbara. 1986. Ideology and Race in American History. *"Race," Writing, and Difference*, ed. Henry Louis Gates, Jr. Chicago: University of Chicago Press.

Frank, Dana. 1991. Gender, Consumer Organizing, and the Seattle Labor Movement, 1919–1929. In *Work Engendered: Toward a New History of American Labor*, ed. Ava Baron, 273–295. Ithaca: Cornell University Press.

Fraser, Nancy, and Linda Gordon. 1994. A Genealogy of Dependency: Tracing a Keyword of the U.S. Welfare State. *Signs* 19: 309–336.

Gelb, Joyce, and Alice Sardell. 1975. Organizing the Poor: A Brief Analysis of the Politics of the Welfare Rights Movement. *Policy Studies Journal* 3: 346–354.

Gluck, Sherna Berger. 1998. Whose Feminism, Whose History? Reflections on Excavating the History of (the) US Women's Movement(s). In *Community Activism and Feminist Politics: Organizing Across Race, Class, and Gender*, ed. Nancy A. Naples, 31–56. New York: Routledge.

Goldberg, Gertrude. 1977. Class Action, Community Organization and School Reform. *Freedomways* 17.

Goodwin, Joanne L. 1995. "Employable Mothers" and "Suitable Work": A Re-Evaluation of Welfare and Wage Earning For Women in the Twentieth-Century United States. *Journal of Social History* 29: 253–274.

Gordon, Linda. 1992. Social Insurance and Public Assistance: The Influence of Gender in Welfare Thought in the United States, 1890–1935. *American Historical Review* 97: 19–50.

Gordon, Linda, Frances Fox Piven, and Richard Cloward. 1988. What Does Welfare Regulate. *Social Research* 55.

Green, Venus. 1995. Race and Technology: African American Women in the Bell System, 1945–1980. *Technology and Culture* 36: (April Supplement), S101–S143.

Hamilton, Charles. 1986. Social Policy and the Welfare of Black Americans: From Rights to Resources. *Political Science Quarterly*, 101: 239–255.

Higginbotham, Evelyn Brooks. 1992. African-American Women's History and the Metalanguage of Race. *Signs* 17: 251–274.

Hine, Darlene Clark. 1994. The Housewives League of Detroit. In *Hine Sight: Black Women and the Re-Construction of American History*, 129–145. Bloomington: Indiana University Press.

King, Deborah. 1988. Multiple Jeopardy, Multiple Consciousness: The Context of a Black Feminist Ideology. *Signs* 14: 42–72.

Kornbluh, Felicia. 2003. Black Buying Power: Welfare Rights, Consumerism, and Northern Protest. In *Freedom North: Black Freedom Struggles Outside the South, 1940–1980*, ed. Jeanne F. Theoharis and Komozi Woodard, 199–222. New York: Palgrave.

_____. 1997. To Fulfill Their "Rightly Needs": Consumerism and the National Welfare Rights Movement. *Radical History Review* 69: 76–113.

Kunzel, Regina. 1994. White Neurosis, Black Pathology: Constructing Out-of-Wedlock Pregnancy in the Wartime and Postwar United States. In *Not June Cleaver: Women and Gender in Postwar America, 1945–1960*, ed. Joanne Meyeerowitz, 304–331. Philadelphia: Temple University Press.

Levenstein, Lisa. 2000. From Innocent Children to Unwanted Migrants and Unwed Moms: Two Chapters in the Public Discourse on Welfare in the United States, 1960–1961. *Journal of Women's History* 11: 10–33.

Levinson, Marc. 1980. Aid to Families with Dependent Children in Georgia. *The Crisis*.

Lipsky, Michael. 1984. The Rationing of Services in Street Level Bureaucracies. In *Critical Studies in Organization and Bureaucracy*, ed. Frank Fischer and Carmen Sirianni. Philadelphia: Temple University Press.

Marchevsky, Alejandra, and Jeanne Theoharris. 2000. Welfare Reform, Globalization, and the Racialization of Entitlement. *American Studies* 41: 235–265.

Matthews, Tracye. 1998. No One Ever Asks What a Man's Place in the Revolution Is: Gender and the Politics of the Black Panther Party, 1996–1971. In *The Black Panther Party Reconsidered*, ed. Charles P. Jones. Baltimore, MD: Black Classic Press.

Mohanty Chandra Talpade. 1991. Under Western Eyes: Feminist Scholarship and Colonial Discourses. In *Third World Women and the Politics of Feminism*, ed. Chandra Mohanty, et al. 51–80. Bloomington: Indiana University Press.

Morrissey, Megan H. 1990. The Downtown Welfare Advocate Center: A Case Study of a Welfare Rights Organization. *Social Service Review* 64: 189–207.

Nadasen, Premilla. 2002. Expanding the Boundries of the Women's Movement: Black Feminism and the Struggle for Welfare Rights. *Feminist Studies* 28: 271–301.

Naples, Nancy A. 1992. Activist Mothering: Cross-Generational Continuity in the Community Work of Women From Low-Income Urban Neighborhoods. *Gender and Society* 6: 441–463.

_____. 1998. Women's Community Activism: Exploring the Dynamics of Politicization and Diversity. In *Community Activism and Feminist Politics: Organizing Across Race, Class, and Gender*, ed. Nancy A. Naples, 327–349. New York: Routledge.

Nelson, Barbara. 1990. The Origins of the Two-Channel Welfare State: Workmen's Compensation and Mothers' Aid. In *Women, The State, and Welfare*, ed. Linda Gordon, 123–151. Madison: University of Wisconsin Press.

Orleck, Annalise. 1997. "If It Wasn't For You I'd Have Shoes for My Children": The Political Education of Las Vegas Welfare Mothers. In *The Politics of Motherhood: Activist Voices From Left to Right*, ed. Alexis Jetter, Annelise Orleck and Diana Taylor, 102–118. Hanover, NH: University Press of New England.

Orshansky, Mollie. 1965. Counting the Poor: Another Look at the Poverty Profile. *Social Security Bulletin* 28: 3–29.

Polatnick, M. Rivka. 1996. Diversity in Women's Liberation Ideology: How a Black and a White Group of the 1960s Viewed Motherhood, *Signs* 21: 679–706.

Quadagno, Jill. 1990. Race, Class, and Gender in the U.S. Welfare State: Nixon's Failed Family Assistance Plan. *American Sociological Review* 55: 11–28.

Reich, Charles. 1965. Individual Rights and Social Welfare: The Emerging Legal Issues. *Yale Law Journal* 74: 1245–1257.

_____. 1964. New Property. *Yale Law Journal* 73: 733–787.

Rosenblatt, Rand E. 1982. Social Duties and the Problem of Rights in the American Welfare State. In *The Politics of Law: A Progressive Critique*, ed. David Kairys, 90–114. New York: Pantheon Books.

Silberman, Charles. 1964. Revolt Against Welfare Colonialism. In *Crisis in Black and White*. New York: Basic Books.

Sparks, Holloway. 1997. Dissident Citizenship: Democratic Theory, Political Courage, and Activist Women. *Hypatia: A Journal of Feminist Philosophy* 12: 74–110.

Spivak, Gayatri. 1988. Can the Subaltern Speak? In *Marxism and the Interpretation of Culture*, ed. Cary Nelson and Lawrence Grossberg, 271–313.Chicago: University of Illinois Press.

Staples, Robert. 1970. The Myth of the Black Matriarchy. *Black Scholar* 2.

Stein, Karen F. 1980. Explaining Ghetto Consumer Behavior: Hypotheses From Urban Sociology. *Journal of Consumer Affairs* 14.

Stone-Mediatore, Shari. 1998. Chandra Mohanty and the Revaluing of Experience. *Hypatia*. 13: 116–133.

Taylor, Ula. "Elijah Muhammad's Nation of Islam: Separatism, Regendering, and a Secular Approach to Black Power after Malcolm X (1965–1975)." In *Freedom North: Black Freedom Struggles Outside the South, 1940–1980*, ed. Jeanne Theoharis and Komozi Woodard, 177–198. New York: Palgrave.

Theobald, Robert. 1966. The Background to the Guaranteed-Income Concept. In *The Guaranteed Income: Next Step in Economic Revolution?* ed. Robert Theobald, 83–96. Garden City, NY: Doubleday and Company.

Tyson, Timothy. 1998. Robert F. Williams, "Black Power," and the Roots of the African-American Freedom Struggle. *Journal of American History* 85: 540–570.

Umansky, Lauri. 1994. The Sisters Reply: Black Nationalist Pronatalism, Black Feminism, and the Quest for a Multiracial Women's Movement, 1965–1974. *Critical Matrix* 8: 19–50.

Valk, Anne. 2000. Mother Power: The Movement for Welfare Rights in Washington, D.C., 1966–1972. *Journal of Women's History* 11: 34–58.

Van Til, Jon. 1971. Reconstruction or Redistribution: Which Way for Welfare Rights? *Social Work* 16: 58–62.

Weems, Jr., Robert. 1994. The Revolution Will Be Marketed: American Corporations and Black Consumers During the 1960s. *Radical History Review* 59: 94–107.

Weems, Jr., Robert. 2000. Consumerism and the Construction of Black Female Identity in Twentieth-Century America. In *The Gender and Consumer Culture Reader*, ed. Jennifer Scanlon, 166–178. New York: New York University Press.

White, Lucie. 1990. Substantive v. Procedural Rights: Goldberg v. Kelley. *Brooklyn Law Review* 56.

Williamson, John. 1973. Beliefs about the Welfare Poor. *Sociology and Social Research* 58: 163–175.

Wright, Gerald C. 1976. Racism and Welfare Policy in America. *Social Science Quarterly* 57: 718–730.

Zinn, Maxine Baca. 1989. Family, Race, and Poverty in the Eighties. *Signs* 14: 856–874.

Zinn, Maxine Baca, and Bonnie Thornton Dill. 1996. Theorizing Difference From Multiracial Feminism. *Feminist Studies* 22: 321–331.

Unpublished Works

Bussiere, Elizabeth. 1989. Social Welfare and the Courts: The Dilemmas of Liberalism. Ph.D. diss., Brandeis University.

Chappell, Marisa. 2002. From Welfare Rights to Welfare Reform: The Politics of AFDC, 1964–1984. Ph.D. diss., Northwestern University.

Chommie, Peter William. 1969. A Study of Differential Participation in an Indigenous Welfare Rights Organization as Related to Value Orientations and Patterns of Alienation. Ph.D. diss., University of Minnesota.

Deneke, Maris Johanna. 1991. Against All Odds: Cleveland Welfare Rights Organization, 1966–1991. Masters thesis, Case Western Reserve University.

Fergus, Devin. 2002. The Ordeal of Liberalism and Black Nationalism in Americas Southern States, 1965–1980. Ph.D. diss., Columbia University.

Frost, Jennifer Ann. 1996. Participatory Politics: Community Organizing, Gender, and the New Left in the 1960s. Ph.D. diss., University of Wisconsin.

Hancock, Ange-Marie. 2000. The Public Identity of the "Welfare Queen" and the Politics of Disgust. P.D. diss., University of North Carolina.

Hertz, Susan Handley. 1974. A Study of the Organization and Politics of the Welfare Mothers Movement in Minnesota. Ph.D. diss., University of Minnesota.

Hogan, Wesley. 2000. "Radical Manners": The Student Non-Violent Coordinating Committee and the New Left in the 1960s. Ph.D. diss., Duke University.

Kornbluh, Felicia. 2000. A Right to Welfare? Poor Women, Professionals, and Poverty Programs, 1935–1975. Ph.D. diss., Princeton University.

Lim, Hilary. 1991. Mapping Welfare Rights. Ph.D. diss., University of Calgary.

Martin, George. 1972. Emergence and Development of a Social Movement Organization Among the Underclass: A Case Study of the National Welfare Rights Organization. Ph.D. diss., University of Chicago.

Mittlestadt, Jennifer. 2000. Dilemmas of the Liberal Welfare State, 1945–1965: Gender, Race, and Aid to Dependent Children. Ph.D. diss., Univeristy of Michigan.

O'Connor, Alice. 1991. From Lower Class to Underclass: The Poor in American Social Science, 1930–1970. Ph.D. diss., Johns Hopkins University.

Rose, Kenneth Wayne. 1988. The Politics of Social Reform in Cleveland, 1945–1967: Civil Rights, Welfare Rights, and the Response of Civic Leaders. Ph.D. diss., Case Western Reserve University.

Sachs, Andrea Jule. 2001. The Politics of Poverty: Race, Class, Motherhood, and the National Welfare Rights Organization, 1965–75. Ph.D. diss., University of Minnesota.

Shreshinsky, Naomi Gottlieb. 1970. Welfare Rights Organizations and the Public Welfare System: An Interaction Study. Ph.D. diss., University of California.

Sparks, Holloway. 1999. Dissident Citizenship: Lessons on Democracy and Courage from Activist Women. Ph.D. diss. University of North Carolina.

Spencer, Robyn Ceanne. 2001. Repression Breeds Resistance: The Rise and Fall of the Black Panther Party in Oakland, CA, 1966–1982. Ph.D. diss., Columbia University.

Spitzer, Scott J. 2000. The Liberal Dilemma: Welfare And Race, 1960–1975. Ph.D. diss., Columbia University.

Springer, Kimberly. 1999. Our Politics Was Black Women: Black Feminist Organizations, 1968–1980. Ph.D. diss., Emory University.

Umoja, Akinyele Kambon. 1996. Eye For an Eye: the Role of Armed Resistance in the Mississippi Freedom Movement. Ph.D. diss., Emory University.

Van Til, Jon. 1970. Becoming Participants: Dynamics of Access Among the Welfare Poor. Ph.D. diss., University of California, Berkeley.

Whitaker, William Howard. 1970. The Determinants of Social Movement Success: A Study of the National Welfare Rights Organization. Ph.D. diss, Brandeis University.

Williams, Rhonda Y. 1998. Living Just Enough in the City: Change and Activism in Baltimore's Public Housing, 1940–1980. Ph.D. diss., University of Pennsylvania.

Zylan, Yvonne. 1994. The Divided Female State: Gender, Citizenship and US Social Policy Development, 1945–1990. Ph.D. diss., New York University.

Index

1935 Social Security Act, 159
1939 Social Security Amendments, 7
1948 United Nations Universal Declaration of
    Human Rights, 241
1962 Social Security Amendments, 12, 69
1962 welfare amendments, 50
1963 March on Washington, 35, 72
1964 Civil Rights Act, 72
1965 White House Conference on Civil
    Rights, 144
1966 Walk fob Adequate Welfare, 163
1966 welfare protests, 2
1967 Social Security Amendments, 160
1967 NWRO annual convention in
    Washington, 136
1967 Social Security Amendments, 49, 135, 171
    NWRO protest of, 136
1969 Detroit Conference, 146
1971 NWRO national convention, 217
1972 Convention in Gary, Indiana, 74
1972 Social Security bill, 187
1973 NWRO convention, 213–214

A

Abernathy, Ralph, 73, 204, 206
Abortion, xii, 166, 197, 216–217
    free, 218
    illegal, 218
    self-induced, 218
"Abrasive" police-community relations, 94
Abuse, 21
    in the system, 40
Abusive welfare practices, 76
Academic interventions, 13–15

ACLU (American Civil Liberties Union), 10, 59
    Welfare Civil Liberties Project of, 54
ACORN (Arkansas Community
        Organizations for Reform
        Now), 202, 222
ADC (Aid to Dependent Children), 4–11, 15,
        18, 20, 32, 48–49, 136
    changing nature of, 9
    cuts in, 7
    establishment of, 48
    history of, 4–5
ADC mothers, 200
Adequate Income Act of 1970, 180
Administrative reform, economic reform
        and, 79
Administrators, bias of, 28
AFDC (Aid to Families with Dependent
        Children)
    budget cuts, xvi, 14–15, 30, 228
    bureaucratic tangles of, 175
    as charity, 46, 59, 61, 76, 117
    disbursement of, 77
    dismantling of, 241
    dissatisfaction with, 81
    freeze on federal payments to states, 49, 171
    heightened criticism of, 135, 145
    history of, 4–5
    humaneness of, 3
    as legitimate income, 117
    negative characterizations of, 173
    patron-client relationship of, 56
    perception of, 77
    as a right, 61, 75–76
    under severe attack, 207
AFDC Leagues, 71

AFDC-Unemployed Parent program, 136
AFDC-UP (Aid to Families with Dependent
    Children—for Unemployed
    Parents), 12
Affluent Society, The, 13, 161
AFL-CIO, 185
African Americans, xvi, 2, 4, 11–12, 18, 23, 28,
    30, 52, 60, 64, 74, 106, 131, 133,
    146–147, 149–150, 197, 203,
    216, 238, 240
  activists, 107, 151, 166, 174
  categorized as undeserving, 207
  challenge to the subordination of, 237
  children, 9
  consumerism and, 112–114
  cultural traits of, 143
  denial of assistance to, 5
  employment of recipients and, 141
  exclusion from welfare rolls, 29
  families, 5, 10
  growing economic clout of, 107
  guaranteed annual income and, 167
  historical oppression of, 137
  migration of to urban areas, 7–8
  northward migration of, 8
  pathological behavior of, 14
  single motherhood and, 143–144
  as "targeted" groups, 207
  women, xv, 4–6, 8, 12, 158, 189, 197–198,
    223, 232, 239
    employment of recipients and, 142
    proper social role for, 9
    relationship to the labor market, 9
    stigmatization of, 3
Aid to black-owned businesses, 225
Aid to Dependent Children. *See* ADC
Aid to Families with Dependent Children. *See*
    AFDC
Aid to Families with Dependent Children—
    for Unemployed Parents. *See*
    AFDC-UP
Aid to Needy Children, 20
Aid to Needy Children Mothers Aid to the
    Blind, 2, 17, 186
Aid to the Blind and Disabled, 195
Aid to the Disabled, 2, 4, 17, 186
Alinksy, Saul, 84–86
  internal tensions and, 131
American Bar Association, 85
American Civil Liberties Union. *See* ACLU
American Public Welfare Association, 10
Annual conferences, 127. *See also* individual
    listings by year

Anti-FAP protests, 181
Anti-social program position, 238
Anti-welfare law, 138
Antipoverty
  activism, 33
  agencies, 38
  reformers, 63
  rhetoric, 50
Antiracist groups, 29
Antiwelfare
  hostility, 218
  sentiment, 194
Appliances, 84. *See also* Household appliances
  working, as a basic right, 81
Area Redevelopment Act, 13
Arkansas Community Organizations for
    Reform Now. *See* ACORN
Association for Voluntary Sterilization, 217
Association of Black Social Workers, 149
Atomized reforms, 226
Autonomy, xii, 130, 139–140, 145, 150, 153,
    164, 166, 196, 210, 213, 222, 229,
    237, 240

B

Baltimore WRO, 151, 224
Barbara Hotel, 60
Barrick, Fred, 209
Basic minimum income, 123, 160, 168, 177,
    180–181, 190
Basic minimum standard of living, 169,
    199, 241
Basic standard of living, 3, 161, 227, 232
  as a right, 100
Beginnings, 1–4
Behind Ghetto Walls, 14
Bell hooks, 68
Bell, Daniel, 91
Benson, Susan Porter, 106
Birth control, 197, 217. *See also* Contraception
  in the black community, 216
  pill, 215
Black activists, 233
Black capitalism, 177
Black caucus, 147–148, 185
Black community organizations, 166
Black culture, renewed interest in, 112
Black electoral power, 74
Black empowerment, xii
Black equality, struggle for, 2
Black family, 238

as "matriarchal," 144–145
policy, 143
Black feminism, xi, 166, 230
Black feminist analysis, 229
Black feminist ideology, 155, 230
Black feminist politics, x
Black freedom activists, 149
Black freedom groups, Poor People's
Campaign and, 71
Black freedom movement, xi–xii, 23, 28–31,
65, 74, 123, 233
as heterogeneous, 33
Black inner-city poverty, 97
Black liberation, 231
movement, 222
Black migration, xvi, 8, 11, 196
Black militancy in the ghettos, 99
Black mothers, 126
Black movement of self-identity, 150
Black nationalism, 31, 153
Black neoconservatives, 238
Black Panther Party, 74, 96–97, 174, 201, 211
guaranteed annual income and, 169
Ten Point Program of, 169
"Black paper," 65
Black poor, 235
Black power, 31, 34, 177
movement, 67, 112
organizations, 97
rising tide of, 148
zslogans, 149
Black Power, 74
Black pride, 112
Black radicalism, 233
Black recipients as politically incompetent, 129
Black single motherhood, 8, 189
Black urban poverty, 144
Black women, 28, 46, 52, 75, 97–98, 126–127,
129, 135, 138, 140–141, 149,
165, 188, 190, 193, 196, 201, 205,
207, 212–214, 217–218, 222,
229–230, 232, 235–240
changing the public's perception of, 155
desire to be recognized as mothers, 142
employment of recipients and, 143
empowerment of, 31
importance of work as mothers, 32
in urban areas, 27
as needing guidance and supervision, 130
sexuality of, 155
single motherhood and, 143
stereotypes of, 29
valued as waged laborers, 32

Black Women's Liberation Group, 217
Black work ethic, notions of, 155
Blackston, Harvey, 224
Blair, Pamela, 153–154
Blakely, Mamie, 154
Bland, Doris, 130, 150
"Blaxploitation" films, 201
Blind persons, 186–187, 207
Boddie, Catherine, 215
Bonfanti, Dora, 128–129
Boston, MA, 2, 18–19, 24, 52, 54, 58, 66–67, 71,
83–84, 94, 118, 125, 147, 149, 197
employment of recipients and, 136, 140
internal tensions and, 129
Bowler, Andrew, 128
Boycotting, 24. *See also* Bus boycott;
Consumer boycotts; Economic
boycotts
"Bread and butter" issues, 214
Breaking point, 208–213
Brinkley, Alan, 105
Bronxvi, the, 98
Tremont Welfare Center in, 82
"Brood mares," 136
Brooklyn Welfare Acdion Council, 67, 109
lobbying and, 71
Brooklyn, NY, 25, 98
churches in, 37
Korvette's store demonstration in, 109
Leadership Development Project in, 86
Welfare Recipients League, 25–26, 40
Welfare Action Council (B-WAC), 83, 86
Brown v. Board of Education, 92
Brown, Barbara, 208
Brown, Jerry, 224
Brumm, Gordon, 145
Buffum, Bill, 154
Bureau of Labor Statistics, mid-Atlantic
regional office of, 136
Bureau of Public Assistance, 5
Bureaucratic control, demands to limit, 46
Bus boycott, 107
Bustamonte, Joanna "Cookie," 203

C

Cabinet, 176
Caesar, Majorie, 48, 142
California, 7, 19–20, 126, 134, 142, 174,
224–226, 228
Alameda County Welfare Rights
Organization, 40

California (*continued*)
  ANC Mothers Anonymous in, 31
  lobbying and, 71
  WRO, 150
Calvert, Mildred, 16, 30, 121
CAP (Community Action Program), 34, 64, 212
Caplovitz, David, 106
CARASA (Committee for Abortion Rights and Against Sterilization Abuse), 218
Carmichael, Stokely, 74
Casework
  advocating an end to, 52
  elimination of, 158
  investigations
    demands to end, 46
    elimination of, 232
Caseworkers, xvi, 4, 6, 12–13, 16, 20, 35, 60, 101, 203
  abusive treatment by, 51
  biases of, 52
  continual monitoring by, 48
  in control of recipients, 114
  challenging decisions of, 54
  dehumanizing treatment by, 15
  demand for efficient service from, 83
  discretionary power of, 175, 190, 231, 237
  divested of power, 96
  establishment of high qualification standards, 48
  fair hearings and, 57–58
  and female recipients, 47
  as "gods," 22, 51
  and lack of understanding, 52
  mistreatment by, 59
  power of, 45, 49–52, 56–58, 66, 76
  and racism, 28, 31
  recipients' battles with, 231
  as servants, 51–52
  special grants and, 80–81, 84, 86, 90, 94
  subjected to standards, 46
  as sympathetic and supportive, 36, 76
  treating recipients with dignity, 125
  unfairness of, 53
  unjust treatment by, 29
  walking off the job, 82
Castro, Clementina, 30
Cazenave, Noel, 239
Celebrezze, Anthony J., 18
Center on Social Welfare Policy and Law, 55, 60–62, 160–161
Chambers, Annie, 224
Charity, 89, 93, 100–101, 206
Cheeks, Bobby, 224

Chicago West Side Organization, 21
Chicago WRO, 152
Chicago, IL, 23, 41–42, 57, 65, 97, 109, 132–133, 152, 174
  Back of the Yards neighborhood, 84
  Jobs or Income Now (JOIN) organization in, 108
  Kenwood-Oakland Community Organization (KOCO), 26
  Poor People's Campaign and, 72
  public welfare workers union, 36
  Woodlawn Organization, 65, 84
Child care, 241
  as legitimate work, 165, 167
Child maintenance, 232
Child Welfare League of America, 10
Children's March on Washington, 205–208
Choice
  lack of, 138
  politics of, 218
Christian Family Movement, 118
Citizen Participation Project, 137
Citizen's Crusade Against Poverty, 39
Citizens United for Adequate Welfare. *See* CUFAW
Citizenship, xiiii, 46
  and participation, 65
Civic action, 226–227
Civic participation, 227
Civil disorders, 131, 173
Civil rights, xi, xii, 3, 15, 22, 27, 29, 45, 62, 74–75, 89, 91, 123, 125, 143–145, 153, 161, 233–235
  activism, 33–35, 107
  of African Americans, 23
  basic guarantees of, 237
  groups, 38
  marches, 2, 30
  movement, 2, 43, 46, 81
    parallels between welfare rights movement and, 59
  organizations, xv, 66
  protests, 107
Civil Rights bill, 63
Clark, Kenneth, 14, 92
Clark, Mamie, 92
Class, xiii, xv–xii, 15, 28–29, 31, 92–93, 105, 114, 142, 155, 167, 188, 197, 212, 221–222, 230
  biases, 48, 140, 239
  divide, 220
  empowerment, 229
  oppression, 126, 130, 219

privilege, 150
    status, 146
Classism, 212
Cleveland Mothers, 18
Cleveland, OH, 1–2, 17–18, 40, 120, 209
    Buyer's Cooperative in, 108
    "Crisis in Welfare" in, 97
    ERAP in, 36
    Welfare Grievance Committee, 82
Client-caseworker relationship, improvement
    of, 51
Clinton, William J., 240
Clothing, 82–83, 86, 88, 91, 95–96, 98, 100,
        113–115, 120–122, 136, 151,
        203, 226
    as a basic right, 79, 81
    grants, 159
    social significance of, 92–93
Cloward, Richard, xiiii, 13, 26, 29, 36, 39
    FAP and, 182
    guaranteed annual income and, 163
    importance in the intellectual
        on single motherhood, 143
    special grants and, 81, 98
    · wage supplements and, 202
Cohen, Wilbur, 169, 172, 177
COLAs (cost-of-living adjustments), 186
Coleman, Dovie, 133–135
Collective action, 20–21, 68
Collective bargaining, 57
Collins, Patricia Hill, 230
Colom, Wilbur, 202
Colonial era, poor relief programs of, 47
Colorado, AFDC Mothers Club in, 31
Columbia University, 97
    School of Social Work, 39
        Center on Social Welfare Policy and
        Law, 54
Columbus, OH, 2, 18
    People's Poverty Board (PPB), 35
    policy making and, 69
    South Side Family Council, 122
    special grants and, 89
    "Toys for Tots" program, 89
    WRO, 61, 131
Committee for Abortion Rights and Against
        Sterilization Abuse. See CARASA
Committee on Consumer Interest, 106
Community Action Program. See CAP
Community activism, 26, 226–227
Community members, 15, 23
Community organizing, 23–28, 226–227
Compassion for the less fortunate, xiii

Compromise bills, 186
Conferences, 221. See also individual listings
        by year
Congress of Racial Equality. See CORE
Consciousness raising, 232
Conservatism, 233–235, 238
Conservatives, 123, 136, 145, 158, 169–172,
        176–177, 188, 195, 198, 201, 236
    groups, 228
    rhetoric of, 123, 171
Constitutional protection, 231
Constitutionality, 174, 205
Consumer boycotts, 107
Consumer campaigns, 107–109
Consumer cooperatives, 108
Consumer power, 111–113
Consumer revolts, 105
Consumer rights, xi
Consumer strategies, 113–117, 233
Consumerism, 103
    as an antidote to class oppression, 114
    in the 1960s, 104–106
        as a core American identity, 114
Consumers, xi, 15, 23
Consumption, 104
    as a basic right and entitlement, 111
Contraception, 215–216. See also Birth control
CORE (Congress of Racial Equality), 24, 29
    National Action Council, 39
Cost-of-living-adjustments. See COLAs
Cost of living increase, 178
Council of Economic Advisors, 63
Council of Federated Organization, 29
Credit
    access to, 232
    as a basic right and entitlement, 111
    and department stores, 103, 109–111
    discriminatory practices of, 117
    strategy, 104
Credit unions, 103, 108, 109, 117
Crow, Jim, 33, 107
CUFAW (Citizens United for Adequate
        Welfare), 18, 36
Cultural activities, 100
Cultural biases, 48, 140
Cutright, Phillip, 217
"Cycle of poverty," 144

D

D. C. Department of Public Welfare, 120
Damaging and dangerous behavior, 91
Dandridge v. Williams, 160

Dangerous living conditions, 60
Dark Ghetto, 14
Dashikis, 112, 153
Davidson, Mary, 130
Davis, Estell, 49–50
Davis, Martha, 220
Day care, 165, 168, 235–236
    centers, 142
    services, 135–136
Day, Edwin, 29, 40
    P/RAC and, 39
Day, Noel, 24
Decent standard of living, 179
Decision making, 125–126, 139, 147, 154,
        184, 211–213, 237
Decline of the welfare rights movement, 238
Dehumanization, 45, 47, 49, 76
Deindustrialization, 13
    in urban centers, 8
DeLeeuw, Bert, 206
Delinquency and Opportunity, 13
Dellinger, Dave, 204
Demands
    for material benefits, 79
    for participation, 70, 73, 75–76
    representation, 65–68, 77
Democracy, 46
Democratic Convention platform fight, 208
Democratic participation, 68, 85
Democratic Party, 66, 172, 190, 198, 234
Democratic Party Convention, 169
Democratic process, 183
Democrats, 136, 171–172, 177–179, 196, 198,
        203, 234, 236, 238–239
    guaranteed annual income and, 169–170
Demolition of homes, 25
Demonization, 184, 222
Demonstrations, 58, 62, 93, 95, 98, 109, 136,
        154–155, 168, 171, 175, 180,
        193, 202, 204, 219, 240
    consumerism and, 107
Department of Agriculture's "economy food
        plan," 168
Department of Health, Education and
        Welfare. *See* HEW
Department of Labor, 137–138
    Bureau of Labor Statistics, 168
Department stores, 231
    credit for recipients, 103, 109–111
Des Moines, IA
    1968 Democratic Platform Committee, 71
    lobbying and, 71

Desertion, 49, 55, 135, 144, 165
Detroit Housewives Leagues in the 1930s, 107
Detroit, MI, 5–6, 19, 40, 97, 99, 105, 127, 139,
        146–155, 174
    1969 annual convention in, 125, 200
    Dodge Revolutionary Union Movement
        in, 134
    internal tensions and, 130
    NWRO conference in, 86
    public welfare workers union, 36
    Westside ADC Mothers, 82, 145
        request for holiday money, 83
Deukmejian, George, 224
Diamond, Renee, 228
Dignity, 47, 62, 64, 73, 75–77, 88, 100, 121,
        123, 129, 134, 139–140, 162–163
    campaign for, 79
    lack of, 45, 79
    maintenance of, 89
    struggle for, 49–52, 59
Direct action, 71
    tactics, 83
Disability insurance, 195
Disability support, 61
Disabled persons, 186–187, 194, 200, 207
Discipline of children, 5, 201
Discrimination, 29, 51, 61, 81, 92, 111, 117, 176
Disempowerment, 21, 51, 57, 59, 75, 77, 85,
        103, 132
Disenfranchisement, 2, 23, 65, 68, 74, 134,
        231, 240
Disposable income, 104
Disproportionate family responsibilities, 220
Disruption, 79, 81–82, 93, 95, 97, 148, 180,
        184, 201
Divorce, 7, 49, 135, 150, 218
    increase in, 144
Dolan, Merrille, 219
Domencich, Loretta, 149, 162
Domestic ideal, the, 142
Domestic work, 4. *See also* Housework
    compensation for, 232
Dominant liberal ideology, 234
Dotson, Ethel, 28, 140, 225, 228
Downer, Cassie B., 51, 166
Downey, Neil, 181
Drake, Guy, 196
Drugs
    abuse of, 63
    counseling for, 225
    use of, 198
        rise in, 238

Due process, 60, 77, 79, 178, 183, 231
   clause, 59
Duncan, Ruby, 203, 205, 225

E

E.J. Korvette, 111
Early welfare rights groups, 3–4
East Kentucky WRO (EKWRO), 225
Economic boycotts, 81, 99
Economic changes, 7
Economic discrimination, xii
Economic dislocations, 8
Economic efficiency, 155
Economic empowerment, 34
Economic exclusion, 240
Economic growth, 122
Economic inequality, 66
Economic justice, 87, 225, 230–231
Economic Opportunity Act. *See* EOA
Economic prosperity, xvi, 107
Economic reform, administrative reform and, 79
Economic rights, xiiii
Economics as a "right" of citizenship, 161
Economists, 91, 173, 188, 232
Edmon, Beverly, 31, 65
Education, xi, 23, 26–27, 32, 42, 50, 53, 55–57,
      75, 92, 112, 122–123, 127,
      132–134, 136, 154, 161, 166,
      169–170, 195, 198, 201, 209,
      212, 215, 226–228
   empowerment of women and, 46
Education Department, 72
Ehrenreich, John, 56
Elderly persons, 134, 163, 186–187, 194, 200,
      207, 214
   consumerism and, 107
Election rigging, 128
Electoral politics, 233
Electoral power, 186, 197
Electoral strategy, 201
Elementary and Secondary Education Act of
      1965, Title I of, 226
Eligibility, 5, 10
   based on declaration of need, 168
   casework and, 52
   criteria, 4, 12, 61
   declaration system and, 52
   restrictions, 9
   restrictive policies of, 218
   separation of, 52
   standards, 207

Emergency grants, 168, 178
Emotional health and well-being, 91–92, 232
Employable mother laws, 6
Employment
   and discrimination, 8
   outside the home, 155
   and single women, 7
   status, 158
   of welfare recipients, 50, 53, 85, 135–139,
      141–143, 165, 232
Empowerment, 50, 56, 58, 61, 75–76, 80, 126,
      132, 134, 154, 201, 212– 213,
      222, 226, 229, 237, 240
   of women, 221
Engelhardt, William, 47
Englewood, NJ, Bergen County Welfare
      Board in, 27
Entitlement, 80, 89, 111, 122, 146, 184, 220,
      227, 232
EOA (Equal Opportunity Act), 34
Equal employment opportunity, 39
Equal housing opportunity, 39
Equal opportunity, 92
   as good business, 112
Equal protection, 30, 60, 160–161
Equal Rights Amendment, 214
"Equality as a fact," 34
Espada, Frank, 25
   P/RAC and, 40
Eugenics movement, 216
"Evaluation of NWRO and Affiliates," 153
Evans, Faith, 212
Evans, James, 210
Exclusionary policies of states, 5
Executive Committee. *See* NWRO Executive
      Committee

F

Fain, Irving, 41
Fair enforcement of laws, 45
Fair hearings, 56–58, 60, 79, 81–82, 168,
      203–204, 237
Fair housing, 233
Fair Housing Associations, 118
Family Assistance Plan. *See* FAP
Family
   breakup of, 136
   planning, 215, 217
   stability of, 50
   status of, 91, 158
   values, decline of, 238

Family (*continued*)
  and wage ideal, 221
  -wage system, 146
Family Planning Digest, 217
Fanueff, Charles, 217
FAP (Family Assistance Plan), 157, 170–176,
        182, 185, 187, 204–205, 208, 211
  criticisms of, 178
  debate, 158, 180, 209
  failure of, 159
  first version voted down, 181
  low monthly payment of, 178
  new version of, 181
  protest song, 181
  recipients' advisory committee, 183
Farm workers as organizers, 23
Farmer, James, 39
Farrell, Robert, 224
Fatherhood, 54–55
FBI Counterintelligence Program
    (COINTELPRO), 95
FDR. *See* Roosevelt, Franklin D.
"A Federal Family Investment Program: The
    Basic Goal of the Philadelphia
    Welfare Rights Organization," 166
Federal government's official poverty line, 168
Federal grants, 34, 225
Federal legislators, 231
Federal subsidization of suburbs, 11
Federal Trade Commission, 106
"Female-dominated" families, 14
Female-headed families, 143, 165, 171
Female-headed households, 144
Feminism, xvi, xii, 126, 211, 213–215, 219,
        221–222, 229–231, 237
  and agenda, 237
  analysis of, 32
  and consciousness, xv
  organizations of, 220
  perspective of, x
  and politics, 214
Feminists, 66, 193, 216, 218, 232
  consumerism and, 112
Field organizers, 127
Finch, Robert, 176, 178, 180, 183
First local welfare rights groups, 15
Fishloe, Dave, 147
Flat grants, 93–96, 98–99, 109, 163–164
Fourteenth Amendment
  due process clause of, 10, 61
  equal protection laws of, 10
Flemming, Arthur, 10
Fonda, Jane, 204

Food, 98
  budget, inadequacy of, 117
  prices, 197
  programs, 227
Food stamps, 172, 181, 187, 194–195
  program, 67, 134, 171, 228
  expansion of, 186
Ford Foundation, 35
Foundation money, 211
Franklin, Olive, 215
Fraser, Donald, 185
Fraser, Nancy, 70, 141
Frazier, Franklin, 144
Free breakfast programs, 174, 226
Free-market advocates, 176
Free Men and Free Markets, 162
Freeman, Roger, 195
Friedan, Betty, 91
Friedman, Milton, 161, 188
  guaranteed annual income and, 170
Friends of Welfare Rights, 42, 110
Funicello, Theresa, 228
Furniture, 67, 80, 83–84, 87, 89, 95, 99, 119,
        136, 159
  as a basic right, 81
  as an enticement, 86
  unfair repossession of, 108

G

Galbraith, John Kenneth, 13, 161, 188
  guaranteed annual income and, 169, 170
Gallup poll, 197
Gays as organizers, 23
Gender, xiii, xv–xii, 4, 8, 14–15, 31, 77, 97,
        112, 114, 126, 142, 146, 150, 155,
        158, 165, 173, 186–191, 193, 195,
        197, 200–202, 207, 211–212, 217,
        222, 238–240. *See also* Sexism
  analysis, 229
  equality, 229
  oppression, 130, 167, 219, 229
  politics, 230
General Assistance, 2, 17
General living standards, 120
Genocidal clinics, 216
Genocide, 216, 217
Ghettos, 173
Gilbert, Neil, 69
Gilchrest, 111
Gilroy, Paul, xii
Ginsberg, Mitchell, 95
Goldberg v. Kelley, 60–62, 75, 205

Goldwater, Barry, 161
Gordon, Linda, 141
Government
    intervention, 13
    job creation, 169
    officials, 107
    responsibility, xiiii
    spending, 195
Graham, Katherine, 41
Grants, 152
Grass Roots Organizing for Welfare
        Leadership. *See* GROWL
Grass-roots, 138, 200, 236
    activism, 107, 113, 147, 153, 165, 236
    base, 158, 213
    groups, 2, 23, 174
        policy making and, 68
    members, 204
    membership, 183
    mobilization versus litigation, 62
    movement, 46, 63, 75, 205
    organizing, 23, 193
    participants, 100
    political movement, 74
    political organizing, 190
    poor people's movement, 199
    recipients, 149, 152, 206
    resistance, 227
    storefront office, 25
Gray Panthers, 186–187
Great Society programs, 194–195, 198
Great Society, the, 176
Groppi, Father James, 30
GROWL (Grass Roots Organizing for Welfare
        Leadership), 241
Guaranteed adequate income. *See*
        Guaranteed annual income
"Guaranteed adequate jobs!," 179
Guaranteed annual income, xv, 39–40, 123,
        159–161, 163–164, 172–173,
        190, 220–221, 226, 232. *See also*
        Guaranteed income
    gender differences and, 165–168
    as an Indian concept, 162
    as NWRO's main strategy, 157
    proposal, 182
    support for, 170
    as a targeted grant, 158
Guaranteed income, 131, 138, 178, 185,
        188–191, 219, 224. *See also*
        Guaranteed annual income
    bill, 158, 193
    debates, 158, 189

    failure of, 199
    plan, 168, 179, 185
    proposals, 187
    struggle, 194
*The Guaranteed Income: Next Step in
        Economic Revolution*, 162
Guaranteed minimum income, 157
Guaranteed minimum standard of living, 189

H

Hagstrom, Warren, 84, 86
"Half-A-Chance" campaign, 223
Hamer, Fannie Lou, 22
Hamilton, Charles, 74
Handouts, 197, 207, 238
Harassment, 48, 87, 94–95, 97, 225
Harrington, Michael, 13, 33
Harris Survey, 178
Head Start, 34, 136
"Health and decency" standards, 159–160
Health care, 161, 187, 200, 227
    agencies, 216
    clinics, 225–226
    insurance, 241
    rights, 200
Health Department, 72
Heineman Commission, 170, 175
Heineman, Ben W., 170
Heller, Walter, 63
Helping-hand approach to poverty, 225
Hennepin County, MN, 27
    Welfare Department, 20
HEW (Department of Health Education and
        Welfare), 10, 53, 57, 137
    employment of recipients and, 141
    family planning and, 217
    FAP and, 172, 176–178, 180, 183, 189
    live-on-a-budget campaigns and, 118
    NWRO and, 184
    Poor People's Campaign and, 72–74
High cost of living, 107
High credit charges, 103
High food prices, 23, 107
High-interest loans, 106
High-school graduation costs, 80
Higher monthly benefits, 231, 232
Hispanics, consumerism and, 112
Hodden, Chuck, 210
Holiday money as a basic right, 79
Home furnishings, 120, 123
Homemakers, 179, 221
    status of, 221

Hoover Institution, 195
Horn, Etta, 47, 71, 89, 111
    empoyment of recipients and, 137
Horton, Myles, 37
Hospital care, 194
Hospital services, 32
Hostility, 119, 191, 193, 209, 235. *See also*
    Public hostility
House of Representatives, 180–181
House Ways and Means Committee, 136,
    178, 180
Household appliances, 119. *See also* Appliances
Household furnishings, 98
    as a basic right, 79
Household goods, 117
Household items, 79–80, 84, 87, 95–96, 100,
    113, 159
Household supplies, 83
Household tasks, 201
Housekeeping as real work, 165
Housework. *See also* Domestic work
    as legitimate work, 167
    wages for, 232
Housing, xi, 15, 23–28, 42, 97, 188, 197, 209,
    224–227
    conditions, 98
    inspectors, 48
HR1, 181
Hudson, Rosie, 151
Huitt, Ralph, 72
Human resources, 164
Human Rights Associations, 118
Hunger Campaign, 134

I

ICPP (Inner City Protestant Parish), 18
Ideological camps, 126
Ideology, materiality and, xi
IFCO (Interreligious Foundation for
    Community Organizations), 37
Illegitimacy, xvi, 6, 8–9, 12, 135–136, 144,
    155, 189, 196
Illiteracy, 35
Immorality, 6–7, 11–12, 32, 49, 238
Improvement of living standards, 79
Inability to work, 13
Inadequacies in the welfare system, 3
    allowances, 26
    clothing, 33
    diet campaign, 119
    housing, 71
    monthly benefit, 121

Income floor, 234. *See also* Minimum income
Income maintenance, 172, 178
    consensus on, 168–171
    plans, 168–170
    program, 173
Increased production, 104
Independence, 114, 142, 220, 237
"Independent" poor, 200
Indian treaties, 72
Indians, 149, 162
Indignities, xvi, 2, 16, 22–23, 26, 95
Individual efforts, 239
Individualism, 226
Individualist ethos, 239
Inequality, 104, 207
    problem of, 119–123
Inflation, 107, 180, 186, 197, 216
Injustice of poverty amid affluence, 117
Inner City Protestant Parish. *See* ICPP
Inner-city poor, 174, 176
Inner-city schools, 166
Interest charges, 117, 121
Internal Revenue Service. *See* IRS
Interreligious Foundation for Community
    Organizations. *See* IFCO
Investment incentives, 105
Involuntary servitude, 136
IRS (Internal Revenue Service), 169, 223

J

J. C. Penney, 110
Jackson, Alice, 132
    employment of recipients and, 139
Jackson, Jesse, 206
Jaffe, Frederick, 217
James, Hulbert, 34, 41, 57, 96, 147–148, 154, 200
    consumerism and, 108, 115
    guaranteed annual income and, 164
    internal tensions and, 127, 129
    Nevada cuts and, 204
Jeffrey, Sharon, 36
Jermany, Catherine, 20, 42, 62, 134–135,
    149–152, 221, 226
    employment of recipients and, 142
    lobbying and, 71
Jeter, Frankie, 150, 214
Job Corps, 34
Job discrimination, end to, 81
Job placement, 177
Job training, 12, 13, 50, 63, 135–136, 138,
    169–170, 172, 177, 189. *See also*
    Training

Jobs or Income Now. *See* JOIN
Johnson administration, 63, 135
Johnson, John, 112
Johnson, Loretta, 17, 134
Johnson, Lyndon B., 106, 144, 171, 173
    guaranteed annual income and, 169–170
JOIN (Jobs or Income Now), 133
Jones, Erla, 18
Jones, Hugh, 95
Jones, Roxanne, 67, 109, 132, 150, 240–241
    as a critic of staff control within
        NWRO, 151
    employment of recipients and, 139–140
Justice Department, 72
Juvenile delinquency, 13, 26

K

Kardiner, Abram, 14
Karenga, Maulana Ron, 149
Karenga, Ron, 134
Katz, Michael, xiii, 195
Kelley, John, 60
Kennedy, Jackie, 142
Kennedy, John F., 13
    1963 income tax cut and, 104
    special grants and, 91
Kennedy, Robert F., guaranteed annual in-
        come and, 169
Kensington Welfare Rights Union, 240–241
Keynesian economists, 104–105
King v. Smith, 60
King, Coretta Scott, 206
King, Martin Luther, Jr., 2, 33, 72
    Poor People's Campaign and, 71
KKK (Ku Klux Klan), 203
Klein Company, 111
Knowledge and power, 52–56, 59
Knowledge of regulations, 79, 82
Kramer, Marion, 241
Kuhn, Maggie, 187
Kwanzaa, 112
Kydd, Andrea, 210

L

Labor organizing, 15, 200
Labor unions, 23, 180
    as organizers, 23
Lampman, Robert, guaranteed annual in-
        come and, 169
Langston Hughes Welfare Rights, 82

Language, x
    of citizenship, 232
    of equality, 111
Larger structural forces, 100
Las Vegas, NV, 203, 225
    Department of Health and Human
        Services, 228
Latinas, 4, 28, 52
Latinos, 2, 31, 238
    consumerism and, 107
Law and order, right for, 234
Lawyers, 46, 54, 58, 79–80, 211
Lay advocates, 55, 56
League of Women Voters, 221, 224–225
Legal aid, 226
    associations, 60
    societies, 54
Legal Aid Society, 61
Legal education, 55
Legal protections, 233
Legal reform, xiiii
Legal services, 168, 225
Legal strategy, 45, 59–63, 161
Legislative Assembly for Adequate Welfare, 159
Lesbians as organizers, 23
Letter-writing campaign, 160
Lewis, John, 147–148, 152
Lewis, Karen, 208
Liberal agenda, 239
Liberal Democratic policies, 198
Liberal economists, 104
Liberal groups, 223
Liberal political climate, 22
Liberal reform, 34, 235
Liberal scholars, 14
Liberal social welfare philosophy, 12
Liberalism, xii, 6, 68–69, 75–77, 96, 122–123,
        136, 145, 158, 161, 169–172,
        176–177, 182, 185–186, 188–190,
        195, 198, 223, 233–236, 239
    consumerism and, 104
Life insurance, 168
Lim, Hilary, 76
Lindsay, John, 174
Linton, Rhoda, 83, 132, 147
    at Syracuse University, 86
Live-on-a-welfare-budget campaigns,
        103–104, 117–119
Living-wage campaigns, 241
Lobbying, 74, 79–80, 115, 137, 158, 164, 169,
        180–181, 185, 187, 190, 212,
        214, 217, 221, 228, 240
    electoral politics and, 70–71

Local WROs, xv, 22, 31, 33, 54, 194
Long Beach, CA, Citizens for Creative
   Welfare, 54
Long, Russell, 136, 137, 188
   as a "one-man blockade" for FAP, 189
Los Angeles County WRO, 20, 42, 49, 51, 55,
      62, 134, 149, 221, 224, 226
   guaranteed annual income and, 164
Los Angeles, CA, 2, 6, 19–21, 135, 150
   ANC Mothers in, 40, 43
   General Hospital, 134
   Police Department, 134
   Welfare Recipients Union in, 31, 65
Louisiana, 5–6, 9, 12, 127, 137, 149, 188, 203
   suitable home clause of, 9–10
   welfare cuts in, 127
Louisville, KY, 2, 41
   West End Community Council, 26
Low benefits, 79
Low wages, 166
"Lower-races," 216

M

Majority class, 151
Male companionship, 20, 48, 94
Male domination, 150
   of staff, 211
Male-headed families, 171, 188
Male-headed family model, xii
Male irresponsibility, 238
Male power-holding groups, 215
Male-centered politics, 201
Malnourishment, 33
"Man-in-the-house" rules, 6, 29
Manhattan, NY, 98
   Dyckman Welfare Center, 82
   Lower East Side of, 16
      Citizen's Welfare Action Group, 35
      Committee of Welfare Families, 35
      Welfare Action Group Against Poverty
         (WAGAP), 35
   protest at City Hall, 41
   upper, 82
   Upper West Side of, 24
Manpower development, 136
   programs, 105
Manpower Development and Training Act, 13
Marble Manor, 203
Marches, 40, 84, 180, 204–205
Marginalization, 75, 235, 239–240
Mark of Oppression, The, 14
Market economy, faith in, xiii

Market strategies, 233
Marshall, T. H., 161
Martin, Rudell, 151
Martinez, Sarah, 96
Masculinity
   as an antidote to racism, 201
   idealization of, 201
Mass mobilization, 80, 205
Mass protest, 75, 93. See also Protests
Mass rallies, 80
Massachusetts, 28, 57, 69, 75, 84, 90, 97, 119,
      147, 163–164, 174, 202
   Department of Public Welfare, 94
   Pittsfield Association of Adequate
      Welfare, 142
   Pittsfield Association of Parents for Ade-
      quate Welfare (PAPAW), 90, 163
   State Welfare Department, special grants
      and, 95
   WRO, 52, 84, 110, 202, 222
      employment of recipients and, 139
      internal tensions and, 129–130
      live-on-a-welfare-budget campaigns
         and, 118
      South Boston committee of, 130
      special grants and, 84–86, 94
      split from MAW, 87
Material benefits, importance of, 88
Material reality, 230
Materiality, ideology and, xi
Maternalist movement, 140
MAW (Mothers for Adequate Welfare), 18–19,
      24, 28, 52–54, 57–58, 149–150,
      211–212
   demands for representation and, 66–67
   formation of, 35
   guaranteed annual income and, 164
   internal tensions and, 130
   lobbying and, 71
   policy making and, 69
   problem of inequality and, 121
   single motherhood and, 145–146
   special grants and, 84, 89
   split from MWRO, 87
Maximum feasible participation, 64
   of the poor, 34
   of ordinary people, 35
Maximum grant limit, 61
Maximum public assistance grants, 160
Mayo, Robert P., 176
McCarthy, Eugene, 179–180, 182, 206
McCarty, Margaret, 137
McClaine, Shirley, 206

McGovern, George, 182
McKissick, Floyd, 39
Median monthly benefit, 205
Medicaid, 70, 178, 195, 216, 225
Medical care, 91, 123, 200, 217
    free, 168
Medicare, 195
MEJ (Movement for Economic Justice), 222
Mental health clinics, 91
Meredith March in Mississippi, 2
Mexican Americans, 72
MFY (Mobilization for Youth), 24, 35, 61, 88
    consumerism and, 108
    guaranteed income proposals and, 177
    neighborhood service centers of, 26
    organizers, 88
Michigan, 6–7, 28, 131–132, 153
    credit campaign in, 110
    State Executive Committee, 154
    WRO, 128, 153–154
        internal tensions and, 128, 130
Middle-class
    activists, 87, 233
    domination, 129, 150
    organizers, 3, 87–88, 209, 212
    participation, 213
    staff, 130, 213, 223, 236
staff members, 153
    standards of respectability, 140
    support, 3, 14–15, 32–37, 54, 117, 126, 233
        domination and control, 38, 42
        inherent problems with, 38
        immense benefits of, 38
    values, imposition of, 128
    white male domination, 147
    women's organizations, 221
Militant actions, 180, 199
Militant movements, 236
Militant protests, 99, 195
Militant strategies, 79, 224
Militants, 185
Mills, Wilbur, 187–188
Milwaukee, WI, 6, 148–149, 151, 199
    guaranteed annual income and, 166
    Milwaukee County WRO, 30, 36, 51, 121
    Milwaukee's Friends of Welfare Rights, 36
    Northside WRO, 16, 30
    WRO, guaranteed annual income and, 162
Minimal resources, 239
Minimum annual income, 171
Minimum income, 158, 161
    as a right, 177

proposal, 186
standard, 179
Minimum standard of living, xv, 1, 62, 80,
        120, 170, 190
    assurance of, 81
    establishment of, 168
    raising of, 121
    rejection of, 168
Minimum standards, 123, 159, 175, 177
    campaign, 87
    national conference on, 87
    checklists, 81, 83
Minimum wage laws, 136
Minneapolis, MN
    Community Union Project, 20
        Welfare Committee, 53, 58
    lobbying and, 71
Minnesota, 179
    AFDC Mothers Leagues in, 31
    WRO, 180
Miss Cleaver life, 221
Misseduc Foundation, 210
Mississippi, 2, 29, 57, 173
    FAP and, 172
    Hinds County Welfare Rights Movement
        in, 54
    suitable home clause of, 10
Mississippi March. See Meredith March in
        Mississippi
Mitchell, Joseph, 11, 29
Mobilization, 85–86, 185–187, 195,
        203–205, 242
    of women, 154
    strategies, 109, 125
Mobilization for Youth. See MFY
Moderatism, 235
Mohanty, Chandra, xi
Montgomery Ward, 109–112, 116
    national agreement with, 115
Moore, Dorothy, 20–21
Moral fitness, 48
Moral guidance, 50
Moral outrage against poverty, 131
Moral standards, 4
Moral values, 116
Morality, 7, 49, 50, 52, 99, 139, 155, 173, 196,
        198, 207, 232, 238
"More money now," 123
"More Money Now!" campaign, 79, 80, 82
Morgan, Roy, 118
Mother laws, 48

Motherhood, xiiii, 9, 12, 23–24, 31–32, 72, 75, 80, 100–101, 103, 119, 126, 154, 158, 185, 194, 198, 200, 202, 212, 215–216, 220, 224, 228, 232, 239. *See also* Single motherhood
as a bulwark against Communism, 92
Children's March and, 206
consumerism and, 107, 114, 117
FAP and, 175, 178–179, 181, 189
as a foundation of civil society, 92
guaranteed annual income and, 158, 166–167
internal tensions and, 128, 130
special grants and, 89–94
white middle-class notions of, 5
as a source of economic prosperity, 92
as work, 237
Mothers for Adequate Welfare. *See* MAW
"Mothers March," 137
Mothers on welfare, 31–33
Mothers' Campaign for Welfare, 18
Mothers' pensions programs, 4, 5, 9, 10, 48, 140
Movement for Economic Justice. *See* MEJ
Moyers, Bill, 238
Moynihan Report, 144–145
Moynihan, Daniel Patrick, 144–145, 171
FAP and, 176, 183
Mud Creek Citizens Health Project, 225
Multiple consciousness, xi, 15, 229
"Multiple jeopardy, multiple consciousness," 229
Murray, Charles, 238
MWRO, 111
consumerism and, 115

N

NAACP (National Association for the Advancement of Colored People), 41, 94
battle to end de facto school segregation, 24
Legal Defense Fund, 29
Nashco, 55, 137
NASW (National Association of Social Workers), 1
Nation of Islam, 29
National Advisory Commission on Civil Disorders, 94, 173
National Association for the Advancement of Colored People. *See* NAACP
National Association of Laymen, 185
National Association of Social Workers, 36, 85. *See* NASW
guaranteed annual income and, 169

National Black Feminist Organization, 214, 218
National Campaign for Jobs and Income Support, 241
National campaign for school and winter clothing and Christmas grants, 82
National campaigns, 93
National Conference on Social Welfare, 110, 132
National Coordinating Committee. *See* NCC
National Council of Churches, 37, 169, 185
National Council of Senior Citizens. *See* NCSC
National day of action, 2
National defense costs, 195
National Federation of Social Service Employees, 185
National Guard, 97
National newsletter, 116
National office, xv, 83, 103, 110, 115–116, 126, 129–130, 133, 137–139, 143, 146–148, 150, 152–154, 165, 179–180, 202, 205, 208–214, 223, 225, 236
closing of, 224
National Organization for Women. *See* NOW
National Security Council, 171
National Self-Help Law Project, 226
National Social Welfare Assembly, 10
National Taxpayers Union, 194
National Urban League, 10, 29
National Welfare Rights Movement, The, xiiii
National Welfare Rights Organization. *See* NWRO
National Welfare Rights Union. *See* NWRU
National Women's Political Caucus. *See* NWPC
National Women's Rights Organization, 214
Nationalism, 233
Nationwide mobilization for welfare rights, 2
Native American women, xi, 71
Native Americans, 2, 28, 67, 133
NCC, 17, 28, 43, 127–128, 133–134, 139–140, 148, 154, 180, 208, 210, 225
Nevada cuts and, 204
NCSC (National Council of Senior Citizens), 186–187
Need, definition of, 70
Negative income taxvi, 161–162, 169–170, 172
Negative Income Tax Experiments, 188
Negative popular attitudes, 193
Negative public perceptions, 49
The Negro Family: A Case for National Action, 144

Neighborhood associations, 22, 233
Neighborhood groups, 15
    transformation into a national political
        movement, 32
Neubeck, Kenneth, 239
Nevada, 62, 135, 181, 228. *See also* Operation
        Nevada
    Clark County WRO, 203, 205, 225
    State Welfare Finance Officers, 135
New Bedford, MA, Wage Supplement
        Organization (WSO), 202
New community activism, 224–230
New Deal, 170, 186, 234
New Deal liberalism, 235
New Jersey, 6, 39, 174, 188, 208
    Bergen County Welfare Board, 51, 57
    Bureau of Assistance Manual, 53
    Englewood WRO in, 51, 53, 57
    WRO, 208
New Left, 112
    movement, 34
    organizations, 66
New York, 7, 28, 58, 86, 108, 132, 160, 165,
        174, 202, 212, 241
    Community Voices Heard, 241
    Board of Social Welfare, 95
New York City, 2, 11, 16–17, 21, 40, 50–51, 60,
        91, 108, 115, 125, 139, 157, 174,
        177, 201, 215, 218
    adoption of flat grant, 95
    Citywide Coordinating Committee for Wel-
        fare Rights Groups, 24, 25, 31, 41,
        52, 56–57, 82, 96, 98–99, 109, 111
    guaranteed annual income and, 164
    Commissioners of Social Service, 61
    Committee of Welfare Families, 38, 81
    credit protests in, 109–110, 113
    Downtown Welfare Advocate Center,
        222, 228
    Kingsbridge Center demonstration, 96
    Legal Aid Society and Mobilization for
        Youth, 56
    Ocean Hill-Brownsville School strike, 24
    organizing in, 88
    policy making and, 69
    public welfare workers union, 36
    "rent revolt," 98–99
    special grants and, 82, 93
    Stryckers Bay Community Action
        Project, 55
    United Welfare League, 55, 96
    Welfare Recipients League, 81
    welfare rights protest, 45
    West Side Welfare League, 55

New York conference on "The Dilemmas of
        Municipal Welfare Policy," 63
New York State, 6
    Board of Social Welfare, 11
    Commissioners of Social Service, 61
Nick, Mrs., 94
Nickerson Gardens, 224
    Planning Organization, 19
Niedzwiecki, Betty, 36
Nxvon administration, 158, 175, 182–185,
        189. *See also* Nxvon, Richard M.
Nxvon, Richard M., 190, 205, 236. *See also*
        Nxvon administration
    election of, 234
    FAP and, 158, 170–179, 181–183, 186,
        188–189, 206
    guaranteed annual income and, 157
    opposition to busing, 181
    war in Vietnam and, 171, 181
No-man-in-the-house laws, 48
Nonprofit support, 33–38
North, the, 6, 8, 27, 74
North Adams, MA, 84
North West Industries, 170
North-South dichotomy, 233
North-South divide, 233
Northward migration, 176
NOW (National Organization for Women),
        219–222
NWPC (National Women's Political
        Caucus), 185, 214, 220
NWRO (National Welfare Rights
        Organization)
    1969 National Conference, 108
    Adequate Income Bill, 185
    annual budget, 152
    annual national convention, 42
    bankruptcy of, 224
    as a black women's organization, 212
    Chicago convention, 82
    churches and, 37
    consumer tactics and, 113–117
    demands for representation and, 66, 68
    Detroit conference, 86
    differences between men and women in, 167
    employment of recipients and, 136–137
    Executive Committee, 43, 127, 147, 153,
        183, 202, 204, 210, 212–214
    FAP and, 172, 178–182
    financial woes, 208, 223
    first meeting in Chicago, 42
    founding convention of, 25
    Friends list, 129

NWRO (*continued*)
    Guaranteed Adequate Income proposal, 129
    HEW and, 184
    internal politics of, 154
    internal tensions and, 127. 129–130, 133
    membership increase, 83–84
    national conference, 65
    National Coordinating Committee of. *See*
        NCC
    national department store credit cam-
        paign, 109–111
    NOW and, 219–222
    Poor People's Campaign and, 71, 73–74
    position on birth control, 217
    riots and, 94
    sexism within, 154
    single motherhood and, 143
    winter action campaign, 87
    Ways and Means Committee, 115
    women leaders of, 71
    as a women's organization, 213–221, 229
NWRU (National Welfare Rights Union), 241

O

O'Callahan, Mike, 203
O'Donnell Heights, 224
Oakland, CA, 23
Obstacles, xiiii
OEO (Office of Economic Opportunity), 34,
        54–55, 169, 170, 188
    consumerism and, 105–106, 108
    demands for representation and, 65
    ideals of participation and, 64
    official history of, 64
    policy making and, 70
Office of Economic Opportunity. *See* OEO
Ohio, 1, 7, 17–18, 57, 115, 129, 149, 159–160,
        190, 202
    Ashtabula County WRO, 209
    demand for holiday money, 83
    Department of Welfare, 61
    General Assembly, 18
    Geneva WRO, 209
    guaranteed annual income and, 165
    march. *See* "Walk for Decent Welfare"
Ohio Steering Committee for Adequate
        Welfare. *See* OSCAW
Ohio Walk for Adequate Welfare, 3, 36
Ohlin, Lloyd, 13
Old age assistance, 4, 17, 186, 195, 202
Old age insurance, 7

Old-age support, 61
Omaha Welfare Rights Council, 182
One-to-one contact, 227
"Operation Breadbasket," 174
Operation Life, 225, 228
Operation Nevada, 203–205, 207
Oppression, 237, 240
Oppressive institutions, 223
Oppressive welfare policies, 15
Ordinary working-class Americans, 238
Organizational control, xv
Organizational platforms, 237
Organizational strategy, 200
Organizational style, 212
Organized labor, 200
Organizers, xv, xii, 180, 204, 211
    domineering behavior of, 208
    motivation of, 15–22
Orshanky, Mollie, 168
OSCAW (Ohio Steering Committee for
        Adequate Welfare), 1, 36, 57, 82,
        159, 160
    demands for representation and, 66
    guaranteed annual income and, 163–164
    lobbying and, 70
Other America, The, 13
Out-of-wedlock births, 7, 49, 135, 145, 171, 198
Ovesey, Lionel, 14

P

P/RAC (Poverty/Rights Action Center), 3, 29
Palladino, Moiece, 93, 150–151, 220, 224, 226
PAPAW, 48, 51
Paraprofessionals, 56
Participatory democracy, 66
Pastreich, Bill, 85–87, 97, 147
    internal tensions and, 129–131
    organizing style of, 84
    wage supplements and, 202
Paternalism, 128
Patriarchal norms, 234, 239
Patriarchy, 229
"Pauper's divorce," 145
Payton, Benjamin, 144–145
Peace Corps, 34, 84
Peaceful negotiation, 180
Peak of the movement, 125
Pennsylvania, 6–7, 28, 132, 151
    "crusade for children" in, 31
    Allegheny County WRO, 34, 150
    Blair County WRO, 194

credit campaign in, 110
empoyment of recipients and, 139
State Department of Welfare, 226
state senate, 240
People of color, 23, 194–195, 227, 234
"People's Hearings," 180
Perkins, Phil, 128
Permanent income support, 100
Personal animosity, 126
Personal behavior, 158
Personal networks, 27
Personal power, 150
Personal Responsibility and Work
Opportunity Act, 239
Personnel and Policy Committee, 153
Philadelphia, PA, 23, 83, 91, 111, 241
credit campaign in, 111
special grants and, 91
WRO, 90, 132, 150, 212, 226, 240
"Petition for Rights and Respect," 51
credit campaign and, 109
demands for representation and, 67
empoyment of recipients and, 139
guaranteed annual income and, 160,
163, 166–167
internal tensions and, 132
Physical abuse, 150
Physically able to work, 48
Picketing, 26, 83, 84, 108, 109, 110, 137, 218
Pierce, Jacquline, 208
Pittsburgh 1970 conference, 200–201
Pittsfield Association of Parents for Adequate
Welfare. See PAPAW
Piven, Frances Foxvi, xiiii, 26, 29, 39, 42, 220
FAP and, 182
guaranteed annual income and, 163
importance in the intellectual develop-
ment of the movement, 40
special grants and, 98
wage supplements and, 202
Planned Parenthood, 215
Playgrounds, 23
Plumbing problems, 224
Polarization, 234
Police
conduct, 97
harassment, 23
repression, 95
Policy analysts, 217
Policy making, xv, 127, 145, 148, 170, 171,
182, 184, 188–189, 207, 217,
231, 232, 235

consumerism and, 107
and the poor, 68–70, 76
Political acumen, 155
Political attacks on welfare, 29
Political climate for legal reform, 46
Political dialogue, xiiii
Political discourse, 5, 236
Political empowerment, 69
Political freedoms, 55
Political ideology, xv
Political isolation, 126
Political mobilization, 69
Political networks, 22
Political priorities, 116
Political process, 66
Political retrenchment, 216
Political rights, xiiii, 161
Politicians
attack on ADC, 7–8
bias of, 28
Politicization, 132, 212, 227
Politics of respectability, 89
"Pollution" of social standards, 11
Pomerance, Rafe, 128
Poor as a political force, 190
Poor black people, 210, 230
Poor construction, 224
Poor housekeeping, 48, 198
Poor maintenance, 224
Poor people as a class of consumers, 105
Poor People's Campaign, 71–77, 143
Poor People's Movements, xiiii, 231
Poor-quality merchandise, 106
Poorhouses, 170
Popular culture, 201, 224, 231, 236, 238
Post-Civil Rights era, 238
Poverty as a women's issue, 219, 222
Poverty lawyers, 59
Poverty/Rights Action Center. See P/RAC
Power in numbers, 58–59
Power of numbers, 80, 84
Power through organization, 115
Powerlessness, 47, 69, 222, 237
Practical change, 222
Preoccupations with personal lives of recipi-
ents, 49
President's Committee on Juvenile Delinquency
and Youth Crime, 13
President's Income Maintenance
Commission, 66
Presidential Commission. See Heineman
Commission

Presidential Commission on Income
Maintenance, 170
Pressley, Ruth, 15
Pressure tactics, 132, 155
Privacy, 54, 60, 123
as an individual right, 232
protection of, 52
Progressive Era, 5, 48, 140, 216
Promiscuity, xvi, 8, 76, 126, 189, 196, 236, 238
Prostitution, 203
Protestant work ethic, 179. *See also* Work ethic
Protests, xiii, 2, 53–54, 69, 79, 81–82, 86, 90,
93, 94, 95, 96, 98, 111, 118, 132,
136, 171, 173, 175–177, 181,
184, 195, 205, 208, 219, 224, 233,
236, 241. *See also* Mass protest
consumerism and, 107
narrowing of avenues for, 103
threat of, 46
Public Assistance Coalition, 228
Public criticism, guarding against, 48
Public hostility, 194–200, 205, 212, 236, 239
Public housing, 161, 195
Public perceptions of recipients, 7, 126
Public safety, 27
Puerto Ricans, 25, 106, 133, 198
Punitive welfare laws, 6
Punitive welfare policies, xvi, 205
Purchasing power, 103, 105
PWRO. *See* Philadelphia WRO

Q

Quality of life, 232
issues, 224
Queens, NY, 24, 98
Jamaica Welfare Center, 82

R

Rabagliati, 88
Race, xiii, xv, xi–xii, 4, 8–9, 12, 15, 29–31, 55,
76–77, 114, 126, 132, 136, 142,
144–146, 148, 150, 155, 158,
167, 173, 186–191, 196–198,
202, 209, 212, 221–222,
229–230, 233, 238–240
as an "excuse," 151
as a factor in the welfare rights movement, 28
Rachlin, Carl, 137, 180

Racial background, 7
Racial characterizations of recipients, 149
Racial control, 239
Racial discrimination, 13, 28, 31, 131
Racial divide, 222
Racial empowerment, 149
Racial equality, 30, 149, 230
struggle for, 23
Racial ideology, 8
Racial inequality, 165
Racial liberation, xvi, 229
Racial oppression, 130, 167, 219
Racial pride, 137
Racial stereotypes, 97
Racial tension, 210
Racism, xii, 3, 5, 7, 14–15, 18, 29–31, 47,
51–52, 59, 81, 94–95, 126, 138,
143–144, 147, 149, 151, 165,
181, 187, 193, 195, 200–201,
207, 210, 212–213, 219, 222,
229–230, 238–239
in the North, 27
Radical change, 227
"Radical citizenship," 66
Radical economists, 162
Radical groups, 201
"Radical organizing," 131
Radical politics, 234
Radical protest, 177
Radical reform, 176
Radical revisions, 214
Radicalism, xi, xii, 86, 123, 131–132, 136, 161,
169–170, 174, 176, 189, 212,
233–236
Rainwater, Lee, 14
Rathke, Wade, 202
Reagan, Ronald, 189
Recipient control, 212
Recipient exclusion, 87
Recipient leadership, 240
Recipient organizers, 154
Recipients
as activists, 27
as consumers with economic clout, 117
as convenient scapegoats, 197
as "dependents," 24, 117, 141
initiative of, 32
as needing political guidance, 134
political actions of, 65
as a potential consumer market, 113
as undeserving, 47
Redress in the legal system, 45, 75

Regional economic depression, 188
Reisman, David, 91
Renewed welfare rights activism, 240
"Rent revolt." *See* New York City, "Rent re-
volt"
Rent strikes, 25, 224
Representation, 77, 123, 226
demands for. *See* Demands, for represen-
tation
in policy-making bodies, 235
politics of, 234
struggle for, 79
Repressive welfare policies, 149, 155, 205, 207
Reproduction, xii
Reproductive control, xii
Reproductive labor, 221
Reproductive rights, xiii, 196, 215–218, 222,
229
Reproductive Rights National Network, 218
Republic of New Afrika, 97, 174
Republican Party Convention, 169
Republicans, 136, 169, 171–172, 178, 198,
224, 234, 236, 238–239
guaranteed annual income and, 170
Resentment toward recipients, 197
Residency laws, 6, 61, 231
constitutionality of, 60
Residential stability, 27
Respect, 62, 150
demand for, 47
Reston, James, 178
Restrictive legislation, x
Restrictive policies, 12
Restrictive welfare laws, 9
"Resurrection Cities," 99
Revolutionary Action Movement, 97
Rhetoric, xiii, xii, 6, 13–14, 45, 111, 198, 209,
213, 234–235, 238–239
of revolution, 115
Rhodes, James, 159
Ribicoff, Abraham, 185
Richardson, Elliot, 183, 189
Richmond, CA, WRO, 28, 140, 225
Richmond, VA, WRO, 17, 228
Right-wing, 190, 234, 236
Rights
to "an adequate hearing," 61
to due process, 161
to life, 164
"to live," 161
to own property, 161
of recipients, 53

to vote, 161
Riots, 97, 131
Ripon Society, The, 169
Rockefeller, Nelson, 160, 174
Roger Baldwin Foundation, 60–61
Roosevelt, Franklin D., 170
Rosado v. Wyman, 160
Ross, Fred, 84

S

Sachs, Andrea Jule, 119
Sampson, Tim, 40, 83, 85, 94, 127, 132, 148,
150, 202
empoyment of recipients and, 138
FAP and, 183
as a white racist, 147
San Francisco, CA, 2, 220
City Wide WRO, 150–151
People Organized to Win Employment
Rights (POWER), 241
WRO, 93
Sanders, Beulah, 24–25, 63
demands for representation and, 66
empoyment of recipients and, 137
FAP and, 178–180
on flat grants, 96
P/RAC and, 40–41
replacement of, 214
Sanders, Viola, 226
Saxon, Corethea, 208
Scarcity of jobs, 166
School clothing, 80, 84, 90, 94
allowances, 2, 88
campaign, 88
School segregation, unconstitutionality of, 92
SCLC, 34, 134, 174
Fair Housing Campaign in Chicago, 34
guaranteed annual income and, 169
Poor People's Campaign and, 71
Scott, AR, 19
Scrutiny, 15, 46, 48, 57, 141
SDS (Students for a Democratic Society),
xiiii, 33–34, 84, 97, 131, 133,
174, 211
Economic Research and Action Program
(ERAP), 35
participatory democracy and, 66
Sears, 109, 111, 116
"right" to shop at, 113
boycott, 110

Campaign, 115
Second-hand clothing, 89
Segregated housing patterns, 85
Segregated South, 92
Segregation, 92
Self-destructive behavior, 63
Senate, 189
    Finance Committee, 137, 180–182, 188
    hearings on FAP, 180
Sexism, 126, 154, 193, 195, 200–201, 207,
        211–213, 218–219, 221, 237,
        239. See also Gender
Sexual abstinence, 217
Sexual behavior, 48
Sexual freedom, 215, 217
Sexuality, xiii, xi, 196, 198, 219, 230, 232
    liberal attitudes about, 215
    proscribed, 229
Shapiro v. Thompson, 60
Sheehan, Susan, 198
Shelter, 120, 123, 151, 160, 232
Shoes, 87, 120, 122–123, 203
Shop-ins, 110
Shrinking the public sector, 198
Shriver, Sargent, 170
Silence, 59, 64, 69, 75–76, 132, 234–235, 239
Simplified payments, 169
Sims, Evelyn, 215
Single black mothers, 22
Single fathers, 212
Single motherhood, 8, 9, 12–15, 76, 154–155,
        186–187, 189, 194, 203, 207,
        229, 231, 237. See also
        Motherhood
    and the black family, 143–146
    as a social problem, 143
Single parenthood, 12, 14
FAP and, 176
rise in, 126
Single-parent families, 238
    FAP and, 172, 176
    rise in, 165
Single-parent households, rise in, 175
Singleton, Clarence, 122
Sisterhood is Powerful, 217
Sit-ins, 24, 26, 40, 66, 71, 81–84, 90, 93, 94,
        97, 137, 155, 180
"Sxv Myths about Welfare" pamphlet, 136,
        199
"Slave labor," 139
Slave masters, 216
Slave South, 107

Slave work force, 166
Slavery, 89, 133, 137, 142, 144, 216
    parallels to, 47
Sloan, Margaret, 214
Slogans, 113
Slum housing, 98
Slums, 11, 24–25, 99
Small government, 187
Smith, Mrs. Sylvester, 60
SNCC, 34, 65, 97, 174, 211
    participatory democracy and, 66
Social activism, 63
Social activities, 100
Social and Rehabilitative Services. See SRS
Social change, 227
Social citizenship, 161–162
Social dislocations, 8
Social disorganization, 173
Social equality, 87
Social exclusion, 240
Social insurance, 4, 195
Social justice, 239
Social mobility, 226
Social movements, 22–23, 62
Social networks, 22
Social participation, 27
Social policy, xiiii, 184, 186, 226
Social reform, 50, 69, 184, 186, 216
Social rights, 161
Social scientists, 13, 168, 173, 202
Social security, 4, 141, 161, 171, 186, 195, 207
Social Security Act, 10, 28, 60
    amendments to, 7, 64. See also individual
        listings by year
    passage of, xiii
    as a watershed development in public
        policy, 4
Social Security Administration, 168
Social Security Board, 5
Social security mechanisms, 105
Social services, xv, 225–227
Social significance of material goods, 89
Social standards, 4
Social workers, 91, 125, 132–133, 159, 180,
        217, 236
Socialism, 66, 218, 221
Socialist-feminism, 218, 221–222
Sociologists, 91
"Sock it to Sears," 110
Solinger, Ricki, 196
Soul food, 112
Soul music, 112

Soundness of character, 13
South, the, 6–7, 9, 23, 136
　　FAP and, 172, 176, 188
Southern black activists, 33
Southern Christian Leadership Conference.
　　See SCLC
Southern congressmen, 4
"Southern strategy," 127
Southwest, 197
Special clothing allowances, 19
Special grants, xv, 231, 237
　　abolition of, 96
　　building a movement and, 83–87
　　campaign for, 79–80, 131, 164
　　emergence of, 80–83
　　flat grants. *See* Flat grants
　　new strategies, 96–101
　　recipients and, 88–89
　　refusal to award, 80
　　as a right, 89
　　system, elimination of, 160
Special interests, 239
Spider, Debby, 129
Spirit of giving, 89
Spot checks, 168, 172
Spring clothing, 82, 94
SRS, Poor People's Campaign and, 73
SSI (Social Security Income), 186–187
St. Louis, MO, 133
　　City-Wide WRO, 215
Staff domination, 127–128, 130, 213
Staff salaries, 152
Staff versus recipients, 126–129
Stagflation, 197
Standard of living, 79
Standard of need, 159, 160
Standardized payments, 169
Stanley, Joy, 49, 50, 51
Stans, Maurice, 176
Starvation, threat of, 164, 190
State repression, 227
Statewide wage supplement
　　associations, 202
Status quo, 76, 95, 234–235
Steinem, Gloria, 206, 220
Steiner, Gilbert, 182
Stereotypes, xiiii, 134–135, 138, 141, 149, 155,
　　158–159, 186, 188–189, 193,
　　195–196, 198–199, 201, 207,
　　224, 236, 238–239
　　of black women, 29
Stereotypical image, 7

Stereotypical welfare recipient, 6
Sterilization, 216–217, 221
　　abuse, 218
Steubenville, OH, 26
　　Community Organization Members
　　　　Build Absolute Teamwork
　　　　(COMBAT), 26
Stigmatization, 15, 21, 24, 45–47, 50, 58, 76,
　　89, 92–93, 100, 114, 117, 121,
　　126, 134, 141, 146, 167, 186, 200,
　　207, 228, 237, 239
Stokes, Carl, 2
Strategic differences, 150
Strength in numbers, 101
Strike fund, 202
Strong-arm tactics, 133
Structural discrimination, 130
Student activism, 33
Student Non-Violent Coordinating
　　Committee. *See* SNCC
Students, 38, 207, 234
　　as organizers, 22–23
　　consumerism and, 107
Students for a Democratic Society. *See* SDS
"Substitute father" rules, 6
Substitute-father laws, 60–61
Suitable home clause, 9, 29
Suitable home laws, 6, 48
　　repealing of, 5
Sunnydale Projects Mothers Group, 150
Supplemental Security Income. *See* SSI
Surplus food program, 35
Swanson, Mabel, 18
Switzer, Mary, 72–73
Sympathy, 236
Syracuse, NY, 40, 84, 119
　　"Poor People's War Council on
　　　　Poverty," 39
Syracuse University, 38–39
　　Community Action Training Center, 84, 86

T

"Talk Black," 149
Talmadge Amendments, 187
Targeted groups, 207
Targeted programs, 206–207
Task Force for Women in Poverty, 219
Tax bill, 63
Tax distribution, 195
Tax protesters, 195

Taxes, xiii
Taxpayer frustrations, 199
Taxpayer organizations, 175, 194
Taylor, Harold, 41
Technological advancements, 188
Teenage pregnancy, 238
Telephones, 82, 120, 121
  as a right, 88
Templson, Maurice, 41
Tenants, xi, 15, 23–24, 26, 64, 98
Tenement offices, 226
Tensions, internal. *See* Internal tensions
Termination, prior notice of, 203
Theft of welfare checks, 19
Theobald, Robert, 162
"Think Black," 149
Tillmon, Johnnie, 19–20, 28, 31, 34, 150–151,
        203, 209, 212–219, 223
  on birth control, 217
  consumerism and, 116
  demands for representation and, 66
  emloyment of recipients and, 139, 142
  FAP and, 182
  guaranteed annual income and, 165
  internal tensions and, 127, 129
  as NWRO chairman, 43
  Poor People's Campaign and, 72
Tobin, James, 169
Tokenism, 89
Top-down affairs, 207
Trade unionists, consumerism and, 107
Traditional notions of manhood, 201
Traditional nuclear families, 165
Trailways, 25
Training, 127, 137, 139, 153, 172, 178, 225,
        227. *See also* Job training
Turner, Mel, 209–210
Tutoring programs, 225
TWA, 117
Two-parent families, 136, 165, 188, 189
  deterioration of, 145
  FAP and, 172, 175
  as the ideal, 234
  reestablishment of, 200
Two-parent working households, 188
"Typical" welfare recipient, 197
Tyson, Timothy, 148

U

U.S. Constitution, 59
U.S. Department of Labor, 11, 133

U.S. Housing Authority, 28
U.S. Supreme Court, 60–61, 72, 92, 160, 174,
        181, 205
Unauthorized income, 203
Unconstitutionality, 10
Undeserving, xiii, xvi, 76, 92, 99, 113, 126,
        141, 186, 194, 199, 201, 207, 212,
        238
Unemployment, 71, 97, 122, 170, 197, 216
  of blacks, 144
  centers, 200
  compensation, 4, 141
  consumerism and, 104–105
  of fathers, 200
  in the postwar period, 33
  problems of, 162
Unexamined assumptions, 237
Unfair consumer practices, 103
Unfair credit practices, 108
Unfair pricing practices, 108
Unfair welfare policies and practices, 15,
        134, 135
Unfit mothers, 76
Ungrateful, 99, 113, 197
Union Benefica Hispana WRO, 30
Union label purchasing, 107
Union organizing, 68, 200
Unions, 52, 241
United Auto Workers, 185
Universal enforcement of regulations, 45
Universal programs, 206–207
Unlawful entry, 137
Unsafe and unhealthy work environments, 241
"Unsuitable" homes, 49. *See also* Suitable
        home laws
Unworthiness, xvi, 6, 12, 47–48, 187, 212, 238
Upstate New York WRO, 215
Urban Affairs, 176
Urban Affairs Council, 171
Urban North, 107
Urban rebellion, 177
Urban renewal, xi, 23, 24, 195, 233
  in Chicago, 26
  in Ohio, 26
  reform, 25
  viewed as "Negro removal," 25
Urbanization, 112

V

Van Til, Jon, 68, 209
Vanishing Family, The, 238

Vee Burke, 185
Vincent, 185
Virginia, 58, 129
    Fayette County WRO, 55
    Mount Hope Baptist Church, 55
    Raleigh County WRO, 55
    Rockbridge County WRO, 32
    WRO, 55, 59, 88
        internal tensions and, 128, 129
Virginia Slims cigarette ad, 112
VISTA, 34, 37, 108, 129, 208
Vocational training, 225
Voter registration, 20
Voting power, 187

W

W.T. Grant, 110–111
Wage discrimination, 220
Wage subsidies, 169
Wage supplement campaign, 202
Wage supplements, 200
Wages for housework movement, 221
"Walk for Decent Welfare," 1, 2, 15, 26, 40, 168
Walker, Lois, 32, 59
Wallace, George, 189
Waltham, MA, 24, 36
"War against the poor," 65
War on Poverty, 34, 54, 56, 100, 105, 136,
      169, 170
    demands for representation and, 65
Washington Afro-American, 147
Washington, D.C., 2–3, 6, 39–41, 83, 99–100,
      111, 118, 127–128, 139, 147,
      180, 202, 205–206, 209, 213–214
    1967 convention in, 125
    Barry Farms Welfare Movement, 159
    Citywide Welfare Alliance, 47, 49, 89, 137
    Citywide Welfare Alliance in, 22, 218
    Citywide Welfare Rights Organization, 108
    low-income merchant study in, 106
    Poor People's Campaign and, 71–72
    special grants and, 95
    United Welfare Rights Organization, 58
    Walker Thomas Furniture Store picket, 108
    winter clothing grant drive in, 89
Washington, Esther, 120
Washington, Jennette, 25, 41, 47, 51, 115, 157,
      201, 215
Weathermen, the, 201
Web of social problems, 23
Welfare abuses, 71

Welfare Action and Community
      Organization, 20
Welfare
    as a benefit to capitalism, 105
    as a black issue, 155
    budget for, xii
    corruption in, 12
    Cadillac, 196
    and fraud, xvi, 6, 12, 94, 135, 189, 198
    as a fundamentally economic problem, 150
    handbooks for, 215
    law of, 86
    manuals, 53–55, 80, 83, 126, 215
    as a metaphor for race, 239
    reform, 26, 45, 59, 86, 93, 97, 99, 116, 138,
        144, 154, 171, 175–176, 181,
        184, 188–189, 228
Welfare Fighter, 153, 202, 217
"Welfare is a right" slogan, 157, 190
"Welfare mess," 198
"Welfare queen," 217
Welfare Racism, 239
Welfare Recipients Demand Action. *See* WRDA
Welfare Recipients in Action, founding of, 15
Welfare Reform Task Force, 220
Welfare as a right, 234
"Welfare a Right; Education a Must," 226
Welfare rights as a militant movement, 233
Welfare rights handbook, 53
Welfare Warriors, 241
Welfare as a women's issue, 222
Wesley, Mary, 225
West, Don, 37
West, Guida, xiiii
"Western" liberal values, 235
Westside Mothers ADC, 19
White domination, 150
    and control in the organization, 148
White feminism, xii
White House, 180, 183
White House Conference on Civil Rights, 105
White House Conference on Food, Nutrition,
      and Health, 185
"White privilege," 151
White women, xi
White, Lucie, 74
Whites, 2, 28
WIC program, 228
Wiley, George, 2–3, 29–30, 38, 66, 97, 148,
      150, 152–154, 185, 199–200,
      208, 211–212, 214, 222
    at 1969 Detroit Conference, 146–147

Children's March on Washington and, 205–206
consumerism and, 108, 115–116
CORE and, 39
emloyment of recipients and, 137–139
Wiley, George (*continued*)
FAP and, 179–183
guaranteed annual income and, 163, 165–166
ideals of participation and, 63
importance in development of national movement, 42
internal tensions and, 127–132
live-on-a-welfare-budget campaigns and, 118
national newsletter, 138
national visibility and, 41
Nevada cuts and, 204
as NWRO executive director, 39, 43
P/RAC and, 39, 41
Poor People's Campaign and, 72
single motherhood and, 144–145
special grants and, 84
Work Incentive Program, 138
Williams, Patricia, 75–76
WIN (Work Incentive Program), 135–136, 138, 140, 187
enacted into law, 137
Winter action campaign, 87
Women
as bad leaders, 129
as organizers, 23
consumerism and, 107, 113–114
Women of color, 48, 141, 155, 216, 219–220, 234, 240–241
"Women's Agenda," 214
Women's freedom, 214
movement, xi
Women's liberation, xii, 113, 165–166, 214, 229–230, 235

movement, 221
Women's movement, 193, 214, 218
Women's oppression, 221
Women's organizations, 81, 214
Women's rights, 201, 206
Women, Infant, and Children (WIC) program, 226
Work ethic, xiii, 165, 171–173, 175–176, 179, 189, 238–239
Work experience program, 19
Work Incentive Program. *See* WIN
Work incentives, 12, 179–180, 188–189
Workers' Alliance to Guarantee Employment, 222
Working poor, 200, 202, 213–214, 223
Working-class consumption, 106
Working-class views, 195
Working-poor strategy, 201
Workplace issues, 91
Workplace organizing, 227
Workshops, 127, 221
World view, x
World War II, 8, 22, 91, 105, 207
WRDA (Welfare Recipients Demand Action), 133, 152–153
WSO, 21

Y

Yearly cost of living adjustment, 159
Yellow Springs, OH, 221
Ylitalo, Sally, 128, 129
Young people, consumerism and, 112
Young, Whitney, 29
Younger, Rev. Paul, 18

Z

"ZAP FAP" campaign, 178